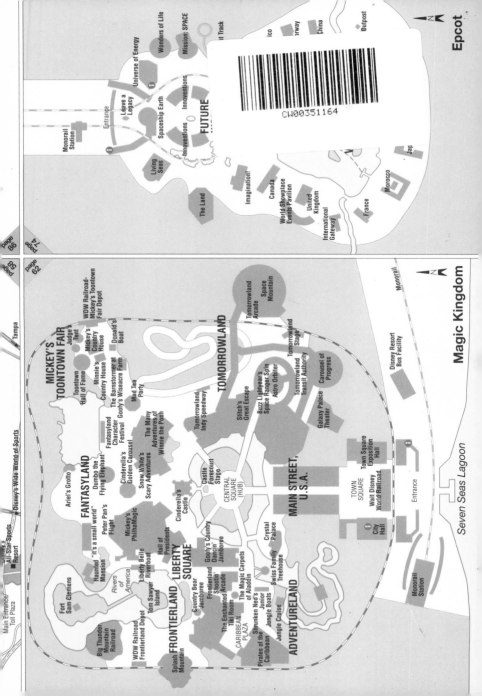

Epcot

N

Wonders of Life
Mission: SPACE
Outpost
Norway
China
st Track
Universe of Energy
Monorail Station
Entrance
Leave a Legacy
Innovations
Living Seas
Spaceship Earth
Innovations
Innovations
FUTURE
Imagination!
Mexico
Japan
Morocco
The Land
World Showplace Events Pavilion
Canada
United Kingdom
France
International Gateway

CW00351164

Magic Kingdom

N

Monorail
Seven Seas Lagoon

Tampa
Disney's Wide World of Sports
All-Star Sports Resort
Main Entrance Toll Plaza

MICKEY'S TOONTOWN FAIR
WDW Railroad-Mickey's Toontown Fair Depot
Judge's Tent
Mickey's Country House
Donald's Boat
Toontown Hall of Fame
Minnie's Country House
The Barnstormer at Goofy's Wiseacre Farm
Mad Tea Party

FANTASYLAND
Ariel's Grotto
Dumbo the Flying Elephant
Fantasyland Character Festival
Cinderella's Golden Carousel
Snow White's Scary Adventures
The Many Adventures of Winnie the Pooh
Peter Pan's Flight
"it's a small world"
Mickey's PhilharMagic
Haunted Mansion

TOMORROWLAND
Tomorrowland Arcade
Space Mountain
Tomorrowland Indy Speedway
Stitch's Great Escape
Buzz Lightyear's Space Ranger Spin
Astro Orbiter
Tomorrowland Transit Authority
Carousel of Progress
Tomorrowland Stage
Galaxy Palace Theater

Disney Resort Bus Facility

LIBERTY SQUARE
Hall of Presidents
Liberty Belle Riverboat
Rivers of America
Fort Sam Clemens
Tom Sawyer Island

FRONTIERLAND
Splash Mountain
Big Thunder Mountain Railroad
WDW Railroad Frontierland Depot
Country Bear Jamboree
Frontierland Shootin' Arcade

ADVENTURELAND
The Enchanted Tiki Room
CARIBBEAN PLAZA
Pirates of the Caribbean
Shrunken Ned's Junior Jungle Boats
Jungle Cruise
The Magic Carpets of Aladdin
Swiss Family Treehouse
Goofy's Country Dancin' Jamboree

Cinderella's Castle
Castle Forecourt Stage
CENTRAL SQUARE (HUB)
Crystal Palace

MAIN STREET, U.S.A.
TOWN SQUARE
Walt Disney World Railroad
Town Square Exposition Hall
City Hall
Entrance
Monorail Station

Page 98
Page 74
Page 58
Page 62

INSIGHT CITY GUIDE

WALT DISNEY WORLD® RESORT & ORLANDO

Part of the Langenscheidt Publishing Group

�֎ INSIGHT GUIDE
WaLT DISNEY WORLD RESORT
& ORLANDO

Editor
John Gattuso
Project Editor
Jason Mitchell
Art Director
Klaus Geisler
Picture Editor
Hilary Genin
Cartography Editor
Zoë Goodwin
Editorial Director
Brian Bell

Distribution

UK & Ireland
GeoCenter International Ltd
The Viables Centre, Harrow Way
Basingstoke, Hants RG22 4BJ
Fax: (44) 1256-817988

United States
Langenscheidt Publishers, Inc.
36–36 33rd Street 4th Floor
Long Island City, NY 11106
Fax: (1) 718 784-0640

Canada
Thomas Allen & Son Ltd
390 Steelcase Road East
Markham, Ontario L3R 1G2
Fax: (1) 905 475 6747

Australia
Universal Publishers
1 Waterloo Road
Macquarie Park, NSW 2113
Fax: (61) 2 9888 9074

New Zealand
Hema Maps New Zealand Ltd (HNZ)
Unit D, 24 Ra ORA Drive
East Tamaki, Auckland
Fax: (64) 9 273 6479

Worldwide
Apa Publications GmbH & Co.
Verlag KG (Singapore branch)
38 Joo Koon Road, Singapore 628990
Tel: (65) 6865-1600. Fax: (65) 6861-6438

Printing

Insight Print Services (Pte) Ltd
38 Joo Koon Road, Singapore 628990
Tel: (65) 6865-1600. Fax: (65) 6861-6438

©2005 Apa Publications GmbH & Co.
Verlag KG (Singapore branch)
All Rights Reserved

First Edition 2003
Second Edition 2004
Updated 2005

ABOUT THIS BOOK

This guidebook combines the interests and enthusiasms of two of the world's best-known information providers: Insight Guides, whose titles have set the standard for visual travel guides since 1970, and Discovery Channel, the world's premier source of nonfiction television programming.

The editors of Insight Guides provide both practical advice and general understanding about a destination. Discovery Channel and its web site, www.discovery.com, help millions of viewers explore their world from the comfort of their own home.

How to use this book

The book is carefully structured both to convey an understanding of the area and its culture and to guide readers through its sights and activities:

◆ The Best Of Orlando section, at the front of the guide, helps you to prioritise what you want to see. Top children attractions, the best festivals, thrill rides, and cultural attractions are listed, together with money-saving tips and a rundown of the area's eccentricities.

◆ To get below the theme park veneer of Orlando today, you need to know something of its past. The first section covers the city's history and culture in a lively, authoritative essay written by specialists.

◆ The main Places section provides a full run-down of all the attractions worth seeing. The main places of interest are coordinated by number with full-colour maps.

◆ A list of recommended restaurants and cafés is included at the end of each chapter in the Places

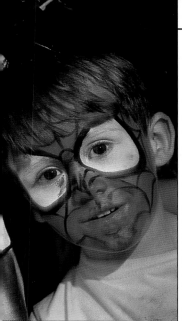

section, and the establishments are plotted on the pull-out restaurants map provided with the guide.

◆ The fact-packed Travel Tips listings section provides a point of reference for information on transport, accommodation, cultural attractions, shopping, and other activities. There is also an A–Z directory of practical information, and a useful language guide. Information may be located quickly by using the index printed on the back cover flap – and the flaps are designed to serve as bookmarks.

◆ A detailed street atlas is included at the back of the book, complete with a full index.

◆ Photographs are chosen not only to illustrate geography and buildings but also to convey the moods of the area and the life of its people.

The contributors

The first edition of this book was produced by **John Gattuso** of Stone Creek Publications in Milford, New Jersey, a veteran of more than two dozen Insight Guides and Discovery Travel Adventures. Gattuso also penned chapters on Universal Orlando and Disney-MGM Studios. His three young daughters, Giovanna, Reina, and Natalia, generously assisted him with research. This relaunched edition was fully updated and edited by **Jason Mitchell**.

Nicky Leach, a regular Insight writer, chronicles the history of central Florida and the development of the Disney empire, then leads readers on a tour of Busch Gardens and dozens of lesser-known attractions around Orlando, including a rich endowment of museums, gardens, and other cultural institutions.

Chapters on Walt Disney World were covered by a team of writers spearheaded by **Chelle Koster Walton**, author of more than half a dozen state travel guides. **William and Kay Scheller** toured the Space Coast and wrote "The Business of Pleasure" and "Licensed to Thrill." The book was indexed by **Helen Peters** and proofread by **Sarah Turner**.

◆ **Trademarks:** This book refers to many attractions, cartoon characters, product names, entities and works that are registered trademarks of their creators and owners. They are used here solely for editorial and descriptive purposes, and Apa Publications makes no commercial claim to their use.

CONTACTING THE EDITORS

We would appreciate it if readers would alert us to errors or outdated information by writing to:

Insight Guides, P.O. Box 7910, London SE1 1WE, England. Fax: (44) 20 7403-0290. insight@apaguide.co.uk

www.insightguides.com

Introduction

The Best of Orlando **6**
A Land of Make Believe **15**

History

The Conquest of Amusement **17**
Decisive Dates **30**

Features

The Business of Pleasure **34**
Licensed to Thrill......................**40**
Survival Strategies **46**

Places

Introduction **55**
Walt Disney World Introduction ..**59**
Magic Kingdom **61**
Epcot **73**
Disney's Animal Kingdom..........**85**
Disney-MGM Studios **95**
Downtown Disney and
    Water Parks **105**
Universal Introduction **117**
Universal Studios **119**
Islands of Adventure **133**
CityWalk **145**
Greater Orlando Introduction ..**149**
SeaWorld **151**
Beyond the Theme Parks **163**
Some Like it Haute **179**
Busch Gardens **193**
Space Coast **205**

Information panels

The Wetter the Better **45**
Disney Cruises **112**
Tampa....................................**203**

Maps

Central Florida **56**
Walt Disney World **58**
Magic Kingdom **62**
Epcot **74**
Animal Kingdom **86**
Disney-MGM Studios **96**
Downtown Disney **106**
Universal Studios **120**
Islands of Adventure **134**
CityWalk **146**
SeaWorld **152**
Beyond the Theme Parks **164**
International Drive **168**
Busch Gardens **194**
Space Coast **209**

Map Legend **241**
Street Atlas **242–247**

Inside front cover:
  Walt Disney World
Inside back cover:
  Orlando and Surroundings

Travel Tips

TRANSPORTATION
Getting There **214**
  By Air **214**
  By Rail **215**
  By Road **215**
Getting Around **215**
  To/From the Airport **215**
  Orientation **215**
  Public Transport **215**
  Driving **216**

ACCOMMODATION
Walt Disney World **219**
Universal Orlando and I-Drive **223**
Further Afield **224**

WHAT TO DO
The Arts **226**
  Museums & Art Galleries **226**
  Theatre **226**
  Ballet **226**
  Opera **226**
  Concerts **226**
Nightlife **227**
  Introduction **227**
  Nightclubs **227**
  Pubs and Bars **227**
  Music Venues **227**
  Comedy Venues **227**
Cinema **227**

Children's Activities **228**
  Little **228**
  Medium **228**
  Teens **228**
Shopping **229**
Sports **230**
  Participant **230**
  Spectator **231**
  Events **231**

A–Z OF PRACTICAL INFORMATION
Budgeting for your trip **232**
Business Hours **232**
Climate **233**
Crime and Safety **233**
Customs Regulations **233**
Disabled Travelers **234**
Embassies and Consulates **234**
Emergencies **234**
Entry Requirements **234**
Gay and Lesbian Travelers **235**
Health and Medical Care **235**
Internet **236**
Left Luggage **236**
Maps **236**
Media **236**
Money **236**
Photography **237**
Public Holidays **237**
Tickets **238**
Time Zone **238**
Tourist Information Offices **238**
Useful Numbers **239**

THE BEST OF ORLANDO

Setting priorities, saving money, unique attractions...
here, at a glance, are our recommendations, plus some
tips and tricks even cartoon mice won't always know

BEST YOUNG CHILDREN'S ATTRACTIONS

These seven attractions are popular with children,
though not all will suit every age group.

● **Mickey's PhilHar-magic.** The Magic Kingdom's newest attraction is a 4-D experience featuring characters that children love. It's the only such cinema in Orlando that leaves aside the creepy crawly effects that so often ruin the experience for younger children. *See page 68.*

● **Seuss Landing.** Perhaps the most imaginative children's play area in Orlando, recreating everything from Seuss' mad landscapes to a helping of Green Eggs and Ham. *See page 135.*

● **Discovery Cove.** A chance to interact with your own private dolphin, given a trainer's assistance of course. You give it a smooch and it will give you a lift back to the beach. *See page 160.*

● **Woody Woodpecker's Kidzone.** Universal Studios wisely gives children ample opportunity and space to just simply play, albeit in a brilliantly designed setting. *See page 123.*

● **Peter Pan's Flight.** Hop aboard one of the best dark rides in the Magic Kingdom (perhaps in all of Orlando) and soar from London to Never-Never Land. *See page 68.*

● **it's a small world.** The quintessential Magic Kingdom ride with dancing animatronic figures that children love and a theme tune parents loathe. *See page 69.*

● **Trainer for a Day.** This is your chance to spend a day with dolphins, orcas, and the humans they train. *See page 151.*

NATURAL ORLANDO

● **Merrit Island National Wildlife Refuge.** Home of endangered manatees and sea turtles. *See page 212.*

● **Blue Spring State Park.** Snorkeling and swimming in crystal clear springs. *See page 181.*

● **Tiger Creek Preserve.** Home of the endangered skinks that swim under the sand. *See page 181.*

● **Orlando Science Center.** Interactive exhibits cover everything from Florida's famous sinkholes to an astronaut's life in zero gravity. *See page 183.*

● **Bok Tower Gardens.** Opened in 1929, these serene gardens are designed along traditional European styles. *See page 188.*

● **Ocala National Forest.** Great hiking and camping in central Florida. *See page 181*

ABOVE: the leatherback turtle is just one of several endangered Floridian species struggling to cope with rapid changes to its environment. **LEFT:** Seuss Landing, with its absence of lines, offers plenty of free playtime for young ones.

LEFT: exhibits at the Orlando Science Center will keep even the most curious kids satisfied. **ABOVE:** gator wrestling is an old-time tourist attraction in Orlando. **BELOW RIGHT:** Epcot's evening fireworks are not to be missed. **BELOW:** Nora Neale Hurston is just one of Florida's famous writers.

HISTORIC ORLANDO

- **Gatorland.** Opened in 1949, this is one of Orlando's first attractions. It still gives you a chance to see, hold, and even eat gators. *See page 165.*
- **Zora Neale Hurston National Museum of Arts.** Revolving exhibitions feature African-American art. *See page 183.*

- **Kissimmee Rodeo.** Harken back to the good old days when the only thing treated like cattle in Orlando was, well, cattle. *See page 166.*
- **Weeki Wachee.** One of Florida's few remaining old roadside attractions and the only one with real live mermaids. *See page 175.*
- **Orange County Regional History Center.** Imaginative exhibits of Florida's 12,000-year history, set in the 1927 Orange County courthouse. *See page 182.*
- **Silver Springs.** Recall the mid-1800s when steamboats carried wealthy tourists down the St John's and Oklawaha Rivers. *See page 174.*

BEST FESTIVALS AND EVENTS

- **Gay Day.** Each June Orlando's amusement parks host over 100,000 gays and lesbians who come with their friends and families for special events held at Walt Disney World and Universal Studios. *See page 235.*
- **Mardi Gras.** Downtown Disney and Universal Studios CityWalk. Don't miss the chance to celebrate the season of all party seasons New Orleans style with jazz bands, Cajun food, and performers.
- **Official Disneyana Convention.** Serious fans and collectors descend on Epcot for a week of memorabilia auctions, seminars, trading, and special tours. Early September.

- **International Food and Wine Festival.** Where better to have wine tastings, cooking demonstrations, and appearances by celebrity chefs than at Epcot's World Showcase. Held from late October through late November.
- **Halloween.** Celebrated at venues throughout Orlando, but the biggest event – Mickey's Not So Scary Halloween Party – featuring parades, costume contests, trick or treating, and fireworks – takes place at the Magic Kingdom.
- **Fourth of July.** Even larger crowds and bigger fireworks celebrate the nation's birthday throughout Disney and Universal Studios.

LEFT: regardless of which dragon you choose, the Dueling Dragons of Islands of Adventure promise to thrill you. **BELOW:** Spider-Man is just one of the famous DC comic characters featured at Islands of Adventure. His "Amazing Adventures" is the park's most sophisticated ride.

BEST IN THRILL RIDES

● **Space Mountain.** Though tame by modern standards, this Magic Kingdom classic still draws the crowds. *See page 71.*

● **Mission: SPACE.** The newest attraction at Epcot is by far its best. You feel you've earned your wings after this simulated trip to the red planet. Barf bag included. *See page 77.*

● **Twilight Zone Tower of Terror.** You go up, they distract you, then you drop. Repeat. Repeat. Repeat. *See page 98.*

● **Rock 'n' Roller Coaster Starring Aerosmith.** If neither the 60 mph launch, nor the dips and inversions get you, then the blaring rock 'n' roll music just might push you over the edge. *See page 99.*

● **Back to the Future…The Ride.** It's just a simulator, but you may forget this, as it's the most exciting simulator ride in Orlando. *See page 124.*

● **Dueling Dragons.** If there is a fine line between terror and exhilaration, it's difficult to remember which side you're on as, at 60 mph, you just miss your dueling coaster as it zooms past you. *See page 138.*

● **The Amazing Adventures of Spider-Man.** Part simulator, part 3-D cinema, part dark ride, and undoubtedly the most sophisticated ride in Orlando. *See page 142.*

● **Incredible Hulk Coaster.** From 0 to 40 mph in two seconds and that's just to get you started. Three rolls, two loops, and the world's highest inversion finish you off. *See page 143.*

● **Kraken.** This floorless roller coaster, which exceeds 60 mph, has been known to scare even the most seasoned roller coaster aficionados. *See page 156.*

● **Montu.** One of the tallest and longest inverted coasters in the world. *See page 197.*

EATING EXPERIENCES

● **Cinderella's Castle.** The Once Upon a Time character breakfast features Disney's female stars, including Snow White, Sleeping Beauty, and Belle. *See page 64.*

● **Medieval Times Dinner Tournament.** Set in the 11th century, it features a well-executed jousting tournament, rowdy atmosphere, and roast chicken. *See page 172.*

● **Wonderland Tea Party.** A one-hour event, hosted by popular Alice in Wonderland characters at the Grand Floridian.

● **Pirates Dinner Adventure.** One of the most impressive sets in Orlando's dinner theater – a life size pirate's ship – and a humorous cast that bumbles its way along trying to save Princess Anita. *See page 173.*

● **Sleuth's Mystery Show and Dinner.** After a humorously-executed murder, the audience deduce the culprit while eating their Cornish hen or prime rib. Undoubtedly the best entertainment on the dinner theater circuit. *See page 173.*

CULTURAL ORLANDO

● **Jack Kerouac House.** This is the house in which Jack wrote *Dharma Bums*. Now it's the home of the current Kerouac-esque writer-in-residence. *See page 180.*

● **Cornell Museum of Fine Arts.** One of the finest art museums in the Southeast, featuring over 6,000 pieces of European and American works of art. *See page 185.*

● **Osceola Center for the Arts.** Home to 10 visual and performing arts groups with an art gallery, a 244-seat theater, and an art school with classes for children and adults. *See page 180.*

● **Charles Hosmer Morse Museum of American Art.** The world's most comprehensive collection of late-19th-century stained glass by Louis Comfort Tiffany. *See page 185.*

● **Orlando Museum of Art.** This well-regarded collection includes ancient artifacts from the American Southwest, Mexico, and Central and South America, plus works by 18th- to 20th-century American painters including Georgia O'Keeffe and John Singer Sargent. *See page 184.*

FREE ORLANDO

● **Orlando City Hall.** In the heart of downtown, City Hall has two galleries amongst the offices that host temporary exhibitions of renowned local artists. Entry to either is free. *See page 179.*

● **Florida Audobon Society's Birds of Prey Center.** Taking in around 600 injured birds a year, the society releases about 40 percent of them. Those whose injuries are too extensive to survive in the wild are kept here in captivity, which gives visitors a rare chance to see tiny screech owls, vultures, bald eagles, and red-tailed hawks. *See page 187.*

● **The Mercado.** Nearly every evening live music acts entertain visitors. Though there are plenty of food and sweet sellers in the courtyard to tempt you to spend, music and parking are absolutely free. *See page 168.*

● **Black Point Wildlife Drive.** A self-guided auto tour through the salt and freshwater marshes along the Space Coast. *See page 212.*

LEFT: the intricate stained-glass artistry of Tiffany at the Charles Hosmer Morse museum.
ABOVE: the Space Coast is home to more than rockets and astronauts: it's one of the best-preserved nature areas in the entire state.

ON THE CHEAP

Stay off-site. Disney hotels are undoubtedly the most convenient, but at a price. Competition immediately outside the resort and along I-Drive makes rooms much more affordable. Plus they are more conveniently located for other attractions. And don't worry, there's hardly a hotel in Orlando that doesn't offer a regular shuttle bus service to and from Disney.

Park the car. Though Orlando is a prime example of urban sprawl and well worth exploring, the Disney resort has fantastic public transportation between parks and hotels plus shuttle buses to and from the airport. You may find the car you've spent a couple of hundred dollars on will just sit in a parking lot while you explore the parks. Wait until you've the time to drive to Orlando's other attractions before spending the money on a car.

Pack your lunch. All theme parks in Orlando charge high prices for their food and often it's difficult to find exactly what you'd like (especially if you've any dietary requirements beyond hamburgers, chicken nuggets, and Coke). A family of four could save about $30 dollars a day just by bringing a packed lunch to the parks.

Book in advance. Booking your Disney tickets in advance, often in a complete package, could save heaps.

Orlando FlexiTicket. From the Orlando tourist office, this provides discounted entry into Universal Studios, Islands of Adventure, SeaWorld, Wet 'n' Wild, and Busch Gardens. Packages, prices, and conditions vary.

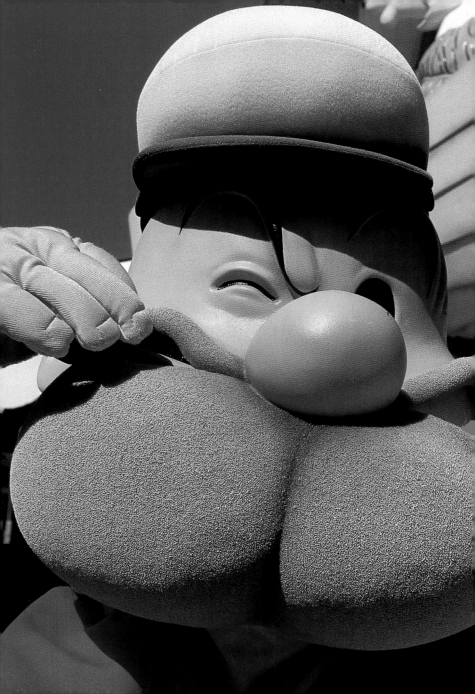

A LAND OF MAKE BELIEVE

Once upon a time, hardly anybody had
heard of the place. Now tourists flock to
Orlando for fun and a taste of fantasy

It's an undisputed fact: Walt Disney invented the theme park when he
opened California's Disneyland and perfected it with Walt Disney
World. When Epcot opened in 1982, the Disney people came up with
another signal accomplishment – the perpetual world's fair. Remember
world's fairs? Conventional wisdom held that they'd become passé – but
Epcot packs in the crowds day after day, year after year. It seems we want
to take rides through the histories of foreign countries – these days, it may
be safer than visiting them – and like our future served up with a healthy
dollop of technological optimism.

We like the movies, too – and here's where the first big non-Disney
operation broke onto the Orlando scene. In 1990, Universal Studios replicated its popular behind-the-scenes Hollywood attraction in Orlando. Disney responded with Disney-MGM Studios, while Universal parried the
Mouse on the theme park front with its Islands of Adventure, containing
some of the most astounding and realistic amusement rides in the world.

SeaWorld brings its own adventure, entertainment and, yes, education into
the mix. Originally the exclusive domain of Shamu the whale and his cohorts
from the watery world, the park has maintained its focus on nature while paying close attention to visitors' taste for thrills: thus Kraken, one of Florida's
wildest roller coasters. Not to be outdone on any flank, Disney has come up
with Animal Kingdom, a terrestrial challenge to SeaWorld's marine realm.

The real wonder is that this game of one-upmanship is played out in a single geographic location – a once-obscure central Florida city called Orlando.
Disney's real-estate scouts kicked things off back in the 1960s, and there's
been no looking back. The result has been a boon for travelers looking for a
one-stop vacation experience but also something of a challenge: how best to
pack so much fun into just so much time? That's been our challenge, too, in
preparing this guide. We hope the result will bring all of those fantasies and
adventures, filmland thrills and undersea wonders, visions of the future, and
Main Street nostalgia, together in a way that delights and never daunts.

And remember, you can always go back again next year. There's sure to
be something new. ❑

PRECEDING PAGES: Hard Rock Café, Universal Orlando; Popeye and Olive Oyl,
Islands of Adventure.
LEFT: Poseidon's Fury at Universal's Islands of Adventure.

THE CONQUEST OF AMUSEMENT

From Seminoles and legal loopholes, to oranges
and amusements, the history of central Florida's
swampland has been anything but stagnant

February 1895. For the second time that winter, icy winds from the north had plunged Florida into a deep freeze. Orlando citrus growers watched helplessly as 95 percent of their crops were wiped out.

Karl Abbott, whose family ran downtown Orlando's luxurious San Juan Hotel, could still shiver in 1950 recalling that long-ago winter. "About 9pm [that night], a fine-looking, gray-haired man in a black frock coat and Stetson hat walked up the street in front of the hotel, looked at the thermometer, and groaned 'Oh, my God!' and shot himself through the head."

Gloom is not something one associates with the modern Sunshine State, that reinvented happy land of theme parks and tourist distractions that grew up after The Mouse roared in 1965. But then the people who have come to Florida, from its earliest days as a 16th-century haven for Spanish conquistadors and colonists, have been dreamers rather than realists, most of them intent on achieving a life of riches and leisure in what early pioneers called the Eden of America. The real Florida – an inconvenient, uncomfortable place of mosquito-infested swamps, dense undergrowth, seasonal freezes, heat waves, unfamiliar animals, and native people – was merely a problem to be solved.

LEFT: Billy Bowlegs, Seminole leader during the Third Seminole War.

RIGHT: orange groves were a cornerstone of Orlando's economy well into the 20th century.

Orange fever

The tropical weather and well-drained soils of Florida attracted orange growers from the moment Spanish colonial governor Pedro Menendez de Aviles founded St Augustine on the northeast coast in 1565. By the time the American Territorial period began, St Augustine was producing 2 million oranges a year. After a freeze in 1835 destroyed the city's crop, a few hardy growers moved into the state's wild interior and planted over 60 varieties of orange trees. So important were these citrus groves that in 1845, the year Florida was made a state, the vast area of central Florida that the first territorial governor,

Andrew Jackson, had dismissed as Mosquito County changed its name to better advertise its chief asset: Orange County.

The 1894–95 freeze was not the first to devastate Florida's citrus groves, but it, as well as another freeze the following year, was a catalyst for far-reaching changes. Many families from citrus-growing communities in the Orlando area, which had grown up with the arrival of the railroad in 1880, moved south or left the state. Many English noblemen, who had first traveled to central Florida on hunting holidays in the 1880s but stayed to enjoy a privileged colonial life of polo, hunting, and fishing while their indentured

packing plant into an ice rink, built a toboggan slide that spilled into the springs, offered picnic facilities, and charged admission. The seed of a new idea – popular tourism – had been planted, 70 years before Walt Disney World would transform Orlando forever.

Greedy land speculators flooded into the state in the early 20th century as the introduction of the motor car ushered in the era of mass tourism. Northern visitors of modest means motored down to Florida for the winter in huge numbers, living in converted Model T Fords called Tin Lizzies and earning the moniker tin-can tourists because they brought all they needed with them. During the Spanish-

workers labored in the groves, took the first boats back to England.

Remaining Floridians became entrepreneurs. General Henry Sanford, whose Sanford community served as a railroad and riverboat link between Jacksonville and Orlando, converted his fields to celery and began to dominate a new market. Others planted winter vegetables among the blackened stumps of their groves or replanted their orange trees, painstakingly pruning back dead wood and grafting on new branches. Still others began what is now an important decorative houseplant business. And one particularly clever chap named John Steinmetz hit upon a brilliant idea: he converted his

American War and World War I, soldiers stationed in Florida developed a taste for life in the American tropics. Following the war, many moved permanently to Florida, attracted by cheap land and good weather. Homegrown roadside attractions like Gatorland and Cypress Gardens sprang up in the 1930s and 1940s, followed by Busch Gardens in 1959. In the 1950s, the air and space industry transformed the central Florida economy. The Glenn L. Martin Company of Baltimore made its headquarters in Orlando and triggered a population boom in nearby Maitland.

By the mid-20th century the citrus industry had not only rebounded from the 1894–95 freeze but was stronger than ever, as advances in technology created the frozen fruit concentrate market, and air freight, started in Florida soon after World War II, transported fresh fruit to distant markets. Despite unpredictable freezes and a post-Disney land grab in the 1970s, the $2.7 billion Florida citrus industry shows no sign of weakening. For many in Orlando, the loss of the orange groves would be a farewell to the Florida of bygone days and a time when life in the South was slower, gentler, and more gracious.

Early arrivals

It's unlikely that Orlando's first American settlers, Aaron and Isaac Jernigan, who arrived in 1843, could ever have envisaged the enormous metropolis that is Orlando today. The Jernigan brothers were the first to take up the government on its offer of 160 acres (65 hectares) of homestead land in return for military duty at Fort Gatlin, which, along with nearby Forts Mellon and Maitland, had been built between 1835 and 1838, during the Second Seminole War.

After this long, expensive, and difficult war against the Seminole Indians, the US government coerced 3,800 Seminoles and runaway African-American slaves onto reservations in Indian Territory, west of the Mississippi river. The government then abandoned the central Florida forts, leaving only citizen-soldiers stationed at Fort Gatlin to defend the new settlements. Skirmishes between Seminoles and settlers led to the Third Seminole War, which lasted from 1855 to 1858. At its close, the last Seminole holdouts, led by chief Billy Bowlegs, were rounded up and sent to reservations in the Everglades and near Tampa Bay, where their descendants – now split into the Seminole and Miccosukee Tribes – live today.

During this period, Florida's Seminole people proved themselves to be brave, implacable foes, and adept at guerilla warfare in Florida's swamps. Like the Sioux and Apache, great leaders grew to prominence among the Seminole. The best known, Osceola, born Billy Powell in 1804 to an English father and

Upper Creek mother in Alabama, was neither Seminole nor a chief. But after moving with his mother to Florida, early in the Second Seminole War, he grew to prominence as a war leader of ruthless daring. In 1837, he was captured under a white flag of truce by US Major General Thomas Jessup, a treacherous action that elevated Osceola in the public imagination to martyr and legend.

Also legendary was Coacoochee, son of Miccosukee chief Philip and nephew of Micanopy, head of the Alachua Seminole. Coacoochee united these two main groups of Florida Indians and fought tirelessly during the Second Seminole War. But in 1842, even

he acknowledged defeat, telling his captors: "The white men are as thick as the leaves in the hammock; they come upon us thicker every year. They may shoot us, drive our women and children night and day; they may chain our hands and feet, but the red man's heart will always be free."

Ancient snowbirds

The fact that others had a prior claim on Florida had been ignored for the previous 300 years by the Spanish, French, British, and, lastly, Americans. Although the landscape the Jernigans and other settlers found seemed a virgin wilderness, it had, in fact,

---

LEFT: tin-can tourists were drawn to the Orlando area by the mild winters, easygoing pace, and good fishing.
RIGHT: Seminole man about 1900.

been home to Florida natives for more than 12,000 years.

Paleo-Indians fleeing the frozen north during the Ice Age were the first to discover the Florida peninsula, then a dry desert with a land mass twice the size of what it is today. The hunters were attracted by the warm climate and abundant game animals, among them now-extinct ground sloths, spectacled bears, mastodons, dire wolves, camels, and giant long-horned bison. They camped along the coastal areas, then, as the glaciers melted and the climate grew wetter, moved inland, where their remains have been uncovered at Silver Springs and other central Florida water sources.

JACQUES LE MOYNE

The first European to document the Timucua was Frenchman Jacques Le Moyne, who made water-colors of the Indians after surviving the 1565 massacre at Fort Caroline on the St John's river by Spanish conquistador Pedro Menendez de Aviles. Le Moyne's drawings show large, handsome people ruled by chiefs and nobles in villages of dome-shaped, palm-thatched huts. Chiefs and nobles were lavishly tattooed and wore feather capes, shell beads, and metal belts. Males wore breechcloths of deerskin, while women dressed in skirts of Spanish moss woven so tightly it shone like green silk.

By 6,000 BC these ancient Floridians had coalesced into hunter-gatherers associated with particular territories, where they hunted otters, rats, squirrels, turtles, alligators, and opossums, fished in lakes, and gathered prickly-pear fruit and other delicacies. These early Archaic people invented tools made of animal teeth and bone fastened to wooden handles. They ceremonially interred their dead wrapped in woven palmettos. The swampy land preserved the corpses so well that 20th-century archaeologists excavating Windover Pond near Titusville were able to extract human brain DNA – a first on the continent. As the climate continued to change and get wetter, more water sources appeared, supporting larger populations.

The people consumed large quantities of oysters in coastal areas, as well as mussels and snails at freshwater sites. The huge shell mounds they left behind were a distinguishing feature of camps and may still sometimes be seen beside inland rivers.

By 1500 BC late Archaic people were making the first fired ceramics in North America, which they strengthened with Spanish moss or palmetto fibers. People along the St John's river, northeast of Orlando, created distinctive effigy pots, which were stamped with corn cob patterns. By the time Spanish conquistador Juan Ponce de Leon landed at Cape Canaveral, in 1513, and named the place La Florida (Land of Flowers) more than 150,000 native people were living on the peninsula. Northern Florida was the province of the Apalachee, the Miami area was home to the Tequesta, and southwestern Florida was the territory of the Calusa, whose shell-tipped arrows took de Leon's life in 1521. The people living in central Florida called themselves the Timucua.

The Seminoles

By the early 1700s, Florida's Indian population had been drastically reduced by continual warfare and introduced diseases. Between 1613 and 1617, half of the 16,000 converted Indians in Spanish missions in northern Florida had died of the plague and other infectious diseases.

In Georgia, meanwhile, Lower and Upper Creek Indians had formed an uneasy trading alliance with the British, bartering deerskins and furs for British guns and accompanying the British on their Florida raids. When that alliance collapsed, Spain invited Creeks into depopulated areas of northern Florida. Sometime between 1716 and 1767, Lower Creeks began colonizing former Apalachee towns, spreading into the center of the state, where they took over former Timucuan farmlands, reestablished trading networks, and lived alongside escaped black slaves, who had been granted sanctuary by the Spanish since 1693 – a situation that led first British and then American plantation owners into a series of battles that resulted in several changeovers in power.

In Florida, the powerful Creek Indians transformed themselves into a new people, the Seminoles. Their name was derived from the

ish Caribbean port. Many Indians and blacks left with the Spanish for Cuba rather than risk being forced back into slavery on British plantations. The Creeks in Georgia and the Florida Seminoles fared better. They used their alliance with the British to continue trading through the powerful Panton Leslie Company, which was owned by Scotsman William Panton, a friend of Alexander McGillvray, a half-English Creek and headman of the Creek Confederacy.

Florida was returned to Spain by the American Government in 1783, as a reward for Spain's loyalty during the American Revolution. Although major settlements were still

Spanish word *cimarron*, meaning "wild and unruly." Always great traders, Seminoles traveled as far as Cuba in their dugout canoes and bartered with ships sailing along the Atlantic Coast. They hunted deer and other game in the Everglades and grew corn, rice, watermelons, peaches, potatoes, and pumpkins in the fertile uplands of central Florida.

In 1764, Spain gave up Florida to the British in exchange for Cuba, a strategic Span-

LEFT: Osceola earned a reputation for great daring during the Second Seminole War.
ABOVE: Bunk Baxter wrestles an alligator in downtown Orlando, circa 1900.

largely on the coasts, swaths of central Florida had now begun to be settled by Seminole, black, and Spanish cattle ranchers and farmers. Late in the 18th century, plantings of cotton replaced corn, rice, and other staples, and interior rancherias raised beef for export to Cuba. Runaway black slaves flooded into Florida in huge numbers. Prince Witten, Zephaniah Kingsley and other African-American entrepreneurs grew to prominence alongside whites and owned property, passed it on to their children, established their own militia, and even had slaves of their own. Many blacks chose to live just outside Seminole villages, where they enjoyed the protection of

The American period

When they arrived in the 1840s and 1850s, central Florida settlers from Georgia, Alabama, and other southern states cleared their land of native pines and oaks, built log cabins, and began running cattle in what was now called Orange County. Jernigan was renamed Orlando in 1857, most likely for an early citizen-soldier whose plantation had been burnt down by Seminoles. Other settlers soon joined them, including cattleman Jacob Summerlin, a native Floridian, in 1873. He built the Summerlin Hotel, donated land around Lake Eola to Orlando in 1883, defeated General Henry Sanford's

their Indian neighbors in exchange for labor and goods – a relationship that would prove both providential and supportive during the Seminole Wars of the American period.

Between 1785 and 1821, numerous Spanish-American border disputes took place along the Florida–Georgia border. American ire over Spain's sanctuary policy for runaway

slaves and its own agenda of Indian removal to reservations west of the Mississippi were at the heart of the clashes, but there was something more: American Manifest Destiny – the vision of one American continent united "from sea to shining sea" – made America's desire to take over Florida insatiable.

In 1818, Andrew Jackson instigated the first Seminole War in northern Florida, earning the name "Sharp Knife" for his ruthless pursuit of Indian removal and extermination. Distracted by wars at home, Spain no longer had the resources to fight the Americans and, in 1821, handed over Florida. Three years later, Jackson became the state's first territorial governor.

effort to change the county seat to Sanford, and served on Orlando's town council. He was an imposing figure, tall and dressed in a dark suit, with a coat over one arm, no matter the weather.

Unlike the aristocratic settlers who preceded them on the coasts, most central Florida settlers were plain folk, poor whites who brought their families and farm animals to Florida seeking a better living. They were often private, mobile, dedicated to popular democracy, and intolerant of those who were different from them. They lived fiercely independent lifestyles in remote rustic cabins in the backwoods, hunting wild turkeys, deer, possums, alligators, and other swamp creatures and raising razorback hogs, sugarcane, and vegetables.

Orlando's first pioneers made almost everything they needed, but every Saturday families would ride into Orlando along sandy routes in ox-drawn wagons to buy provisions. Teenagers made eyes at each other at taffy pulls while cowmen and turpentine workers spent the week's wages in the local bars, letting off steam by shooting into the floors and evading Orlando's policy of no public drunkenness with the aid of bar owners who locked their doors and allowed their customers to sober up before escorting them to their waiting families.

Most of the men hired themselves out as poorly-paid cowmen, rounding up cattle in the palmetto prairies, and sandhill pines around Kissimmee. On drives, they rode small, sturdy marsh ponies, descended from Spanish ranchero ponies, working 18 hours a day. Grub was hauled in a long, covered oxcart containing biscuit, bacon, salt pork, syrup, and 3 to 4 quarts (3 to 4 liters) of coffee per man.

Western artist Frederic Remington, who had made his living celebrating the noble western cowman, was decidedly unimpressed by Florida's cow operations when he visited in the 1890s. He adjudged the cattle "scrawny creatures not fit for a pointer-dog to mess on," the men who herded them as scrawny as their cows, lank, unkempt, and wild, and the landscape "flat and sandy, with miles of straight pine timber, each tree an exact duplicate of its neighbor, and underneath the scrub palmettos, the twisted brakes and hammocks, and the gnarled water-oaks festooned with the sad gray Spanish moss – truly not a country for a high-spirited race of moral giants."

The dawn of tourism

By the time of the Great Freeze of 1895, Orlando had been incorporated for 20 years and was serving as the county seat. In the 1870s, over 50,000 visitors a year were cruising the St John's and Oklawaha rivers to Silver Springs, inspired by the words of naturalist William Bartram, who had written about the beauty of the Florida backcountry

in his *1870 Travels*, the state's first guidebook. President Ulysses S. Grant traveled the Oklawaha river to Silver Springs in 1880. "The steamers that thread the very narrow and wonderfully crooked waters of that stream are an aquatic curiosity," wrote one reporter on the trip. "Built especially for the route, they are altogether unique. Upon the roof of the wheel-house of our special steamer was a large iron box where a bonfire of pitch-pine knots lighted up the scenery by night."

The steamboat that Grant traveled on was the Osceola, part of James Brock's shipping line. Brock's wealthy customers, kept out of

European destinations by the Franco-Prussian War, demanded luxury. To serve them, Brock built the famous Brock House at Lake Monroe in Enterprise, where guests danced the schottische, the waltz, and the lancers in a grand ballroom as alligators bellowed in the marshes.

Once-thriving riverside communities like Enterprise and Palatka died, along with steamboat tourism, after the building of Henry Plant's and Henry Flagler's railroad networks in the 1880s and 1890s. The railroad opened central Florida to greater visitation and settlement. Upper-class Englishmen, attracted by the idea of being

LEFT: trick photos were a popular tourist souvenir.
RIGHT: Walt Disney and celluloid friend, 1935.

plantation owners and enjoying an easy out-doors lifestyle far from home, rushed to pur-chase land from state and railway corporations at a dollar an acre. The new land also lured working-class Englishmen hoping to escape the strictures of home, among them Joseph Bumby, a railway man, who with his many sons opened the largest hardware store between Tampa and Jack-sonville in downtown Orlando.

The first African-American township in the United States, Eatonville, was built north of Orlando in 1887 and named in honor of a Maitland resident who had helped get the project completed. It was here that African-

The mouse has landed

Walt Disney and members of his entourage gazed out of the plane window at the small central Florida city of Orlando (pop. 87,000). As the pilot of the aircraft borrowed from radio personality Arthur Godfrey circled the city that November day in 1963, the founder of the world's most famous theme park – Dis-neyland, in Anaheim, California – and his associates leaned forward to take in the view.

East of Orlando was McCoy Jet Airport, forerunner to Orlando International Airport, then a military base with a second runway used for commercial passengers. But what interested Disney and his colleagues was the

American writer Zora Neale Hurston was born in 1891. Civil rights were still a long way off for blacks, but writing in her auto-biography, *Dust on the Tracks*, Hurston remembered her Florida birthplace with great affection. It was "a country where per-sonal strength and courage were the highest virtues. People were supposed to take care of themselves without whining... Bears and alligators raided hog-pens, wildcats fought with dogs in people's yards, rattlesnakes as long as a man and as thick as a man's fore-arm were found around back doors."

By the mid-1900s, however, things were very different.

major highway intersection rising out of miles of alligator-infested swampland. Bisecting the city was I-4, then under construction through old Orlando neighborhoods and citrus groves. When finished, it would link Florida's Gulf and Atlantic coasts from Tampa to Daytona Beach and join Florida's Turnpike, the main artery between Miami and Orlando.

Orlando fulfilled everything he needed to make his dream a reality. It had enough virgin land to accommodate a park 10 times the size of Disneyland and buffer it from the develop-

ABOVE: Walt Disney, brother Roy, and Governor Haydon Burns announce plans for a new theme park in Florida.

ment that now marred its southern Californian location. The Sunshine State's warm, tropical climate ensured year-round visitation, but most important of all, Orlando already had good roads, an essential part of the Walt Disney Company's business plan to achieve national dominance in the tourism market.

It turned out to be a momentous day: November 22, 1963 – ever after etched in the nation's psyche as the date of the assassination of its popular young president, John F. Kennedy – and equally important for the future of Orlando.

Through the mouse hole

By October 25, 1965, the day Florida Governor Haydon Burns announced that Walt Disney would build "the greatest attraction yet known in the history of Florida," locals knew something was afoot. A total of 27,300 acres (11,000 hectares) of swamps, rivers, and lakes – pieced together from tracts of land of 5,000 (2,000 hectares) and 20,000 acres (8,000 hectares) in size – had been acquired by a mysterious buyer at an average price of $200 per acre, for a final investment of just over $5 million. Some thought it might be Howard Hughes; others, the space program. Local real estate agents dealt with a William Lund, a financial analyst for Economic Research Associates, the corporation secretly doing site consultation for Disney.

All sales were made through local dummy corporations. Secrecy was of the utmost importance to Walt Disney, who wanted to buy the land cheaply and shut out the specu-

lators who had inflated the price of building Disneyland.

Even Orlando's primary movers and shakers, lawyer and Sun Trust banker Billy Dial and the *Orlando Sentinel's* rough-hewn publisher Martin Andersen, found themselves, unexpectedly, left out in the cold.

Disney's search for a site for a new East Coast theme park had not been a secret. Only two percent of Disneyland's visitors came from east of the Mississippi, where three-quarters of the US population lived, and Walt saw a huge market waiting to be tapped on the opposite coast. The studio head had angrily pulled out of a deal with the city of St Louis overnight, when that city's major entrepreneur, brewery owner Augustus Busch (whose other family businesses – SeaWorld and Busch Gardens – would eventually go head to head with Disney in Florida), publicly told Disney that no theme park could succeed without serving alcohol.

Publisher Martin Andersen sent reporter Emily Bavar on a press tour of the Disney Studios in early October 1965. Bavar asked Walt Disney point-blank if he was buying up land in Florida, and Disney's surprised but ambiguous reply convinced Bavar that Disney was indeed doing exactly that. Andersen cautiously buried Bavar's first two stories in the back of the paper, but finally on Sunday, October 24, the *Sentinel* led with a page-one scoop, headlined "We Say It's Disney." Orlando, so long bypassed by tourists headed to Miami beaches, would now become a destination in itself.

DISNEY'S HOMETOWN

Those who wondered what had become of Walt Disney's vision of an experimental City of Tomorrow got their answer in 1991, when the company announced the residential community of Celebration. Lot sales for the nostalgically-designed homes began selling in 1996, but there have been bumps in the road for the new community.

Disney promised a visionary town charter founded on five principles: wellness, community, technology, place, and education; and the forward-thinking Celebration School that emphasized a small enrollment, personalized learning plans, and narrative reports rather than grades.

In practice, the school's mission proved impossible,

and in 1999 Disney struck a deal with Osceola County to build a public school at Celebration. In pleasing the county, however, Disney angered parents.

Even Disney's future ownership of Celebration is uncertain, yet the town remains an oasis amid the frenetic strip malls on Highway 192. Buildings by, well-known architects have made it something of a tourist attraction. Philip Johnson, known for the New York State Theater at Lincoln Center and the Glass House of New Canaan, Connecticut, designed the town hall. Michael Graves, whose projects include Disney World's Swan and Dolphin hotels, gets credit for the post office.

I-Drive debut

By the time Walt Disney, his brother Roy, and the Project Winter team arrived at Orlando's Cherry Plaza on November 15 to officially announce the new park, land prices around the new Disney property on the Orange County-Osceola County line had skyrocketed to $1,000 an acre. Developers jumped aboard the Mouse wagon. One of the first was Orlando Hilton owner Finley Hamilton, who held land north of the new Disney property. Hamilton built a new 114-room Hilton Hotel at the Sand Lake Road/I-4 interchange, the southern end of a road that Hamilton named International Drive. At a time when no other developers had ventured south of the city, the lodging seemed a long shot and Hamilton's friends took to calling it "Finley's Folly." The hotelier was eventually vindicated when Disney staff commandeered the hotel as their principal lodging during the four years of Walt Disney World construction, setting off a rush to buy plots and develop hotels, restaurants and, eventually, competing themed attractions along the 12-mile (19-km) commercial strip dubbed I-Drive by locals.

Disney insisted on far-reaching powers of self-government and immunities from Orange County regulations that might otherwise delay construction. Walt Disney

THE FLY BOY OF PINE CASTLE

Pine Castle Army Air Field, now Orlando International Airport, played a crucial role in the development of the Bell XS-1, dubbed Glamorous Glennis, which on October 14, 1947 became the first airplane to brake the sound barrier. Built just before World War II, Pine Castle was chosen to test the new plane because it had a 10,000-foot (3,000-meter) runway – one of the longest in the nation. In early 1946, the Bell Aircraft's lead pilot, a 29-year-old named Jack Woolams, tested the plane ten times before pilot Chuck Yeager flew the plane when it broke the sound barrier at California's Muroc Dry Lake.

died of lung cancer 13 months after the initial announcement. His successor, Roy Disney, argued in 1967 that the 43-square-mile (111-sq-km) Florida property would need to be a city within a city, with its own power and sewage plants, police, firefighters, regulations, and inspectors. In an unprecedented move, the Florida legislature greenlighted the creation of a separate Disney government, the Reedy Creek Improvement District, in just 12 days. It was a decision that did more than allow Walt Disney World to open its doors by 1971; it set a standard for corporate bargaining power unmatched before in Florida.

Building a better mousetrap

Disney's careful business planning was matched by its attention to detail in the actual construction of Walt Disney's dream park. Preparing the site took 18 months, with 9,000 workers and 200 pieces of heavy equipment working seven days a week, around the clock, under powerful portable spotlights. When they had finished, 8 million cubic yards of earth had been moved and the wetlands had been drained with the aid of 18 miles (29 km) of levees, 13 water control structures and 40 miles (64 km) of canals. The centerpiece of the park – Bay Lake – was dredged, and a new 200-acre (80-hectare) entrance lake named

MORTIMER OR MICKEY?

Walt Disney initially wanted to name his famous cartoon mouse Mortimer. Walt's wife Lillian thought the name stuffy and suggested Mickey instead. The name stuck and a star was born.

for costumed Disney employees, for whom being seen with their "heads off" is a no-no.

Disney wrote the Southeast's strongest building codes to accommodate its technological innovations and new structures. Fire sprinklers, smoke detectors, and other safety features were mandatory in every building, far ahead of what was required by Orange County at the time.

Seven Seas Lagoon created. The lake was then lined with 4 million gallons of white sand to make the brackish Florida water appear blue, and more than 60,000 trees were planted around the property.

During the next two years, a 3½-mile-long (5.5-km) monorail and 5-mile (8-km), two-lane highway were built, along with an environmentally-friendly energy plant, paid for by tax-free municipal bonds. Tunnels were built to contain utilities and for use as a staging area

LEFT: the monorail under construction.
ABOVE: CEO Michael Eisner and director George Lucas at a ribbon cutting for the new Star Tours ride in 1987.

D-Day

By the time Walt Disney World opened on October 1, 1971, with much fanfare and many dignitaries in attendance, including President Richard Nixon, the park had cost nearly $400 million to complete. But the immediate success of the new Disney park more than made up for the price tag. During the Magic Kingdom's first year, 10 million visitors came to central Florida, nearly three times the number before Disney. Everyone, it seemed, was smitten. NBC anchorman David Brinkley was particularly impressed with the new town outside the park, noting that the roads, transportation systems, lakes, golf courses, campgrounds, stores, and motels "all fit together in a setting of land, air and water better than any other urban environment in America." The well-coordinated architecture and design, state-of-the-art technology, and efficiently-run public works were universally praised and sparked a debate about the future of urban planning in the US.

In Orlando itself, that debate took on a particular urgency, as Orange County struggled to accommodate overnight growth. By 1969, the city had become one of the top 10 fastest-growing cities in the nation, riding a diversified economy of agriculture, high-tech industry and the expected tourist boom. Downtown was undergoing the first of two major

rebirths. And new housing developments were sprouting up all over the Orlando area as the city rushed to meet the demand for housing and services for thousands of low-paid workers attracted by the spate of new service industry jobs. *Sentinel* publisher Martin Andersen felt that city and county officials could take a page from Disney's book. "As Disney has planned, we, too, must plan," he opined in a front-page editorial. "Disney has taught us that, knowing the facts of life as to what is to come, we should plan for the great confrontation."

For better or worse, the democratic process, with its emphasis on public debate, regulation, and tax levies, is vastly different from the benign dictatorship of corporate giants like Disney. This became obvious in the 1980s when the Disney Company, under the leadership of Michael Eisner, began to extend the Disney empire in directions even Walt Disney had never imagined.

The Mouse roars

With the growth of Orlando tourism beyond Disney's walls, the Walt Disney Company, under the direction of its new chairman, Michael Eisner, began competing hard to keep visitors on its property. Disney took advantage of its special relationship with Orange County to fast-track new onsite hotels and entertainment facilities ahead of competitors, and, in 1988, announced plans for the Swan and Dolphin Hotels, designed by nationally-known architect Robert Stern, and a $373 million convention complex. Growth-challenged Orange County adopted the Florida Growth Management Plan in 1985. Looking for a solution to traffic congestion, it backed a Matra light rail in 1986 and a Mag-lev high-speed train in 1989, linking the Disney property with Orlando International Airport and I-Drive. Both plans were vetoed by Disney, invoking criticism from county officials whose calls for a mutually beneficial partnership went unheeded.

The Mouse's long dominance of the Orlando market met its first big challenge in the late 1980s when Disney's Californian rival, Universal Studios, announced that it would build a theme park in Orlando. The Walt Disney Company's response was to prioritize the construction of its own studio tour. Disney-MGM Studios, the company's third Orlando theme park, opened in 1989, more than a year ahead of Universal Studios, along with Typhoon Lagoon, a water theme park. In 1998, Disney introduced its own cruise line, unveiled its fourth Orlando park, the wildlife-themed Animal Kingdom, and renamed its West Side, Pleasure Island, and Disney Village Marketplace as Downtown Disney, anchored by the House of Blues and Cirque du Soleil.

A competitive market

Only those with deep pockets can afford to take on the Mouse. Of the many theme parks operating in Florida, Universal Studios, Sea-World, and Busch Gardens are the only major competitors, cutting into Disney's market share with innovation, speed of construction and hot technology. In 1998, Universal opened its own nighttime complex, CityWalk, and the following year a second theme park, Islands of Adventure. In 2002, it opened its third hotel, offering visitors a destination resort rivaling Disney.

In 2000, Anheuser-Busch also rose to the challenge by opening the exclusive destination resort, Discovery Cove, next to Sea-World Orlando, the popular marine park that opened in 1973 and had undergone a major expansion in 1993. Anheuser-Busch also upped the ante for ride enthusiasts by installing the fearsome roller coaster Kraken at SeaWorld. Three other state-of-the-art roller coasters were installed at Busch Gardens, the company's original 1959 exotic zoo and bird gardens in Tampa Bay.

Before the arrival of Disney, Busch Gardens had undergone constant expansion, beginning in 1965, with the addition of the country's first open-range habitat for its African animals. Later it would build a new water park next door, improve its Africa-themed exhibits, and introduce an up-close African safari and offroad adventure ride, Rhino Rally, in 2001, boosting its popularity among locals and post-Disney vacationers.

Early Orlando theme parks that fill unique niches have also retained their markets. The 1949 Gatorland is unmatched for its alligators and crocodiles and alligator wrestling shows. And Ocala's Silver Springs, which began the theme park ride craze with its glass-bottomed boats in 1878, is as popular as ever, after being taken over by the state and designated a historic site. It is now run by a concessionaire.

The road ahead

At the dawn of the 21st century, Orlando is proving that it is more than a one-mouse town. The City Beautiful is now the fastest-growing urban area in the nation. The population in the four-county region that includes Orlando stands at more than 1½ million, three times the number of residents who lived here in 1971, the year

LEFT AND RIGHT: Orlando then and now – the City Beautiful has become one of the fastest-growing urban areas in the United States.

before the Magic Kingdom opened its doors. Orange County now has a major university, numerous world-class cultural institutions, and a downtown undergoing a second renaissance, with a sensitively-restored historic district, a renovated Lake Eola Park, and a new performing arts center, city hall, courthouse, hotels, restaurants, art galleries, and other buildings on Orange Avenue. There are more than 110,000 hotel rooms in the Orlando area, second only to Las Vegas as the largest in the United States. More than 17 million air passengers fly into Orlando International Airport each year.

But there are clouds on the horizon. Even as new hotels and themed attractions open,

old ones close their doors, unable to weather the cut-throat competition. Periodic downslides in tourism, such as the catastrophic fallout for the travel industry that followed the September 11, 2001, terrorist attacks in New York City and Washington, D.C., hit Orlando hard. Such events are a continual reminder that too much reliance on tourism can be devastating to a community. A more chronic problem not yet addressed is the traffic congestion that has plagued Orlando since city boosters hitched their star to the motor car and issued a call for entrepreneurs. A call that a man named Walt was happy to answer. ❏

Decisive Dates

Native cultures

15,000–7500 BC: Paleo-Indian hunters – Florida's first "snowbirds" – flee Ice Age glaciers in the north and begin living on the Florida peninsula.

7500–5000 BC: Archaic hunter-gatherers occupy Florida. Archeologists later uncover the first human burials in North America near Cape Canaveral.

3000–500 BC: Late Archaic people, living along the Wekiva and St. John's rivers, make the first pottery in North America.

500 BC–AD 15: Early farming of corn, squash, and pumpkins along the St. John's River. Unique

St. John's culture includes effigy pots, pottery stamped with corn cobs, and 6-foot (2-meter) high carved totem animals. Clam bakes create huge shell mounds.

AD 15–early 1500s: Timucua farmers, descended from the St. John's culture, occupy central Florida, encompassing nearly 40 major chiefdoms.

Colonial power struggle

1497–1514: French and Spanish claim discovery of Florida. The peninsula appears on a Spanish map in 1510, and Peter Martyr writes in 1514 of a land near the Bahamas with water of eternal youth. Spanish explorers are shipwrecked off Cape Canaveral. Rescued by Timucuans, they

marry into the villages and act as interpreters for later Spanish arrivals.

1513: Ponce de Leon lands in Cape Canaveral area in search of gold, treasure, and the Fountain of Youth. He claims the territory for Spain, naming it La Florida – the Land of Flowers. He is killed in 1521 by an Indian arrow.

1528: Panfilo de Navaez lands in Tampa Bay in April. After attempting to colonize the west coast of Florida and being repelled by Indians, he dies at sea. Hernando de Soto and 600 soldiers land in Tampa Bay on May 30, but fare no better.

1564: Frenchman René Oulaine de Laudonnière builds a fort on the St. John's River and names it Caroline for Charles IX.

1565: Pedro Menendez de Aviles enters a harbor, which he calls San Agustin, on August 28. Capturing Fort Caroline, he renames it San Mateo. San Agustin becomes St. Augustine, and the Spanish mission system in Florida is begun.

1567–68: Frenchman Dominique de Urgues avenges the massacre at Fort Caroline by recapturing the Spanish outpost San Mateo and hanging the Spaniards there.

1586: British seafarer Sir Francis Drake conquers and burns St. Augustine.

1672: Construction of El Castillo de San Marcos, the fortress at St. Augustine, begins. It is completed 23 years later.

1702–04: The British raid Spanish settlements, including a 52-day siege of St. Augustine. Governor James Moore of Carolina invades middle Florida, forcing the Spaniards and Christianized Indians to abandon Apalachee missions. The mission era comes to an end shortly after.

1740: A British general, James Oglethorpe, invades Florida from Georgia and seizes outlying forts. He lays siege to St. Augustine for 27 days, but is stymied by lack of fresh water and provisions.

Mid-1700s: Creek Indians – dubbed Seminoles – and runaway African-American slaves, driven south by American settlers, enter Florida.

1764–83: Britain rules Florida. The first local newspaper, The East Florida Gazette, is published in St. Augustine.

1774: Quaker naturalist William Bartram of Philadelphia tours Florida. His account inspires many travelers to come to the region.

1783: Britain returns Florida to Spain.

1785–1821: Numerous Spanish-American border

disputes occur. A republic is proclaimed by patriots in northeastern Florida in 1812.

1813: Future American president Andrew Jackson captures Pensacola.

1818: First Seminole War. Jackson campaigns against Indians and African-Americans.

1821: Jackson receives Florida from Spain at Pensacola on July 17 and is later appointed the territorial governor.

1824: The territorial government creates Mosquito County, a vast area extending from near St. Augustine to south of Cape Canaveral and west to Alachua County.

1835: The Second Seminole War begins.

1837: Osceola, a half-English, half-Upper Creek Indian fighting with the Seminoles, is imprisoned after entering an American camp under a flag of truce and dies a martyr in 1838.

1842: The Second Seminole War ends with 3,824 Indians and African-Americans being relocated to Arkansas. The federal government offers land to anyone willing to settle near Fort Gatlin, south of Orlando, and act as a citizen-soldier.

1843: Aaron and Isaac Jernigan migrate from Georgia to settle near Fort Gatlin, naming their settlement Jernigan.

1845: Florida becomes a state with 57,921 residents. Mosquito County changes its name to Orange County in an effort to lure settlers.

1857: Jernigan is renamed Orlando.

1875: Orlando is incorporated (pop. 85) and becomes the seat of Orange County.

1880: Henry Plant's South Florida Railroad is extended to central Florida, allowing expansion of Orlando's agricultural markets.

1884: Fire destroys most of Orlando's downtown business district.

1887: The first African-American township in the United States, Eatonville, is built north of Orlando.

1891: The African-American writer Zora Neale Hurston is born in Eatonville.

1894–99: Severe frosts kill 95 percent of the county's citrus groves.

Modern times

1903: The first automobile is sold in Orlando; the speed limit is 5 miles per hour (8 kph).

1910–25: A land boom hits Florida. "Tin can tourists" motor to Florida for the winter.

1929: Mediterranean fruit flies devastate the citrus industry. Bok Tower Gardens in Lake Wales is opened by President Calvin Coolidge. African-American physician W.M. Wells opens the Wells' Built Hotel in Orlando as a lodging for jazz musicians.

1936: Cypress Gardens opens.

1949: Gatorland opens.

1950s: Postwar automobile tourism skyrockets.

1957: The Glenn L. Martin Company of Baltimore relocates to Orlando, starting a population boom.

1959: Busch Gardens opens in Tampa Bay.

1964: Walt Disney quietly buys more than 28,000 acres (11,300 hectares) of central Florida farmland.

1965: Disney announces plans to build Walt Disney World in Orlando. Interstate 4 opens.

1966: Walt Disney dies.

1971: The Magic Kingdom opens.

1973: SeaWorld Orlando opens.

1990: Universal Studios opens in Florida.

2001: September 11 attacks depress Florida's tourist industry. The effects have yet to fade.

2003: Space Shuttle *Columbia* explodes on re-entry. All seven astronauts die.

2004: Controversy engulfs Disney: a takeover bid is thwarted, while Roy Disney, the family's last representative on the board, resigns over disagreements with CEO Michael Eisner. Hurricanes rock Florida, but Orlando escapes any serious damage.

2005: Disney World announces plans to celebrate Disneyland's 50th anniversary. ❑

LEFT: a keepsake from the early days of tourism.
RIGHT: a Seminole woman and baby, 1905.

THE BUSINESS OF PLEASURE

It takes a heap of logistics to keep theme parks up and running and ahead of the competition. Lots of toilet paper helps, too

For the Disney Company, Mickey, Goofy, and the gang are big business: the estimated 46 million people – that's one and a half times the population of Canada – who pass through the gates every year will spend an average of $100 each on tickets, meals, refreshments and souvenirs. It's no wonder so much hard work goes into assuring that everyone has fun.

The Disney folks produce and package pleasure. They provide a safe, clean, and controlled environment staffed by cast members (the Disney term for employees) who are always neat and well-groomed, and who never sport beards, long nails, tattoos, or visible body piercings. They buff and polish a place where youngsters can frolic and parents can relive their childhood fantasies alongside Cinderella, Peter Pan, and a host of cartoon characters that by now seem part of the American family. And the cast does it well: Walt Disney World is the most visited vacation destination on earth.

Day-to-day Disney

Disney World functions well because it was planned that way from the beginning. When Walt and his brother Roy began scouting sites for an East Coast theme park, they wanted to avoid mistakes they'd made in building Disneyland in California. One mistake was not purchasing enough land to accommodate a self-contained vacation resort – one that could offer visitors everything they would want or need, so that they wouldn't have to go off-property to spend their money. Under a blind trust, Disney purchased 27,300 acres (11,000 hectares) of rural central Florida for an aver-

Each evening, after approximately 117,000 guests exit the turnstiles at Walt Disney World, the park's night crew swings into action. Almost 25,000 people work until morning refreshing the cobwebs and "antique" grime in the Magic Kingdom's Haunted Mansion, mowing almost 2,000 acres (800 hectares) of grass, distributing over 3 tons of food to more than 1,000 animals at Animal Kingdom, even refilling the toilet tissue holders that dispense 19,000 miles (31,000 km) of paper in a year. This crew is about half of the "cast" of 55,000 hired by central Florida's largest employer to help keep Disney World "the happiest place on earth" – and also, perhaps, the best maintained.

SAY CHEESE

Kodak estimates that roughly 4 percent of all the amateur photographs taken in the United States are snapped at Walt Disney World or Disneyland.

age of $200 an acre. Although it was mostly swamp, the 43-square-mile (111-sq-km) parcel – a piece of land twice the size of Manhattan – allowed Disney to create a buffer large enough to keep competition well at bay.

Equally important as having enough land was having the authority to develop and manage the property as the Disney people saw fit. The Florida legislature knew that the park would be a cash cow for the state: it was estimated that during construction and the first 10 years of operation it would generate $6.6 billion. A sizable cut of its income would go to the state, before new construction and permanent service jobs were added in.

The legislature thus approved a bill granting Disney permission to establish the Reedy Creek Improvement District, an area some wags have dubbed "the Florida Vatican." The legislation gave Disney authority to develop and manage every aspect of its property, including decisions about zoning, establishing building codes, levying taxes and even building an airport or nuclear power plant if and when the need arises.

Beneath the kingdom

From the outset, Disney planned to retain complete control of its environment. With an initial investment of $400 million, the company built an energy plant which generates approximately 35 percent of the electricity needed to operate the park. (Each year, Disney World uses about half as many kilowatt hours as Maine.)

Disney also set up its own waste disposal system, which now handles a daily load of up to 50 tons of trash – much of it generated at the park's restaurants. Each day more than 500 employees prepare and distribute 8,000 different menu items, a gigantic enterprise that incorporates the services of bakers (more than 40,000 pounds/18,000 kg of flour go into each

week's supply of bread, rolls, and pastries); people to oversee machines, including automated pizza makers that pump out pies at the rate of one every two seconds; and delivery personnel to service 450 food vendor locations throughout the property.

The heart of the disposal system is a giant underground vacuum called an AVAC (automated vacuum-assisted collection), which sucks refuse from points throughout the park and scoots it at 60 miles per hour (100 kph) through tubes leading to a central repository, where it is compacted and transported to a landfill. Enormous amounts of material, including 6,500 pounds (3,000 kg) of aluminum cans each day,

are processed at the park's recycling center.

When the Magic Kingdom was in its planning stage, designers came up with an elegant way to hide from guests the day-to-day operations necessary to run the park. They built a 2.8-mile (4.5-km) utility corridor, or "utilidor," with 15-foot-high (5-meter) tunnels at ground level, covered it with 8 million cubic yards (6 million cubic meters) of soil dug to create the Seven Seas Lagoon, and built the park over it. The utilidor houses the park's computer operations, the AVAC tubes, wires, offices, make-up operations, and costuming rooms. Color-coded connecting corridors lead to each of the Kingdom's four themed areas, permitting Mickey and the

PRECEDING PAGES: Oh, the places you'll go in Orlando. **LEFT:** lifeguard on duty at Wet 'n' Wild. Theme parks are Orlando's largest employers. **RIGHT:** a Busch Gardens staff member is ready to help.

gang a quick and easy way to suit up and then scoot to different parts of the park. A smaller utilidor is used at Epcot, where the central computer bank is located 20 feet (6 meters) under the Innovations East pavilion.

Vying for dollars

The Orlando Convention and Visitors Bureau estimates that in 2005, 38 million people will visit the city. The hundreds of hotels (with a combined total of more than 110,000 rooms), restaurants, stores, and attractions all want a share of the money these visitors will spend, and most of them pool a portion of their advertising budgets to get it. Theme parks, includ-

ing Universal Orlando, SeaWorld, and Gatorland, offer discounts in a myriad of free coupon books and offer substantial discounts through programs including the Convention and Visitors Bureau's MagiCard.

Disney managers have taken a different route. Not only do they decline to advertise cooperatively with other businesses, they've pursued a policy of building attractions in an attempt to monopolize tourist dollars: hence the additions in recent years of Typhoon Lagoon (to compete with Wet 'n' Wild), Disney-MGM Studios (to combat Universal Studios) and Animal Kingdom (to draw clientele from Busch Gardens and SeaWorld). The building of Down-

town Disney to compete with Universal's City-Walk and downtown Orlando's Church Street Station was so effective that the latter closed its doors temporarily in 2002 (though now new businesses are slowly re-opening). The $100 million Wide World of Sports Complex – a 200-acre (80-hectare) development that includes an 8,000-seat baseball stadium, four major league practice fields and a 5,000-seat fieldhouse with six basketball courts – is Disney's attempt to capture another segment of the tourist market.

Disney does offer a few discounts – generally on packages which include the purchase of 4-day park hopper tickets – through its own Disney Club, as well as in cooperation with AAA, AARP, and American Express. A few retail outlets offer discounted packages. But in an unusual move for a company that retains ironfisted control over its marketing, Disney in January 2000 signed a distribution agreement with Travelocity.com giving the travel website authority to book theme park tickets and onsite hotels for its customers.

Disney World, here I come

The Travelocity deal may well be an acknowledgement of the fact that attendance figures are down at Disney, as well as at parks throughout the country. This decrease may also be the reason that Orlando theme parks, and Disney in particular, have stepped up their advertising campaigns. In fact, "stepped up" may be an understatement for a company that, until Michael Eisner became chairman in 1984, did no direct advertising. Until then the company relied on word of mouth and co-advertising: when Epcot opened, in 1982, corporations such as Kraft and General Motors paid a total of $300 million to have their companies associated with Disney, which, of course, was the recipient of all that free advertising.

The day after the New England Patriots won the Super Bowl championship in 2002, their quarterback Tom Brady was the guest of honor at the Magic Kingdom. After hitting his record

73rd home run for the 2001 season, Barry Bonds announced to the media, "We're going to Disney World." Even President George W. Bush got into the act, exhorting the American public, after September 11, to "Get down to Disney World in Florida... take your families and enjoy life the way we want it to be enjoyed."

Brady and Bonds were part of the enormously successful "What's Next" campaign launched in 1987, designed to present Disney World as the place for people – especially winning athletes – to go when they're celebrating. President Bush used the park as a metaphor for America's ultimate vacation ideal, just as astronaut Sally Ride evoked Disney when she

its nearest competitor by nearly four times. In 1999, 42½ million people paid admission to Disney World's four major theme parks, 11½ million went to Universal Orlando, and 4.7 million flocked to SeaWorld.

But management knows that to stay on top, the park has to continue to meet – better yet, to exceed – the expectations of its guests, approximately 70 percent of whom are repeat customers. So, amid a business climate in which workers are being laid off, hours of operation are being shortened, perks are being curtailed, and expansions are being put on hold, quality must be maintained and image burnished even more aggressively. Efforts include Epcot's

described her journey into space as an "E-ticket ride" (referring to the early days when the best rides in the park went by that designation).

Staying on top

Despite a decline in admissions over recent years, Disney World remains the 800-pound gorilla of Orlando theme parks, outdistancing

LEFT: costumed characters, like this one at Universal studios, delight young and old. And no, the costumes aren't air-conditioned.

ABOVE: nighttime entertainment at Downtown Disney (right) and Universal's CityWalk (left) are designed to keep visitors, and their money, at the resorts.

state-of-the-art Mission: SPACE, opened in 2004, which turns an ordinary centrifuge ride into an ultra-realistic trip to outer space, and the announcement of Beastly Kingdom, a new land scheduled to open in 2006, which will feature an E-ride projected to cost in excess of $120 million (although there are reports that this project, too, has been put on hold).

In addition, there are new rides and shows, such as the Magic Carpets of Aladdin and Mickey's PhilharMagic. But there's grumbling among some Disney aficionados that these new entries don't measure up to the last generation of E-rides such as Epcot's GM Test Track. Indeed, that's what the folks at Universal and

SeaWorld might well be counting on to boost their own attendance figures in the years ahead. Since it opened its Orlando venue in 1990, Universal's East Coast working studio has evolved into an entertainment empire, with two distinct parks, a water park, the CityWalk entertainment complex, and three huge theme hotels.

The words most often used to compare Universal with Disney are "hipper," "edgier," and "newer." It's hard to imagine two more different experiences than listening to a calm, carefully-scripted presentation at the Magic Kingdom's Jungle Cruise (ad-libbing by Disney cast members is forbidden) and hearing a sweating, frantic guide at

Hospitality Center, where customers can sample the wares of its parent company, Anheuser-Busch. Alcohol, in fact, was forbidden at Disney World for years, because Walt didn't feel that it was appropriate in a family environment. (This policy almost sank Disneyland Paris when it first opened: Parisians, incredulous that they couldn't have a glass of wine when they relaxed between rides, boycotted the park until management gave in and began serving alcohol.) It was only in 1984, when Epcot opened, that beer, wine and spirits were approved for sale at restaurants in the World Showcase. Management realized that customers did not want ginger ale to wash down bangers and mash at the

Universal's Poseidon's Fury scream "open the friggin' door."

Because it's so much newer than much of Disney and is not as concerned with overall family image, Universal's rides tend to be much more state-of-the-art and hair-raising. Revenge of the Mummy – the Ride, "a psychological thrill ride" is a wild, five-minute ripping roller-coaster ride through the set of a haunted Egyptian tomb that uses every single trick in the book to leave you terrified. If the g-forces don't disturb you, they hope the dark forces will.

SeaWorld also offers a very un-Disney-like attraction: free beer. The drink that is banned in the Magic Kingdom flows at the marine park's

Rose & Crown pub or sip Coke while dining on sumptuous French cuisine. Alcohol is also available at Universal Orlando – for a price, of course – and it's not unusual to see visitors strolling the park with a tall glass of beer in hand.

The war of more

Orlando is a land of superlatives. "Universal Orlando Resort is a spectacular vacation destination which includes the world's two most amazing theme parks… a dazzling entertain-

ABOVE: a SeaWorld audience waits for Shamu. Theme parks have turned crowd control into a science.
RIGHT: taking a break from the crowds at Water Mania.

ment complex, and magnificently-themed on-site hotels," proclaims the brochure. SeaWorld boasts of the Kraken roller coaster, "Nothing like it in Orlando… The highest, fastest, longest and only floorless coaster." Downtown Disney is "the epicenter of excitement… a waterfront 'wonderland' of top-notch, world-famous shopping, entertainment, and dining."

Every attraction in the Orlando area wages a daily battle for tourist dollars. But the big three are engaged in a war of "more." Universal and Disney are also locked in a battle to keep tourists from leaving their properties. Guests who stay at one of Universal's resort hotels, including the new, 1,000-room Royal

Pacific Resort, enjoy a variety of special park privileges, including complimentary on-site transportation, priority restaurant seating, complimentary package delivery, and, most important at a park where lines for major attractions can be up to 90 minutes long, express ride access on certain rides. Not to be outdone, Disney offers similar perks to guests at its hotels.

Each year the parks raise their admission fees, and the average cost for the big three has now reached $60. So it's more important than ever for each of them to continue to make their customers believe they are the biggest and best. That's only good business. ❏

MOB MANAGEMENT: FOLLOW THE WIENIE

Crowd control designed to keep guests docile, mannerly, and patient in lengthy queues starts at Walt Disney World before visitors even enter the park. Cars funnel into lanes at parking toll booths and drivers thread their way through the cones to assigned spaces. It continues as visitors listen to a barrage of instructions on the tram ride to the ticket booth, then wait in line to buy an admission ticket, pass through security, and, finally, clear a park turnstile.

Inside, guests are moved along with what the Disney people call "wienies": lures like Cinderella's Castle and Big Thunder Mountain that draw them from one spot to another. As Walt said, "you've got to have a wienie at the end of every street." Other controls include peppy music to keep guests moving and a "flow-through" ride protocol, whereby passengers enter on one side and leave on another, reducing loading time.

Many attractions have hidden lines: no one is waiting outside, but once inside, guests are channeled through winding corridors toward the loading zone. Because the scenery changes as they move, they sense progress. A variation is the pre-show – usually presented on video screens – that keeps guests entertained and fills them in on the ride's story line. In essence, the queue becomes an extension of the ride – yet another Disney innovation.

LICENSED TO THRILL

Hold on tight! The rides at central Florida's biggest parks are faster, wilder, and more imaginative than ever before

When you get right down to it, we don't visit theme parks for the themes. There's no denying that much of Walt Disney World's lure is the familiarity of its characters and the Disney way of storytelling and at Disney-MGM Studios or Universal Studios, the magic of the movies is a big part of the draw. But beneath the gloss and the story lines, the reason millions flock through the gates of theme parks is the same as it was for our grandparents when they frolicked at Coney Island in Brooklyn or on midway rides at county fairs. We simply want to be tossed around until our insides can barely stand it, shot through space at traffic-ticket speeds, and

plummeted earthwards with harrowing abandon. When we surrender ourselves to the untender mercies of the best thrill rides, what we really want is to feel like we are about to die… forgetting for just a moment that the brakes will work, the tracks will turn from the abyss, just in the nick of time.

Of course, not every ride is a calculated dance with dread. Many rides, meant for children or merely for transportation through a themed environment, operate at a continuous and predictable pace. One popular example – a takeoff on the traditional "dark ride" – is "it's a small world" at Disney's Magic Kingdom, a boat trip through a multicultural audio-animatronic wonderland that leaves patrons powerless to get the title tune out of their heads. At Disney-MGM Studios, The Great Movie Ride is a gentle meander through "movieland." Without the familiar stars and sets along the way, however, it would be an awfully tedious experience. So would Disney's Haunted Mansion, if there were no hologrammatic spooks around.

The marquee thrill rides at the big parks are another thing altogether: motion first, visuals and concept second. They are close cousins to the great amusement park gut-wrenchers, and they use the same reliable tricks of physics and physiology to make you delightfully terrified.

Faster, faster

It all began without rollers, hundreds of years ago, when Russians passed long winters by building wooden ramps, glazing them with snow and ice, and sliding down them on sleds with runners. Added wheels then extended the fun into summer. By the early 1800s, the craze had spread to France. It struck the United States as an outgrowth of railroad technology: when a hill-climbing coal railway in Pennsylvania closed in the 1870s, it soon reopened as a pleasure ride.

By the late 1800s, pleasure railways built solely for amusement were hurtling thrill-seekers along at all of 12 miles per hour (19 kph). As more amusement parks were built, roller coaster technology advanced by leaps and bounds – or by drops and loops. The 1920s saw the construction of some 2,000 wooden coasters in the United States alone, many with speeds that exceeded 40 miles per hour (64 kph). During this era, the coaster's fundamental components came into play – underwheels to lock cars onto the track; guide wheels to prevent lateral sliding; passenger restraints; and braking systems.

Most important of all, though, was the mechanical ascent system for the first incline on a track, called the "lift hill." Traditional roller coasters still rely on this basic principle: a train of cars is hauled via a chain-and-ratchet system to the top of the first big drop. From here on in – except in those few coasters in which a second lift hill is employed – gravity does all the work, pulling the cars through a series of lesser hills and the dips and curves between them. All of those other hills have to be lower than the lift hill, or else there won't be enough momentum for the cars to reach the end of the line.

G-force and air time

If roller coaster cars traveled downhill in a straight line, the only thrills involved would be those of speed and forward motion. The most exciting sensations on a coaster are the result of shifting g-forces, alternately lessening and magnifying the force of gravity upon the riders.

A force of 1 g is what we feel under normal circumstances. Double the g-force and gravity's apparent effect is doubled: in other words, a 170-pound man feels like he's packing 340 pounds (154 kg). Most American roller coasters exert forces under 3 gs – approximately the force space shuttle astronauts feel at launch time. A scant few pin riders back into their seats with 5 gs; several overseas coasters, however, achieve 6 gs or more.

The g-force effect also works in the opposite direction. At less than 1 g, there is a sensation of lightness; at zero gs, we experience a feeling of total weightlessness.

Much of the thrill of coaster riding occurs at the points where there is a sudden transfer from positive to negative g force, such as at the top of a hill in the moment before a drop. This is the coaster enthusiast's trea-

sured "air time," achieved on Universal's Incredible Hulk coaster in the roll that immediately follows a lightning ascent through a 150-foot (46-meter) tunnel.

Air time should not be confused with "hang time" – that mini-eternity of suspended motion right at the crest of a lift hill before the plummet begins. Coaster designers often deliberately prolong hang time in order to enhance anticipation and make the payoff all the more delicious.

All of these external effects focus on a tiny but crucial component of our anatomies, contributing not only to exhilaration but to the disorientation and outright nausea that make

LEFT: a corkscrew in Busch Gardens' Python. Believe it or not, this is one of the park's milder coasters.
RIGHT: an elaborate Egyptian theme sets the stage at Montu, another Busch Gardens roller coaster.

rapid, twisting rides less than appealing for many theme park patrons. The inner ear is our gyroscope, an apparatus that enables us to stand and walk upright and react appropriately to changing spatial circumstances.

But when those circumstances are manipulated as quickly and unnaturally as they are on a coaster ride, the fluid in the inner ear and the nerves leading to the brain simply can't keep up. The result is dizziness, occasionally nausea, compounded by the sloshing and squeezing of the stomach. Unless you have an iron constitution, it's best to avoid large meals or acidic foods before a challenging ride. Don't ride on an empty stomach, though – have a few

crackers to absorb stomach acid. It also helps to look straight ahead while on a coaster, or, if worse comes to worst, to close your eyes altogether. Those prone to motion sickness can always resort to Dramamine, an over-the-counter medication best taken at least two hours before you intend to board your first ride.

The steel age

The classic, clattering wooden coaster is a favorite of thrill-ride aficionados and, in some cases, can deliver much the same impact as its high-tech cousins. One example is Gwazi, unveiled in 1999 at Busch Gardens in Tampa. Built of more than 1.25 million feet (400,000

meters) of lumber, it's actually two coasters on intertwining tracks that hurtle past each other at 50 miles per hour (80 kph) or, as the park likes to boast, a "fly-by" speed of 100 miles per hour.

Coaster design was revolutionized, however, by the development of the tubular steel track, first introduced in 1959 at California's Disneyland in the Matterhorn Bobsled. Steel liberated coaster cars from having to remain more or less right side up and made possible rides incorporating corkscrews, double helixes, barrel rolls, camelbacks and other gravity-defying effects. Tubular steel tracks also enabled the construction of the newer "suspended" coasters, in which seats hang from their tracks rather than ride upon them, and swing from hinges. Since the connection to the track is out of sight, riders have the sensation of flying through space.

On "inverted" coasters, seats are suspended but not hinged. This setup allows the maneuvers that actually turn passengers upside down. Universal Orlando's Dueling Dragons compounds the topsy-turvy routine with sheer terror, as dual coasters careen towards each other at 60 miles per hour (100 kph) – only to loop out of the way at the very last moment. Conventional coasters with their wheels on the bottom can also turn upside down on steel track, as they do on Universal's Incredible Hulk. For sheer muscle, however, it's hard to beat Busch Gardens' Montu or SeaWorld's Kraken, both floorless coasters with hairy drops and multiple loops. Kraken, at a top speed of 65 miles per hour (105 kpm) and a drop of 144 feet (44 meters), is the faster and taller of the two, but Gwazi wins plaudits for overall design, with huge inversions, tight corkscrews and g-forces of 3.85.

Kick start

As if all this weren't thrilling enough, new propulsion systems are replacing the old chain-lift approach to launching a coaster, delivering more explosive acceleration and higher speeds. Among the methods now in use are blasts of compressed air and – in the case of Universal's Incredible Hulk Coaster – a tire-driven launch. This latter system is really no more complicated than the simple friction of tires against the underside of the coaster cars – but, then, tires are what race cars travel on. The Hulk climbs 150 feet (46 meters) and reaches a launch speed of 67 mph (108 kph), more than enough to fire passengers through seven subsequent inversions on a 3,700-foot (1,130-meter) track.

Many engineers and thrill-ride enthusiasts feel that the future of coaster propulsion lies in the use of linear induction (LIM) and linear synchronous motors (LSM) – the same devices associated with magnetic-levitation (maglev) trains being developed for high-speed rail corridors. A true maglev train also uses electromagnetic energy to hover slightly above its track, thus avoiding friction. Roller coasters simply aren't that advanced… yet.

Disney World's LSM coaster is the Rock 'n' Roller Coaster at Disney-MGM Studios. Themed around a rock 'n' roll story involving the rock band Aerosmith – which created the pulsing theme music, served up via 120 speakers mounted in the limousine-style coaster cars – the electromagnetic track-side motors launch riders from zero to 57 miles per hour (92 kph) in 2.8 seconds, with a force of nearly 5 gs. This coaster may not climb 400 feet (120 meters), but it is hardly tame. The entire ride takes place on 3,400 feet (1,000 meters) of indoor track, incorporating two rollovers and a corkscrew.

Beyond the coaster

It's hard to think of roller coasters and related rides as subtle, but there are theme park attractions that make an even sharper point of their g-force assaults. The most outrageous g-force manipulators are "drop" rides. These attractions are sheer verticality, employing gravity in its crudest form.

The two Orlando standouts in this category are Doctor Doom's Fearfall at Universal and Twilight Zone Tower of Terror at Disney-MGM Studios. Story lines aside – and Tower

---

LEFT: inverted, or floorless, coasters give riders the sensation of soaring through space.
RIGHT: the Hulk, at Universal's Islands of Adventure.

of Terror has a doozy, all about a haunted hotel with a wing that seems to have disappeared into another dimension – both of these rides are all about plunging to your apparent demise. Fearfall has sheer altitude on its side: passengers secured into a battery of seats are fired 150 feet (46 meters) up the sides of two towers, then, following a moment of weightlessness, they go into a power-augmented descent before braking at the bottom. The Tower of Terror also employs power assistance to exceed the velocity of free fall, but the 13-story drop is made all the creepier by the fact that passengers are in an "elevator." The ride thus simulates a real-life fear, with

one insidious fillip: the elevator is on the outside of the building.

Virtual thrills

Given the fact that jet-fighter pilots black out at 10 gs, there are obvious limits to the thrills raw acceleration and sudden turns can provide. Total integration of themed graphics with the motion of the ride itself is the object of the latest generation of simulator rides, based on technology originally developed to train military and commercial pilots.

Simulators are essentially metal pods mounted on hydraulic lifts that shake, twist and jolt the riders seated inside. Together with visual displays, they give riders the sensation of traveling through space, although the pod doesn't actually move more than a few feet in any one direction. Concept is essential to the overall effect, as in the Star Tours ride at Disney-MGM Studios, which takes you on a mad-cap journey through the galaxy with familiar characters from the movie, or Universal's Back to the Future, an even more intense experience in a time-traveling DeLorean.

Roller coaster enthusiasts will be especially thrilled at Disney Quest on the west side of Downtown Disney, where an attraction called CyberSpace Mountain allows visitors to design their own roller coaster on

(120 meters) into the city streets below. This isn't to say that the vehicles don't actually move; they do, around a 1½-acre (0.5-hectare) set simulating a city besieged by super-villains. But each move of the vertically- and laterally-mobile vehicles is coordinated to effects created by 25 large-format 3-D projectors, several dozen smaller projectors, various hydraulic pistons, and all sorts of smoke machines, lasers and blasts of air. Computer graphic imaging makes the comic-book characters seem like living entities, and their actions merge seamlessly with the precisely controlled motion of the vehicles. The world they inhabit is one in which projected moving images enhance and magnify

a computer screen, then experience the ride in a simulator.

The next level

Perhaps the most creative new development in thrill rides is represented by the Adventures of Spider-Man at Universal Orlando, which combines simulator technology with 3-D movies and traditional dark rides. Universal describes it as "immersive entertainment," and it involves "moving point of convergence" technology.

What all this adds up to is a skillful weaving together of visual, aural, and physical sensations that, in one heart-stopping sequence, makes riders feel as if they're plunging 400 feet

the effect of actual movement, as with that 400-foot plummet – in reality, the vehicles move no more than 4 feet (1.2 meters).

For all its high technology, Universal's Spider-Man is still a ride. Beyond such interactive experiences lies a realm that might not fit that description quite so accurately – true virtual-reality entertainment, in which participants might not go anywhere at all, other than those places a personal simulator might take them. It might even be an ice slide down a frozen ramp in Russia. ❏

ABOVE: Adventures of Spider-Man dazzles with 3-D images and motion simulation.

The Wetter the Better

Some of the simplest old-time amusement park rides – and some of the most sophisticated attractions at Orlando's big theme parks – are based on moving through water.

The earliest water rides involved nothing more complicated than towing or otherwise propelling small boats along a specially-built trough. That's the concept behind many of the first kiddie rides we enjoyed as well as the tunnels of love we looked forward to a few years later. With the addition of a global village of animatronic figures and a maniacally catchy theme song, this is the low-tech underpinning of Disney's "it's a small world."

Water-rides then harnessed gravity on flume and raft rides to duplicate the thrill of white water. They combine the lifts and drops of a roller coaster with the fun of getting splashed on a hot day.

On many raft rides, gravity does most of the work, with assistance from computer-controlled water circulation systems. The slope will generally be 9 or 10 degrees, with twists and turns engineered into the ride for added thrills.

Flume rides incorporate a succession of mechanically-assisted lifts and free-fall drops. On the level passages in between, designers weave themes and story lines into the experience.

Disney World's top flume attraction is Splash Mountain, which intersperses three lifts and four drops into the *Song of the South* story of Br'er Rabbit and the briar patch. Eleven minutes long, the part-indoor, part-outdoor ride ends with the raft plummeting five stories at an angle of 45 degrees and a top speed of 40 miles per hour (64 kph). At that angle and speed riders expect to get wet, but only front-row passengers get thoroughly soaked.

At Sea World's Journey to Atlantis, the big finale is a 60-foot (18-meter) plunge at a 60-degree angle in a "fishing boat" caught up in the story of the lost continent. And at Universal's Jurassic Park River Adventure, tour boats exploring a dinosaur habitat are "accidentally" shunted into a channel that leads into raptor country and over the highest precipice of all – no less than 84 feet (26 meters) at an angle in the 60-degree range, though it feels like you're falling straight down.

Today's water parks, such as Disney's Typhoon Lagoon and Blizzard Beach, as well as Water Mania and Wet 'n' Wild, can resemble a cross between elaborately-themed dreamscapes and the

nightmares of a lunatic plumber. As with water parks worldwide, the formula is simple: combine a steady flow of water with a looping or arrow-straight chute canted at an angle of descent generally ranging from 12 to 20 degrees.

But in Orlando, things get carried to extremes. The Summit Plummet at Blizzard Beach is angled at 60 degrees, and riders attain speeds of up to 60 miles per hour (100 kph) along its 500-foot (150-meter) course. That's about as far from the slide at the kiddie pool, or from the tunnel of love, as any of us may care to get. ❑

RIGHT: Jurassic Park River Adventure.

SURVIVAL STRATEGIES

Having a fun time gets easier with a bit of foreknowledge, a dash of patience, and some plain old common sense

Taking on Orlando's theme parks can be a daunting prospect, especially with young children. The crowds, the heat, and the outlandish prices can sap your strength and empty your wallet before you know what hit you. But it doesn't have to be that way, if you think things through before leaving home and arrive prepared. So, in the interest of mental and financial health, here are a few tips to prevent your dream vacation from turning into a nightmare.

Rule no. 1: Have fun

Sounds simple enough when you're perusing brochures, but it's another matter when you're waiting in line, sweat trickling down your back, and your kids – exhausted from a day of overly ambitious touring – are whining like police sirens. A worst-case scenario? Maybe, although it's the rare family that tours a theme park unscathed. The ones who have the most fun, while enduring the fewest minor hassles and outright meltdowns, are those who remember the cardinal rule of theme park touring: slow down. This is a vacation, remember?

OK, this is easier said than done. After all, you only have so much time, and it's difficult to resist the hype surrounding the parks, but consider the hazards of trying to do too much. Unrealistic expectations will lead only to disappointment and exhaustion. Forget about packing as much as possible into your visit or even following some preordained schedule. Instead, select three or four "must-dos" for each day and fill in with other attractions as time allows. Remember, if you find yourself feeling more stressed-out than at a typical day of work, you are probably missing the point.

Timing is everything

The second most important rule is to use your time wisely. The key here is to visit the parks at the least crowded time of day, which in almost all cases is first thing in the morning.

Arrive at the parks about an hour before the posted opening. That way you can park, buy a ticket, and enter as soon as the gates swing open. Parks at Disney World and Universal Orlando usually open at least 30 minutes prior to the official time, although all attractions may not yet be running. You can often do more in the first two hours when lines are short and temperatures are mild, than in the remainder of the afternoon. Attendance peaks between 11am and 4pm – a good time for meals, shopping, and less popular attractions. If you're staying at an on-site resort, you might even sneak back to your hotel for a swim and a snooze. Keep in mind also that the Disney parks stop selling tickets when they reach capacity – another inducement to stake your claim early.

Granted, waking up at 6.30am in order to get to the Magic Kingdom by 8am isn't everyone's idea of taking it slow. For those who prefer a late start, another good time to do the rides is in the evening, when the early birds have already gone home. This is especially true at Universal, which often stays open for about an hour after the official closing. You can squeeze in two or three attractions with virtually no waiting, while most of the crowd is filing toward the exit.

'Tis the season

The least crowded season is from right after Thanksgiving weekend to the week before Christmas. Two other good windows are from immediately after Labor Day until the weekend before Thanksgiving, and from the second week of January to the first week in February (excluding Martin Luther King weekend). During these periods, waiting times for rides and attractions generally don't exceed 30 minutes.

You can count on the theme parks being swamped over Thanksgiving weekend, from Christmas to New Year's Day, and during Easter Week. It's prudent to avoid these times like the plague.

Also crowded are Presidents' week in February, spring break (the third week of March through the third week of April), and summer break. Be prepared to wait in line for up to two hours at popular attractions during these peak periods, which coincide with school vacations.

Sit, eat, relax

You should allow time for a decent sit-down meal at least once a day. This is especially important if you're traveling with young children, who are sure to be tired and grumpy after a couple of hours of schlepping from one

attraction to another. As always, the best time to eat is during off-hours, so plan on a late breakfast or an early lunch or dinner.

Reservations are absolutely essential. At Disney, reservations are known as "priority seating." Essentially, your party has dibs on the first available table at or after your appointed time. You should arrive about 15 minutes early in order to check in. If the restaurant isn't too busy, you'll be seated within 10 or 15 minutes.

Universal takes a more varied approach. Only Emeril's, Mythos, and Lombard's Landing accept reservations by phone. Others run on a first-come, first-served basis, though

LEFT: character greetings are a highlight for children.
RIGHT: plan on at least one sit-down meal a day.

WHICH PARK FIRST?

If you're visiting Disney with young children, save the Magic Kingdom for last. Kids find it the most exciting, and if you visit it first, they may be disappointed in the other parks. If you're not with kids, visit the park you're most excited about first. Bad weather, blisters, and fatigue might interfere with later plans.

At Universal, it's more or less a toss-up, since you can walk between the three main areas in less than 20 minutes. Islands of Adventure has the hairiest coasters, and Universal Studios has movie-related attractions and more shows. CityWalk, the entertainment complex, doesn't get hopping until about 8pm.

some give you a beeper so you can browse at nearby shops while you're waiting for a table. At some times, in some restaurants, priority seating is also an option. Call 407-224 9255 for information or check at the CityWalk information booth as you enter the complex.

With the exception of a few premier restaurants, food at the theme parks is notoriously mediocre and expensive, although the offerings at Universal are certainly a big improvement over Disney. As a general rule, the simpler dishes are the most satisfying. Be suspicious of complicated entrées with fancy descriptions and ethnic flair, especially at restaurants that are clearly not geared for high-end dining.

directed to an express lane. The maximum wait is usually 15 to 20 minutes, often much less.

If you don't mind splitting up your party, you can also take advantage of single rider lines, which offer time savings similar to the express system without having to return later. Another shortcut is designed for couples with children too small for certain rides. After waiting in line, one parent goes on the ride while the other stays with the kids at a switching off or baby swap area. When the first parent returns, the second one boards with no waiting in line again.

Both Disney and Universal give special privileges to visitors staying at on-site hotels. Guests at Disney resorts with multi-day passes can pur-

Know the shortcuts

The biggest gripe people have about visiting theme parks is the long lines. Both Disney and Universal have heard your grumbles and now offer several programs that greatly reduce the amount of time you'll spend staring at the back of another person's head.

The cornerstone of this effort is an electronic system that allows visitors to reserve a ride on the most popular attractions. Disney calls the system Fastpass, Universal calls it Universal Express, but they work essentially the same way: you stick your ticket into a kiosk stationed near the attraction and are given a window of time to ride. When you return, you'll be

chase tickets (about $12 for adults) for an after-hours "E-ride night" at the Magic Kingdom. Ticket holders are permitted to stay in the park for three hours after closing. Only about 5,000 tickets are issued, so riders are guaranteed ride if any waiting. The nine or ten "E-rides" (Disney-speak for the really good ones) that remain open include Space Mountain, Splash Mountain, Buzz Lightyear, and the Haunted Mansion. The schedule changes often, however, and E-ride nights may not be offered during your visit.

When it comes to perks, Universal offers the biggest plum of all. Guests at Universal hotels have only to flash their room key (it looks like a credit card) at an attendant to be whisked to the front of the line. It applies to all but a few rides and – in an obviously calculated move – trumps Disney by a mile.

Both Universal and Disney offer guided behind-the-scenes tours, with express access to select rides and a fascinating look at the operation of a theme park. Universal calls it the VIP Tour Experience and charges about $125 per day for a one- or two-day tour, including park admission. Disney offers more than a dozen options, including a backstage look at the Magic Kingdom, an informative tour of Disney-MGM's animation studio, and a scuba diving adventure at Epcot's Living Seas pavilion.

Both Disney and Universal have a maddening habit of canceling or changing such programs at a moment's notice, so ask for the latest information before arriving.

Be prepared

To be a successful tourist, you have to dress the part. Most visitors walk 4 to 8 miles (6–13 km) in a typical day at a theme park, so comfortable shoes are essential. The Florida sun is unmerciful, so wear light-colored clothing, a hat and sunglasses, and use plenty of sunscreen.

If you're traveling with kids, a backpack is also essential. Soft drinks are expensive, and you won't want to go hunting for a water fountain every time a kid gets thirsty, so pack water bottles or freeze individual juice boxes and sip them as they thaw. A few snacks will sustain everyone between meals. Don't forget a camera and perhaps an autograph book for Mickey and other characters you'll meet along the way.

Brief downpours are common in summer, so bring a poncho or umbrella and a towel and change of clothes if you intend to do the water rides. Lockers can be rented at all the parks, so you can stow clothes. If your party is going to split up, you may want to bring cell phones or beepers, or invest in a couple of walkie-talkies. A stroller is a must for all but the hardiest young children. You can bring your own or rent one at the parks. Tie a ribbon around the handle so you can identify it quickly among the dozens that are parked outside the attractions.

LEFT: you can pick up maps and entertainment schedules at the entrance gates.
RIGHT: it doesn't all have to be hectic.

Plan ahead

No matter how you cut it, this is bound to be an expensive vacation. A family of four will probably spend about $350–$400 a day, not including lodging and transportation. If you want to get your money's worth, therefore, you need to have a plan.

Request information from Disney, Universal, SeaWorld, and other theme parks (and/or the Orlando Convention and Visitors Bureau) well in advance, and allow at least four weeks for delivery. If you're planning to stay at a Disney or Universal property, allow even more time so you can pick the hotel you want (see Travel Tips for descriptions) and

reserve your lodging as far in advance as possible. Booking six or nine months in advance is not too early.

Buy park tickets before arriving. They're sold by phone, by mail, on the Internet, at the Orlando airport, in Disney stores at shopping malls, at Disney and Universal hotels, and by travel clubs like AAA (which offers a small discount). Some of these venues, such as mall stores and the Orlando airport, sell only multiple-day tickets. Do not buy tickets of any kind from sidewalk vendors or fly-by-night discounters: the savings will be small and they may not be legal. It's not worth taking a chance. ❏

PLACES

A detailed guide to the resorts and
the city, with the principal sites clearly
cross-referenced by number to the maps

The title of this book – Walt Disney World Resort and Orlando – reflects a basic fact about vacationing in central Florida: for most people, there's Disney, and then there's everything else. Situated off I-4 about 16 miles (26 km) from downtown Orlando and sprawling across an area roughly equal in size to Boston, Disney World truly is a city in its own right.

It has its own police, fire, and sanitation departments and an average daily population of over 100,000 people. It even has quasi-governmental status, thanks to a deal that Walt Disney and brother Roy cut with the state of Florida to create the Reedy Creek Improvement District, a public corporation that gives Disney powers usually reserved to municipalities.

There's a whole other world of entertainment outside Disney. About 9 miles (15 km) down I-4 is Disney World's chief competitor, Universal Orlando. Its two theme parks – Universal Studios and Islands of Adventure – offer some of the wildest and most technologically advanced rides in the Southeast. With the addition of a nighttime entertainment complex, and three new hotels, it has positioned itself as a self-contained, multi-day resort.

Between Universal and Disney World is SeaWorld, the third big player in Orlando's theme-park triumvirate. Famous as the home of Shamu, the killer whale, SeaWorld is a cross between an aquarium and an amusement park, with beautifully presented shows and exhibits featuring dolphins, seals, penguins, and other marine creatures as well as two world-class thrill rides.

Clustered along International Drive is an array of smaller attractions like Ripley's Believe It or Not Odditorium, and shopping and dining complexes such as the Mercado. Downtown Orlando houses the city's main cultural venues, including the Orlando Museum of Art and Orlando Science Center.

Farther afield, the area is scattershot with worthy destinations like old-time favorite Gatorland, and for those who don't mind a short drive, Busch Gardens in Tampa and the Kennedy Space Center on Cape Canaveral. The choices are rich indeed. Little wonder that Orlando and Disney World are the most visited tourist destinations in the United States. ❑

PRECEDING PAGES: the entrance to Dueling Dragons at Universal's Islands of Adventure, and screaming through the coils of the Python, Busch Gardens.
LEFT: Bullwinkle greets an appreciative fan at Universal Studios.

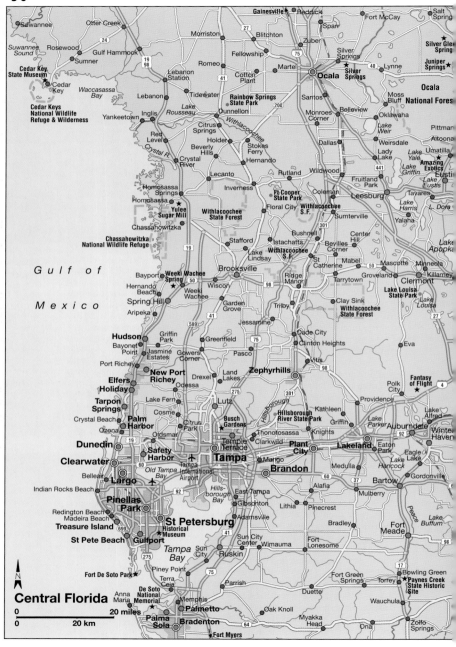

Gainesville · Reddick · Fort McCay · Salt Spring

Suwannee · Otter Creek · Morriston · Blitchton · Zuber · Spar · Silver Glen Spring

Rosewood · Gulf Hammock · Fellowship · Silver Springs · Lynne · Juniper Springs

Suwannee Sound · Sumner · Romeo · Martel · Ocala · Silver Springs · Ocala National Forest

Cedar Key State Museum · Cedar Key · Lebanon Station · Tidewater · Rainbow Springs State Park · Santos · Moss Bluff

Waccasassa Bay · Lebanon · Lake Rousseau · Dunnellon · Monroes Corner · Belleview · Oklawaha

Cedar Keys National Wildlife Refuge & Wilderness · Yankeetown · Inglis · Citrus Springs · Withlacoochee · Dallas · Lake Weir · Weirsdale · Pittman · Altoona

Red Level · Holder · Stokes Ferry · Lady Lake · Lake Yale · Amazing Exotics · Eustis

Crystal R. · Beverly Hills · Hernando · Rutland · Wildwood · Fruitland Park · Lake Griffin · Lake Eustis

Homosassa Springs · Lecanto · Inverness · Coleman · Leesburg · Tavares · L. Dora

Homosassa · Yulee Sugar Mill · Ft Cooper State Park · Floral City · Withlacoochee S.F. · Sumterville · Lake Harris · Yalaha

Chassahowitzka · Withlacoochee State Forest · Bushnell · Bevilles Corner · Center Hill · Mabel · Mascotte · Minneola · Lake Apopka

Chassahowitzka National Wildlife Refuge · Stafford · Istachatta · St Catherine · Groveland · Killarney · Clermont

Bayport · Weeki Wachee Spring · Brooksville · Ridge Manor · Tarrytown · Lake Louisa State Park · Lake Louisa

Hernando Beach · Weeki Wachee · Wiscory · Garden Grove · Trilby · Clay Sink · Withlacoochee State Forest

Spring Hill · Aripeka · Jessamine · Dade City · Clinton Heights · Eva

Hudson · Griffin Park · Greenfield · Pasco · Vitis · Fantasy of Flight

Bayonet Point · Jasmine Estates · Gowers Corner · Land Lakes · Zephyrhills · Polk City · Providence · Lake Alfred

Port Richey · New Port Richey · Drexel · Lutz · Kathleen · Griffin · Lake Parker · Auburndale · Winter Haven

Elfers · Holiday · Lake Fern · Odessa · Busch Gardens · Hillsborough River State Park · Knights · Eaton Park · Eagle Lake

Tarpon Springs · Cosme · Citrus Park · Thonotosassa · Clarkwild · Plant City · Lakeland · Medulla · Lake Hancock

Crystal Beach · Palm Harbor · Oldsmar · Temple Terrace · Marigo · Brandon · Alafia · Bartow · Gordonville

Dunedin · Safety Harbor · Tampa · East Tampa · Mulberry · Lake Buffum

Clearwater · Bellear · Old Tampa Bay · Tampa International Airport · Gibsonton · Lithia · Pinecrest · Fort Meade

Largo · Indian Rocks Beach · Pinellas Park · Adamsville · Bradley · Bowling Green

Redington Beach · Madeira Beach · Treasure Island · St Petersburg · Historical Museum · Sun City Center · Wimauma · Fort Lonesome · Paynes Creek State Historic Site

St Pete Beach · Gulfport · Tampa Bay · Sun City · Ruskin · Fort Green Springs · Torrey · Zolfo Springs

Fort De Soto Park · Piney Point · Terra Ceia · Parrish · Duette · Wauchula

De Soto National Memorial · Anna Maria · Memphis · Palmetto · Oak Knoll · Myakka Head · Ona

Palma Sola · Bradenton · Fort Myers

Central Florida

0 — 20 miles
0 — 20 km

Gulf of Mexico

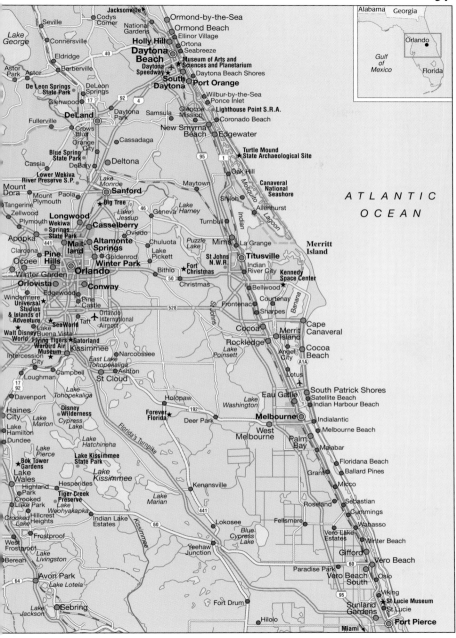

Alabama   Georgia

Orlando

Gulf
of
Mexico

Florida

*Lake
George*

Seville

Codys
Corner

Jacksonville

National
Gardens

Ormond-by-the-Sea
Ormond Beach
Ellinor Village
Ortona
Seabreeze

Connersville

Holly Hill
Daytona
Beach

Museum of Arts and
Sciences and Planetarium

Eldridge

Barberville

Daytona
Speedway

South
Daytona

Daytona Beach Shores

Port Orange

Astor
Park

Astor

De Leon Springs
State Park

DeLeon
Springs

92

4

Wilbur-by-the-Sea
Ponce Inlet

Lighthouse Point S.R.A.

Glenwood

17

Fullerville

DeLand

Daytona
Park

Samsula

Glencoe
Mission

Coronado Beach

Crows
Bluff

Cassadaga

New Smyrna
Beach

Edgewater

Orange
City

Blue Spring
State Park

Cassia

Deltona

95

1

Turtle Mound
State Archaeological Site

Oak Hill

Lower Wekiva
River Preserve S.P.

DeBary

*Lake
Monroe*

Canaveral
National
Seashore

Mount
Dora

Mount Paola
Plymouth

Sanford

Maytown

Shiloh

Tangerine

Big Tree

*Lake
Harney*

Allenhurst

Zellwood

Plymouth

*Lake
Jessup*

Geneva

Turnbull

Longwood

Wekiwa
Springs
State Park

Casselberry

Oviedo

Merritt
Island

Apopka

441

Altamonte
Springs

Chuluota

*Puzzle
Lake*

Mims

La Grange

Clarcona

Mait-
land

Goldenrod

*Lake
Pickett*

St Johns
N.W.R.

Titusville

Pine
Hills

Winter Park

Bithlo

Fort
Christmas

Indian
River City

Kennedy
Space Center

Ocoee

Orlando

Winter Garden

50

Orlovista

Conway

Christmas

Bellwood

Edgewood

Pine
Castle

Frontenac

Windermere

Universal
Studios
& Islands of
Adventure

528

Orlando
International
Airport

Tatt

Courtenay

Sharpes

Walt Disney
World

SeaWorld

Lake
Buena Vista

Cocoa

Cape
Canaveral

Flying Tigers
Warbird Air
Museum

Gatorland

Kissimmee

Rockledge

Merrit
Island

Cocoa
Beach

Intercession
City

East Lake
Tohopekaliga

Ashton

*Lake
Poinsett*

Angel
City

A1A

Loughman

Campbell

St Cloud

Lotus

17
92

*Lake
Tohopekaliga*

Holopaw

*Lake
Washington*

Eau Gallie

South Patrick Shores

Davenport

Satellite Beach

Indian Harbour Beach

Haines
City

Disney
Wilderness

*Cypress
Lake*

Forever
Florida

192

Deer Park

Melbourne

Indialantic

*Lake
Marion*

Melbourne Beach

*Lake
Hamilton*

Dundee

*Lake
Pierce*

West
Melbourne

Lake Kissimmee
State Park

Palm
Bay

Malabar

Bok Tower
Gardens

*Lake
Kissimmee*

Floridana Beach

Lake
Wales

Hesperides

Grant

Ballard Pines

Highland
Park

Micco

Crooked
Lake Park

Tiger Creek
Preserve

*Lake
Weohyakapka*

Kenansville

441

Roseland

Sebastian

Hillcrest
Heights

Indian Lake
Estates

Cummings

Crooked
Lake

Frostproof

*Lake
Marian*

60

Lokosee

Fellsmere

Wabasso

West
Frostproof

*Lake
Livingston*

Vero Lake
Estates

Winter Beach

Bereah

64

Yeehaw
Junction

*Blue
Cypress
Lake*

Gifford

Avon Park

Lake Lotela

60

Vero Beach

Oslo

*Lake
Jackson*

Sebring

Fort Drum

Paradise Park

Vero Beach
South

Viking

95

St Lucie Museum

St Lucie

Hilolo

Sunland
Gardens

Fort Pierce

Miami

A T L A N T I C

O C E A N

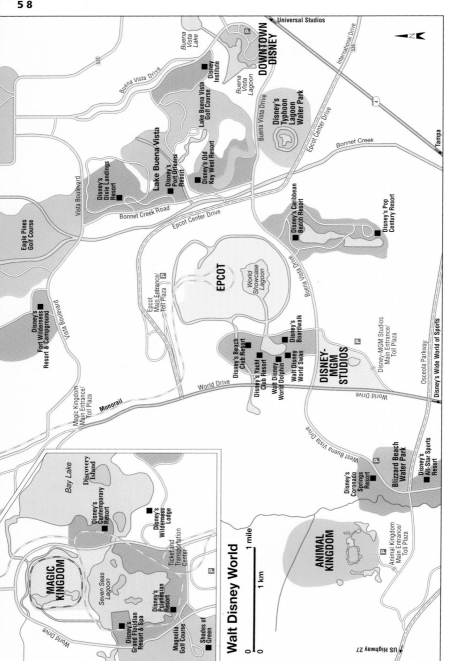

Walt Disney World

WALT DISNEY WORLD

Beyond the house that Walt built is a vast
entertainment complex that keeps
pleasure-seekers coming back for more

I f you're under the impression that Walt Disney World is nothing but an overgrown amusement park, think again. Its 43 square miles (111 sq. km) – an area twice the size of Manhattan – encompass not one, but four of the world's most elaborate theme parks. The sentimental favorite, the Magic Kingdom, opened in 1971 and is the most closely attuned to Walt Disney's original (and now somewhat dated) vision of fun and fantasy. If you're traveling with very young children or just enjoy classic Disney magic, this is the place to go. In 1982, Disney World expanded to include Epcot, a permanent world's fair with an emphasis on technology and world culture. In response to theme-park rival Universal Studios, Disney-MGM Studios opened in 1989, with rides and shows inspired by television and the movies. The most recent addition, Animal Kingdom, unveiled in 1998, is a state-of-the-art zoo with naturalistic habitats and an array of rides and attractions.

But that's only the beginning. Disney has added a host of other inducements, including two water parks, two nighttime entertainment districts, six golf courses, three spas, and a professional sports complex, not to mention over a dozen hotels and 100 restaurants. The idea is to provide an all-in-one vacation experience. Indeed, there are so many diversions that some people come back year after year and never feel that they've done everything.

A note about pictures

Part of Disney's success is the control it maintains over the guest experience. Nearly every aspect of your stay at Disney World – from the Mickey Mouse waffles to the lilting melodies piped into the public toilets – is scripted in advance. No detail is too minor. It's all part and parcel of the "Disney magic."

The same goes for the company's efforts to control its public image, including – and of particular relevance to an illustrated book like this one – the publication of pictures showing Disney characters, logos, and attractions. That's why the photographs in the next few chapters capture the spirit of Disney World without actually showing much of the place itself. Disney restricts the use of photos in travel guides unless the publisher agrees to submit text for prior approval. We respectfully declined the offer, preferring to retain editorial independence so as to speak straight about Disney World – the good, the bad, the merely so-so. The result, we feel, is a more informative book for readers who want to get the most out of their Disney vacation. ❑

THE MAGIC KINGDOM

Fantasy continues to thrive here, just as Walt imagined. The park remains a magnet for millions of starry-eyed visitors – young and old

More than a quarter century after it was opened to the public, the Magic Kingdom remains the enchanting place that Walt Disney imagined. Though attractions have been updated over the years and a few are targeted at seasoned thrill-seekers, the park remains a gentle, almost quaint place whose power to enchant lies more in extravagant design (what the Disney people call imagineering) than in thrill rides or special effects. This is, at heart, a children's park, although the painstaking detail, good humor, and whimsy with which Walt's vision is brought to life rarely disappoints even the most jaded traveler.

If there's a downside to the Magic Kingdom it's that the place is too darn popular. This is the most visited theme park in North America, and in some respects it's the victim of its own success. About 15 million people a year pass through the gates – 75,000 or more on a busy day – and the sheer density of bodies can be oppressive. There are ways to avoid the worst of the rush – arrive early, visit during the slow season, use Fastpass and priority seating – but waiting in line for rides, shows, restaurants, and transportation is virtually unavoidable. Disney managers have learned to make queues as painless as possible, but waiting

half an hour or more (sometimes a lot more) for a ride that lasts only a few minutes can wear down even the most buoyant tourist.

Main Street, U.S.A.

If you're staying at a Disney resort, you'll be transported to the entrance of the Magic Kingdom by bus or, depending on the resort, by boat or monorail. If you're traveling by car, you'll have to park and buy tickets at the **Transportation and Ticket Center**, then take a 10-

Map on page 62

LEFT: Walt Disney and Mickey Mouse in a publicity photo from the early days of the Disney Company.
BELOW: celebrating Easter, Disney style.

Magic Kingdom

↑ N

MICKEY'S TOONTOWN FAIR
29
Judge's Tent

Ariel's Grotto

FANTASYLAND
Toontown Hall of Fame
23
"it's a small world"
20
Dumbo the Flying Elephant

Mickey's Country House
WDW Railroad-Mickey's Toontown Fair Depot

Fort Sam Clemens

Big Thunder Mountain
14

18
Haunted Mansion

Minnie's Country House

22
Peter Pan's Flight

Fantasyland Character Festival

30
Donald's Boat

WDW Railroad Frontierland Depot

Mickey's PhilharMagic
21

24
Cinderella's Golden Carousel

The Barnstormer at Goofy's Wiseacre Farm

Rivers of America

25
Mad Tea Party

Splash Mountain
13

Tom Sawyer Island
15

Liberty Belle Riverboat

27
Snow White's Scary Adventures

26
The Many Adventures of Winnie the Pooh

FRONTIERLAND
12

Hall of Presidents
19

LIBERTY SQUARE
17

Cinderella's Castle
5

28
Fairytale Garden

Tomorrowland Indy Speedway
32

16
Country Bear Jamboree

Liberty Tree Tavern

TOMORROWLAND

Shops and Restaurant

Frontierland Shootin' Arcade

Goofy's Country Dancin' Jamboree

Castle Forecourt Stage

Shops and Restaurant

31

The Enchanted Tiki Room

CARIBBEAN PLAZA
11

10
The Magic Carpets of Aladdin

CENTRAL SQUARE (HUB)

Stitch's Great Escape

Tomorrowland Arcade
33

Shrunken Ned's Junior Jungle Boats

35
Buzz Lightyear's Space Ranger Spin

Space Mountain

9
Pirates of the Caribbean

7
Swiss Family Treehouse

Crystal Palace
4

Astro Orbiter

Jungle Cruise
8

Tomorrowland Stage

ADVENTURELAND
6

MAIN STREET, U.S.A.
1

Tomorrowland Transit Authority

Carousel of Progress
34

Galaxy Palace Theater

Tony's Town Square Restaurant
3

TOWN SQUARE

Walt Disney World Railroad

Town Square Exposition Hall

2
City Hall

Disney Resort Bus Facility

Monorail

Entrance

Monorail Station

Seven Seas Lagoon

minute monorail or ferry ride to the park entrance.

Dozens of artfully-decorated Mickeys greet you at the entrance plaza, foreshadowing the endless ears that lie ahead. Follow the walkway under an ornate, Victorian-style railroad station to **Main Street, U.S.A. ❶**, a picture-perfect evocation of an American town circa 1900. Shops and restaurants occupy buildings scaled down to four-fifths of their normal size, a trick called forced perspective that Disney designers borrowed from Renaissance artists.

Allow yourself enough time to soak in the scene – the architectural details, the fanciful signs (look for familiar names such as Walt and Roy Disney in the windows above the shops), the lilting strains of Disney tunes, the ever-present smell of popcorn and homemade cookies – all coming together to give Main Street a dreamy, movie-set quality.

There are no major attractions along Main Street, but there's no lack of distractions, either. Horse-drawn trolleys, double-decker buses, and an old-fashioned fire truck transport visitors up and down the street. A barbershop quartet serenades passersby and shoppers browse in more than a dozen stores, including a few where candymakers, glassblowers, silhouette artists, and other artisans demonstrate their work.

At the top of Main Street, near the entrance, is the **Walt Disney World Railroad**, which takes passengers on a 1.5-mile (2.5-km) journey around the Magic Kingdom with stops in Frontierland and Mickey's Toontown Fair. The steam engines were built around the turn of the century and purchased in Mexico, where they were being used to haul sugarcane. The whole circuit takes about 20 minutes and offers a few good views of the park. Unless you're a train aficionado, it's best to leave the railroad for later in the day, when footsore kids will be glad for a ride back to Main Street.

To the left of the train station is **City Hall ❷**, where you can pick up a map and entertainment schedule, arrange priority seating at park restaurants, and ask knowledgeable staffers for information. Just across the plaza, the **Town Square Exposition Hall** houses a camera shop, an exhibit on the history of photography, and a theater that screens classic Disney movies. It makes a great retreat from the crowds, especially for those who prefer vintage Disney animation. Costumed characters often greet visitors near the entrance in the morning.

Main Street eats

Of the many restaurants and food vendors along Main Street, two are noteworthy: **Tony's Town Square Restaurant ❸** serves pasta, pizza, salads, and other Italian fare in an atmosphere reminiscent of the trattoria in *Lady and the Tramp*. **The Plaza Restaurant** at the opposite end of Main Street sells chicken strips and

Map on page 62

TIP

Do popular rides during parades. Avoid them immediately after nearby shows let out.

BELOW: the premiere of Disneyland in California in 1955 – an excuse for 50th-anniversary celebrations in 2005.

big sandwiches but has plenty of outdoor seating with a great view of Cinderella's Castle. The **Crystal Palace** ❹ features an all-you-can-eat buffet with Winnie the Pooh, Piglet, and other characters from the Hundred Acre Wood in a glass pavilion inspired by San Francisco's Conservatory of Flowers.

Main Street is also the principal route for Magic Kingdom **parades** – one in the afternoon and one (sometimes two) in the evening. Themes change every couple of years, but you can count on seeing plenty of Disney characters and interesting floats. High school bands often warm up the crowd before the main attraction.

Main Street leads to a roundabout known as the **Hub**, beyond which is **Cinderella's Castle** ❺, the visual anchor of the park and a Disney icon second only to Mickey Mouse himself. There are no rides in the castle, but a restaurant on the second floor, **Cinderella's Royal Table**, is decked out like a medieval banquet hall, with stone walls, banners, and suits of armor. The "Once Upon a Time" character breakfast is

Rope-drop

It's an event in the tradition of the Oklahoma Land Rush, the London Marathon, or opening time at your favorite shopping mall on the day after Thanksgiving. Only this mad dash occurs every single day of the year.

We're talking about Disney World's "rope drop," the morning signal for mustering crowds at the entrance to the Magic Kingdom. It's preceded by an entertaining show involving Mickey and all his friends. Disney PR agents insist there is only one Mickey at Disney World, though they do admit he's quite magical. Indeed, as he appears at the opening of all the parks, even when they open at the same time.

Main Street, U.S.A, which lies immediately beyond the main gate, is the first part of the park to admit guests. Thirty minutes to an hour later, the rest of the park opens with yet another "rope drop." Entryways to the Magic Kingdom beyond Main Street are roped off at three points adjoining the hub at the street's far end. When the ropes drop, you want to be in the right place: on the left side of the hub for Adventureland and Frontierland; on the right for Tomorrowland; or at center for Fantasyland and Liberty Square.

extremely popular and features appearances by a roster of Disney royalty – Snow White, Belle, Sleeping Beauty, Jasmine, and, your hostess, Cinderella. Lunch and dinner are quite pricey and the subject of much grousing about the quality of the food. The open-air Forecourt Stage, just in front of the castle, is used for a musical show starring several well-known Disney characters. In May 2005, a new show, Cinderellabration, will open to commemorate the 50th anniversary of Disneyland California. Check your guide map for show times.

Adventureland

Pathways radiate from the Hub into five distinct lands, starting on the left (as you face Cinderella's Castle) with **Adventureland** ❻. Adventure in this case takes in a wide range of geography, from the Amazon river and Pacific Islands to the Spanish Main and ancient Arabia. All are rendered in detailed and imaginative style, with elaborate sets, gorgeous landscaping, and a subtle but persistent soundtrack of jungle noises, drums, and exotic melodies.

The first attraction is a classic. **Swiss Family Treehouse** ❼ brings to life the treetop home of Johann Wyss's fictional castaways, the Swiss Family Robinson. Children will get more out of the experience if they first read the book or see the movie, but they'll enjoy exploring the various rooms perched in the canopy of this huge, artificial banyan tree even if they haven't. Especially intriguing is the bamboo plumbing and the intricate system of ropes and pulleys that sets it in motion.

Next up is the **Jungle Cruise** ❽, a Magic Kingdom original that, frankly, is beginning to show its age. Canopied river boats take you on a 10-minute float trip through the jungles of Asia, Africa, and South America. Along the way you encounter a menagerie of animatronic (Disney's term for robotic) animals, including hippos, pythons, elephants, and an ill-tempered crocodile. Teenagers will probably be bored by the experience, though young children will find it amusing and adults may get a chuckle or two out of the guide's corny schtick. **Shrunken Ned's Junior Jungle Boats**, a minor attraction near the exit of the Jungle Cruise, gives you a chance to pilot a miniature remote-controlled vessel around a little lagoon, although you'll have to pay a few bucks for the privilege.

If the line is long for the Jungle Cruise – and it often is – you may want to skip ahead to **Pirates of the Caribbean ❾**. Here you'll find some of Disney's most spirited animatronic work. After inching your way into the bowels of what looks (and smells) like the dungeon of an old Spanish castle, you board a ship for a slow, dark ride back in time, only to find yourself smack in the middle of a pirate invasion. The action has been toned down over the years in deference to politically-correct sensibilities, but there is still plenty of rum-soaked debauchery on view. Buccaneers fire cannon, chase wenches, squabble over booty, and quaff beer on overhead bridges. The technology is hardly cutting edge, but the whole thing comes off with a "yo-ho-ho" high-spiritedness that's hard to resist. A word of warning: very young kids may find the dungeon scenes a little too creepy for comfort.

Right in the center of Adventureland are the **Magic Carpets of Aladdin ❿**, a hub-and-spoke ride familiar to anyone who's been to a county fair. Passengers sit in colorful four-seater cars tricked out like flying carpets, then zoom round and round and up and down while fountains resembling camels spit at them from the sides. A control stick makes the car ascend or descend and pitch forward or back. A new shopping area here, the **Agrabah Bazaar**, is fashioned after the market in the Aladdin films.

Disney's first animatronic venture in 1963 featured hundreds of animated birds in a classic show known as the **Enchanted Tiki Room ⓫**.

Map on page 62

BELOW:
Walt Disney inspects an early version of the Jungle Cruise.

Now "under new management," the 300-bird show stars *The Lion King*'s wise Zazu and *Aladdin*'s smart-mouthed Iago. The old birds protest that their show has been successful since 1963 and doesn't need a change. Iago comes back with a squawky pastiche of the song "You Ain't Never Had a Friend Like Me," then proceeds to anger the vengeful fire gods, who let loose a barrage of fire and brimstone. Other contemporary numbers like "Hot, Hot, Hot" give the show a much-needed bounce. Overall, it makes for an amusing, if not spectacular, 15 minutes, especially appealing to younger children, although some may be frightened by the volume and intensity of the effects.

Frontierland

The rides are more exhilarating over at **Frontierland** ⓬, a slice of the Old West done up in Disney style, with stockade fences, worn wooden boardwalks, and trading posts (OK, they're souvenir shops) stocked with coonskin hats, sheriff badges, and American Indian crafts. The most popular attraction is **Splash Mountain** ⓭, a 10-minute log flume ride that takes you on a journey into the world of Br'er Rabbit, Br'er Fox and Br'er Bear from Disney's 1946 *Song of the South*. Dozens of animatronic figures reenact scenes from the movie as riders dip and turn through caves, swamps, and forests before making a drenching, five-story plunge. Those in the front seats will be soaked. Everyone else can expect a cooling spritz at the very least. Another thing you can count on are long lines. Your best strategy is to arrive first thing in the morning or reserve a riding time with Fastpass.

Only slightly less crowded is **Big Thunder Mountain** ⓮, a roller coaster that's light on thrills and heavy on concept. The 2,780-foot (847-meter) track leads in and around an elaborate recreation of southern Utah's red-rock country. Scenes of crusty miners, ornery mules, and ramshackle mining camps whiz by as your runaway train careens through canyons and caverns and over rickety bridges. Though the experience is more intense than, say, the Barn-

BELOW: strollers are convenient for much-needed naps.

stormer over at Mickey's Toontown Fair, it's a piece of cake compared to Space Mountain and strictly minor league compared to the big coasters at other Orlando parks. This is a good choice for children who consider themselves too grown-up for "kiddie rides" but who aren't yet ready to take on the big guns.

Opposite Big Thunder Mountain you can hitch a ride on one of the rafts that crosses the Rivers of America (actually a circular lagoon) to **Tom Sawyer Island ⓯**, a refreshingly low-tech attraction, where kids explore caves, trails, and a pioneer fort under their own steam.

Best of all, mom and dad can enjoy a cool glass of lemonade on the porch of **Aunt Polly's Dockside Inn**, an out-of-the-way spot for sandwiches, ice cream, and cold drinks, and a good choice for lunch or a midafternoon break.

Back on the mainland, the **Country Bear Jamboree ⓰** is the Magic Kingdom at its down-home best, or worst, depending on how you feel about this hillbilly hoedown starring a cast of animatronic bears. Opinions are divided on this long-running show. Some people find the scripting stale and corny; others say it's a real kid-pleaser, a Disney classic. Judge for yourself, if you don't mind standing in line; a waiting time of 30 to 45 minutes is not unusual during the busy season. Next door is the **Frontierland Shootin' Arcade**, where for a few quarters you can take target practice with old-fashioned rifles that emit laser beams instead of bullets.

Another choice for those who like Western-style singing and dancing is **Goofy's Country Dancin' Jamboree**, a live show that's presented regularly throughout the day. In addition to Disney's beloved dog, Chip and Dale join a real live human to lead the singing and dancing. Try to stay downstairs. It will give your kids a chance to dance with the characters later in the show. Sitting upstairs, though, gives you a great view of embarrassed parents trying to learn the two-step.

Liberty Square

The Wild West melds into colonial America at **Liberty Square ⓱**, where you can see a replica of the Liberty Bell, cool off in the shade of the 150-year-old Liberty Tree, or hop aboard the triple-decker *Liberty Belle* **Riverboat**, a steam-powered paddlewheeler that takes a relaxing, 15-minute cruise around Tom Sawyer Island.

The most popular attraction here – and, according to some Disney aficionados, the best in the park – is the **Haunted Mansion ⓲**, a masterful combination of set design and special effects that most people find more funny than frightening. After waiting in a lobby whose walls appear to get closer and closer, you board a doom buggy for a tour of the house and its incorporeal residents. There's a library full of ghost writers, spectral dancers, a skeleton who plays the

Map on page 62

TIP

Height requirements are 35 inches (89 cm) for The Barnstormer, 40 inches (102 cm) for Splash Mountain and Big Thunder Mountain, 44 inches (112 cm) at Space Mountain, and 52 inches (132 cm) for Tomorrowland Speedway.

Mr Toad's Last Ride

In the hierarchy of the Disney pantheon, J. Thaddeus Toad ranks well below Mickey, Donald, and Goofy. But the irrepressible hero of Kenneth Grahame's 1908 book *The Wind in the Willows* – and of a 1949 Disney film – became one of Fantasyland's highest-profile denizens when his attraction, *Mr Toad's Wild Ride*, was threatened with dismantling in 1997.

The Toad ride was an oddity at Disney World, involving a madcap train ride to the least Disney-esque place imaginable – hell. But it had fiercely loyal supporters. When Disney management announced that they wanted to replace Mr Toad with a tame-hearted Winnie-the-Pooh ride, protestors responded with a web site, letter-writing campaign, and even a series of "Toad-Ins." Their T-shirts read, "Ask me why Mickey is killing Mr Toad."

All the action was for naught. Mr Toad's end was nigh. He took his last ride in September 1998. Though childhood may seem eternal at Disney World, a cartoon frog's lifespan is as ephemeral as his fame to the park's executives. Pooh, said a Disney spokesman, "is a lot more relevant than Mr Toad." *Bon voyage,* Mr Toad.

The Sword in the Stone Ceremony is performed several times a day behind Cinderella's Castle. The show stars Merlin, who selects a worthy child from the audience to remove Excalibur from the stone.

bones, a woman in a crystal ball, and, in a clever bit of astral projection, an apparition that appears in your car. The holographic effects – cutting edge when the ride opened some 25 years ago – still hold up pretty well. Despite the mansion's popularity, waiting times aren't usually a major problem. If the line is long, try back in 30 minutes or so.

On the opposite side of Liberty Square, the **Hall of Presidents** ⑲ occupies a Federal-style building reminiscent of those around Philadelphia's Independence Hall. Exhibits in the waiting area include a few odd pieces of presidential memorabilia, including George Washington's silver tongue scraper and Jimmy Carter's fly-fishing box. Inside the theater, a brief multimedia presentation on the US Constitution sets the program's patriotic tone. Then the screens part to reveal animatronic models of all 43 US presidents. Each figure nods his head or otherwise gestures at the mention of his name. Introductions made, George W. Bush makes a few comments on America's role as the guardian of freedom (this animatronic

Bush's speech comes off rather smoother than usual). Notice how the presidents fidget during the presentation and the detail in their costumes, each painstakingly researched and recreated in period style.

You'll find one of the Magic Kingdom's better eateries just across the plaza from the Hall of Presidents. It's the **Liberty Tree Tavern**, a full-service restaurant decked out like a colonial inn. The all-you-can-eat dinner features visits from Minnie Mouse, Pluto, Goofy, and others.

Fantasyland

For many visitors, **Fantasyland** ⑳ is the heart and soul of the Magic Kingdom, a place that Walt Disney described as a "timeless land of enchantment." Among the most winning attractions here is **Mickey's PhilharMagic** ㉑, a 3-D show presented continuously throughout the day in a 500-seat theater. The Magic Kingdom's newest attraction doesn't disappoint. Donald Duck guides you through a world of 3-D animation, music, and special effects.

The show includes appearances by Ariel, Simba, Peter Pan, and Tinkerbell and characters from *Aladdin* singing songs from their respective films. In the ensuing chaos, the audience is sprinkled with mop water and blown by the winds of London while following Peter Pan's Flight. The show lasts about 15 minutes but the theater's large capacity keeps crowds manageable at most times of day.

Just around the bend, the real (well non-celluloid) **Peter Pan's Flight** ㉒ is a beautifully-executed dark ride that takes passengers on a journey to Never-Never Land aboard a two-person pirate ship. After soaring through the night sky over London, you learn that Captain Hook has kidnapped the Darling children, and off you go on a whirlwind tour involving such familiar characters as Tinker Bell, the Lost

Hidden Mickeys

Though you may feel that every time you turn around you see a new way of presenting the familiar silhouette of Mickey Mouse's trademark ears, Disney imagineers have made a game out of hiding them. You don't win any prizes for spotting Mickey-shaped ice cream or shrubbery (well you don't win any prizes at all actually), but lurking in the midst of nearly every Disney attraction is a hidden Mickey.

Strangely enough, this most ubiquitous presence at Disney World can sometimes be quite tricky to find. This concept originated as an inside joke. In their simplest form, hidden Mickeys consist simply of the head-and-ears Mickey silhouette, subtly incorporated into a structural or graphic design. Later, imagineers got even more creative, slipping Mickeys into such unexpected places as a table setting in the Haunted Mansion, the dwarfs' stone fireplace in Snow White's Scary Adventures, and an arrangement of rusty old gears on Big Thunder Mountain. Mickey really is everywhere at Disney World, but he's not always easy to find. Souvenir shops sell guides to help you find your way through the world of hidden Mickeys.

Boys, Princess Tiger Lily, and a certain pirate-munching crocodile.

Working your way clockwise around Fantasyland, you come next to the ride that Disney critics love to hate – **"it's a small world" ㉓**, – made all the smaller, cynics say, by the incessant singing of hundreds of animatronic dolls. A slow-moving boat floats through chambers representing various corners of the world, each one populated with scores of the chirpy cherubs in folksy costumes. There are Italian gondoliers, German oompah bands, American Indians with drums, and feathers, and many, many more. Love it or hate it, you have to experience it, although you run the risk of having the melody seared permanently into your brain.

Young children will be delighted by the two classic rides in the middle of fantasyland: **Cinderella's Golden Carousel ㉔** is a meticulously-refurbished merry-go-round built in 1917 and salvaged from an amusement park in New Jersey. **Dumbo the Flying Elephant** is another hub-and-spoke ride, this one created in the image of the floppy-eared pachyderm. A joystick in each car lets kids go up or down at will.

Nearby, the **Fantasyland Character Festival** is a meet and greet with Pluto, Goofy, Pinocchio, and other characters. Around the other side of the lagoon is **Ariel's Grotto**, where tots can get their photo taken with the Little Mermaid and cool off in a play area with interactive fountains.

Remember when you were a kid and enjoyed twirling around until you could barely stand up? That's the sensation you get on the **Mad Tea Party ㉕** – what folks in the amusement-park biz call a "spin-and-barf" ride. Riders sit in whirling teacups, mounted on giant-sized whirling discs, set on a whirling turntable. A steering wheel controls

just how fast your teacup spins. The ride lasts only about two minutes, just long enough to make you wish you had taken some Dramamine.

As soon as your head stops spinning, saunter over to the **Many Adventures of Winnie the Pooh ㉖**, a whimsical journey through the storybook world of the Hundred Acre Wood. Riders in oversized hunny pots bounce along with Pooh and his mates – Piglet, Owl, Eeyore, Tigger, and others – as they encounter Heffalumps, Woozles, and a bit of blustery weather. Long lines are a given here. Fortunately, this is one of the rides at the Magic Kingdom that utilizes the Fastpass system.

The mood is decidedly darker at **Snow White's Scary Adventures ㉗**, a frightening experience for some preschoolers despite a recent overhaul that softened the story line. The problem is the wicked witch, who makes several sudden appearances, poison apple in hand. Not to worry: the prince eventually delivers the fateful smooch, and he and Snow White live – what else? – happily ever after. If your little ones

Map on page 62

Coins tossed into the fountain to the left of Cinderella's Castle in Fantasyland are donated to children's charities.

BELOW: putting on a game face.

were frightened by the movie, the ride is probably too intense.

The last attraction in Fantasyland is perhaps the simplest and sweetest. **Storytime with Belle** is presented in the **Fairytale Garden** ㉘, a pleasant little theater made to look like the ruins of a stone courtyard behind and to the right of Cinderella's Castle. Here Belle, played by a live actress, retells Beauty and the Beast, using children from the audience as the cast. One lucky dad gets to portray the Beast and dance with Belle, who hangs around after the show for autographs and photos.

Mickey's Toontown Fair

Squeezed between Fantasyland and Tomorrowland is **Mickey's Toontown Fair** ㉙, a 3-acre (1-hectare) slice of Mickey's cartoon universe brought brilliantly to life by Disney imagineers. Unveiled in 1988 to celebrate the rodent's 60th birthday, the park's newest land proved so popular it was allowed to stay on indefinitely. The charm of this area lies almost entirely in the loopy, toon-ish set design and the freedom with which young visitors can explore their surroundings. Three attractions – **Mickey's Country House**, **Minnie's Country House**, and **Donald's Boat** – invite kids to explore at will. You can look inside Minnie's refrigerator and check for messages on her answering machine, wander through Mickey's garden, peruse the baby pictures in his bedroom, or get soaked aboard Donald's leaky boat, the Miss Daisy, a play area where just about everything drips, sprays, or splashes.

There's only one ride in this section of the park, the **Barnstormer at Goofy's Wiseacre Farm** ㉚, a roller coaster styled like an old-fashioned biplane and scaled down for young riders and their parents. Mickey himself greets visitors in the red-and-white-striped **Judge's Tent**, and an all-star lineup of Disney characters, including Snow White, Alice in Wonderland, and Winnie the Pooh, hang out at the **Toontown Hall of Fame**. There's often a separate line for those who prefer to hobnob with Disney's best – that is, worst – villains.

TIP

The day ends at Magic Kingdom with a spectacular fireworks display called Wishes. Jiminy Cricket guides a cast of Disney characters through a story told amongst the stars in the sky.

BELOW: ice-cream stands and other food vendors are situated throughout the park.

Tomorrowland

The problem with the future is that it never stands still. What seemed cutting edge just a few years ago is passé today. That's why, in the late 1980s, Disney designers revamped the badly-dated **Tomorrowland** 31, shifting the emphasis away from a vision of the future as it might actually unfold to a vision of the future as it was imagined in classic science fiction books and movies. The result is an architectural environment of sleek steel spires and blazing neon that takes its cues from sources as varied as Buck Rogers, Jules Verne, and *Fritz Lang's Metropolis*.

What the **Tomorrowland Indy Speedway** 32 has to do with the future is a mystery, as is why this attraction – essentially a go-cart ride – has remained so popular over the years. Though the cars are sleek and have their own gas-powered engines, they actually run on a track, are difficult to steer and achieve a top speed of only 7 miles per hour (11 kph). Add to this the chronically long lines, the mind-numbing roar of the engines, and the haze of exhaust fumes, and you'd be better off riding the go-carts at an amusement park back home.

Space Mountain 33, on the other hand, is a perennial favorite, and deservedly so. The Magic Kingdom's most challenging coaster rides on an indoor track replete with whiz-bang visual effects and, weirdest of all, stretches of inky darkness. The ride, lasting only about three minutes, is actually quite tame compared to brawnier coasters at SeaWorld and Universal Orlando but, like so many Disney rides, it's the ancillary effects that make it worth the wait. You exit into the **Tomorrowland Arcade**, a good place to escape the heat, avoid the crowds and empty your pockets of spare change.

At **Walt Disney's Carousel of Progress** 34, the audience sits in a rotating theater that chronicles the way technology has changed the lives of an animatronic family. Old folks seem to enjoy the show. Kids, especially teens, find it a snooze.

The railway you've been seeing overhead is part of the **Tomorrowland Transit Authority**, which offers a relaxing, 10-minute ride aboard trams powered by non-polluting, electromagnetic linear induction motors. A portion of the tracks actually pass through Space Mountain. Just a few steps away from the boarding area is the entrance to **Astro Orbiter**, yet another hub-and-spoke ride à la Dumbo, this one with rocket ships straight out of the old Buck Rogers flicks.

Far more dynamic is **Buzz Lightyear's Space Ranger Spin** 35, an interactive dark ride. Every car is equipped with a joystick, a couple of laser cannons and electronic scoreboards. The idea is to help Buzz Lightyear save the universe from the evil Emperor Zurg by blasting as many of the bad guys as possible. The line moves quickly, but shorten the wait by using Fastpass. ❏

Map on page 62

The Galaxy Palace Theater in Tomorrowland features Disney characters and live bands. Check the entertainment schedule for performance times.

RESTAURANTS

Cinderella's Royal Table
Cinderella Castle
(priority seating)
Festive medieval setting serves up Once Upon A Time character breakfast. Salads and sandwiches at midday. Dinner menu includes spice-crusted salmon and beef tenderloin. **$$**

Liberty Tree Tavern
Liberty Square
(priority seating)
Decorated in the style of an 18th-century inn. Cooking has a New England touch with stews, chowders, fresh fish, and bread bowls. All-you-can-eat dinner feast includes roast turkey and honey mustard ham. **$$**

Tony's Town Square Restaurant
Main Street USA
(priority seating)
As close as the Magic Kingdom gets to fine dining, this Italian restaurant serves a healthy selection of salads and pastas. **$$**

• • • • • • • • • • • • • • •
Price includes dinner and a glass of wine (when available), excluding tip.
***$$$** over $30, **$$** between $20–30, **$** under $20. For priority seating, stop by City Hall or call 407-939 3463. Dialing *88 from a public phone in Disney will give you free access to this number.*

EPCOT

Technology and world cultures are at the forefront
of this theme park, intended by Walt Disney to
demonstrate advanced urban design but
created in the spirit of a world's fair

Orlando

Epcot

Kissimmee

Walt Disney originally con-
ceived of Epcot as a living
laboratory – an Experimental Prototype Community of Tomorrow (EPCOT) that would blaze a trail
into a brave new world of urban
design and technology. Alas, the
vision perished with its creator.
Shortly after Walt's death in 1966,
park planners reconfigured Epcot
along commercial lines, transform-
ing his pie-in-the-sky city into a
marketable theme park. What they
came up with can best be described
as a permanent world's fair, where
the themes of international brother-
hood and technological progress are
laced with more than a little corporate shilling.

Despite the lofty ideals behind
its conception, Epcot is arguably
the least successful of the Disney
parks – moderately entertaining,
moderately educational, but not a
home run on either count. Its focus
on foreign cuisine and education
appeals generally to an older audience. The characters kids so love
are scarce, and the rides (with the
exception of Mission: SPACE and
Test Track) are tame, even by Disney's low-intensity standards. As
for education, many exhibits are
similar to those at a good science
museum, and it's sometimes difficult to put much stock in lessons

that are packaged and presented by
corporate sponsors.

That's not to say that Epcot
doesn't have its high points. Mission:
SPACE is a fantastic ride. Honey, I
Shrunk the Audience is a crowd-
pleaser and among the first of the
new 3-D movies loaded with special
effects. World Showcase offers crib
notes and cuisine to travelers unable
to trek the globe. And IllumiNations,
Epcot's pyrotechnic extravaganza, is
a spectacle unlike anything you are
likely to have seen elsewhere.

**Map
on page
74**

LEFT: IllumiNations
lights up the sky
over the World
Showcase Lagoon.
BELOW: a contented
Epcot visitor.

Epcot

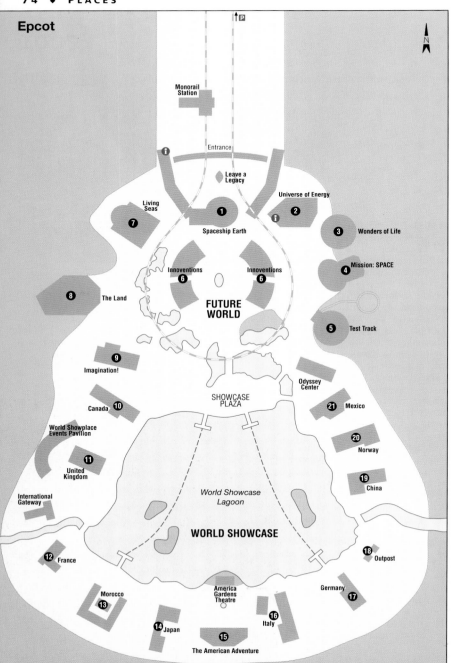

P

Monorail Station

Entrance

Leave a Legacy

1 Spaceship Earth

2 Universe of Energy

3 Wonders of Life

7 Living Seas

4 Mission: SPACE

6 Innoventions

6 Innoventions

FUTURE WORLD

8 The Land

5 Test Track

9 Imagination!

Odyssey Center

SHOWCASE PLAZA

21 Mexico

10 Canada

World Showplace Events Pavilion

20 Norway

11 United Kingdom

19 China

International Gateway

World Showcase Lagoon

WORLD SHOWCASE

12 France

18 Outpost

13 Morocco

America Gardens Theatre

Germany

17

14 Japan

16 Italy

15 The American Adventure

In the end, it's a matter of taste. If you're traveling with an older crowd and you like a little edification sprinkled in with your entertainment, then Epcot may be just the ticket. If you have young children or enjoy thrill rides, you may want to invest your time in another park.

Small world, big park

The first thing you'll notice about Epcot is its size – 300 acres (120 hectares), nearly three times as big as the Magic Kingdom. This means two things: Epcot feels less crowded than the other parks (unfortunately, this doesn't translate into shorter lines), and you're going to do a lot of walking, much of it across open plazas with little cover from the sun.

If you're blessed with short lines and cooperative kids – unlikely at best – a single long day is sufficient to see most of the park, provided you don't tarry too long at the walk-through exhibits. If what you read here sounds intriguing, plan an extra half day or sign up for one of the special behind-the-scenes tours.

The park is laid out in two roughly circular areas. The first, **Future World**, anchored by that monumental silver golf ball – that is, a geosphere – called Spaceship Earth, is devoted to science and technology. Its attractions are housed in pavilions that contain rides, shows, and exhibitions sponsored by big corporations.

The other part of Epcot is **World Showcase**. It encompasses 11 pavilions arrayed around a 40-acre (16-hectare) lagoon, each representing a different country and featuring live entertainment, some spectacular films, exhibits, and restaurants with native cuisine.

Future World

Looming over Epcot's front entrance is **Spaceship Earth ❶**, the huge, aluminum-clad orb that is both a park icon and an architectural summation of Disney's visionary aspirations. Before getting there, however, you first have to negotiate a curious piece of public art that Disney calls the **Leave a Legacy Sculpture**. Installed for the millennium, the project consists of several granite

Map on page 74

TIP

Fastpass is available at Honey, I Shrunk the Audience, Mission: SPACE, Test Track, Living with the Land, and Maelstrom.

BELOW: Spaceship Earth under construction in 1982.

Opening in May 2005, is Epcot's newest attraction: Soarin' – a simulator ride that recreates a majestic flight over California ending, where else, but Disneyland.

BELOW: Walt Disney in 1959 presenting a concept drawing of the monorail.

plinths slowly gaining a skin of customized metal plates. For about $25, you purchase the dubious honor of having a snapshot engraved onto a steel tile and fastened to a shiny stone monolith. Aside from separating you from your money, it's hard to say what the point is. A monument to the future? An elaborate sham? Either way, thousands of people have added their images to the growing montage of smiling faces.

Inside Spaceship Earth is a 14-minute dark ride sponsored by AT&T that takes passengers on a journey through the history of communications. The ride passes through a series of dioramas populated by animatronic figures, starting with primitive humans painting pictures on cave walls and progressing through scenes of ancient Rome and Egypt, the Middle Ages and Renaissance, the invention of the printing press, radio, television, satellites, and computers. At the end of the ride, you're deposited at the **Global Neighborhood**, a large exhibition space with interactive games and kiosks. Spaceship Earth tends to be swamped in

the morning when guests pour through the park entrance. If the line is long, try back after 10am.

Universe of Energy

Exit Spaceship Earth and head over to **Universe of Energy ❷**, presented by ExxonMobil. The main attraction here is **Ellen's Energy Adventure**, a combination film and dark ride that is perhaps the most plodding, poorly-scripted show at Epcot. Its only saving grace is the cast of celebrities Disney roped into the project: television personalities Ellen Degeneres, Alex Trebek, and Bill Nye the Science Guy, plus screen star Jamie Lee Curtis. They manage to lend a little charisma to a convoluted tale involving a trip back to the Age of Dinosaurs so that Bill Nye can teach Ellen about energy in order to defeat her know-it-all college roommate (played by Curtis) and Albert Einstein on the television game show Jeopardy (hosted by Trebek) in a bizarre dream sequence. Follow that? Don't bother. The important thing to know is that halfway through the film the theater breaks up into individual

trams that pass through animatronic tableaux illustrating where energy comes from. Perhaps the only thing more ill-conceived than the script is the choice of an oil company to present a balanced picture of the world's energy needs. Do yourself a favor and cross this one off your to-do list.

Wonders of Life

The picture is a lot brighter, and the scripts a lot snappier, at the **Wonders of Life ❸** pavilion, featuring three of Epcot's better attractions. The most exciting is **Body Wars**, a motion simulator ride designed by George Lucas and his crew of special-effects wizards. The concept here is that you've been shrunk down to the size of a blood cell and injected into a human body in order to assist in the reconaissance of a splinter. Your "fantastic voyage" takes an unexpected turn, and you're soon whisked off into the circulatory system for a rollicking ride through inner space. Though not particularly scary, it does give passengers a good bounce and may be too intense for young children and those prone to motion sickness.

Step over to **Cranium Command** and into the brain of a 12-year-old boy during a typical day at school. He wakes up late, meets the girl of his dreams, narrowly escapes a fistfight, gets called to the principal's office, and raids the refrigerator. All the while, his brain is under the direction of Captain Buzzy, an animatronic guide, who tries desperately to coordinate various organs played on film by a cast of well-known actors – Jon Lovitz as the right brain, Charles Grodin as the left brain, Bobcat Goldthwait as the adrenal gland, and Dana Carvey and Kevin Nealon (Hans and Franz of *Saturday Night Live*) as the heart. The show is clever, funny and appealing to all ages.

Equally well-done is *The Making of Me*, a film that addresses that most sensitive question: where do babies

come from? It stars Martin Short as a man who goes back in time to learn how his parents fall in love and make a baby. Animated segments are combined with real footage, creating a humorous and touching portrait of one life's beginnings. If you haven't already talked to your kids about the birds and the bees, this is a good way to break the ice.

Interactive exhibits outside the theater offer a computer analysis of your golf stroke, a workout on video-enhanced exercise bicycles, and a review of the latest developments in medical technology. An improv group called the **AnaComical Players** uses comedy to address health issues in another small theater.

But most people milling around this area are building up the nerve to ride Epcot's newest ride – **Mission: SPACE ❹** – the only ride in all of Disney that offers you two chances to change your mind and provides a sick bag for those who should have taken the chance to get out when they had it. The ride simulates a mission to Mars. For the most part, it's the same as any other quality simulator ride in

Map on page 74

Height requirements are 40 inches (102 cm) for Body Wars and Test Track, 44 inches (112 cm) for Mission: SPACE.

BELOW: kids can't resist playing in the elaborate fountains around Future World. Bring a towel and change of clothes.

Orlando. What makes this one exceptional is its beginning, when you experience the g-force of lift-off as an astronaut would. It's so convincing that as the force releases and you see a beautiful (and seemingly weightless) view of the earth below, you have to remind yourself that, unlike a real astronaut, you're still in Florida. Disney is clearly out to snatch a piece of the Kennedy Space Center's pie. They even brought in NASA consultants to help design the ride.

Test Track

Continuing around the outer edge of Future World brings you next to General Motors' **Test Track** ❺. This is one of the most popular attractions at Disney World, but it's not altogether clear why. It's a fun ride and technologically complex (translation: it has a tendency to break down a lot), but when it comes to sheer thrills it doesn't hold a candle to the Tower of Terror or the Rock 'n' Roller Coaster at Disney-MGM Studios, or even the Space Mountain at the Magic Kingdom. Nor is it, as you might think, the kind of ride that you control yourself. When Disney says that "you're the test driver," they don't mean you actually steer the thing. It works more like a roller coaster. The car does all the work; you do all the screaming.

After you negotiate the queue, you get a ride in a six-seater car simulating the course at a GM proving ground, including a uphill acceleration test, a kidney-bouncing suspension test, a neck-jerking road-handling test, and a simulated crash. The five-minute excursion ends with a speed test that sends your vehicle whipping around banked turns at a top speed of 65 miles per hour (105 kph).

The line for Test Track is almost always one of the longest in the park. Your best bet is to ride first thing in the morning or make a Fast-pass reservation for later in the day. A word of warning: Fastpass tickets are often completely allotted by noon, so snag one early, before they're gone. If you don't mind splitting up your party, you can opt for the single rider line, which cuts waiting time significantly.

TIP

Future World often opens and closes earlier than World Showcase. Call 407-824 2222 or inquire at your hotel for exact times.

RIGHT:
a fascinating variety of plants are nurtured in an experimental greenhouse at The Land pavilion.

Take the Plunge

You can get an inside view of Epcot's Living Seas with Dive-Quest. All you need is a C-card, a reservation, and about $140. Divers are provided with equipment, a pre-dive briefing, and a dive master who accompanies them into the tank for a 40-minute dive.

Beneath the surface, you are surrounded by a living rainbow of angelfish, sergeant majors, jacks, snappers, and other tropical species, as well as brown sharks, stingrays, and a couple of green sea turtles. Dolphins are prevented from entering the tank, but they sometimes come to the barrier to investigate what's going on next door. There are even portions of a real shipwreck, salvaged off the Florida Keys and deposited here, along with an anchor and a pile of cannonballs.

You might see something else down there, too – people. And not the kind with scuba tanks and dive masks on. These folks are wearing street clothes, and they're looking at you – because you're not merely enjoying a Disney attraction, you're part of one.

Reservations for DiveQuest can be made by phoning 407-939 8687. It's an extremely popular program, so call several weeks in advance in order to secure a spot.

Innoventions

With all the lofty rhetoric about Epcot's vision of the future, it's nice to know that someone at Disney hasn't forgotten about life's little problems. Who among you has never suffered the shock of a cold toilet seat in the morning or discovered there's no milk in the fridge only after pouring a bowl of cereal? Well, good people, you need suffer no longer, thanks to the clever folks at **Innoventions ⑥**, a pair of parenthesis-shaped pavilions at the heart of Future World.

Here you'll find high-tech solutions to mundane problems – a heated toilet seat, for instance, or a refrigerator that compiles its own grocery list. Elsewhere at this sprawling exposition are sections devoted to entertainment, communications, home electronics, and medicine. Exhibits change periodically, but highlights from a recent visit included a huge display of Sega games, a robotic pet puppy, and an interactive product-testing area.

A cursory tour of Innoventions won't be very rewarding, as some of the gizmos take a while to figure out. Plan to visit during a hot afternoon, or, if technology isn't your thing, skip it altogether.

Sea, land, and imagination

Flanking Innoventions to the west are three pavilions: Living Seas, The Land, and Imagination! The centerpiece of **Living Seas ⑦** is a 5.6-million-gallon (18-million-liter) saltwater aquarium – the world's largest when it was opened in 1986 – containing an artificial coral reef populated by grunts, jacks, parrots, and other tropical fish, as well as sharks, sea turtles, and the occasional scuba diver. Dolphins are kept in an adjacent tank and manatees are given their own area where visitors can get a close-up view.

After a brief film, you file into hydrolators – elevator-like chambers – that create the illusion of sinking beneath the waves to an exhibition called **Sea Base Alpha**, where you can explore interactive displays recently rebranded in a *Finding Nemo* theme, aquariums, and a deep-sea diving suit. You can extend your undersea adventure at the **Coral Reef** restaurant, which features pricey seafood dishes and underwater views of the aquarium.

Next up is **The Land ⑧** pavilion, sponsored by Nestlé and devoted to agriculture, nutrition, and the environment. More interesting than it sounds, the 6-acre (2.5-hectare) structure houses three attractions. **Living with the Land** is a boat ride through a series of ecosystems – rainforest, desert, prairie – then into an experimental greenhouse where research is conducted (with partners like the US Department of Agriculture) in hydroponics, aquaculture, pest management, and farming in inhospitable environments such as the desert and even space.

The tone is lighter at **Food Rocks**, which stars a troupe of animatronic performers such as the Peach Boys,

Map on page 74

TIP

See the tip board in Innoventions Plaza for approximate waiting times at Epcot attractions.

BELOW: brilliant tropical fish populate a huge aquarium at the Living Seas, dubbed "the world's sixth largest sea."

Pita Gabriel, and Chubby Cheddar, who belt out nutrition-related songs to the tune of rock classics. Environmental stewardship is the message of *The Circle of Life*, a 20-minute film featuring characters from *The Lion King*. Curiously, the story features Timon and Pumba, who are about to clear a huge swath of wilderness in order to make room for a fancy new resort. Sound familiar? Fortunately, Simba intercedes with a valuable lesson about the environmental cost of progress. Kids who are anxious to meet Disney characters will have their chance at the **Garden Grill**, which serves all-you-can-eat, family-style meals in the company of Mickey, Pluto, and other Disney characters. By the way, much of the produce served at the Garden Grill and **Sunshine Season Food Fair** (a fast-food court) is grown in the pavilion.

Wrap up your tour of Future World at the **Imagination!** ❾ pavilion, home of **Honey, I Shrunk the Audience**, a 3-D film (4-D counting the effects built into the theater) that draws big crowds. The story is a spin-off of the *Honey, I Shrunk the Kids*

movies, starring Rick Moranis as inventor Dr Wayne Szalinski. Heres the good doctor manages to muck things up by shrinking the audience, which is then left to the mercy of a slobbering dog, a hungry snake, and a curious toddler, not to mention the hundreds of mice you'll swear scurry up your legs. It's all played for laughs, but the effects (and the volume) may overwhelm young children.

Much less successful is a dark ride called **Journey into Your Imagination**, presented as a tour of Dr Szalinski's Imagination Institute in which riders are subjected to a series of optical illusions. Skip it if the queue is long or time is short.

World Showcase

Strolling the 1.3-mile (2-km) promenade around **World Showcase** is like perusing a stack of travel brochures. Each of the 11 pavilions is a collection of fleeting impressions, delivered by giant-screen films, replicas of landmark buildings, live entertainers, unique shops, ethnic restaurants, and employees that come from the countries they represent. Stereotypes loom large.

The tour begins on the lagoon's west side with **Canada** ❿, which features the breathtaking film *O Canada!*, projected on a 360-degree screen that surrounds the audience. Viewers tumble over waterfalls, find themselves at the business end of a bison, and feel the whoosh of a dogsled racing through snow. Nearby, in the **Hotel du Canada** (inspired by Canada's grand railroad hotels), **Northwest Mercantile** sells maple syrup, coonskin hats, Inuit crafts, and other souvenirs.

The Union Jack flies proudly over the **United Kingdom** ⓫, executed in a variety of architectural styles ranging from stately Georgian and Tudor to the modest thatched huts of the 1500s. Pub crawlers are drawn to the **Rose & Crown**, so accurate that

It's a punny world after all...

There must have once been a time when the gratuitous use of puns in naming attractions seemed cutting edge. But, like Spaceship Earth, it's faded away now, leaving behind an oily residue at Epcot that is difficult to wash away.

No sooner have you stopped shaking your head at the "Behind the Seeds Tour" at The Land pavilion then you realise Food Rocks features musical acts such as the Peach Boys and Pita Gabriel.

Sadly, the situation only worsens at World Showcase. Off Kilter, at the Canada pavilion, features a band in – wait for it – kilts. Don't worry, there's no need to cover the little ones' eyes. The kilts stay securely on, and only those in the front row know if they are worn with traditional ventilation. But there is very little excuse for naming the indigenous musical act in Morocco, MO'ROCKIN.

For some visitors, this is the kitsch that makes Disney special for them. To others it betrays an underlying problem at Epcot – instead of presenting complex cultures accessibly, nations are simplified to be accessible. Those who crave more than Italian-clad Goofy dolls and Top of the Pops culture may leave sadly disappointed.

you'll be shocked you can't smoke indoors and it's not raining outdoors. Enjoy fish 'n' chips and a pint of Guinness, then shop for Beatles T-shirts, tea, and toy soldiers. Performers appear in the pub and on the street, including Cockney buskers in an abridged Shakespeare comedy and an occasional appearance by Fab Four look-alikes.

From croissants to kaki-gori

The five-screen film in **France** ⑫ is spectacular, but as anyone who has dined here will tell you, the food is … how do you say? … *magnifique*. After viewing the 18-minute ***Impressions de France*** at the cozy **Palais du Cinema**, indulge yourself at one of Disney World's finest restaurants, **Les Chefs de France**, developed by renowned French chefs Paul Bocuse, Gaston Lenôtre, and Roger Vergé (priority seating is essential). If time (or finances) don't permit a full meal, stop in for a quick bite at the **Boulangerie Patisserie**, where you can nibble on pastries, quiche, and other light bites at the foot of a scaled-down model of the Eiffel Tower.

A few steps farther on is **Morocco** ⑬, the only Moslem country represented at World Showcase. The centerpiece of the complex is **Koutoubia Minaret**, a replica of a Marrakesh prayer tower. Changing exhibits of art and artifacts are displayed in the **Gallery of Arts and History**. Casbah merchants sell baskets, pottery, soapstone carvings, leather goods, and brass, while traditional weavers make rugs before your eyes. **Restaurant Marrakesh** treats guests to spicy couscous, lamb, and authentic belly-dancing.

Japan's ⑭ traditional gardens, with bonsai trees, babbling brooks, and faux rocks, are a peaceful place to escape the crowds. Shop for kimonos, geisha dolls, Pokemon cards, and shrimp-flavored snacks at the **Mitsukoshi Department Store**,

inspired by the Gosho Imperial Palace in Kyoto. Pause for sushi and a Kirin beer at **Yakitori House** or a kaki-gori (Japanese snow cone) at one of the stands. The **Bijutsu-Kan Gallery** hosts changing exhibitions focusing on various aspects of Japanese art and culture, and the traditional Matsuriza drummers deliver one of Epcot's most rousing performances.

Of thee I sing

Situated at the southern tip of World Showcase, **The American Adventure** ⑮ is housed in a replica of Philadelphia's Independence Hall. The show inside is an elaborately-staged civics lesson in which Ben Franklin and Mark Twain – played by animatronic figures – condense 200 years of history into a 30-minute review. Also on offer is a sample of America's native cuisine – fast food. The **Liberty Inn** has hot dogs, hamburgers and, of course, apple pie. An amphitheater on the edge of the lagoon showcases live entertainers.

Replicas of the Doge's Palace and campanile from St Mark's Square in Venice dominate the **Italy** ⑯ pavil-

Need a lift? Double-decker buses circle World Showcase, and ferries cross the lagoon from docks near Germany and France.

BELOW:
strollers can be rented at all the parks.

Map on page 74

Map on page 74

Kids can make masks, kites, and do other small projects at Kidcot Fun spots. There's one at each country in World Showcase.

BELOW:
a visitor from Pakistan takes in the sights of World Showcase.

ion, given over mostly to shops selling Venetian glasswork, Florentine leather, and a delectable array of wines, sweets, olive oil, and pasta. The elegant **L'Originale Alfredo di Roma Ristorante** competes with the park's best dining experiences (priority seating recommended).

Germany , on the other hand, looks like something out of a Bavarian folktale. The center of activity is the **Biergarten**, a buffet restaurant offering hardy German sausages, breads, spatzle, and beer. An oompah band is usually on hand, and guests are invited on stage with a group of lusty lederhosen-clad yodelers. Shops around a cobblestone platz carry traditional goods, ranging from handmade toys and cuckoo clocks to beer steins and delicate Hummel figurines.

The park pays lip-service to Africa at **Outpost** ⓲, offering performances of traditional music and a golden opportunity to sell even more *Lion King* souvenirs.

Enter the more elaborate **China** ⓳ pavilion through a gate styled after the summer palace in Beijing. **Land of Many Faces** introduces China's multi-ethnic population with displays of traditional clothing and other cultural artifacts. A reincarnated Chinese poet guides you through *Reflections of China*, another Circle Vision film, this one shown in a replica of Beijing's Temple of Heaven. The **Yong Feng Shangdian Department** Store is stocked with puppets, Chinese lanterns, painted screens, and other merchandise; **Nine Dragons** restaurant serves specialties from various Chinese provinces; and the **Dragon Legend Acrobats** perform gravity-defying feats in the courtyard.

Float trips

In **Norway** ⓴, you wander among buildings rendered in an assortment of traditional styles, including a replica of Oslo's 14th-century fortress Akershus and a 13th-century stave church. **Maelstrom**, the main attraction, is a tame longboat journey back through the mists of time. After encountering trolls, Vikings, and stunning fjords, you return to the present and a view of oil rigs in the North Sea. Your boat docks at a seaside village and everyone files into a theater for a short film that will leave you wanting to see more of this remarkable country. Kids can play on a replica of a Norse ship, while parents make plans at the Norwegian Tourist Board, conveniently located for impulsive travelers.

Your whirlwind tour ends in **Mexico** ㉑, where a Mayan temple rises above a lively plaza marketplace filled with colorful handicrafts and the music of a roaming mariachi band. Inside is the romantic **San Angel Inn**, serving authentic Mexican cuisine, much of it a surprise to diners who have never ventured beyond tacos and enchiladas. Pass up **El Río del Tiempo** – a boat ride similar to the Magic Kingdom's "it's a small world" – in favor of an exhibit of ancient artifacts housed inside the pyramid. ❑

RESTAURANTS & BARS

Future World

Coral Reef
The Living Seas Pavilion
(priority seating)
Dramatically-situated restaurant with underwater view of artificial reef. The menu features seafood bisques and grills, fresh fish, and pasta selections. **$$$**

Garden Grill
The Land Pavilion
(priority seating)
Revolving restaurant overlooking scenic ecosystems and boat ride. Salads and vegetables are grown in The Land greenhouses. Full country breakfast stars Mickey, Minnie, and Chip 'n' Dale. **$$$**

World Showcase

Akershus
Norway Pavilion
(priority seating)
Norwegian buffet of cold and hot dishes, from herring and salmon to goat cheese and desserts. **$$**

Biergarten
Germany Pavilion
(priority seating)
Hearty buffet includes veal, spaetzle, bratwurst, and other German specialties, with Bavarian entertainment by musicians, dancers, and yodelers. **$$**

Bistro de Paris
France Pavilion
(priority seating)
The first of two fantastic French restaurants. The elegant atmosphere and gourmet cuisine makes this one a bit more pricey. **$$$**

Le Cellier Steakhouse
Canada Pavilion
(priority seating)
Maple-glazed salmon, prime rib, Canadian specialties and beers. **$$**

Les Chefs de France
France Pavilion
(priority seating)
Exceptional service and innovative cuisine, including specialties by chefs Paul Bocuse and Roger Vergé, as well as master pastry chef Gaston Lenôtr all accompanied by a selection of fine French wines. **$$**

L'Originale Alfredo di Roma Ristorante
Italy Pavilion
(priority seating)
Colorful, festive offshoot of the famous Roman restaurant. Specialty is fettuccine Alfredo. All pastas are made fresh. Strolling musicians entertain guests. **$$$**

Restaurant Marrakesh
Morocco Pavilion
(priority seating)
Moroccan specialties and sampler platters: couscous, kebabs, and roast lamb. Musicians and belly dancer accompany the meal. **$$$**

Rose & Crown
UK Pavilion
(priority seating)
Roast beef and Yorkshire pudding, Harry Ramsden fish and chips, and other traditional pub fare served in a polished dining room or on an outdoor terrace. Lagers, ales, and Guinness served in a perfectly-recreated English pub. **$$**

San Angel Inn
Mexico Pavilion
(priority seating)
Mexican dishes range from the familiar to the unusual, served in a scenic indoor setting. **$$**

Teppanyaki Dining Rooms
Japan Pavilion
(priority seating)
Sushi, tempura, and stir-fry reign at this complex of Japanese eateries. At the Teppanyaki Dining Room, chefs entertain while cooking at tableside grills. Martinis made with sake. **$$$**

• • • • • • • • • • • •

*For priority seating call 407-939 3463. Dialing *88 from a public phone in Disney allows toll-free access to this number.*

PRICE CATEGORIES

Price includes a three course dinner and a glass of wine (when available), excluding tip:
$ = under $20
$$ = $20–$30
$$$ = over $30

RIGHT: enjoy sushi at Japan's Matsu No Ma Lounge, one of more than 18 notable restaurants at World Showcase.

DISNEY'S ANIMAL KINGDOM

**Nature's creatures – living and extinct – are the stars
of a theme park that mixes wildlife habitats and
elaborate architecture with state-of-the-art thrill rides**

Orlando

Disney's
Animal
Kingdom

Kissimmee

One thing about animatronic animals: they're predictable. They don't smell. They don't eat the landscaping. They don't bite. And they never really die. Moreover, you can't train a real crocodile to rise from the water, bare its teeth, and politely sink back.

That's why Walt Disney, despite his reputed love for animals, decided against the real thing in his first Californian park and its counterpart in Orlando. To the once wildlife-rich wetlands of Florida, Disney managers imported animatronic alligators and talking stuffed birds. That was in the early 70s, before eco-tourism became popular and neither SeaWorld nor Busch Gardens had yet to incorporate wild animals into a profitable theme park.

Once it had been proved possible, the Disney company jumped into the fray with both feet, and launched Animal Kingdom in 1998. Neither a zoo nor a traditional amusement park, Animal Kingdom combines the allure of exotic wildlife exhibited in naturalistic habitats with Disney's architectural and landscape design, high-concept attractions, and extravagant live performances.

The grand opening was marred by the death of more than two dozen animals (federal investigators found no evidence of mistreatment or neglect on Disney's part). Early visitors also complained about congestion and poor crowd management, plus several attractions were delayed, modified or scrapped altogether.

Most of the bugs have now been worked out of the system, but Animal Kingdom remains a park still in the making. **Animal Kingdom Lodge**, a 1,307-room resort about a mile from the park with its own 35-acre (14-hectare) wildlife reserve, was launched in 2001 *(see Accommodations page 219)*, and there are persis-

**Map
on page
86**

LEFT: a white rhino grazes on the savanna.
BELOW: a colony of meerkats can be viewed along the Pangani Forest Trail.

Animal Kingdom

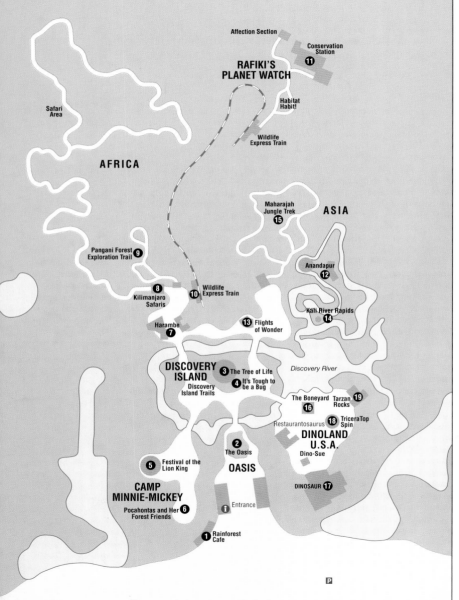

tent reports of a major expansion at Animal Kingdom itself. Disney execs aren't talking, but theme-park watchers speculate that the project is the long-awaited Beastly Kingdom, a new land dedicated to imaginary creatures like dragons and unicorns, and perhaps a second area devoted to Australian wildlife.

Early birds

To make the most of your visit, plan on arriving at the park early in the morning when the animals are most active and easily seen. Animal Kingdom usually has shorter hours than the other parks, typically opening about 8am and closing at 5 or 6pm. (The schedule changes often, so confirm hours before arriving.) If possible, hit a couple of rides – especially Kilimanjaro Safaris – first thing and save the shows and nature walks for later in the day.

With some 500 acres (200 hectares), this is Disney World's largest park (five times larger than Magic Kingdom), although the space where visitors can wander about freely is actually smaller than the others. This gives the park a rather congested feeling on busy days, and with fewer traditional rides and shows, queues tend to be quite long. If you arrive early and step lively, one day is enough time to see just about everything, though you could easily come back for a return visit without running out of fun things to do.

The Oasis

The experience starts even before you pass through the park gates. Situated just outside the entrance is the **Rainforest Cafe ❶**, a full-service restaurant with a lavish jungle theme. On the outside it looks like the side of a mountain with a huge waterfall gushing over the top. Inside it's all leafy green foliage and animal calls. There's even a (simulated) thunderstorm. The food's pretty good, too,

with dishes like coconut shrimp, pot roast, thick burgers, and rasta pasta that make up in quantity what they lack in finesse. A word to the wise: waits of an hour or more are not unusual without priority seating.

The moment you walk through the park turnstiles, you realize that Disney has made some interesting changes to the standard theme-park layout. Unlike the Magic Kingdom or Disney-MGM Studios, the entrance into Animal Kingdom doesn't funnel visitors into the center of the park down a wide boulevard lined with shops and restaurants.

What you find instead is a choice of several branching pathways that pass through an outcropping of simulated rock, then meander through a lush tropical garden known as **The Oasis ❷** that brims with jacaranda, tabebuia, orchids, ferns, and dozens of other plants.

Tucked into the foliage are discrete alcoves separated by waterfalls, grottoes, and walls of greenery containing the first of approximately 1,700 animals that reside at the park. There are parrots, scarlet ibis, river

Map on page 86

TIP

Fastpass is available at It's Tough to Be a Bug, Kilimanjaro Safaris, Kali River Rapids, Primeval Whirl, and DINOSAUR.

BELOW:
the Oasis features tropical birds like this blue and bold macaw.

otters, iguanas, wallabies, a giant anteater, a two-toed sloth, and many others, although some animals may be difficult to see. Knowledgeable guides stroll the pathways with spiders, snakes, birds, and other small creatures and are always willing to talk about their charges and answer questions.

Discovery Island

Emerging from The Oasis, you're greeted by your first unobstructed view of the **Tree of Life ❸**, a huge, artificial banyan-like tree that rises 14 stories above a section of the park called **Discovery Island**, set in the middle of a large lagoon connected by bridges to the park's four main lands.

What looks at first like the tree's gnarled bark turns out on closer inspection to be a melange of carved animal figures – more than 300 in all – that swirls around the trunk and limbs. Constructed of steel, rockwork, and more than 103,000 vinyl leaves, and sculpted by a team of 20 artists, the Tree of Life serves the same landmark function as Cin-

The male mandrill – the model for the character of Rafiki in The Lion King – *is known for its brightly-colored face and buttocks.*

derella's Castle at the Magic Kingdom or Spaceship Earth at Epcot. Think of it as a work of art and it won't seem so odd that the icon of a park dedicated to nature is not itself organic.

The **Discovery Island Trails** meander around the Tree of Life past meadows, ponds, and leafy enclosures populated by axis deer, capybaras, ring-tailed lemurs, red kangaroos, Galapagos tortoises, and dozens of colorful birds. Housed within the base of the tree, in a large indoor theater, is the park's most comical attraction, **It's Tough to be a Bug! ❹**, based loosely on the Disney–Pixar movie *A Bug's Life*. Calling this a 3-D film doesn't quite do it justice, because many effects are built right into the theater and engage the sense of touch and even smell. The story involves seeing life from an insect's point of view. You experience what it's like being on the receiving end of a fly swatter or a can of bug spray and encounter several noxious members of the insect family, including an acid-spraying termite and a stinkbug with, shall we say, a bad case of gas. Parents should use discretion: the effects are loud and intense, and, while the show is basically light-hearted, it can frighten small children or anyone who's afraid of bugs.

Arranged around the edge of the island, in brightly-colored buildings that recall a tropical African village, are clusters of shops and restaurants where you can stop for smoked chicken and ribs (**Flame Tree Barbecue**) or pizza and pasta (**Pizzafari**), or pick up an assortment of trinkets, T-shirts, and African imports.

Camp Minnie-Mickey

Walking around Discovery Island in a clockwise direction, the first bridge on the left leads to **Camp Minnie-Mickey**, designed in Adirondack style and devoted entirely to live

Mouse Conservation

After being lambasted by the press in 1988 for exterminating a flock of buzzards, Disney learned the hard way that being bad to the environment is bad for the bottom line.

Since then, Disney has burnished its environmental record in ways both small and large. You may have noticed brownish napkins made of recycled paper or heard about Lyocell, a renewable wood fiber used in costumes. On a much larger scale was the creation in 1993 of the Disney Wilderness Preserve, now run in partnership with Nature Conservancy, and another conservation area at Disney World itself. The Wilderness Preserve includes a three-mile hiking trail to help visitors learn about the resident plants and animals.

In 1995, the company launched the Disney Wildlife Conservation Fund. Supported largely by visitor donations, the fund gives money to organizations such as the Jane Goodall Institute that protect threatened animals. The fund also supports the Florida Audubon Society's Bird-of-Prey Center, devoted to the study of raptors such as hawks, owls, eagles – and buzzards.

shows and character greetings. The big attraction here is **Festival of the Lion King** ❺, an uplifting 30-minute pageant based loosely on the animated film, with song, dance, acrobatics, moving stages, and flamboyant costumes. Arrive at least 30 minutes before curtain time. The covered theater-in-the-round seats 1,400 people, but the show is extremely popular and those at the end of the line sometimes have to wait for the following performance.

Less exuberant is **Pocahontas and Her Forest Friends** ❻, a 15-minute morality tale on the importance of caring for the natural world, with the Indian princess, a talking tree (Grandmother Willow), and a cast of skunks, oppossums, snakes, rabbits, rats, and other live animals. Sappy even by Disney standards, the show appeals to preschoolers more than most other attractions in the park.

Children get a kick out of the four **Character Greeting Trails**, which lead back to pavilions housing costumed characters who spend a few minutes posing for pictures, signing autographs, and joshing around with little ones and adults. Mickey and Minnie are almost always on hand. The other lines usually feature characters from *The Lion King* and *Jungle Book*. See the signs posted out front for details. Queues are usually longest immediately after the theaters let out; there's virtually no waiting early in the morning.

Africa

Return to Discovery Island and cross the first bridge on your left to **Africa**, where you immediately find yourself amid a clutch of shops and restaurants called **Harambe** ❼, modeled loosely on the real-life village of Lamu in Kenya. Disney imagineeers have gone to great lengths to give the place the time-worn appearance of a backcountry settlement. Tattered clothes hang on a clothesline, fishing nets are draped along the riverbank, and buildings are covered with peeling paint and crumbling stucco. Disney even imported a crew of Zulu craftsmen to construct thatched roofs for some of the buildings.

If you skipped breakfast, you may want to stop at the **Kusafiri Coffee**

Map on page 86

TIP

Health-conscious visitors will find fresh fruit and wholesome juices at the Harambe Fruit Market near the entrance to Kilimanjaro Safaris in Africa.

BELOW: zebras roam freely in a recreation of the African veldt. Their stripes are designed to disorient predators.

TIP

Mickey's Jammin'
Jungle Parade features
costumed characters,
stylized floats, rolling
drums, and a lively
call-and-response
theme. The parade
starts in Africa and
circles Discovery
Island. Check the
entertainment schedule
for details.

Shop for a shot of espresso and a freshly-baked pastry. Otherwise, the **Tusker House Restaurant** serves African dishes and American favorites like roasted chicken and beef stew; the **Dawa Bar** has tropical cocktails, Safari Amber beer (brewed especially for Animal Kingdom) and several South African wines; **Mombasa Marketplace** carries handmade African wares, such as woven baskets and wood carvings, along with safari attire and Disney doodads.

At the end of Harambe, next to an enormous, artificial baobab tree, is the Animal Kingdom's most popular attraction, **Kilimanjaro Safaris** ❽. Here, visitors board safari vehicles for a 20-minute ride across a recreated patch of the African veldt. The type and number of wildlife you encounter depend largely on the time of day and the mood of the animals, although strategically-placed water holes, feeders (disguised as tree stumps), and even artificially-cooled rocks tend to keep the animals close to the road. As the truck rumbles over rutted tracks, you may see zebras, giraffes, or rhinos grazing on the savanna, gazelles

Backstage Safari

For a behind-the-scenes look at Animal Kingdom, book a 3-hour Backstage Safari (tel: 407-939 8687). The tour starts first thing in the morning at the Conservation Station and includes a visit to the veterinary hospital, animal barns, and food warehouse. The cost is $65 per person, and participants must be at least 16 years old.

The highlight is a close-up encounter with several animals and discussions with their handlers about nutrition, behavior, and some of the research projects under way at the park. The tour changes daily, but it's not unusual to view giraffes, rhinos, or elephants in the backstage housing area or on the savanna.

With more emphasis on the set of Animal Kingdom than its inhabitants, Wild by Design is a three-hour tour revealing how the park's designers created the natural appearance of the park by recreating authentic-looking architecture, incorporating actual historical artifacts, and throwing in a large quantity of native art. The cost is roughly the same at $58, but the tour is not as intriguing. You only have to be 14 to attend this tour. For a booking telephone 407-939 8687.

bounding through the undergrowth, or elephants cooling themselves by the side of a pond. There are lions lounging on boulders, crocodiles wallowing beneath a rickety bridge, hippos bathing in a water hole, and a great many less-familiar animals such as klipspringers, bongos, kudus, and elands. The barriers are ingeniously camouflaged so most animals look as if they're roaming freely. Some even approach the truck for a close encounter with visitors. This being Disney, merely seeing the animals isn't excitement enough. About halfway through the tour, your driver learns that poachers are threatening a mother elephant and her calf, and off you go on a wild ride to rescue the threatened beasts and catch the bad guys. There are a few bumps and thrills along the way, but nothing that young children will find too alarming.

It's only a few steps from the safari exit to the **Pangani Forest Exploration Trail** ❾, a self-guided nature walk laced with streams, waterfalls, and abundant vegetation. Along the way you can watch endangered species such as dik-diks (a diminutive member of the antelope family) and black-and-white colobus monkeys as well as hippos (an observation window gives an underwater view), a family of lowland gorillas, and a band of ever-watchful meerkats. An indoor research center harbors a colony of naked mole rats and other unusual small animals, and a cleverly-disguised aviary houses a rainbow of free-flying tropical birds. Interpreters are on hand to answer questions and discuss conservation issues. One gripe: the trail is often crowded, and it can be difficult for children to get close enough to the observation areas for a good view.

Rafiki's Planet Watch

If you're looking for a break from the crowds, you might consider a side trip from Africa to **Rafiki's Planet**

Watch, a small behind-the-scenes area dedicated to environmental education. The journey starts at a train station a short walk from the Pangani Forest Exploration Trail exit. Here the **Wildlife Express** ⓾, a replica of an 1890s British colonial steam locomotive, picks up passengers for a 5-minute ride through the not-terribly-scenic backstage area where animals are housed at night. **Habitat Habit**, a collection of small exhibits along the trail from the station, teaches guests about local wildlife and encourages them to make their backyards more animal friendly. At the end of the line is the **Conservation Station** ⓫, a veterinary facility with walk-through exhibits on various aspects of conservation and animal care. Sound booths with headphones allow you to experience the sounds of a rainforest, live video feeds from the park's habitats are displayed on overhead monitors, and observation windows view a working research lab and veterinary clinic. The outdoor **Affection Section** – a petting zoo – gives visitors a chance to get close to goats, ducks, and other barnyard critters.

Asia

Rather than return to Discovery Island, look for a hidden trail that connects Africa to Asia. It starts near the Africa bridge and runs along the edge of the lagoon through an overgrown patch of jungle and over stepping stones across a stream. Upon reaching Asia, you find yourself in the village of **Anandapur** ⓬, yet another example of Disney's genius for set design. Situated in a re-creation of a Southeast Asian rainforest and taking architectural cues from Thailand, Nepal, India, and Indonesia, the village is a pastiche of thatched huts, stone spires, palace walls, and trickling fountains. Among the most impressive structures are temple ruins surrounded by

bamboo scaffolding that serve as a habitat for a troop of howler monkeys, whose resonant hoots can be heard throughout the park.

Eateries in Anandapur include the **Chakranadi Chicken Shop**, which serves chicken satay and a few other Asian specialties, and, for something sweet, the **Anandapur Ice Cream Shop**. **Mandala Gifts** carries a variety of Asian handicrafts and a predictable assortment of toys and clothing.

Asia encompasses three main attractions. To your left as you enter Anandapur, the open-air **Caravan Stage** presents **Flights of Wonder** ⓭, a live 20-minute show featuring hawks, falcons, parrots, and more than a dozen other birds in a story involving a treasure hunter and a wise old wizard. It's hardly a blockbuster, but the birds are beautiful and the script, though stilted, has a few laughs. You may even learn a thing or two.

Down a long path to the right of Anandapur is **Kali River Rapids** ⓮, a conventional whitewater ride that Disney imagineers have given a lav-

Map on page 86

TIP

Height requirements are 38 inches (96 cm) for Kali River Rapids, 40 inches (102 cm) for DINOSAUR, and 48 inches (122 cm) for Primeval Whirl.

BELOW: fruit bats occupy a scenic enclosure on the Maharajah Jungle Trek in Asia.

ish jungle setting and an unexpected environmental twist. After passing through a queuing area resembling an ancient temple, you climb aboard a colorful 12-person raft and are immediately swept away by the current through a cloud of jasmine-scented mist. Your raft bobs over a series of chutes and cataracts past crumbling ruins and dense jungle foliage before skirting a final hazard: a fiery log jam created by illegal loggers who have devastated a patch of forest. The ride lasts only about 5 minutes, all too brief considering the time you'll probably spend waiting in line. If the queue is long – and it almost always is – make a Fastpass reservation and come back later. Be sure to stow cameras, dry clothes, and maybe shoes and socks in the waterproof compartment in the center of the raft. You will get wet and probably drenched.

The final stop in Asia is the **Maharajah Jungle Trek** ⑮, a nature walk with close-up views of Komodo dragons, Malayan tapirs, Asian deer, and blackbuck antelope. Bengal tigers lounge amid the toppled remains of a rajah's palace;

giant fruit bats dangle from ropes in an overgrown courtyard; unusual birds strut and flutter around an aviary decorated with a lotus pool, intriguing stone idols, and peeling murals. Visually compelling, the setting alone is worth the walk.

Look out for a new attraction coming in late 2005. Expedition EVEREST will be a new thrill ride recreating the legend of the yeti.

DinoLand U.S.A.

Return again to Discovery Island and cross the first bridge on the left into **DinoLand, U.S.A.** You'll notice a more campy, carnival-like atmosphere here, injecting a welcome dose of humor into the mostly straight-faced approach elsewhere in the park.

The entrance to DinoLand passes under the skeleton of a 40-foot (12-meter) Brachiosaurus. The giant beast stands astride a bridge connecting two sections of **The Boneyard** ⑯, an elaborate playground resembling an archaeological dig, with tunnels, tubes, rope ladders, and giant dinosaur bones to climb on. Kids especially love the sand pit, where they can uncover fossils diligently buried by the park staff every night. The only drawback is that with so many places to hide it's sometimes difficult to keep track of your kids, much less gather them up when it's time to leave.

Next to The Boneyard is **Restaurantosaurus**, a sprawling eatery featuring an all-you-can-eat buffet with Mickey Mouse, Donald Duck, Goofy, and Pluto. Priority seating is highly recommended. Lunch and dinner are more prosaic – burgers, fries, and chicken nuggets à la McDonald's, DinoLand's corporate sponsor.

Farther along, toward the back of DinoLand, is **DINOSAUR** ⑰, the area's biggest thrill ride. En route, you'll pass a replica of Dino-Sue, the largest, most complete T-Rex ever unearthed. The original was

"I have learned from the animal world. And what everyone will learn who studies it is a renewed sense of kinship with the earth and all of its inhabitants."
—WALT DISNEY

BELOW: the golden lion tamarin is a small monkey found in the rainforests of Brazil. Only a few hundred exist in the wild.

housed temporarily at Animal Kingdom before being shipped back to the Field Museum in Chicago.

More bones are displayed in the ride's queuing area, which is modeled after a museum gallery, with large dinosaur models and exhibits on extinction. The conceit here is that you're a visitor at the Dino Institute, a facility dedicated to "Exploration, Excavation, and Exultation" and, you soon learn, the developer of a time machine that is about to transport you back to the age of Dinosaurs.

Your mission: save the last surviving Iguanodon before an asteroid collides with Earth. What follows is a jolting ride through a misty Jurassic forest that's being pelted by meteors. dinosaurs abound, of course, not the least of which is a Carnotaurus, a ferocious predator with razor-sharp teeth, a sour disposition and – an often overlooked detail – a wicked case of bad breath. The experience is quite intense, so exercise discretion with young children. Lines tend to be long but usually advance quickly. If time permits, use Fastpass and return later in the day.

Memory lane

At the ride's exit, take a stroll down the **Cretaceous Trail**, a short, self-guided pathway through a primeval forest brimming with cycads, ferns and other green plants that survived the dinosaur age. There are a few animal survivors, too, including turtles and Chinese alligators who, judging by their behavior here, probably slept through the extinction.

Next on the agenda is **Chester & Hester's Dino-Rama**, a mini-carnival intended primarily for children. There are two rides here. The first, **Primeval Whirl**, is a cross between a roller coaster and a spinning teacup that sends passengers through curves, short drops, and a final descent into the gaping jaws of a giant dinosaur fossil. **TriceraTop Spin** ⓲ is a hub-and-spoke ride that resembles a giant top, with 16 dinosaur-shaped cars that zoom around a central pylon. A midway area features classic boardwalk games adapted to the dinosaur theme. The main shop is **Chester & Hester's Dinosaur Treasures**, which is packed to the rafters with dino-related toys and novelties. Towering over the entire scene is a vivid yellow concrete brontosaur, recalling the wacky roadside attractions popular in the 1950s and 60s.

The last big attraction in DinoLand is **Tarzan Rocks** ⓳, a live stage show at the 1,500-seat, open-air **Theater in the Wild**. There are those who claim this is the best live show at Disney World. It's probably the loudest, and certainly the most unusual. Featuring music by Phil Collins, it combines the energy of a rock concert and the high-flying acrobatics of the X Games with characters from the animated film. The band is tight, the in-line skaters are astounding, and the staging is spectacular. It's Disney World at its over-the-top best and a fitting way to end your day at the park with a bang. ❑

Map on page 86

In May 2005, Disney is introducing the world to Lucky, a free-roaming animatronic dinosaur. This amazing creature laughs, sneezes, brays, and even signs autographs.

RESTAURANTS

Restaurants

Tusker House
Africa
An unexpectedly great counter-service dining experience with fried chicken in African spices, roasted vegetables on focaccia bread, and other unusual choices. $

Rainforest Cafe
Entrance
This chain restaurant with a recreated jungle environment has found its spiritual home. If you are going to eat at any of its outlets this is the one to enjoy (see page 87). $$

Flame-Tree Barbecue
Discovery Island
Who can visit wildlife without craving a bit of barbecue. $

Bar

Dawa Bar
Africa
Cocktails served up with live contemporary African music and a beer brewed specially for Disney. $

• • • • • • • • • • • • • • •

Price includes dinner and a glass of wine (when available), excluding tip. **$$$** *over $30,* **$$** *between $20–30,* **$** *under $20.*
For priority seating, call 407-939 3463.
*Dial *88 from a public phone in Disney for toll-free access to this number.*

DISNEY-MGM STUDIOS

Caught in the spotlight here is the magic of movie making – the glamour, the technical wizardry, the elaborate sets and costumes: the nuts and bolts of fantasy

Opened to the public in 1989, Disney-MGM Studios was the first major addition to Walt Disney World since the unveiling of Epcot seven years earlier and one of the first big projects launched under CEO Michael Eisner. It was a daring move for a company that was still recovering from a slump and had only recently fended off a hostile takeover. What's more, Universal Studios was already operating a theme park in California dedicated to "the magic of the movies" and had announced its intention to build a second one in Orlando.

The race was on. Disney imagineers set to work creating a park that evoked the Golden Age of Hollywood and gave visitors a behind-the-scenes look at film and television production. Along the way, they forged partnerships with special-effects wizard George Lucas and inked a licensing agreement with MGM, giving Disney access to a vast archive of Hollywood classics. The Studios, as the park came to be known, premiered to rave reviews only four years after the plan was announced and more than a year ahead of Universal.

In some respects, this is Disney World's most satisfying park, especially for adult visitors or those with older children. About the size of

Magic Kingdom but with half the attractions, it's easy to do everything in a day without exhausting yourself, and the Hollywood theme appeals to folks of every age. There are good shows, lots of character greetings, several interesting restaurants, and two of Disney's hairiest thrill rides. If there's anything to complain about, it's that there's less actual movie-making than you might expect. But then, as anyone in the movie biz will tell you, the day-to-day work of a film crew can be deadly boring.

Map on page 96

LEFT: Maureen O'Sullivan and Johnny Weissmuller in *Tarzan*, an MGM classic featured in the Great Movie Ride.
BELOW: Graumann's Theater is replicated in the park.

Disney-MGM Studios

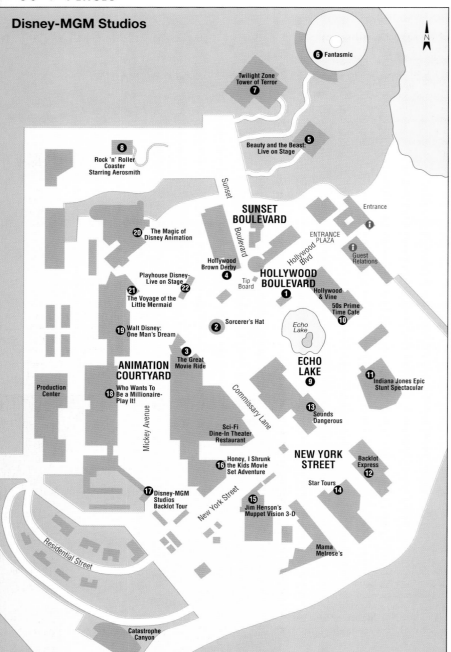

Hollywood Boulevard

Done up in Art Moderne style, the main gate funnels visitors (Disney calls them audience members) down **Hollywood Boulevard ❶** past scaled-down replicas of iconic Tinseltown buildings from the 1930s and 40s. Inside, shops peddle an array of merchandise – T-shirts, key chains, toys, and other goods emblazoned with Disney characters – as well as practical items such as film and sunglasses. The most interesting shop is **Sid Cahuenga's One-of-a-Kind**, where you'll find a collection of autographed head shots, movie posters, and other movie memorabilia.

Hollywood Boulevard is also the first place you're likely to encounter costumed characters. The roster changes often, but you might find Cruella DeVil from *101 Dalmations*, Princess Jasmine and Jafar from *Aladdin*, and Belle from *Beauty and the Beast*, all of whom mug for the camera, josh around with kids, and sign autographs. Some of the funniest moments come from a troupe of actors playing stock Hollywood types (a struggling actress, an imperious director, a rapacious agent, and so forth) who do street skits and often drag audience members into the act.

Towering over a circular plaza at the end of Hollywood Boulevard is a 12-story **Sorcerer's Hat ❷** like the one worn by Mickey Mouse in *Fantasia*. Costumed characters are often stationed around the plaza, too. The most pleasant spot is to the left of Hollywood Boulevard in a shady grove of trees.

Behind the Sorcerer's Hat, in a full-scale replica of Graumann's Chinese Theater, is **The Great Movie Ride ❸**, which promises to take guests on a "spectacular journey into the movies." A few dozen celebrities such as Sylvester Stallone, Steve Martin, Warren Beatty, and, in happier times, Billy Joel and Christie

Brinkley, have left their handprints (footprints in the case of Donald Duck) in the cement just outside.

An interior queue snakes through the theater's lobby past an exhibit of old props and costumes – a carousel horse from *Mary Poppins*, Dorothy's ruby slippers from *The Wizard of Oz*, Bruce Willis's space suit from *Armageddon*. Visitors then file through a standing-room-only theater to view a continuous reel of clips from classic flicks such as *Singing in the Rain*, *The Searchers*, *Fantasia,* and *Raiders of the Lost Ark*. The audience is eventually loaded onto trams that glide through a series of stage sets populated with animatronic figures – Julie Andrews and Dick Van Dyke in *Mary Poppins*, Johnny Weismuller in *Tarzan*, Sigourney Weaver in *Alien*, Bergman and Bogey in *Casablanca*, and many others. There's a little hijinx along the way involving a live-action shootout, but nothing too traumatic. This is a mostly gentle, occasionally plodding ride. Teenagers may find it a snooze, but the pace is just

**Map
on page
96**

TIP

A tip board at the corner of Hollywood and Sunset Boulevards lists waiting times for all attractions.

BELOW:
Ingrid Bergman and Humphrey Bogart appear in animatronic form in the Great Movie Ride.

about right for young children, old folks, and those who merely want an excuse to get out of the sun.

Sunset Boulevard

The Hollywood iconography continues on Sunset Boulevard, which veers off to the right of the plaza. On the corner is the **Hollywood Brown Derby ❹**, one of the most elegant restaurants in any Disney park, with snappily-attired waiters, starched white table linens, and a leafy, candlelit atmosphere. The menu changes often but usually features Cobb salad (invented at the original Brown Derby in the 1930s), filet mignon, rack of lamb, and a variety of seafood and pasta dishes. The list of California wines is brief but sensible, and the desserts are just short of sinful. **Starring Rolls Bakery**, just next door, is a good spot for a quick cup of joe and a sticky sweet pastry.

Sunset Boulevard is lined with several more shops and a cluster of food vendors and picnic tables. Those with an appreciation for the darker side of life should stop at the

Beverly Sunset, a souvenir shop dedicated to Disney villains.

Farther along and to the right, in a roofed amphitheater modeled after the Hollywood Bowl, is **Beauty and the Beast: Live on Stage ❺**, a spirited if not exactly inspired encapsulation of the animated film, with a live cast singing (and in part lip-syncing) to a prerecorded track. The 30-minute show plays several times a day. Check an entertainment guide for the day's schedule.

Just a few steps away is the entrance to a second open-air venue, the Hollywood Hills Amphitheater, situated around a circular lagoon at the end of a long path. This is the site of **Fantasmic ❻**, Disney-MGM's big finale, which plays nightly just before the park closes (sometimes twice in busy seasons). The special-effects crew pulls out all the stops for this one, dazzling the audience with a barrage of lasers, fountains, watery explosions, and fire balls during a 25-minute show that pits Mickey Mouse against Disney's most unsavory characters. There's not much of a story, but the pyrotechnics are rousing and some effects, like the projection of moving images on veils of water, are quite remarkable.

Scream machines

Also at this end of Sunset Boulevard is a pair of Disney World's most intense thrill rides. Disney imagineers have never met a ride they couldn't improve with elaborate theming, and these two are no exception.

The tall forbidding structure hulking over the end of Sunset Boulevard is the **Twilight Zone Tower of Terror ❼**. To reach it, you first stroll through the gates of a misty, overgrown garden that clearly went to seed a long time ago. A sign at the entrance says Hollywood Tower Hotel. An eviction notice is dated October 31, 1939.

TIP

Seating for Fantasmic begins two hours before curtain time. You can reduce the wait by arranging a dinner-and-show combo at the Hollywood Brown Derby or Mama Melrose's Ristorante Italiano, which entitles you to priority seating at one of the eateries as well as the theater.

BELOW: Rod Serling welcomes visitors to the Twilight Zone at the Tower of Terror.

In the lobby are more signs of abandonment – luggage left unattended at the concierge desk, an unfinished mahjong game, a thick coat of dust. A bellhop dressed in a threadbare uniform shows you into the library. The lights go out, a television sparks to life, and there on the screen is Rod Serling, creator of *The Twilight Zone*. He explains that the hotel was struck by lightning on Halloween night, 1939. An entire wing disappeared, including an elevator with five guests inside. Where did they go? You're about to find out.

The queue files through a boiler room and finally into an elevator. The doors close, and, in the wink of an eye, you're hurtling skyward. The doors open and five ghostly figures appear before your eyes. They snap shut and again you're flying through space, up, down, up, down, like a salt shaker given a vigorous shake. There are other stops and other eerie sights. When you finally disembark, Rod leaves you with a friendly word of advice: "The next time you check into a deserted hotel… make sure you know just what kind of vacancy you're filling, or you may find yourself a permanent resident of… *The Twilight Zone*." And, oh yes, in the future, use the stairs.

The excitement (and nausea) continues over at the **Rock 'n' Roller Coaster Starring Aerosmith ❽**, an indoor coaster with enough dips and inversions to satisfy even a hardcore thrill-seeker. The cars look like limousines and each is equipped with a sound system blasting an Aerosmith tune synchronized to the twists and turns. The launch is especially riveting, achieving a top speed of about 60 miles an hour (97 kph) in less than 3 seconds. A word of warning: while Rock 'n' Roller Coaster isn't quite as gut-wrenching as Sea-World's Kraken or Universal's Hulk, it's not a ride for lightweights.

If you thought Space Mountain was a challenge, this one will knock you for a loop.

Rock 'n' Roller Coaster and Tower of Terror are almost always packed. Use Fastpass or try riding early in the morning or during Fantasmic.

Around Echo Lake

Return to the Sorcerer's Hat the way you came and explore the area on the opposite side of the plaza around little **Echo Lake ❾**. The ship on the near side – actually a fast-food counter serving milkshakes and soft drinks – recalls the tramp steamer in the 1931 film *Min and Bill* with Marie Dressler and Wallace Beery. On the opposite side, an ice cream stand operates out of the belly of a brontosaur modeled on Gertie the Dinosaur, an early cartoon that inspired Walt Disney. It's designed in a style known as California crazy, and is typical of the roadside attractions of the 1930s.

Two restaurants are worth noting on the triangular plaza to the left of the lake. **Hollywood & Vine** is an Art Deco cafeteria decked out in tile, stainless steel, and huge murals

Fastpass is available for Indiana Jones, Star Tours, Voyage of the Little Mermaid, Rock 'n' Roller Coaster, and Tower of Terror.

BELOW: Indiana Jones, originally played by Harrison Ford, is brought to life in a popular stunt show.

A new stunt show is due to open in May 2005. Lights, Motors, Action! Extreme Stunt Show includes cars, motorcycles, and jet skis making mayhem in the studios backlot.

of old-time Hollywood landmarks. Breakfast and lunch are all-you-can-eat buffets with visits from Minnie Mouse, Goofy, Pluto and others. Next door is the **50s Prime Time Café** , a culinary time warp that's a little like eating at Ward and June Cleaver's house. Before seating you, a hostess calls out, "Kids! Dinner's ready!" Pot roast, meatloaf, and other comfort foods top the menu, televisions at every table play clips of 1950s sitcoms, and waiters have been known to refuse serving dessert until you've eaten all your vegetables. And keep those elbows off the table! Priority seating is recommended at both restaurants.

In a 2,000-seat theater just across from Gertie the Dinosaur is the **Indiana Jones Epic Stunt Spectacular** , one of the park's longest-running shows. Stuntmen reenact several scenes from *Raiders of the Lost Ark*, then show you how it's done. A few audience members get in on the act, too. (If you want to be chosen, sit front and center and look perky.) There are gunfights, fistfights, pratfalls, and other feats

of derring-do, not to mention a couple of explosions, and a giant boulder that nearly flattens the star. A recent overhaul gives the show even more bang for the buck.

A big restaurant next door, the **Backlot Express** , is tricked out like a studio workshop, with props, paint cans and bits of scenery scattered about a warehouse-like setting. The fare is strictly fast food – burgers, fries, chicken nuggets – but the indoor dining area is blessedly cool on a hot day.

Across the way is **Sounds Dangerous** , a comedy starring Drew Carey, who plays an undercover reporter on the trail of a smuggler. Most of the show takes place in darkness, while the audience listens in with headphones. The script is silly, but the experience illustrates how sound is used to advance a story. Interactive exhibits outside the theater let you add sound effects to video clips.

An Imperial walker, one of those spacey war machines that sprang from the mind of George Lucas, stands in front of **Star Tours** , the park's only simulator ride. Upon entering the building, you discover that you're a tourist preparing for a pleasure trip to the Moon of Endor. Unfortunately, your travel agents – R2-D2 and C-3PO, the bickering androids from the movie – have you booked on a flight with a rookie pilot. You're ushered into a starspeeder and before you can say "May the force be with you," you're dodging comets, zooming around space-borne icebergs, and evading laser blasts. The ride isn't particularly frightening, but it does give passengers a good shake.

New York, New York

The atmosphere takes on an urban, brick-and-mortar quality as you drift into the area around New York

BELOW:
Miss Piggy and Kermit the Frog star in Muppet Vision 3-D.

Street. Here you'll find a statue of Miss Piggy perched regally atop a fountain. She stands in front of a theater showing **Jim Henson's Muppet Vision 3-D** , a raucous 25-minute romp with Kermit, Piggy, Fozzie Bear, and the rest of the muppet crew. The 3-D effects are amazing, and a few animatronic figures, including an orchestra of penguins and two wisecracking codgers – Waldorf and Statler – add to the experience.

Working your way along the path that loops around the theater, you can gobble down a slice of pizza and play the latest video games at **Pizza Planet Arcade**, modeled after the arcade from the Disney-Pixar film *Toy Story*. For something more substantial, try **Mama Melrose's Ristorante Italiano**, serving pasta, chicken marsala, risotto, wood-fired pizza, and other Italian dishes in a setting reminiscent of a family trattoria of the 1930s. Next door, **Al's Toy Barn** is the place to meet *Toy Story*'s Woody, Jessie, and Buzz Lightyear.

Exit the theater and wander over to New York Street, a backlot rendition of the Big Apple. This is the least crowded part of the park and the place you're most likely to catch a glimpse of a film crew at work. Take a few moments to appreciate the extraordinary detail that went into its design and construction. The subtle street sounds – a distant siren, car horns, a jackhammer – are an especially nice touch.

A side street leads to the **Honey, I Shrunk the Kids Movie Set Adventure**, a super-sized playground designed from an insect's point of view. Kids zoom down slides on a blade of grass, explore tunnels in a giant mushroom, and get a good soaking around a leaky hose. On the downside, the playground is sweltering on a hot day, there's not much room for adults to sit, and once children disappear into the tunnels it takes a while to find them, much less convince them that it's time to leave. **The Writer's Stop** is where one would come to write the great Disney novel. It also sells stationary, Disney books, and

TIP

Height requirements are 40 inches (102 cm) for Star Tours and Tower of Terror, and 48 inches (122 cm) for Rock 'n' Roller Coaster.

LEFT: television personality Drew Carey is featured in Sounds Dangerous.

Disney-MGM or Universal?

How does Disney-MGM Studios compare with Universal Studios? Generally, Universal is more intense and adult-oriented. The explosions are bigger, the soundtrack is louder, the action is more violent. At Universal, the big 3-D attraction features Arnold Schwarzenegger battling killer robots on a mission to exterminate the human race. At Disney-MGM, the 3-D show stars Kermit the Frog trying to keep the lid on a bunch of rambunctious muppets. The Terminator is made of titanium and is armed with a sawed-off shotgun. Kermit is made of cloth and has a boutonniere that squirts water.

The shows at Disney-MGM – nearly all musicals – tend to be sweet and schmaltzy. At Universal Studios, they're hipper, louder, and are usually set to a rock beat. Interestingly, both parks try to play against type. Disney-MGM ratchets up the adrenaline level with two first-class thrill rides – Tower of Terror and Rock 'n' Roller Coaster, while Universal Studios tries to capture the kiddie market with its Woody Woodpecker's KidZone. Heck, they even have Barney.

So which park should you visit? For an action-packed adventure, go to Universal. For a kinder, gentler theme park, stick with Disney.

best-sellers to be enjoyed with the in-store coffee and pastries.

Feeling hungry? Swing around the corner for a bite at the **Sci-Fi Dine-In Theater Restaurant**, where the 1950s drive-in theme is wonderful and the food is, well, not. Diners are seated in car-shaped booths and watch trailers of hokey horror flicks like *Cat Women of the Moon* and *Frankenstein Meets the Space Monster*. Stick to something simple like a burger and milkshake and you'll be fine. Or skip the entrée altogether and go directly to dessert. The food next door at the **ABC Commissary** is equally uninspired and the cafeteria ambience is nothing to write home about. The advantage: it's fast and relatively cheap. Just across the road is a chance to meet characters from *Monsters Inc* throughout the day.

Mickey Avenue

It's a quick stroll down Commissary Lane and across the central plaza to Mickey Avenue. To the far left is the **Disney-MGM Studios Backlot Tour** ⓱, a 35-minute tram ride with glimpses of the wardrobe

department, scenery workshop, and what appears to be a quiet suburban street lined with trim little houses. The buildings are nothing more than shells, of course, used for exterior shots in countless television commercials and programs like *The Golden Girls* and *Empty Nest*. In another highlight of the tour, you file into a soundstage equipped with an enormous special-effects water tank. Here, a few audience members are chosen to reenact a splashy battle sequence from the 2001 film *Pearl Harbor*. Later, the tram pulls into Catastrophe Canyon, which you're told is a movie set for a film currently under production. Within moments the earth begins to shake, an oil tanker explodes, and 70,000 gallons (270,000 liters) of water come barreling down at you. The flood subsides with only a moment to spare, and as you pull away, the set automatically reassembles itself. The tram then takes a quick spin around New York, where you learn that the brick and steel facades are really fiberglass and Styrofoam. The tour ends with an exhibit of show biz memorabilia at the **American Film Institute Showcase**.

Back on Mickey Avenue, the next attraction is **Who Wants To Be a Millionaire – Play It!** ⓲, a faithful recreation of the television game show, though contestants win Disney swag instead of cash. Audience members play along on individual keypads. Whoever gets the highest score becomes the next contestant.

Next up is **Walt Disney: One Man's Dream** ⓳, a movie and walk-through exhibit on the life and career of the man who started it all. In the same building **Making of the Haunted Mansion Movie** is nothing more than a short film describing just that. The only novelty is that it's presented in the set of the ballroom of the Haunted Mansion– a

BELOW:
Star Tours takes riders on a virtual adventure in space.

recreation of the ride at the Magic Kingdom. This attraction is not that special and is probably nothing more than a short-lived attempt to self-promote a film Disney realizes is likely to struggle.

At the end of Mickey Avenue in a little plaza called the **Animation Courtyard** is **The Magic of Disney Animation ⓴**, a tour of a working animation studio. The tour starts with an amusing film featuring Walter Cronkite and Robin Williams, who give an overview of the animation process. Next up is a presentation by an artist on how Disney characters are developed and brought to life. The amazing thing is that he or she draws (usually a character from a recent film) throughout the entire talk. When the spiel is over, the drawing is done. Then it's a walk through a glassed-in corridor with views of artists at work on an upcoming project. The finale occurs in yet another theater, showing a flashy montage of Disney animated classics.

Visitors with small children will find two delightful shows at the Ani-mation Courtyard. **The Voyage of the Little Mermaid ㉑** is a sweet retelling of the 1989 movie that's credited with starting a new era in Disney animation. Cleverly staged in a misty under-the-sea setting, the show makes use of live actors, puppets, film, and a host of special effects. It's all a bit schmaltzy, but kids are enthralled and most adults walk out humming one of the infectious tunes.

If you have a preschooler at home, you probably know about Bear, Tutter, Rolie Polie Olie, and Stanley. They're characters from the Disney Channel, and they're the stars of **Playhouse Disney – Live on Stage ㉒**. The appealing thing about this 20-minute song and dance revue is that kids are encouraged to jump to their feet (the audience sits on the floor) and join in the fun. There are bouncy tunes, cute dance routines, and lots of interaction with the characters. Few people, even adults, fail to leave happy.

Come to think of it, that can be said about the park as a whole. ❏

Map on page 96

The water tower capped with giant mouse ears near Mickey Avenue is known as the Earffel Tower. It's empty, a prop meant to evoke the look of a Hollywood studios in the 1940s.

BELOW: Walt Disney collaborates with conductor Leopold Sokowski (far right) during the making of *Fantasia,* the landmark animated film.

RESTAURANTS

50s Prime Time Café
Sit by a black-and-white TV playing 1950s sitcoms and eat favorites from the era such as meatloaf, fried chicken and pot roast. Thick milk shakes, apple pie and banana splits for dessert. $$

Hollywood Brown Derby
The Derby features fresh fish, pasta, and steaks served by snappily dressed waiters in an elegant recreation of the original Tinseltown restaurant. You must try the grapefruit cake. $$

● ● ● ● ● ● ● ● ● ● ● ● ● ● ● ● ● ●

*Price includes dinner and a glass of wine (when available), excluding tip. $$$ over $30, $$ between $20–30, $ under $20. For priority seating, call 407-939 3463. Dial *88 from a public phone in Disney for toll-free access to this number.*

DOWNTOWN DISNEY & WATER PARKS

At the hub of this particular universe is a complex of emporiums and night spots offering all manner of goods, goodies, and not so cheap thrills for the grownup set

Map
on page
106

LEFT: R&B musician
Sony Rhodes at the
House of Blues.
BELOW:
sushi chefs at work
at Wolfgang Puck Café.

The name Downtown Disney is a bit misleading: some tourists have even gone looking for it in Orlando's business district. At Walt Disney World, however, "downtown" is a dining, shopping, and entertainment complex that sprawls along the shore of Lake Buena Vista, about a mile east of Epcot. The impetus behind the development was a desire to recapture visitors being siphoned off by Orlando's own Church Street Station. Sometimes referred to as Disney for adults, its target audience is the over-21 crowd, although – ever sensitive to the needs of families – there are plenty of attractions for kids.

The complex is divided into three sections – West Side, Pleasure Island, and Marketplace. Many businesses here are non-Disney operations, so there's a greater variety of food and merchandise than you typically find at the theme parks. Admission is free during the day; after 7pm Pleasure Island has a cover charge good for all eight nightclubs, so you can wander from one to another without having to pay for each separately.

Fun, food, and fanfare

West Side, the newest part of Downtown Disney, is a mixed bag of food, entertainment, and retail. Anchoring one end of the complex is the huge white circus tent of **Cirque du Soleil ❶** (407-939 7600), a troupe of about 100 performers who blend traditional circus art with theater, mime, and cabaret. The show, *La Nouba*, is as difficult to describe as it is entertaining. It's safe to say you've never experienced anything like it – at least not at Disney World. The experience doesn't come cheap – about $87 for an adult – comparable to a Broadway show, but most people say it's worth every penny. See it if you can.

Next door is the **House of Blues**  ② (407-934 2583), founded by actor, comedian, and original Blues Brother Dan Aykroyd and others, and done up like the kind of ramshackle wharfside warehouse you might find in the Mississippi Delta. The food is surprisingly good for a chain operation, with spicy Southern favorites like fried catfish, seafood gumbo, jambalaya, and bread pudding dribbled with brandy sauce.

The music hall features everything from heavy metal to acoustic blues, with a healthy mix of established artists and up-and-comers. A few recent acts include Sammy Hagar, Pat Benatar, and LL Cool J. If you're traveling with kids, consider booking a table for the **Sunday Gospel Brunch**. You'll jump up for Jesus and chow down on all the Southern vittles you can eat. It's a soulful way to finish your week at Disney.

The ambience at **Wolfgang Puck** ❸ (407-939 3463) is a bit more

Top-name rock, blues, and gospel acts appear at the House of Blues.

sedate, though the cavernous rooms and chatty clientele aren't exactly conducive to an intimate conversation. The atmosphere is all color and energy, with open kitchens, video monitors showing chefs at work, and a bustling wait staff. The menu runs the gamut from sushi and gourmet pizza to lamb chops and seafood, all prepared with the celebrity chef's Californian flair (except perhaps the Weiner schnitzel). The upstairs dining room is quite expensive. The downstairs café is cheaper and more casual, and the food is just as tasty.

Just a few steps away is **Bongos Cuban Café** ❹ (407-828 0999), the creation of pop star Gloria Estefan and her husband Emilio. A giant pineapple sprouting from the roof sets the tone of the place, which throbs with Latin music and brilliant colors. Aficionados of Cuban cuisine may have better luck elsewhere, but the lakeside patio is a pleasant place to sip a fancy tropical drink.

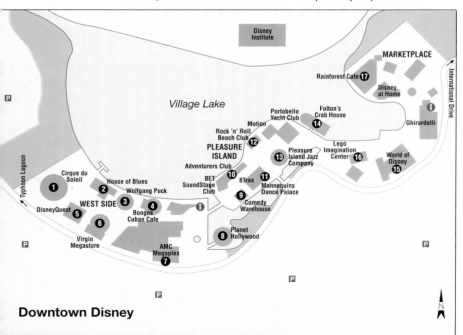

Downtown Disney

DisneyQuest

What do you get when you compress all the thrills of a theme park into a five-story building? Well, something like **DisneyQuest ❺** (407-828 4600), a high-tech pleasure dome packed with simulator rides and souped-up video games in a wavy, aquamarine building across from the House of Blues. Like a real theme park, Disney Quest is divided into distinct areas, each spread over several levels connected by a labyrinth of elevators (known here as cyberlators), ramps, and twisting slides. Also like a real theme park, admission isn't cheap – $34 for adults, $28 for children – and afternoon crowds can be extremely thick.

Some of the best virtual-reality attractions are in the **Explore Zone**. At **Aladdin's Magic Carpet Ride**, for example, you don a VR helmet and mount something that looks like a motorcycle. Your team's mission is to free the genie as you wing your way over the streets of Agrabah and through the Cave of Wonders. At **Pirates of the Caribbean: Battle for Buccaneer Gold**, a four-person crew boards a ship (a motion platform with a wraparound screen) equipped with six cannons and does battle in a 3-D world of storm-tossed seas, fortress islands, and erupting volcanoes. On the **Virtual Jungle Cruise**, you paddle a raft down a raging river; an inflatable mattress under the raft simulates the motion of water as your crew tries to navigate a series of rapids, waterfalls, and other perils that appear on a projection screen in front of you.

In the **Create Zone**, you can utilize digital technology to paint a picture, alter an image of your face, or design a toy and have it shipped to your home (for a fee). Learn to draw like a Disney animator at the **Animation Academy** or produce your own musical opus at **Songmaker**. The coolest attraction in the Create Zone – and perhaps in all of Disney-Quest – is **CyberSpace Mountain,** which allows you to design a roller coaster at a computer station (with the assistance of Bill Nye the Science Guy), then experience the ride in a motion simulator.

There are more virtual-reality games in the **Score Zone**. At **Ride the Comix** you slip on a head-mounted display and battle comic-book villains with a virtual saber. At **Mighty Ducks Pinball Slam**, you stand on a moving hockey-puck-shaped platform and use a joystick and body English to maneuver your ball on a huge video screen.

The **Replay Zone** comes closest to a traditional arcade, albeit bigger, louder, and with a number of high-tech twists. The standout is **Buzz Lightyear's Astro-Blaster**, a version of bumper cars – called astro-blasters – equipped with cannons that fire spongy balls. A direct hit sends your opponent's car into a dramatic tailspin.

Map on page 106

BELOW:
shoppers, diners, and revelers crowd the walkways of Downtown Disney at night.

Guitars, cigars, & superstars

The next couple of buildings are devoted to retail. **Virgin Megastore** ❻ (407-828 0222) is a virtual archive of contemporary pop culture, with more than 250,000 music, book, and movie titles. Don't expect any bargains. Several shops are ensconced in the gargantuan structure next door, including **Guitar Gallery** (407-827 0118), filled with the stuff of guitar-god fantasies. **Sosa Family Cigar Company** (407-827 0114) is the place for a premium smoke. A cigar roller works in the front window, and a walk-in humidor is stocked with more than 80 brands of cigar. At **Starabilia** (407-827 0104) you'll find autographs and memorabilia. Prices range from about $200 (for Willie Nelson or Geraldo Rivera) to $250,000 (for a guitar signed by the Beatles). Other shops sell refrigerator magnets, decorative arts, and fashion. A 24-screen **AMC** megaplex ❼ (407-298 4488) shows the latest flicks in theaters with stadium seating, digital sound, and floor-to-ceiling screens.

The illuminated sphere with a flying saucer embedded over the entrance is the Orlando headquarters of **Planet Hollywood** ❽ (407-827 7827), the worldwide restaurant chain launched by Arnold Schwarzenegger, Bruce Willis, Sylvester Stallone, and entrepreneur Robert Earl. Every inch of the dome-shaped dining room is jammed with movie props, memorabilia, and other eye candy. The good news is that the food has improved since the company's brush with bankruptcy in 1999. The bad news? The wait can be terribly long, especially when the theaters let out; so it's sensible to make reservations well in advance.

Pleasure Island

The next section of Downtown Disney – **Pleasure Island** (407-939 2648) – operates in a slightly different manner than the rest of the complex. This is, for lack of a better term, Disney's nightclub district. An admission fee covering all eight clubs is charged after 7pm, at which times guests must be at least 18 to enter, unless accompanied by an adult. As elsewhere in Florida, the drinking age is 21. A separate

RIGHT: the Guitar gallery stocks more than 150 guitars, ranging in price from $90 to $17,000.

Behind the scenes

If you're curious about those secret corridors under the Magic Kingdom, want to learn about the art and history of Disney animation, or yearn to swim with the fish in the Living Seas aquarium, sign up for one of Walt Disney World's Behind-the-Scene Tours.

There are about 10 tours in all, guided by enthusiastic cast members or staff experts. Among the most popular are the five-hour Keys to the Kingdom tour, limited solely to the Magic Kingdom; Backstage Magic, a daylong excursion through the Magic Kingdom, Disney-MGM Studios and Epcot; Wild by Design, which traces the planning and development of Animal Kingdom; Gardens of the World, a study of plants at Epcot's World Showcase; and Backstage Safari, which includes a visit to a wildlife housing area and veterinary hospital. Although most tours require that participants be at least 16 years old, Disney's Family Magic, a two-hour interactive exploration of the Magic Kingdom, is open to visitors of all ages.

Tours range in price, frequency and duration. Some require the purchase of separate park admission. All require a 24-hour advance reservation. For information, call 407-939 8687.

admission may be required for special events and concerts.

Things don't start rolling here until about 9 or 10pm, so you may want to catch a couple of shows or a meal in the early evening before getting into serious party mode. A show at the **Comedy Warehouse ❾** starts the night on an upbeat note. The improvised routines are a hoot, and the comics are experts at working an audience. There are five 45-minute shows a night; the first two are the least crowded.

Perhaps the most unusual place is the **Adventurers Club ❿** – part bar, part interactive theater, part Disney imagineering. The conceit here is that this is a dusty old gentlemen's club established by long-lost explorer Merriweather Adam Pleasure. The place is decked out in primitive masks, shrunken heads, archaeological relics, and stuffed animals (some of whom talk), and staffed with actors who draw guests into improvisational encounters. Be sure to hang around for one of the 20-minute cabaret-comedy shows held in the library, and don't be surprised if you get dragged into the act.

Excellent live bands crank up the volume at the open-air **West End Stage** between the Adventurers Club and Comedy Warehouse. There are usually four sets a night, culminating at midnight with fireworks, confetti and a light show.

If dancing is your thing, you have five venues to choose from. **Mannequins Dance Palace ⓫** is the most extravagant – a multilevel mannequin warehouse (at Disney, everything has a back story) with a revolving dance floor, state-of-the-art laser lights, several bars, and an earthshaking sound system. Disney cast members sometimes come here after hours, and there are occasional outbreaks by professional dancers. Ask at the desk if there's anything scheduled.

Other dance halls cater to a variety of musical tastes. **BET SoundStage Club** plays hip-hop, reggae, and R&B; **8Trax** breathes new life into the disco hits of the 1970s; and Motion, the island's newest club, spins top 40 and alternative rock. The **Rock 'n' Roll Beach Club ⓬** – a three-story beach house tricked out in a surf club motif – features top-notch bands bashing out rock classics from the 1960s to today. There's a dance floor on the first level and barroom games like air hockey, darts, and billiards on the floors above.

The vibe is laid-back at the **Pleasure Island Jazz Co. ⓭**, a showcase for first-rate local talent and an occasional big-name touring act. This restaurant is currently closed for renovation and due to reopen in late 2005. Two other restaurants offer full-service dining, too: the **Portobello Yacht Club** serves up Italian cuisine, including tasty wood-fired pizza, and **Fulton's Crab House ⓮**, in a replica of a Mississippi riverboat, offers seafood with a few beef, poultry, and pasta dishes. Both have decent wine lists.

Map on page 106

BELOW: a three-level restaurant is housed within the distinctive blue sphere of Planet Hollywood.

Marketplace

The final section of Downtown Disney – **Marketplace** – is devoted almost exclusively to shopping. The hub is the **World of Disney** , the largest Disney store on the planet, with 12 themed rooms sprawling across 38,000-square feet (3,500-square meters) and bursting with nearly half a million items. The next building over is the **Lego Imagination Center** ⑯ (407-828 0065), where kids and adults can create their own Lego masterpieces in an outdoor play area, have their pictures taken with amazing Lego sculptures (a dragon, a sleeping tourist, a UFO, and more), then stock up on kits and educational toys in the shop.

A plethora of other Disney-themed stores hawk sporting goods and clothes, animation cels, housewares, Christmas decorations, and just about anything else you can slap a logo on.

Dining options include **McDonald's**, **Wolfgang Puck Express**, **Earl of Sandwich,** and the **Ghirardelli Soda Fountain & Chocolate Shop**. For something more substantial, try **Cap'n Jack's Restaurant** (407-828-3971) for seafood and pleasant views of the lake. The smoke you've been seeing billowing in the distance is from a smoldering volcano that sits atop the **Rainforest Café** ⑰ (407-827 8500), a cavernous restaurant with an extravagant jungle setting. Even with priority seating, you'll have a good long wait. Management hopes you'll spend the time (and at least a few extra dollars) in the adjoining gift shop. A marina at this end of the lagoon rents powerboats and operates fishing excursions for largemouth bass.

On the boardwalk

Smaller in scope and generally more sedate than Pleasure Island is **Disney's Boardwalk**, situated at the Boardwalk Resort on Crescent Lake within walking distance (or a short boat ride) of Epcot and Disney-MGM Studios. The complex recalls the look and spirit of a seaside resort à la Atlantic City about 1925, with boardwalk buskers, midway games, ice-cream stands, and gingerbread architecture. Evenings are the most pleasant time to visit, with music

BELOW:
Cirque du Soleil is presented in a tent-like structure at Downtown Disney's West Side.

from the nightclubs filling the air, cool breezes blowing off the lake, and party lights shining on the water.

For serious dining you might try the seafood specialties at the **Flying Fish Café** (407-939 3463) or tapas and other Mediterranean dishes at **Spoodles** (407-939 3463). More gimmicky is the **ESPN Club** (407-939 5100) which, in typical theme-restaurant fashion, is crammed with all things sports, including more than 70 television screens; there's even one in the restroom, lest you miss a minute of the big game. Beer lovers can sample a selection of handcrafted suds at Disney's first brewpub, the **Big River Grille & Brewing Works** (407-560 0253). The pub grub is nothing to write home about, but the outdoor seating is a good spot to sip a brew and watch the crowd pass by.

Club hoppers have two choices here. The **Atlantic Dancehall** (407-939 2444) has switched identities over the years – first swing, then modern rock, now Latin. DJs provide music during the week; Latin bands appear on Friday and Saturday nights. **Jelly Rolls** features a raucous music and comedy act, with comedians at dueling pianos and lots of audience participation. Shops peddle the usual variety of Disney merchandise – T-shirts, hats, souvenirs, sweets. One exception is the **Wyland Gallery** (407-560 8750), selling the work of the well-known marine-life artist.

Water parks

Walt Disney World has two water parks, each with a distinct personality. Cleverly designed and beautifully landscaped, they are thrilling – and usually crowded – places to cool off during a scorching Florida afternoon. Like the theme parks, the trick to beating the crowds is to arrive about 30–45 minutes before opening and make a beeline to the most popular slides. By noon on a hot day, the queues can be prohibitively mobbed. Another option is to arrive in the late afternoon – say 4pm–5pm – after the early birds have pooped out and gone home. Consider too that frequent electrical storms in summer will cause the

Map
on page
106

Sweet Indulgence

What could be more relaxing after spending a day or two trampling around the parks than a long, luxurious soak in a lavender-scented bath followed by a Swedish massage, gentle facial to wash away the grime and ease away the stress that inevitably accompanies the magical world at Disney?

If that sounds enticing, make a reservation at one of Disney World's three spas. Each offers a wide range of services, ranging from seaweed wraps, saunas, aromatherapy, and several styles of massage to manicures, pedicures, and hydro-therapy.

Treatments last from one or two hours to a full day and vary in price from $50 to $300. Special packages are offered for athletes, couples, brides, even children. Clients are not required to be guests at Disney resorts to take advantage of these services.

For more information, call the Grand Floridian Spa & Health Club at 407-824 2332; The Spa at the Disney Institute at 407-827 4455; or The Spa at the Wyndham Palace Resort at 407-827 2727. But remember to leave the evening free. You may be too relaxed to lift a foot until morning.

Disney Cruises

Only on Disney Cruise Line's two 1,750-passenger ships, Disney Wonder and Disney Magic, do passengers head out to sea to the tune of "When You Wish Upon a Star." The line offers several cruising options, including a seven-night, land-and-sea vacation that includes a three- or four-night stay at a Walt Disney World resort, and three-, four- and seven-night cruise-only packages. Ships sail from Port Canaveral, an hour east of Orlando.

The three- and four-night cruises stop at Nassau, Freeport, and Castaway Cay in the Bahamas. Once known as Gorda Cay, Castaway was a notorious rendezvous for international drug smugglers. Disney bought the island, cleaned it up, and renamed it. At 1,000 acres (400 hectares), it's a lovely spot for hiking, biking, swimming, snorkeling, and sunbathing.

Weeklong cruises alternate between the eastern Caribbean (St Maarten, St John, and St Thomas) and the western Caribbean (Key West, Grand Cayman, and Cozumel), with a stop at Castaway Cay.

Modeled on the luxury liners of the 1920s, the two vessels offer similar amenities and are designed for those traveling with or without children. Special areas and activities are reserved for children only, others are exclusively for adults. Supervised programs for kids aged 3–12 and 13–17 run from 9am to midnight; babysitting is available for infants.

Adults-only areas include a swimming pool, an ESPN sports bar, several nightclubs, a restaurant and a secluded beach on Castaway Cay. Activities include winetasting, lectures and comedy shows. For families, there are several swimming pools, first-run movies, an interactive play area, and a lounge with live entertainment. Teens have their own café and music bar and activities on the sports deck.

Of course, Disney characters are very much in evidence, from the bronze Mickey Mouse in the three-story atrium to a full schedule of parades, appearances, and photo ops. Familiar characters, songs and Disney's signature super-sweet attitude are featured each night in lavish stage shows.

Most of the 875 staterooms aboard each ship have baths-and-a-half; 73 percent are outside rooms; nearly half have small, private verandahs. All have telephones, televisions and safes. There are 12 stateroom classes, corresponding to room rates at the Walt Disney World resorts. Passengers who opt for land-and-sea packages receive rooms comparable in size and amenities to those they book at Disney World.

Passengers rotate among several theme restaurants. Interestingly, your wait staff and companions move with you. An indoor-outdoor café serves breakfast, lunch, and a children's buffet dinner, and 24-hour room service is available. One restaurant aboard each ship is reserved for adults and serves candlelight dinners.

Other shipboard amenities include shops, whirlpools, a spa and salon, and a well-equipped fitness center. ❑

LEFT: Disney cruises include a stop at the company's own island.

water parks to close. A long storm can work in your favor, however, since some guests will get discouraged and return to their hotels. Bring a towel, sunscreen, snacks, and enough cash to last you the day. Locker rental runs $5–$7 a day; $2 is refunded when you return the key.

Water rides are notorious for giving wedgies and stripping off bathing suits. Tie your suit tightly and leave the teeny-weeny bikini at home.

Blizzard Beach (407-560 3400) is Disney's newest and largest water park, and the one with the most bizarre concept. The story goes that Blizzard Beach was hastily constructed as a ski resort after Florida was hit by a freak snowstorm. When the snow melted, management decided to cut its losses and turn the area into a water park. At its center is **Mount Gushmore**, a 90-foot (30-meter) peak serviced by what may be the state's only ski lift (there are also stairs and a gondola for disabled guests).

At the top, guests choose among an assortment of routes to ride back down. The most exciting, the **Summit Plummet**, actually begins on a platform 30 feet (10 meters) above the mountaintop. Said to be the world's highest free-fall slide and the fastest in the country, it zips riders down a 350-foot (107-meter) ramp at an angle of 60 degrees and speeds approaching 60 miles per hour (97 kph). Needless to say, this is not an experience for the faint of heart.

For the less adventurous, the **Slush Gusher**, a double-humped water slide, transports riders through snow-banked gullies at a slightly more civilized top speed of 50 miles per hour (80 kph). On **Teamboat Springs**, the world's longest white-water raft ride, guests in five-person rafts twist and turn through 1,200 feet (360 meters) of rushing waves and cataracts. Other options include **Toboggan Racers**, where riders on mats travel headfirst down an eight-lane chute, **Downhill Double Dipper**, a tubing route that plunges through a partially-enclosed run at a mere 25 miles per hour (40 kph); and **Snow Stormer**, a 350-foot

Map on page 106

TIP

You can sign up for a 90-minute surfing lesson at Typhoon Lagoon. Lessons are offered Tuesday and Thursday at 6.30am. The fee is about $125.

BELOW: Planet Hollywood anchors Downtown Disney.

Map
on page
106

(106 meters) long flume ride. For kids, **Tikes Peak** and the **Ski Patrol Training Camp** have tubes, body slides, and a bungee cord slide. If you're looking for a milder experience, Runoff Rapids is a tamer flume ride and Cross Country Creek is a very lazy half mile innertube ride. Blizzard Beach is also home to Disney's **Winter Summerland Miniature Golf**, with two elaborately-designed 18-hole courses.

Slip sliding away

The back story is a bit more sensible at **Typhoon Lagoon** (407-560-4141), which, we are led to believe, is the waterlogged remains of a tropical resort drowned by a hurricane. In the center of the park is the **Surf Pool**, which generates waves more than 5 feet tall (1.5 meters), high enough for the surfing competitions that are held here. Rising above this scene is the summit of the 85-foot-high (26-meter) **Mount Mayday**, crowned with the wreckage of Miss Tilly, a washed-up trawler.

The action is a bit tamer here than at Blizzard Beach, but not by much. You can lounge on a sandy beach, frolic in the waves, and take a relaxing 45-minute float trip through rainforest grottoes and waterfalls. At **Shark Reef**, you get a brief snorkeling lesson, then fin around a sunken tanker accompanied by tropical fish and real (friendly) sharks. This is one adventure you want to do just after the park opens. By midday, the lines are too long and the tank too crowded to be much fun.

There's no lack of high-speed slides, either. Daredevils shoot the rapids and careen through caves at **Mayday**, **Gangplank**, and **Keelhaul Falls**, fly down a trio of 214-foot (65-meter) speed slides at **Humunga Kowabunga**, and whoosh down winding fiberglass chutes at **Storm Slides**. The thrills are toned down at **Ketchakiddee Creek**, designed especially for children aged two to six. **Castaway Creek** is this park's version of the lazy river. Its size is impressive – it takes over 45 minutes to complete it. ❑

BELOW:
Disney World offers three elaborate water parks, with slides and chutes suitable for children of all ages.

RESTAURANTS & BARS

Restaurants

Bongos Cuban Café
Downtown Disney
West Side
Tel: 407-828 0999
Cuban cuisine in a restaurant owned by Gloria and Emilio Estefan and showcasing the tastes of Miami and South Beach. **$$**

Cap'n Jack's Oyster Bar
Downtown Disney
Marketplace
Tel: 407-828 3971
Pier house restaurant featuring crab, lobster, clams, and oysters, plus "land lubber" specials. **$$**

ESPN Sports Club
Disney's BoardWalk
Tel: 407-939 5100
Jocks will love this theme restaurant crammed with all things sports, including more than 70 television screens; there's even one in the restroom, lest you miss a minute of the big game. Bring a big appetite. Entrées, including hamburgers, hot dogs, sirloin and grilled chicken, are oversized. Desserts are big and yummy. **$$$**

Flying Fish Cafe
Disney's BoardWalk
(priority seating)
One of Disney's best restaurants, in a whimsical setting with a busy stage kitchen. Potato-wrapped yellowtail snapper and other creative dishes. Chocolate lava cake for dessert. **$$$**

Fulton's Crab House
Downtown Disney
Pleasure Island
(priority seating)
Seafood specialties with fresh fish flown in daily. Raw seafood bar. **$$$**

Planet Hollywood
Downtown Disney
West Side
Tel: 407-827 7827
Predictable version of this chain restaurant. Expect big portions and long lines. **$$**

Portobello Yacht Club
Pleasure Island
Downtown Disney
Tel: 407-934 8888
First-rate Northern Italian cuisine and seafood specialties. **$$**

Rainforest Café
Downtown Disney
Marketplace
Tel: 407-827 8500
Eat in the midst of volcanoes, waterfalls, dense foliage, simulated rainstorms, and a colorful troop of rainforest animals. Pasta, sandwiches, salads, ribs, and other American specialties. **$$**

Spoodles
Disney's BoardWalk
(priority seating)
Mediterranean specialties, yogurt-marinated chicken kebabs, fish. One of Disney's best breakfast buffets. **$$–$$$**

Wolfgang Puck Express
Downtown Disney
(priority seating for upstairs dining room)
California creations featuring Puck's famous pizza, Thai specialties, sushi and killer salads. **$–$$$**

Bar

Big River Grille & Brewing Works
Disney's BoardWalk
Tel: 407-560 0253
Beer lovers can sample a selection of handcrafted suds at Disney's first brewpub. The pub grub is nothing to write home about, but the outdoor seating is a good spot to sip a brew and watch the crowd pass by. **$$**

House of Blues
Downtown Disney
West Side
Tel: 407-934 BLUE
Live music nightly. Menu specialties include jambalaya, etouffee, gumbo and bread pudding. The Sunday Gospel Brunch is a roof raisng breakfast with hymns and hominy. **$$**

• • • • • • • • • • • • •
*For priority seating call 407-939 3463. Dialing *88 from a public phone in Disney allows toll-free access to this number.*

PRICE CATEGORIES

Prices for three-course dinner per person with a half-bottle of house wine:
$ = under $20
$$ = $20–30
$$$ = $30–45
$$$$ = more than $45

RIGHT: movie memorabilia fill Planet Hollywood's spacious dining rooms.

UNIVERSAL ORLANDO

Recent expansions have transformed this newcomer into a full-fledged resort poised to give Disney World a run for its money

If there's one word that describes the difference between Disney World and Universal Orlando, it's *attitude*. Everything is a little more intense here. The rides are wilder, the soundtracks are louder, the special effects are more explosive. It's also a much newer place, with an emphasis on cutting-edge technology. Rides like Revenge of the Mummy and The Amazing Adventures of Spider-Man pioneered a new level of realism and excitement, and continue to lead the pack in the creative possibilities of motion simulators and virtual effects.

What you don't find here is the Disney knack for storytelling or the infectiously hummable Disney tunes. For some people, that's a relief. Others – especially those with very young children – may find Universal a bit too intense for comfort, despite the addition of two new lands (Woody Woodpecker's KidZone and Seuss Landing) designed specifically for tots.

Universal is also smaller and more compact than Disney World, with two theme parks to the Mouse's four: Universal Studios, which opened in 1990, and Islands of Adventure, which debuted in 1999. CityWalk, an entertainment district with restaurants, nightclubs and shops, is situated between the two and serves as a gateway for visitors arriving by car. Three theme hotels and an affiliated water park (Wet 'n' Wild) complete the picture, making Universal, like Disney World, an all-in-one resort where visitors can spend several days or more without needing to leave the property. As a bonus, Universal grants on-site guests express access to nearly all the attractions. With a wave of your room key, you're whisked to a special entrance. It's the best perk offered by any theme park.

If, like most visitors, you're one of the plebes who has to wait in line (and the lines at Universal can be very, very long), follow the same advice as at other theme parks: arrive early (15 minutes to an hour before the official opening) and stay late (the parks often close about an hour after the posted time). You can often do more in the first and last two hours than in the rest of the day. Devote the busiest midday hours to eating, shopping, and seeing the big amphitheater shows. Or, if possible, sneak back to your hotel for a swim, a snooze, and a relaxing meal. ❏

LEFT: Marilyn offers visitors a Christmas kiss at Universal Studios.

UNIVERSAL STUDIOS

Visitors are invited to "ride the movies" at this expansive park and learn a thing or two about the art and science of cinema

In 1915, shortly after the haberdasher-turned-filmmaker Carl Laemmle established Universal Pictures in Los Angeles, he discovered that people were willing to pay good money to watch movies being made in the back lot. As a result, guests were given a tour of the studio, served lunch, and invited to watch Rudolph Valentino, Lon Chaney, and other silent-film stars at work – all for the princely sum of 25 cents.

The fee at Universal Studios today is a heck of a lot steeper, but the idea is basically the same. Inspired by the romance and technology of Hollywood movies, Universal has created a state-of-the-art theme park with white-knuckle rides, lively shows, and a bevy of familiar characters. The property sprawls across more than 400 acres (160 hectares) and is arranged around a lagoon in richly-conceived neighborhoods – Hollywood, New York, Production Central, and others.

As Universal likes to remind us, this is a working film production facility. Sections of the park are designed to double as movie sets, and there are several soundstages run by Nickelodeon Studios, where television programs are taped for the popular children's network.

The Front Lot

If you're arriving by car, pass through CityWalk *(see page 145)* and bear right toward the beige arches and the palm-lined boulevard at the park entrance. This staging area, known as the **Front Lot**, is the place to pick up a map, rent a stroller or wheelchair, check Nickelodeon's taping schedule at the **Studio Audience Center**, or fatten your wallet at the ATM.

Pass through the turnstiles and stroll down **Plaza of the Stars**. At

Map on page 120

LEFT: character greetings are part of the fun. **BELOW:** a photo-op near the entrance.

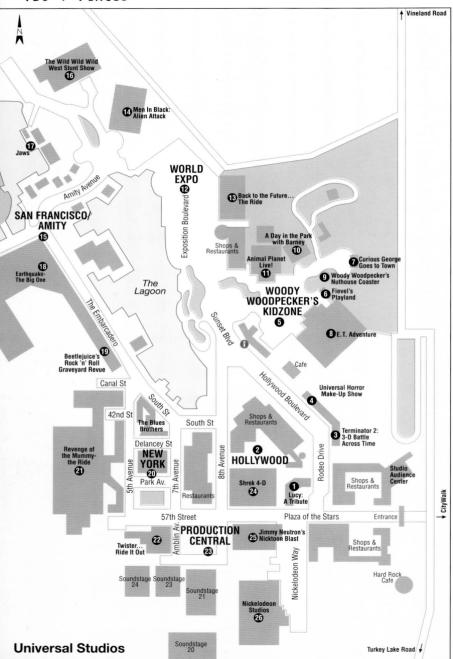

N

↑ Vineland Road

The Wild Wild Wild West Stunt Show **16**

Men In Black: Alien Attack **14**

17 Jaws

WORLD EXPO 12

13 Back to the Future… The Ride

Amity Avenue

SAN FRANCISCO/ AMITY 15

Exposition Boulevard

Shops & Restaurants

A Day in the Park with Barney **10**

Animal Planet Live! **11**

7 Curious George Goes to Town

9 Woody Woodpecker's Nuthouse Coaster

18 Earthquake- The Big One

The Lagoon

WOODY WOODPECKER'S KIDZONE

6 Fievel's Playland

5

The Embarcadero

Sunset Blvd

ℹ

8 E.T. Adventure

Beetlejuice's Rock 'n' Roll Graveyard Revue **19**

Cafe

Universal Horror Make-Up Show

4

Canal St

Hollywood Boulevard

42nd St

South St

The Blues Brothers

South St

Shops & Restaurants

3 Terminator 2: 3-D Battle Across Time

Delancey St

NEW YORK

8th Avenue

2

HOLLYWOOD

Rodeo Drive

Revenge of the Mummy- the Ride **21**

Park Av.

20

5th Avenue

7th Avenue

Restaurants

Shrek 4-D **24**

1 Lucy: A Tribute

Shops & Restaurants

Studio Audience Center

→ CityWalk

57th Street

Plaza of the Stars

Entrance

Twister… Ride It Out **22**

Amblin Av.

PRODUCTION CENTRAL

Jimmy Neutron's Nicktoon Blast **25**

Shops & Restaurants

23

Soundstage 24

Soundstage 23

Soundstage 21

Nickelodeon Way

Nickelodeon Studios **26**

Hard Rock Cafe

Soundstage 20

Universal Studios

Turkey Lake Road ↓

most times of day, you'll find a knot of tourists here, consulting maps, checking backpacks, and generally milling about, while the strains of "Hooray for Hollywood" blast from the ever-present soundtrack. To the left is the world's largest **Universal Studios Store**, stocked from floor to ceiling with hundreds of plush toys, key chains, coffee mugs, and just about anything else you can slap a logo on. It's best to save serious shopping until you're ready to leave the park, so you don't have to lug your booty around all day.

Costumed characters are often stationed near the store entrance. You might find Rocky and Bullwinkle, Angelica Pickles, Sponge Bob Square Pants, and an assortment of characters from recent Universal movies. Some of them even talk, although they aren't much for conversation beyond a few stock lines.

Hollywood

Turn right onto **Rodeo Drive** at the **Beverly Hills Boulangerie**, a good place to fortify yourself with coffee, pastry, or a decent sandwich before attacking the rides. On the opposite corner is **Lucy: A Tribute ❶**, a low-tech exhibition on the career of actress-comedian Lucille Ball, with video clips, costumes, memorabilia, and the obligatory gift shop. This is one of the few attractions at Universal Studios where nothing explodes or leaps out at you. Kids who are eager to do the rides may find this a snooze, but those who grew up with Lucy and Ricky, Fred and Ethel, will be instantly charmed. One startling fact: at its peak, the *I Love Lucy* show reached more than 12 million viewers, nearly 95 percent of the television sets in the United States – numbers that any network executive would gladly give an appendage for today.

Rodeo Drive winds through a version of **Hollywood ❷** plucked from America's collective unconscious –

Ciro's, the Beverly Wiltshire Hotel, the Max Factor Studio, the Brown Derby (which, in this incarnation, sells hats) and the Montmartre. Also here is a recreation of **Schwab's Pharmacy** where, legend has it, a casting agent discovered the young, curvaceous Lana Turner sipping a soda in 1936. Here it sells ice cream, turkey sandwiches, and soft drinks in a set that lovingly recreates the soda shops of the 1940s.

As always, costumed characters are never far away. Scooby-doo might cruise by in the Mystery Machine, the Blues Brothers in a souped-up hearse, or Fred and Wilma Flintstone on a fanciful streetcar. Other appearances might include Marilyn Monroe or Harpo Marx, who kid around with visitors and mug for photos. Heightening the festive mood are live shows that seem to erupt spontaneously on the sidewalk. One notable show features Lucy and Ricky look-alikes doing a "Ricky, I want to be in the show" routine familiar from the TV program, then breaking into a rousing rendition of Ricky's signature num-

Map on page 120

Height requirements are 36 inches (91 cm) for Woody Woodpecker's Nuthouse Coaster, 42 inches (107 cm) for Men in Black and Revenge of the Mummy, and 40 inches (102 cm) for Back to the Future.

BELOW: Groucho has fun with a guest on Hollywood Boulevard.

ber, Babalu, with Lucy leading a conga line of tourists. Another show has a Carmen Miranda clone performing with a sizzling Latin band.

High-tech thrills

This is also where you'll find the first of the park's high-tech, high-adrenaline attractions, **Terminator 2: 3-D Battle Across Time ❸**, featuring original cast members Arnold Schwarzenegger, Linda Hamilton, and Eddie Furlong as well as live actors in a 3-D extravaganza produced by James Cameron to the tune of some $60 million.

The interior holding area accommodates more than 1,000 people, so expect a long wait even if you don't see a queue outside. While you're waiting, video screens and a sugary hostess fill you in on the concept behind the show: you're on a tour of Cyberdyne, the evil technology consortium from the *Terminator* movies, for a preview of its new global defense system called Skynet.

Things go awry shortly after the film begins, as the audience is caught in the crossfire between robots and

rescuers. There are gunshots, explosions, smoke bombs, and amazing 3-D effects. The only trouble is that the action unfolds so rapidly, and the sound is so earsplitting that it can be difficult to follow the story – not that storytelling is really the point. Suffice it to say, you will be dazzled, if a little shell-shocked, by the experience. Parents should use discretion; young children will probably be frightened.

About a half block farther along is the **Universal Horror Make-Up Show ❹**, the funniest attraction at the park. The show features a wise-cracking special-effects expert and a straightman host, who freely mix shtick with a short course on the finer points of stage blood, rubber knives, explosive squibs, foam rubber masks, and other staples of the horror genre. They use movie clips, props from several well-known films, and the perennial victim – er, volunteer – from the audience. It's a good-natured 25 minutes, filled with inside jokes, deft improvising, and – a rarity at theme parks – a dose of off-color humor. One wishes other theme-park shows

BELOW: dining options in Hollywood include Café La Bamba (right) and Mel's Drive-In.

were half as witty. The effects really are creepy, so use caution with young children who may not understand the difference between what happens on the stage and what happens in real life.

If you haven't lost your appetite, you'll find two places to eat at the end of the block. On one side is a replica of **Mel's Drive-In** from the George Lucas film *American Graffiti*. Like the original, it's a burger joint, although, sadly, there are no roller-skating waitresses. In the afternoon, a doo-wop group performs favorite tunes from the 1950s on an open-air stage just out front.

For something a bit more relaxing try **Café La Bamba**, housed in a Spanish Mission-style building across the street. The menu features rotisserie chicken, wrap sandwiches, burgers, and a few Cajun dishes. Even if you don't eat, it's a good place for a break. Order a cocktail at the cantina, snag a table in the pretty outdoor courtyard, and spend a few minutes watching tourists parade down the street.

Woody's Kidzone

Continue on Hollywood Boulevard toward the lagoon. If you're traveling with young children, bear right into the checkered green-and-gray plaza of **Woody Woodpecker's Kidzone ❺**. This is Universal's attempt to cater to its youngest customers, and it does a bang-up job. Although there are two shows and two rides here, the best feature is that Kidzone gives children the opportunity to do what they do best – play. Two interactive play areas – OK, they're elaborate playgrounds – give kids plenty of space to run, climb, jump, and get themselves soaking wet.

The first, **Fievel's Playland ❻**, a takeoff on Steven Spielberg's *American Tale* movies, gives kids a mouse-eye view of the world as they explore multi-level tunnels, slides

and nets in the shape of a gargantuan gramophone, a giant cow skull, tin cans, and barrels. An elaborate pump-handle fountain and a mini-water slide guarantee a good soaking.

Kids (and brave adults) have a second chance to get drenched just a few steps away at **Curious George Goes to Town ❼**, a watery playground where everything squirts, leaks, drips, and gushes. In the back is a two-level space where visitors use air-powered cannon to bombard each other with harmless foam balls. A clever system of vacuum tubes transports the balls up to the second level and into big baskets near the ceiling that gradually tip with the ever-increasing weight, raining down balls on everyone below.

The two rides in Kidzone are equally child-friendly. **E.T. Adventure ❽** is a dark ride in which visitors mount bicycles in order to guide E.T. back home. Video screens in the waiting area feature none other than Steven Spielberg explaining the premise, a convoluted tale about E.T. having to find his teacher, a new character named Botanicus, in order

Map on page 120

Fireworks light up the sky every night shortly before closing time. Find a spot aound the edge of the Lagoon for a good view.

BELOW:
Fievel, from Steven Spielberg's *American Tale*, welcomes youngsters to an elaborate playground.

WELCOME TO THE SET!
You'll feel like you're the size of a MOUSE

Actor Rip Torn, as Agent Zed, makes a guest appearance in Men in Black: Alien Encounter.

to save his ailing planet. As with so many rides, the story line is almost incidental. What kids enjoy most is seeing the bizarre animatronic creatures, including a gaggle of singing baby E.T.s and a talking mushroom. Overall, this is a sweet and gentle ride without the climactic payoff typical of those designed for an older audience. Teenagers may be bored stiff, but young children (and nerve-jangled parents) will be grateful for a break from the pyrotechnics.

A bit more exciting is **Woody Woodpecker's Nuthouse Coaster** ❾, a steel roller coaster with just enough twists and turns for riders under 10 years old. One complaint: the wait is rarely less than 20 minutes, and the ride itself is a scant 90 seconds long. Still, kids love it and – lines or not – may want to ride more than once.

Visitors with preschoolers will appreciate **A Day in the Park with Barney** ❿, a 25-minute sing-along starring the cuddly purple dinosaur of television fame. Cynics love to grumble about Barney's squeaky-clean brand of entertainment, but the under-five crowd will be enchanted. Barney hangs around after the show for hugs and photos. The theater is adjacent to yet another play area, this one designed especially for tiny tots.

A fairly recent addition, **Animal Planet Live!** ⓫, is presented in a covered amphitheater near the Kid-zone entrance. The show mixes live animal performances with video clips from such popular Animal Planet programs as *Emergency Vets* and *The Jeff Corwin Experience* in order to demonstrate how animals and their trainers work together behind the scenes. It's a varied and fast-paced show, with sight gags and other tricks performed by dogs, birds, a skunk, a cheeky orangutan, and a hawk that swoops dramatically over the audience. Many of the actors have appeared in well-known movies and television shows. Two special performances at the time of writing are Crocodile Hunter and Animal (police) Precinct – the first shows on Sunday and Monday respectively.

World Expo

Walk back to the lagoon and turn right, past a series of booths with snacks, games, and talented carica-turists. A large cafeteria on the corner, the **International Food and Film Festival**, serves fast food in several flavors – Italian, Mexican, Chinese, American – though you may want to skip the main course and head directly to the ice-cream bar for banana splits and gooey sundaes. Movie clips play on video monitors stationed around the eatery.

Known as **World Expo** ⓬, this section of the park is supposed to resemble a typical World's Fair, although the theming here isn't as detailed or imaginative as elsewhere. Instead, the area is dominated by two of the park's biggest attractions.

If thrill rides are your thing, you're going to love **Back to the Future… The Ride** ⓭, a bone-rat-

tling, head-spinning journey through time that sends you skittering over Ice Age glaciers, through a volcano, into the gullet of a dinosaur, and, well, back to the future.

The story behind the ride goes something like this: You're at the Institute for Future Technology for a test drive of Doc Brown's latest time machine. While waiting on line, security cameras reveal that Biff Tannen (the villain from the movies) has hijacked one of the contraptions, and you've been drafted to capture him and save the universe. Your conveyance is an eight-person DeLorean – actually a motion simulator – that moves in sync with the images projected on a curved seven-story screen. What follows is five minutes of nonstop (some might say harrowing) special-effects action.

The warnings posted at the entrance are no exaggeration. If you are prone to motion sickness, have a heart condition, or a bad back, sit this one out. If, on the other hand, you can't get enough twists, turns and white-knuckle thrills, don't miss this ride. A word of advice: lines are long nearly all day. Waits of an hour or more are not uncommon during the busy season. The best time to ride is first thing in the morning or the hour before closing.

Queues are also usually quite long at **Men in Black: Alien Attack** ⓮, which Universal bills as a ride-through video game. What you have here, essentially, is a combination of a traditional dark ride and a shooting gallery. The story is that you're trying out for the MIB. But what starts as a fairly ho-hum test of marksmanship quickly turns into a full-blown battle with a batch of bloodthirsty aliens who, we learn in a bulletin delivered by *Men in Black* star Will Smith, have crash-landed in Manhattan. Each rider is equipped with a laser gun; the more

aliens you zap, the higher your score. The only hitch is that the aliens shoot back, sending your vehicle into a wild tailspin with every hit. Just when you think the ride is coming to an end, you find yourself in the belly of a gargantuan bug and the only way out is to blast your way through. As you cruise toward the landing zone, an electronic scoreboard tallies your team's points, and Will Smith reappears for an assessment of your performance. Are you MIB material or bug bait?

Although the cars spin rapidly, the ride isn't nearly as nauseating as Back to the Future. Nor is it especially scary. Most young children will do just fine, provided they meet the height requirement. A tip to shorten your wait: if you don't mind breaking up your party, single riders move quickly to the front of the line.

San Francisco/Amity

Cross the bridge over the lagoon and you find yourself on the cobblestone streets of **Amity** ⓯, the cinematic home of Sheriff Brody, Captain Quint, and a certain ill-tempered

Map on page 120

TIP

Shutterbugs can take advantage of Photo Spots stationed throughout the park, with instructions on how to get the most out of their pictures.

BELOW: Elwood Blues and a friend after a performance on Delancey Street.

shark with a predilection for human flesh. Tourists can't resist posing for photos with a fiberglass shark hung from a scaffold in the main plaza, usually with their heads in its gaping maw.

Tucked behind a bank of trees a short walk from the plaza is a covered theater featuring the **Wild Wild Wild West Stunt Show** . Cowboys don't really fit the seaside theme at Amity, but in Orlando, like Hollywood, reality is what you make it. The show is a 20-minute, bare-knuckle romp replete with gunfire, pratfalls, explosions, mock fistfights, and slapstick humor. Bottles are smashed over skulls, chairs are broken over backs, a guy falls off of a roof, and the bank goes boom. It's goofy, good-natured, and generally benign and, being Universal, full of pyrotechnics.

Also just a few steps from the plaza, in a convincingly-rendered wharfside village, is **Jaws** ⓱, Amity's signature attraction. Jaws follows a fairly standard script: while you're waiting in line (which tends to be quite long), a news flash

from Amity TV suggests that this seaside town may not be quite as sleepy as it appears. Your cruise starts pleasantly enough, just another sunny day in the harbor until, as always, something goes dreadfully wrong. It's that pesky shark, who shakes things up considerably, despite the grenade launcher your guide fires at him. There are bumps, surprises, screams, a 30-foot (9-meter) wall of fire, and the requisite number of explosions before you are returned to the safety of the dock, somewhat soggier but none the worse for wear.

Jaws exits onto **Amity Avenue**, which winds past a bank of games and food vendors dressed up like a boardwalk arcade, with a ring toss, a guess-your-weight, a funnel cake stand, and, across the way, several excellent caricaturists. **Captain Quint's Seafood and Chowder House**, a fast-food place on the left, serves fish and chips, clam chowder, fried shrimp, and other seaside fare. **Lombard's Seafood Grille**, a little farther on, where Amity magically transforms into **San Francisco**, is a

BELOW: the Wild Wild Wild West Stunt Show.

full-service seafood restaurant and one of the best places for a sit-down meal in the park.

Just across the street is **Earthquake – The Big One ⑱**. The educational portions of this attraction may be a bit tedious for thrill-seekers. There's a payoff at the end, however, and few people walk away disappointed. In the first part of the show, the audience is ushered into a standing-room-only theater for a short film narrated by Charlton Heston, star of the original *Earthquake*, who explains how models, matte paintings, and high-speed photography are used to create the illusion of a city in the throes of a catastrophic temblor. Genuine film models, including the one used in his film, are on display here. The detail is extraordinary. In the next portion, several volunteers reenact a scene from a movie in order to demonstrate the use of blue-screen technology, a process in which images of actors are married with a background that's dropped in electronically.

The much-anticipated finale starts when you board a subway train for a simulated ride from Oakland to San Francisco. The train passes through a tunnel under San Francisco Bay and rolls into Embarcadero Station when – Wham! – the earth begins to tremble. "There's nothing to worry about," says a voice over a loudspeaker (with a certain lack of conviction), but you know better. In the wink of an eye, you're in the midst of a seismic event that registers 8.3 on the Richter scale. The train shakes, the platform buckles, the ceiling collapses. A propane tanker comes crashing in from above and erupts into a ball of flame. Then the water starts pouring in, thousands of gallons gushing through every crack and crevice in only a few seconds. And just when you think it's over, a runaway train comes hurtling straight at you. "Cut!" a director yells, and the mayhem subsides just as quickly as it began. Your last sight as the train pulls away from the station is of the set automatically reassembling itself for the next crew of extras. Pretty cool stuff.

Exit Earthquake and continue along the Embarcadero to **Beetle-**

Map on page 120

LEFT: a visitor gets an inside view of Jaws.

Of Mice and Rabbits

Disney vs. Universal is a rivalry that stretches beyond theme-park competition. It was Carl Laemmle, the man behind Universal Studios from its founding in 1912, who inspired Walt Disney's cartoon career with the character Oswald the Lucky Rabbit.

Laemmle proposed some kind of funny rabbit to an associate, film distributor Charles Mintz. So in March 1927, Walt began work on Poor Papa as the initial episode in the Oswald series. A year later, Disney headed to New York to negotiate a new Oswald deal for a higher fee. Mintz informed him that there would be a new fee all right – it would be 20 per cent lower, take it or leave it. Universal could always find other artists to do the work, including some of Disney's own people.

Disney was often underestimated. Relinquishing any claim to the unlucky rabbit, he sent a telegram to brother Roy in Hollywood – don't worry everything okay – and headed for home and super-stardom via a happy mouse. Laemmle did OK. He sold Universal in 1936, and his estate was valued at $4 million upon his death in 1939, a year after Oswald was laid to rest as a cartoon character.

BELOW:
night in New York.

juice's Graveyard Revue . The star of the show is Beetlejuice, the wacky, stream-of-conscious ghoul from the Tim Burton flick who, along with Frankenstein's monster, Dracula, Wolf Man, and the Bride of Frankenstein, sing and dance to a recorded backing track of rock classics. It's a goofy, raucous, almost painfully loud routine. What the performance lacks in finesse it makes up for in energy and, no surprise, pyrotechnics.

New York

The movie-set metaphor becomes a reality in **New York** ⑳, which is a working back lot. It's not unusual for a section of this area to be roped off while camera crews are at work.

New York offers something rarely found at a theme park – room to roam in a relatively quiet atmosphere. If you need a break from the crowds and rides, you might take some time to wander about here, a special treat just before the park closes, when the neighborhood is particularly empty. You can explore

the back alleys and brownstones of downtown, examine the scaled-down replicas of the Guggenheim Museum and New York Public Library, have a seat on one of the stoops, and enjoy an ice-cream or cold drink.

Two shows are performed in the street: the **Blues Brothers** feature Jake and Elwood look- and sound-alikes who do an enthusiastic 20 minutes of R&B standards on a tiny stage on Delancey Street. **Street Breakz**, a break-dancing troupe, performs at the intersection of 57th Street and Seventh Avenue. Both are crowd pleasers.

Unless you are a very seasoned thrill seeker you will be wishing for such lighthearted entertainment not long after you've set off on **Revenge of the Mummy – the Ride** ㉑. Universal's newest ride, in development for over 10 years, has attempted to push fright levels even further. Much like Disney-MGM's Rock 'n' Roller Coaster, Revenge is set indoors. Billed as a "psychological thrill ride" it takes full advantage of set design, high-

speed coaster tricks and optical illusions to scare you again and again. The concept is that you are on a journey deep into an ancient Egyptian tomb and before you know it you are confronted by an army of rotting mummies, fireballs, and swarms of scarb beetles.

Coming out, you'll be near the New York Public Library, the scene for **Extreme Ghostbusters: the Great Fright Way**, a live action, singing, and dancing comedy show that casts Beetlejuice as the antihero and seems anything but extreme if you've just ridden the Mummy.

Across the scaled-down Grammercy Park from Penn Station, on 57th Street, is **Twister... Ride It Out ㉒**, based on the 1996 action movie starring Helen Hunt and Bill Paxton. Twister employs the same basic formula as Earthquake, funneling guests through two stages of edutainment before delivering the finale. In this case, you first hear a spiel on tornadoes given by Hunt and Paxton, then walk through a re-creation of one of the movie sets – a farmhouse ravaged by a twister –

while video monitors educate viewers about the special effects used to create tornado conditions on film. The payoff doesn't start until you file into a standing-room sound stage where the audience sees what appears to be a quiet Oklahoma drive-in theater.

What happens next is little short of amazing, as the sky darkens, lightning flashes and rain begins to patter on a tin roof overhead. Just when you think the storm might pass, a five-story, 12-foot-wide (4m) funnel cloud descends on the scene, unleashing the fury of an F-5 tornado. The wind roars, power lines spark, roofs peel off, a gas pump explodes, and an assortment of objects – including a billboard, truck, and cow – go flying across the stage. It's all over in about two minutes, but they are two minutes worth waiting for.

Two restaurants reflect the real New York's immigrant culture. **Finnegan's Bar and Grill** is a faithful reproduction of a downtown Irish pub with a decent selection of domestic and imported beer. A large

Map on page 120

BELOW: Universal's new Revenge of the Mummy – the Ride promises to be Orlando's most terrifying ride yet.

Shrek signs an autograph for an appreciative fan. Be sure to have pen and paper ready when you meet the characters

BELOW: have lunch surrounded by memorabilia from classic horror flicks at the Monster Café.

dining room with table service has traditional dishes like fish and chips, bangers and mash, corned beef and cabbage, and shepherd's pie. The atmosphere is more winning than the food at **Louie's Italian Restaurant**, a cafeteria with pizza, pasta, and other Italian standards.

Production Central

Still hungry? How about a bite with Frankenstein or the Creature from the Black Lagoon? At **Monsters Café**, catercorner from Twister, you can dig into pizza, roasted chicken, and a variety of salads surrounded by props and memorabilia from Universal's classic horror flicks.

The monster-movie theme suits this section of the park, called **Production Central ㉓**, which is the most directly related to the art and science of film and television. Housed in a castle-like building about a block from Monsters Café on Plaza of the Stars, is **Shrek 4-D ㉔**, a multisensory experience that picks up the story of the soft-hearted ogre where the 2001 animated film left off. While waiting in the lobby,

you learn that the ghost of Lord Farquaad (who was swallowed by a lovesick dragon in the first film) is plotting to exact revenge against Shrek and his new bride Princess Fiona by crashing their honeymoon with a host of ghoulish monsters. The action starts off with a bang and quickly evolves into an aerial dogfight involving fire-breathing dragons and a breathtaking plummet down a 300-foot (90-meter) waterfall. The 3-D images are enhanced by special effects built into the theater itself. Seats move up and down and from side to side, and are equipped with tactile transducers, pneumatic air propulsion, and water spray nodules. The show is enormously popular, but with a capacity of 2,400 guests per hour, the queue moves fairly briskly.

Just across the street is **Jimmy Neutron's Nicktoon Blast ㉕**, featuring yet another computer-generated character – Jimmy Neutron, Boy Genius. After watching a video setting up the action, guests file into a movie theater equipped with several rows of motion simulators

Map on page 120

arrayed in front of a huge screen. What follows is a madcap tour of Nickelodeon's cartoon universe in a spaceship piloted by the young Mr Neutron, who has to save the world from wicked egg-shaped aliens known as Yokians. Adults may be mystified by the unfamiliar characters, but kids – at least those kids who watch Nickelodeon – will be tickled by the appearance of such well-known figures as SpongeBob SquarePants, the Fairly Odd Parents, and the Rugrats. Like much else at Universal, the experience is silly, fun, and extremely bumpy.

The finer points of slime

Tucked behind The Funtastic World, fronted by a fountain that belches green, gooey slime, is **Nickelodeon Studios ㉖**, the main production facility for the popular children's television network. Ask any 10-year-old in America and he'll tell you that slime is a Nickelodeon trademark, often poured by the bucket-load on hapless game-show contestants.

The 30-minute studio tour is your best opportunity for a behind-the-scenes look at the making of real-life television shows. The itinerary changes, but you're likely to get a glimpse of the wardrobe and makeup departments, see stage sets being constructed, talk to a member of the production staff, or watch actors in rehearsal. In one highlight, a studio rep expounds on the finer points of slime, also known as "gak" or "goo," depending on its lumpiness. At the end of the tour, kids and adults compete against each other in the Game Lab, where Nick tests wacky stunts and contests for upcoming programs. The show ends with one lucky child receiving Nick's highest honor – getting drenched with slime.

Watching the taping of a broadcast is a hit or miss proposition, depending on what's in production when you visit. Tickets are available on a first-come, first-served basis. Call 407-224 6355 for scheduling information or go directly to the Studio Audience Center just inside the park to the right of the main entrance. ❏

LEFT:
a make-up artist displays his skills in Production Central.

RESTAURANTS & BARS

Restaurants

International Food and Film Festival
World Expo
Sample fast-food versions of Mexican, Italian, Chinese and American dishes, though you may want to skip the main course and head directly to the ice-cream bar for banana splits and gooey sundaes. Food-related movie clips play on video monitors stationed around the eatery. $$

Lombard's Landing
San Francisco
A full-service seafood restaurant and one of the best places for a sit-down meal in the park. $$

Bars

Finnegan's Bar & Grill
New York
Full-service restaurant in New York area serving traditional Irish-American food. Live entertainment and Happy Hour. $$

● ● ● ● ● ● ● ● ● ● ● ● ● ● ● ●
Price includes dinner and a glass of wine (when available), excluding tip.
$$$ *over $30,* **$$** *between $20–30,* **$** *under $20.*

ISLANDS OF ADVENTURE

Universal's cutting-edge pleasure palace has no educational ambitions – it's an elaborate tour-de-force combining themes, thrill rides, and high-tech fun

niversal took the theme park concept and ratcheted it up a notch when it unveiled Islands of Adventure (IOA) in 1999. Even more elaborately designed than Universal Studios, which is only about 10 minutes away on foot, IOA is divided into five compact islands arranged around a central lagoon known as the **Great Inland Sea**. Cutting-edge rides, including two of the wickedest steel roller coasters on the East Coast, keep hardened thrill-seekers happy, while gentler attractions like those at Seuss Landing – inspired by the work of the children's book author – enchant kids.

What you won't find at IOA is a strict tie-in with the movies. The park takes its cues from a variety of sources – comic books, myth, the funny pages, and cartoon characters. There are fewer shows and street performances, and virtually no attempt to educate visitors or give them a behind-the-scenes look at the entertainment industry. Fun is the only order of business here, and – despite often lengthy queues – that's one commodity you will find in abundance.

Port of Entry

Unless you're staying at an on-site hotel, the only way to enter IOA is to pass through CityWalk, then bear left toward a fanciful stone light-house. After clearing the turnstiles, visitors are funneled through the **Port of Entry ❶**, a narrow passage lined with shops and eateries designed to evoke the mysterious and exotic ports of the East. Palms and colorful canopies wave in the breeze; fountains trickle (including a Rube Goldberg affair of ropes, poles, and giant clam shells); and the rousing strains of pipes and strings heighten anticipation almost as much as the roar of the Incredible

Map on page 134

LEFT: Popeye & Bluto's Bilge-Rat Barges.
BELOW: Seuss Landing.

Hulk roller coaster, visible just above the roofline.

There aren't any attractions here, but it's a good place to buy last-minute necessities – sunglasses, film, bottled water, and such – all about 50 percent more expensive than outside the gate. Most visitors will press on quickly, though two shops may be worth a second look: **Island Market & Exports**, which carries thick blocks of fudge and exotic candy (ever seen M&Ms in violet, silver, pink, teal? You will here), and **Croissant Moon Bakery**, a good spot to

tank up on coffee and a pastry before entering the park proper. **Cinnabon**, a chain operation known for sinfully sweet Danishes, is at the far end. **Confisco Grille**, just a few steps away, is one of the better restaurants in the park, with the ambience of an exotic-port and a menu that ranges from fajitas and *pad thai* to barbecued ribs and yummy desserts. Drinks are available at the **Backwater Bar**. Its small patio is perfect for a few minutes of people-watching.

The Port of Entry is also where you'll find a variety of guest ser-

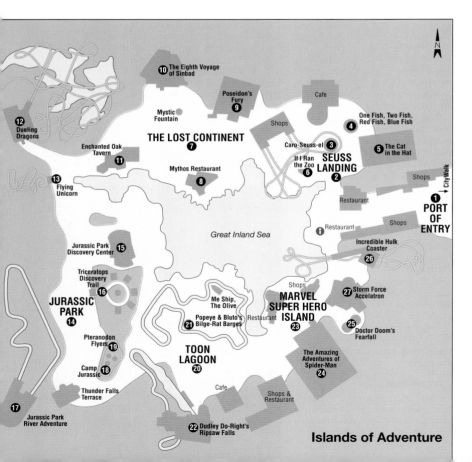

Islands of Adventure

vices, including telephones, a mail drop, lockers, stroller- and wheelchair-rental, and a first-aid station. You're also likely to have the first of the day's character encounters, perhaps with Rocky and Bullwinkle, Boris and Natasha, or stiltwalkers dressed like harem slaves.

In a rocky little harbor at the end of the Port of Entry is **Island Skipper Tours**, where one of three fanciful boats will take you on a gentle trip across the Great Inland Sea. The ride takes about five minutes each way. It's not much of a shortcut, but it gives a useful overview of the park, and footsore tourists are usually happy to hitch a ride.

Seuss Landing

Bear right at the lagoon and cross a whimsical multicolor bridge into the loopy, droopy world of **Seuss Landing ❷**, inspired by the books of Theodor Seuss Geisel, aka Dr Seuss. Teenagers may feel out of their element here, but young children and adults will be tickled by this imaginative realization of Seuss's Technicolor universe. It's a tour-de-force

of set design, where everything tilts, sags, and pitches to one side, with nary a right angle in sight. Take a few minutes to soak in the details – the lopsided lampposts, the curvy benches, the bizarre topiary shrubs.

Even the palm trees bend at unnatural angles. They were permanently contorted by Hurricane Andrew and carefully transplanted here by Universal's groundskeepers *(see page 141)*.

The rides are geared down for the younger set (and their middle-aged chaperones). Most are based on familiar amusement park attractions cleverly interpreted à la Seuss. The **Caro-Seuss-el ❸**, for example, is a traditional merry-go-round, with a bestiary of Seuss's fantastical creatures for kids to ride upon. **On One Fish, Two Fish, Red Fish, Blue Fish ❹**, riders go round and round and up and down while fountains squirt them from the sides. Don't care to get wet? Listen to the song. It instructs you (in rhyme) how to avoid a soaking.

The Cat in the Hat ❺ is a traditional dark ride, although here passengers sit in a couch that takes

Map on page 134

One Fish, Two Fish, Red Fish, Blue Fish – a classic amusement park ride with a Seussian twist.

LEFT: characters like Dudley Do-Right wander about the park.
BELOW: stiltwalkers greet visitors at Seuss Landing.

TIP

Universal Express in Seuss Landing and the Lost Continent is available at The Cat in the Hat, One Fish, Two Fish, Caro-Seusse-el, Poseidon's Fury, the Eighth Voyage of Sinbad, Dueling Dragons, and the Flying Unicorns.

BELOW: the park features many elaborately-themed restaurants.

them through the story of one of the good doctor's most beloved books. Costumed characters like the Cat in the Hat, Sam I Am, Thing 1 and Thing 2, and the Grinch congregate near the ride entrance every half hour between 11am and 4pm and are happy to pose for photos and sign autographs. Across the plaza, **If I Ran the Zoo** ❻ is a small interactive play area where young children can explore tunnels and frolic in a mini water park with various fountains and sprayers.

There are several places to eat. The most elaborate is **Circus McGurkus Café Stoo-pendous**, a cafeteria with Day-Glo colors and otherworldly creatures. A costumed organist serenades diners several times a day, and costumed characters make the rounds during lunch (12–2pm). Or stop by the **Green Eggs and Ham Café** for burgers, frings (a deep-fried combo of fries and onion rings) or a green-egg-and-ham sandwich. And yes, the contents of the sandwich are really green – well, pale green anyway. If

you're feeling especially decadent, skip the real food and head directly to the **Hop on Pop Ice-Cream Shop**, where you can indulge your sweet tooth with a sundae on a stick, a waffle cone banana split, an upside-down sundae, or something called an Itzakadoozie – a glorious, artery-clogging confection of ice-cream, hot fudge, caramel sauce, whipped cream, peanut butter, sugar cones, and oodles of sweet and crunchy sprinkles.

Shopping is fairly predictable – mugs, T-shirts, children's clothes, plush toys, and backpacks emblazoned with images from *The Cat in the Hat* and other Seuss characters. It's heartening to see one shop, **All the Books You Can Read**, stocked with the complete catalog of Dr Seuss titles.

The Lost Continent

The adventure takes a decidedly dark turn when you cross over a massive timber bridge into **The Lost Continent** ❼ – a dungeons-and-dragons fantasy come to life, about equal parts Middle Ages,

Middle East, and Middle Earth. To the left, a waterfall gushes from the mouth of a monumental visage – the face of some long-forgotten god, perhaps – that appears to be carved into the side of a rocky outcropping. Within this mountain is **Mythos ❽**, the park's finest restaurant full of waiters with classical sounding names – Adonis, Pan, Hera. In the tradition of overworked concepts so familiar at theme parks, staff members are assigned names from Greek mythology *(see page 143).*

Wrath of the gods

Across the way is yet another extravagant example of set design. It's the ruins of Poseidon's temple, a giant trident still in the grasp of a king-sized fist rising at the entrance. The temple contains **Poseidon's Fury ❾**, a 21st-century update on the classic haunted house in which visitors are led through a series of chambers (actually theaters) by a rather excitable guide. The tour hums along just fine until, as usual, something goes awry, and the guide is drafted into a grudge match between Poseidon and Zeus. What follows is about 5 minutes of finely-orchestrated chaos replete with fireballs and watery explosions. The action is way over the top and loud enough to wake the dead, though the effects – including a walk-through vortex involving more than 17,500 gallons (66,200 liters) of water – are quite dazzling.

The same incendiary impulse is evident in **The Eighth Voyage of Sinbad ❿**, a stunt show presented in a 1,200-seat amphitheater. The story behind the show is fairly straightforward and almost entirely beside the point: Sinbad and his accident-prone sidekick rescue a beautiful princess (who, it turns out, is quite handy with a sword herself) from the clutches of a wicked sorceress and her band of evil minions.

There are fistfights, pratfalls, sword play, sight gags, and a scorching barrage of pyrotechnics. In the end, a nasty evildoer is set on fire and falls 20 feet (6 meters) into a bubbling pool. "Masterpiece Theater" it's not, but kids – especially those weaned on video games and action cartoons – think it's grand. They get a kick out of meeting the actors after the show, too. Arrive 15 or 20 minutes before showtime in order to claim the best seats, although you can usually find something at the last minute.

Don't be surprised if you hear strange voices near the front of the theater, where a fountain – **The Mystic Fountain**, in fact – is apparently possessed by a wisecracking oracle with a penchant for squirting innocent bystanders. A clutch of shops nearby is dressed like a medieval bazaar, with fortune tellers and several midway-style games (try shooting a ball into a cup with a miniature catapult). Glassblowers and metalworkers are occasionally on hand, and an assortment of merchandise, rang-

"Would you try them here or there? Would you try them anywhere?" Green eggs and ham are served in Seuss Landing.

BELOW: Sinbad cast member poses for photos with visitors after the show.

ing from hand-struck medallions and carved wooden chests to ornamental swords, is for sale.

The Enchanted Oak Tavern , just around the bend resembles a weathered tree stump. Inside, sitting at wooden tables under a dome of gnarled roots, customers gnaw on barbecued ribs, turkey legs, and chicken. The park's own brew, Dragon Scale Ale, and a good many other potent potables are served next door at the **Alchemy Bar**.

The dragons' lair

Any roller coaster aficionado will tell you that there is a deliciously fine line between terror and exhilaration. **Dueling Dragons** ⑫, one of the park's two big-deal coasters, zooms along that razor's edge for more than 2 minutes.

Three elements make this one of the best rides in the Southeast. First, it's an inverted coaster. This means the cars attach to the track overhead, while your legs dangle freely below (and sometimes above). Next, it's not merely one coaster but two. Fire Dragon and Ice Dragon ride on intertwining tracks devilishly engineered for several near misses. A computer system monitors the trains in order to minimize the flyby distance between the trains – and maximize the terror. Last, the attraction is elaborately themed, with a long, long queuing area that passes through castle ruins ostensibly destroyed by the feuding dragons. Merlin the Magician appears and warns you to turn back before it's too late, and tells the story of the legendary beasts – Pyrrock and Blizzrock – and the ill-fated knights whose charred and frozen remains are strewn about the place.

Eventually, you are given a choice. Will you ride Fire or Ice? Fire is slightly faster – 60 miles per hour (97 kph) compared to Ice's 55 miles per hour (89 kph) – and has a bit more snap, but both deliver multiple loops, corkscrews, rolls, and up to 5 gs. Expect an extremely long wait for all but the earliest and latest few rides; the wait is even longer if you are one of those peculiar gluttons for punishment who elect to sit in the front cars. Do yourself a favor and get a Universal Express ticket as soon as you reach the Lost Continent.

Children and others who aren't up to Dueling Dragons can take a spin on **The Flying Unicorn** ⑬. The queue moves fairly quickly, so you can ride two or three times while others take on the dragons.

Jurassic Park

Jurassic Park ⑭ is the largest and most fully-realized island of the park. Here a lush, tropical jungle is lined with high-voltage fences, bushes rustle ominously, and mysterious roars sound in the distance.

Pass through the imposing stone gateway – the **Watering Hole** provides frozen, alcoholic refreshment – then make your first left down to a spacious palm-shaded plaza on the shore of the Great Inland Sea. This

TIP

Height requirements in the Lost Continent and Jurassic Park are 54 inches (137 cm) for Dueling Dragons, 36 inches (91 cm) for the Flying Unicorn and Pteranodon Flyers, and 42 inches (107 cm) for Jurassic Park River Adventure.

BELOW: dinosaur fossils are mounted in the atrium of the Jurassic Park Discovery Center.

is the entrance to the **Jurassic Park Discovery Center** ⓯, a re-creation of the lodge from the movie, including dinosaur skeleton replicas in the center of an atrium stairway.

Around the edges are a variety of interactive computer displays designed more for entertainment than education. On one you can meld your DNA with that of a dinosaur. The resulting dino-human hybrid – actually a composite of your face and a dinosaur's – is displayed on a video monitor. Other exhibits allow you to analyze the contents of dinosaur eggs created in the Jurassic Park nursery and includes a light-hearted game show, You Bet Your Jurassic, that pits three contestants against a computerized game-show host. The second floor of the building is a fast-food joint with burgers and fries.

Farther along the main pathway is the **Triceratops Discovery Trail** ⓰, a low-key stroll through a veterinary compound where visitors can watch animatronic dinos being weighed, measured, and fed. At the end, a vet examines a triceratops.

It's a reasonably convincing effect and, depending on the vet's acting skills, quite informative and entertaining, though you may be more amused by watching young children puzzle over the possibility that the beast is real. A few kids are selected to step up and pet the gentle giant's snout. Hang around long enough and you may see him sneeze on an unsuspecting customer. In all, it's a diverting 15 or 20 minutes for kids and a blessedly quiet interlude for shellshocked parents.

Across the way from Discovery Trail is the island's big ride – the **Jurassic Park River Adventure** ⓱. Almost always crowded (you may want to make an express ticket kiosk your first stop), the attraction takes you on what's billed as a peaceful float trip through dinosaur habitat. It's lovely drifting past half-submerged dinosaurs until – you guessed it – something goes dreadfully wrong. The raptors have gotten loose and your raft is diverted into the restricted zone, where you find an overturned jeep, a demolished containment pen, and other signs of

Map on page 134

A sign warns visitors about the highly aggressive Velociraptor, a resident of Jurassic Park.

BELOW: Dueling Dragons.

T-rex at the Jurassic Park River Adventure.

BELOW: Spider-Man swings through Marvel Super Hero Island.

carnage (including a couple of small raptors scrapping over the tatters of a staff member's uniform). The climax is a face-to-face encounter with T-rex and a stomach-flipping, 85-foot (26-meter) plummet. As the video monitors warn at the beginning of the ride: you will get wet and probably soaked. You may want to stash dry clothes in lockers near the queuing area.

You can celebrate surviving your adventure at **Thunder Falls Terrace**, a cafeteria with barbecued chicken and ribs, conch chowder, roast corn, and other tasty choices. The food is quite satisfying, and the setting works beautifully – a safari lodge with a bank of windows and a patio overlooking the big splashdown.

On the opposite side of the pathway is **Camp Jurassic** ⓱, the playground of every child's dreams. Inside, kids climb a two-story maze of dinosaur nets, rope bridges, ladders, and twisting stairways. There are tunnels (amber mines) to explore, boulders to scramble on, waterfalls to cross, and, in a delightful touch of naughtiness, high-powered squirt guns that the little imps can use to ambush passersby.

You'll also find one of the park's better rides for young children: **Pteranodon Flyers** ⓳, a modified ski lift that takes you on a 90-second flight over Camp Jurassic. In a nice twist, the park requires all guests over 56 inches (142 cm) tall to be accompanied by a child. The ride's capacity is extremely low, however, so expect unpleasantly long lines at most times of day. Try riding first thing in the morning or just before the park closes. Universal Express is not available for this attraction.

Toon Lagoon

The atmosphere turns giddy a little farther along at **Toon Lagoon** ⓴, an entire island devoted to cartoon characters like Blondie, Popeye, Betty Boop, and other familiar faces from the funny papers. **Comic Strip Lane** is a crazy quilt of wacky storefronts, colorful statues, whimsical fountains, and strategically-placed thought balloons with statements like "Is this a great bod or what?" and "Betty Boop eat your heart out." Costumed characters appear several times a day in a brief street show, followed by a photo-op and autograph session, and it's not unusual to see Bullwinkle, Dudley Do-Right, Olive Oyl, and other characters wandering about.

Popeye & Bluto's Bilge-Rat Barges ㉑ follows a fairly standard formula for whitewater rides, although the setting brims with playful details. A circular, 12-person raft bumps and bobs through a series of rapids, while passengers are soaked with waterfalls, fountains, and, in one section, spectators wielding water cannons. There are a few thrills and spills along the way but nothing too traumatic. Most of the fun comes from watching your shipmates getting doused, and wondering when your turn will come around.

Afterward, kids can explore **Me Ship, The Olive**, a three-story play area decked out like Popeye's trusty vessel, with slides, ladders, and all sorts of squirters, sprayers, and other ways to get wet.

On the opposite side of Comic Strip Lane is a log flume ride called **Dudley Do-Right's Ripsaw Falls** **㉗**. There's nothing new in the basic concept, although, like the Popeye ride, the set design is cleverly executed, employing the same off-the-wall humor as Dudley Do-Right's creator, animator Jay Ward. This one has more dips and drops than Bilge-Rat Barges, with a 75-foot (23-meter) plunge at the end that will make your stomach do a somersault and probably soak you to the skin.

There are no full-service restaurants at Toon Lagoon, but you can order up a thick, two-handed sandwich at **Blondie's** ("The Dagwood," named after Blondie's husband, recalls his mountainous concoctions), burgers and hot dogs at **Wimpy's**, and your choice of Mexican, Chinese, Italian, or American food at the cafeteria-style **Comic Strip Café**. Collectors may want to check out the **Betty Boop Store**, chock full of dolls, T-shirts, postcards, and other merchandise dedicated to the squeaky-voiced chanteuse who made "boop-oop-a-doop" an American catchword.

Marvel Super Hero Island

Set to a booming soundtrack with a driving beat, **Marvel Super Hero Island** **㉓** tears a page from the comic book publisher who made super heroes out of muscle-bound guys in colorful tights. Billboard-sized cutouts of the X-Men, Captain America, Iron Man, and other flamboyantly attired fellows line a winding path through a gauntlet of rides, shops, and eateries. The overall design is more subdued here than in Toon Lagoon, recalling the mean streets of New York with foreshortened skyscrapers and lots of faux chrome, steel and glass, plus those socko sound effects drawn in the comics in big flashy letters – Wham! Splat! Aaarrgghhh!? Other shops are branded with the sort of generic shorthand

Hagar the Horrible crowns a storefront in Toon Lagoon.

LEFT: Comic Strip Lane, Toon Lagoon.

The Story Behind the Plants

The landscaping at Islands of Adventure is more than a backdrop. It's part of the overall theme, creating each island's unique identity. "The intent," says Barry McKently, Universal's director of horticulture, "is to create absolute immersion in the surroundings."

For Seuss Landing, McKently and his team chose plants that "reflected the two-dimensional images in the Seuss books." A group of Mexican sand palms curved by storm damage fit the bill perfectly. Some were leaned in the opposite direction to complete the S shape in the trunk. In some cases, pruning a tree yields the desired look. A few snips of a weeping holly, for instance, creates hundreds of the dangling pom-poms familiar to Seuss readers. Other plants have a natural Seussian shape, like ponytail palms, that recall the trufffula trees from Dr Seuss's environmental fable, *The Lorax*.

The landscaping in Jurassic Park is even more impressive, though more subtle. It evokes a lush primeval jungle by using cycads, treeferns, monkey puzzle trees, and other plants that existed during the age of dinosaurs. "The effect is almost subliminal," McKently says, but "its landscape is the anchor of the park."

typical of Marvel comics: Diner, Store, Bank, Hotel.

The first attraction to the right, **The Amazing Adventures of Spider-Man** , is hands down the best ride in the park and perhaps in all of Orlando. Spider-Man combines a traditional dark ride with simulator technology, and 3-D visuals. A band of evil-doers known as the Sinister Syndicate is kidnapping the Statue of Liberty with an anti-gravity gun. Your mission: get the story and bring it back to J. Jonah Jameson, editor of the *Daily Bugle*. Along the way you encounter a variety of villainous characters who bang, blast, and bomb your floating tram, sending it into wild spins and lurches. The tour culminates in what feels like a 400-foot (120-meter) headlong plunge into the city streets below, only to be saved at the last moment by – who else? – your friendly neighborhood Spider-Man. The amazing thing about this last maneuver is that your tram never moves more than 4 feet (1.2 meters) in any direction, although

you'll have a hard time convincing your brain of that fact.

Children and adults enjoy it equally. It's thrilling without being terrifying and, because it relies more on tricks of perception than physical jolts, it gives a good jostle without scrambling your innards. For sheer imagination and technical skill, the ride is worth the wait, which you can expect to be quite long. Spider-Man is a technical tour-de-force. This is one attraction you don't want to miss.

The other two big rides in this area should be reserved for the seasoned thrill seeker. **Dr Doom's Fearfall** ⑳ is a common amusement-park ride. This version, however, is turbo-charged with extra propulsion and a futuristic design. Riders are strapped into a four-person fear-sucking chamber at the base of one of two towers. The chamber is rocketed 150 feet (45 meters) straight up at a force of 4 gs, then pushed down faster than the speed of gravity. And just when you think you're safely back on earth, you do it all over again.

TIP

Universal Express in Jurassic Park and Toon Lagoon is available at Jurassic Park River Adventure and Bilge-Rat Barges, and at all rides in Marvel Super Hero Island.

BELOW: the Incredible Hulk roller coaster zooms over Islands of Adventure.

Fearfall exits through **Kingpin's Arcade**, a clanging pinball emporium with all the latest video games. You'll need tokens to play.

Mean green machine

A bit farther along, snarled in the sky like green and white ribbon, is the **Incredible Hulk Coaster** , a roller coaster on a par with (and some would say even more challenging than) Dueling Dragons. Rather than gently ascending the lift hill as most other coasters do, the Hulk catapults riders skyward with the g-force of an F-16 fighter, accelerating from 0 to 40 miles per hour (64 kph) in a scant two seconds. What follows in the next two-and-a-half minutes is a short course in vertigo, as the cars scream through three rolls, two carousels, two loops (including the world's highest inversion, at 109 feet/33 meters), and two subterranean passages, one of them under the lagoon. Top speed: a searing 67 miles per hour (108 kph).

Much tamer, although nauseating in its own way, is **Storm Force**

Accelatron ㉗, a Marvel-ized version of the teacups – a spinning cup on a spinning disk on a spinning turntable. The effect, predictably, is dizzying.

Several times a day a group of super heroes and villains ride out on four-wheelers for a meet and greet with visitors. Photos and autographs are cheerfully offered – except by Dr Doom, who tends to be a grouch. The super heroes are apparently enjoying the good life here at IOA; some are a bit more plump in their Spandex than their paper-and-ink counterparts.

Marvel fans will want to browse in the shops for a selection of the latest comic books and everything from coffee mugs to underpants emblazoned with the image of their favorite characters.

Marvel's two cafeterias aren't particularly distinguished eateries. **Café 4** serves pizza, pasta, and other Italian dishes. **Captain America Diner** has burgers, frings, and apple pie; a small outdoor patio has a good view of the Lost Continent across the lagoon. ❑

Map on page 134

TIP

Height requirements in Toon Lagoon and Marvel Super Hero Island are 44 inches (112 cm) for Dudley Do-Right, 42 inches (107 cm) for Bilge-Rat Barges, 40 inches (102 cm) for Spider-Man, 52 inches (132 cm) for Fearfall, and 54 inches (137 cm) for Hulk.

LEFT: Captain America towers over passersby in Marvel Super Hero Island.

RESTAURANTS

Confisco Grille
Port of Entry
Tel: 407-224 9255
Decorated as an exotic wharf-side tavern, Confisco Grille offers ethnic dishes ranging from fajitas and pad thai to barbecued ribs. Drinks are available at the Backwater Bar, which has a small patio perfect for people watching. **$$**

Green Eggs & Ham Café
Seuss Landing
A dream come true for Seuss fans if not for culinary critics, with burgers, fries, and green-egg-and-ham sandwiches tinted with minced parsley. **$$**

Mythos
Lost Continent
Tel: 407-224 4533
The park's best restaurant is ensconced in a regally appointed cavern with sculpted walls, purple upholstery, and lagoon views. Entrees include wood-roasted lobster with wild mushroom risotto, cedar-planked salmon with orange horseradish mashed potatoes, and wood-fired pizza, plus child-friendly dishes. **$$$**

● ● ● ● ● ● ● ● ● ● ● ● ● ●

Price includes dinner and a glass of wine (when available), excluding tip. ***$$$*** *over $30,* ***$$*** *between $20–30,* ***$*** *under $20.*

CITYWALK

This entertainment complex functions by day as a gateway to the parks. At night, it's a grown-up playland for schmoozing, boozing, dining, and dancing

Orlando

Universal CityWalk

Kissimmee

CityWalk is an all-in-one, adult-oriented entertainment district with restaurants, shops, and nightclubs. It's also Universal's front yard, funneling visitors from parking areas to the theme parks and, management hopes, encouraging them to stay for dinner and dancing.

Larger, louder, and hipper than Pleasure Island, **CityWalk** (407-363 8000) occupies a two-tiered, 30-acre (12-hectare) complex arranged around a central **Plaza**. It's quiet during the day. Some visitors retreat here for a peaceful lunch when the theme parks are most crowded. At night, however, it's a different story. The place wakes up around 10pm as nightclubs fill, liquor flows, and the bands – some of them on outdoor stages – crank up the volume. Nightclubs have an evening cover charge (times and fees vary), but if you want to hop from club to club it's cheaper to buy a Party Pass, available for $10 plus tax at the guest services kiosk as you enter. Guests must be at least 21 years old to enter the nightclubs (there are a few exceptions for minors accompanied by adults). The drinking age is 21 and strictly enforced.

Motown and Marley

The first large structure you see if you enter CityWalk from the car park is the **Universal Cineplex ❶**, a 20-screen theater playing blockbusters, some on more than one screen. It's a shame they don't devote at least one theater to foreign and alternative films or revivals of the golden oldies that must be collecting dust in a studio vault.

Across the main walkway is the **DECADES Cafe ❷** serving standard American fare of burgers and fries. Each room is decorated with every sort of imaginable memorabilia and accompanied by the

Map on page 146

LEFT: nightlife on CityWalk's Plaza.
BELOW: the sound of New Orleans at Pat O'Brien's.

Theme restaurants such as NBA City feature elaborate settings.

BELOW: rock hard hair at the Hard Rock Café.

music and popular culture of the last several decades.

Exiting DECADES from the second floor puts you on the **Promenade**, a strip of nightclubs that ramps down to ground level. At **Bob Marley – A Tribute to Freedom ❸**, you can chow down on yucca chips, jerk chicken, and plenty of Red Stripe beer while jammin' to reggae. The exterior is modeled after Marley's Kingston, Jamaica, home. Inside, photos and other artifacts chronicle his life and career. Live bands perform nightly on the courtyard stage.

An older crowd inhabits **Pat O'Brien's ❹**, a replica of a landmark New Orleans watering hole. The sing-along crowd loves the dueling pianos, and foodies enjoy jambalaya, muffeletta, and other Big Easy specialties. Wash it down with a hurricane, O'Brien's signature rum drink.

The crowd is mostly young and single at **the groove ❺**, a cavernous dance club equipped with kaleidoscopic lights, a mist machine, and a mind-numbing sound system that pumps out techno, house, and hip-hop. A warren of intimate themed rooms with color-coded drinks is the place for conversation.

Spice of life

Both the food and the music are spicy next door at the **Latin Quarter ❻**, dedicated to the culture and cuisine of 21 Latin American nations. After dinner, an orchestra and dance troupe take the stage. Dance instructors initiate neophytes into the wonders of merengue, salsa, and the mambo.

For a laid-back beach-bum, Jimmy Buffet is quite the entrepreneur. Decked out in beachy, tropical style, **Jimmy Buffet's Margaritaville ❼** – the third restaurant in his empire – leans toward Caribbean flavors – conch fritters, seafood chowder, grilled fish – with a sprin-

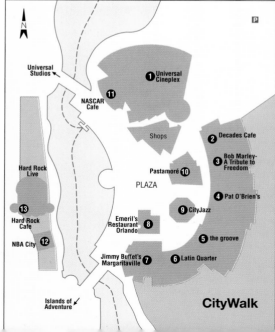

Map
on page
146

kling of American standards, including the inevitable "cheeseburger in paradise." Three bars – one with a margarita-spewing volcano – keep the crowd lubricated, and a house band rolls through Buffet's songbook.

Around the corner is **Emeril's Orlando ❽**, CityWalk's finest and most expensive restaurant. Behind it is **CityJazz ❾**. Styles range from Chicago blues to bebop. The menu features light fare and about 60 wines. Or simply choose a drink from the rolling martini cart. More than 500 objects are on display here in Downbeat magazine's Jazz Hall of Fame. It also doubles as **Bonkers?** with early evening comedy shows Thursday–Saturday.

Pastamoré ❿, serves up abundant portions of eggplant parmigiana, veal Marsala, and a dozen varieties of pizza and pasta. An option to dine family-style lets you taste a little bit of everything, including the *dolci assortiti*, a selection of yummy desserts.

Fan base

Anchoring the far end of the Plaza, near the bridge to Universal Studios, is **NASCAR Cafe ⓫**, a testament to the popularity of stock-car racing. Fans munch on chicken wings, chili and burgers in a boisterous room with video games and live acts, where every square inch is plastered with racing paraphernalia. There's even a couple of racing cars suspended from the ceiling.

You'll find more fan worship at the two restaurants across the waterway. **NBA City ⓬**, if you hadn't guessed, is the one with the statue of a basketball player towering over the entrance. Inside is hoopster heaven, with skill games, shrines to b-ball stars, and a battery of video monitors replaying the game's greatest moments. There are tasty grilled salmon, roasted chicken, and strip steak as well as kid-friendly choices like burgers, pizza, and sandwiches. The milk shakes are a slam dunk; for $7, they ought to be.

When it comes to theme restaurants, the big daddy of 'em all is the **Hard Rock Café ⓭**. With seating for 600 in the restaurant and 3,000 in the concert hall, this is the largest Hard Rock in the world and, like its humbler brethren, its walls are plastered with gold records, album covers, flashy costumes, and instruments that have been strummed and drummed by some of the rock world's biggest names. A pink Cadillac revolves over the bar; a Sistine Chapel-like mural featuring a heavenly host of dead rock stars adorns the ceiling; and stained-glass panels pay tribute to a trinity of rock legends – Elvis Presley, Chuck Berry, and Jerry Lee Lewis. It's a bit much to take in over a meal, which is why the Hard Rock offers free tours in the afternoon. The concert hall brings in contemporary stars and classic rockers as well as up-and-coming bands. ❏

Lounging on the patio at Jimmy Buffet's Margaritaville.

RESTAURANTS

Emeril's Orlando
Tel: 407-224 2424
Featuring the creations of television chef Emeril Lagasse. Assertive Creole flavors bubble up through artfully prepared specialties like grilled pork chop with caramelized sweet potatoes. Wine connoisseurs can choose from more than 10,000 bottles. The desserts are equally glorious; homey favorites like root beer floats and banana cream pie become decadent masterpieces **$$$**

Hard Rock Café
Tel: 407-351 7625
Burgers and sandwiches, fries and shakes, in an over-the-top shrine to rock's biggest stars. **$$**

The Latin Quarter
Tel: 407-224 FOOD
One of the newest additions to the CityWalk complex. Menu reflects the diversity of cultures and cuisine encompassed by Latin America. Entertainment includes a hot Latin orchestra and free mambo lessons Tuesday–Saturday. **$$**

● ● ● ● ● ● ● ● ● ● ● ● ●
Price includes dinner and a glass of wine (when available), excluding tip.
***$$$** over $30, **$$** between $20–30, **$** under $20.*

GREATER ORLANDO

With destinations such as SeaWorld and the Space
Coast within easy driving distance, Orlando
is no longer a one-mouse town

Newcomers to Orlando are often surprised at the variety of tourist attractions beyond the gates of Disney World and Universal Studios. Not only are there more theme parks, but also many excellent museums, performing arts venues, wilderness preserves, and quirky attractions.

Right in the thick of things is SeaWorld, near the junction of Interstate 4 and the Beeline Expressway, a combination aquarium and amusement park that celebrates marine life of every kind. Orcas and dolphins are the stars of the show, but there are also thrill rides, including one of the biggest roller coasters in Florida. Adjacent to the main park is Discovery Cove, a self-contained tropical hideaway where you can snorkel with colorful fish, float lazily down a river, and – the biggest thrill of all – swim with a dolphin.

Wildlife is also the main attraction at Busch Gardens in Tampa Bay, a 90-minute drive from Orlando. More than 2,700 animals reside at the park, most in enclosures simulating their native habitats. Touring the 29-acre (12-hectare) savanna is about as close as you can get to an African safari without actually being in Africa. There are rides too, including a trio of monster roller coasters that make thrill-seekers scream for more – or beg for mercy.

Old Florida is much in evidence as well. Before Disney came to town, places like Weeki Wachee attracted visitors with such down-home diversions as garden tours, boat rides, and real-live mermaids. One longtime Florida native, alligator mississippiensis, looms large at Gatorland, where handlers put on quite a show wrestling the fierce-looking creatures. Even old-fashioned sideshows have made a comeback – at least in spirit – at Ripley's Believe It or Not and the Guinness World Records Experience, which specialize in displays of the sensational, the grotesque, and the just plain weird.

Lest you think Orlando is all kitsch and no culture, visit a museum or two. The Orlando Museum of Art has a first-rate collection of works by John Singer Sargent, Georgia O'Keeffe, and Ansel Adams. The stained-glass artistry of Louis Comfort Tiffany highlights the Charles Hosmer Morse Museum, or for budding scientists there's the Orlando Science Center. And, of course, the Kennedy Space Center, only 75 miles (120 km) from Orlando, is the locus of NASA and America's gateway to the heavens. ❏

LEFT: Orlando skyline from Lake Eola Park.

SEAWORLD

Marine life is the focus of this easygoing theme park, where the star of the show is a three-ton killer whale and visitors can swim with dolphins

SOAK ZONE. TIDAL WAVE ALERT. Anyone sitting in the first 14 rows of SeaWorld's enormous Shamu Stadium is given due warning. When the stars of the show – Shamu, Namu, and six other killer whales – arrive and their trainers put them through their paces, it's not just the beauty and intelligence of these giant marine mammals that make for lasting memories; it's the fact that you will get unceremoniously, shiveringly… wet.

Therein lies the perennial appeal of **SeaWorld** (407-351 3600 or 800-327 2424), Orlando's third most popular theme park, situated off I-4 between Disney World and Universal. While those two parks rely on knock-your-socks-off rides in themed lands and sets, SeaWorld knows that today's technological wizardry pales next to the enduring appeal of nature's creations: a three-ton orca shooting into the air and beaching itself for a photo op, the flap of a stingray's wings as it brushes your fingers in a touch tank, the gaze of a manatee as it grazes on sea grass, or the clicking noises of a dolphin as it eats fish right out of your hand.

Cleverly designed aquatic habitats allow some remarkably close encounters, but SeaWorld offers more. Daily **Backstage Tours** and other special programs, costing between $12 and $300, provide even closer access. Small numbers of guests accompany the park's education staff behind the scenes and learn about caring for polar bears, seals, beluga whales, and manatees. The popular **Trainer for a Day** program pairs visitors and trainers for a full day with the park's orcas and dolphins.

If that isn't enough, reserve well in advance for a day at SeaWorld's sister park, **Discovery Cove**, where, for a hefty all-inclusive fee, you can sun yourself on a sandy beach, feed

Map on page 152

LEFT: an Orca gives one of his trainers a lift during the Shamu Adventure Show.
BELOW: Shamu's Happy Harbor, a play area for kids.

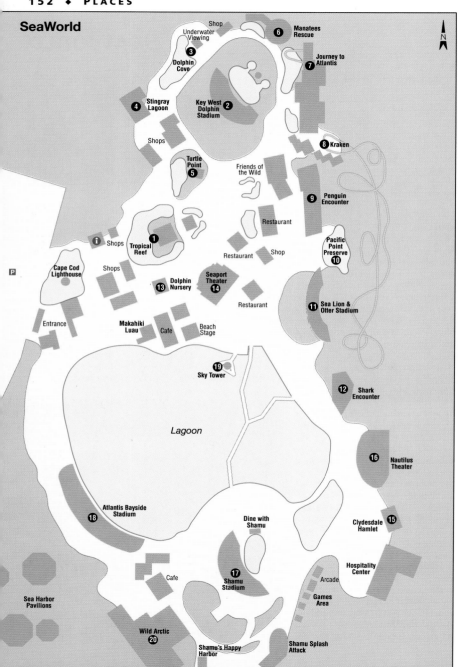

SeaWorld

N

Shop
Underwater Viewing
6 Manatees Rescue

3 Dolphin Cove

7 Journey to Atlantis

4 Stingray Lagoon

2 Key West Dolphin Stadium

Shops

8 Kraken

Turtle Point **5**

Friends of the Wild

9 Penguin Encounter

Restaurant

Pacific Point Preserve **10**

Tropical Reef **1**

Shops

Restaurant

Shop

Cape Cod Lighthouse

P

Shops

13 Dolphin Nursery

Seaport Theater **14**

Restaurant

Sea Lion & Otter Stadium **11**

Entrance

Makahiki Luau

Cafe

Beach Stage

Sky Tower **19**

12 Shark Encounter

Lagoon

16 Nautilus Theater

Atlantis Bayside Stadium

18

Dine with Shamu

Clydesdale Hamlet **15**

Hospitality Center

Cafe

Arcade

Games Area

Sea Harbor Pavilions

Shamu Stadium **17**

Wild Arctic **20**

Shamu's Happy Harbor

Shamu Splash Attack

exotic birds in an aviary, snorkel among stingrays and tropical fish, and, the highlight, swim with a dolphin. A one-week pass to SeaWorld is included in this package.

Easy does it

With three top-of-the-line rides, nine shows, over a dozen restaurants, and a host of top-notch entertainers – from comedians, mimes, and unicyclists to jugglers and singers – SeaWorld is much more than just the world's foremost aquarium. But the animals remain the stars, and, with careful planning, you can see most of them in one full day, if you arrive early.

Because the emphasis is on shows and exhibits rather than rides, there tend to be fewer lines and a more easygoing pace than at Disney World or Universal. Spacious grounds, beautiful landscaping, and the absence of themed lands encourage visitors to meander from one attraction to another instead of marching doggedly from beginning to end.

Attendance peaks around the middle of the day, so plan to arrive early; about 30 minutes prior to the official opening is best. Park in the large lot, then ride the tram to the entrance, where you can purchase tickets, get cash from an ATM, exchange foreign currency, make a phone call, use a restroom, or stash a change of clothing in a rented locker. (More phones, lockers, and restrooms are sprinkled throughout the park.) Stuffed Shamu toys, postcards, T-shirts, hats, and safari-style clothing, as well as the usual disposable cameras, film, and other souvenirs, are sold at gift shops in the park, the theme usually tied in with nearby exhibits.

It's showtime, folks!

Animal shows featuring killer whales, dolphins, and sea lions are the heart and soul of SeaWorld and take place eight or nine times a day in large stadiums with plenty of shaded seating. Other venues present musicians, circus performers, and a cast of four-legged comedians.

Check show times and build your day around them. Distances between venues are generally quite far, so avoid doing two shows beginning less than half an hour apart. You'll also want to check times for dolphin, sea lion, stingray, and other animal feedings. These are varied each day and disguised as animal enrichment exercises, often involving toys, tricks, and hiding food, to prevent these highly intelligent animals from getting bored and engaging in negative, repetitive behavior.

All three SeaWorld rides are hugely popular, so you may want to do a couple of them first thing in the morning before the lines become unpleasantly long. The terrifying Kraken, Florida's highest, fastest, loopiest roller coaster, and the unusual Journey to Atlantis, are conveniently adjacent to each other on the park's north side. Wild Arctic, a

Map on page 152

A lighthouse signals your entrance to SeaWorld.

BELOW:
a cheeky walrus is one of the cast members of Clyde and Seamore Take Pirate Island.

5-minute motion simulator ride through an outstanding polar exhibit, is located on the other side of the large lagoon, just southwest of Shamu Stadium.

Making an entrance

Pass through the gate near the Cape Cod Lighthouse and head to the **Information Center** to pick up maps and daily schedules and rent two-way radios (useful if members of your party have a tendency to wander off). You can book a behind-the-scenes tour here (tours are limited to 12 people, so call ahead to avoid disappointment). You will be given a tour time, meeting location, and ticket. If you arrive before 10.30am you can also sign up for the pricey six-hour **Adventure Express** tour, which allows priority entry to all the park's rides and shows. Reservations for the **Dine with Shamu** buffet and nightly **Makahiki Luau** can be made here. Strollers and wheelchairs are available next to the Information Center.

Orient yourself (there are signposts throughout the park), then sit down for a few minutes to plan your

A SeaWorld guide introduces visitors to a sloth.

BELOW: false killer whales perform at the Key West Dolphin Stadium.

day. **Cypress Bakery**, across from the Information Center, has umbrella-shaded tables and serves delicious espresso drinks, cakes, and pastries made on the premises. Nearby, you'll find ice-cream at **Polar Parlor**.

Morning in Margaritaville

The first area you come to is known broadly as **Key West** and is so lushly landscaped and full of fascinating creatures you could easily spend a whole day there. Just beyond Cypress Bakery is the **Tropical Reef ❶**, a darkened pavilion housing thousands of colorful fish. A flock of flamingos wades in the horseshoe-shaped pond around the building.

If you time things right, you should be able to catch the day's first showing of the **Key West Dolphin Fest**, usually presented at 10am at the **Key West Dolphin Stadium ❷**, the hub of this side of the park. To ensure good seats and enjoy the preshow, queue up about 20 minutes before curtain time. A Jimmy Buffet-style entertainer acts as emcee, and when the show starts, dolphins and false killer whales – an unusual dark-coated dolphin midway in size between an orca and an Atlantic bottlenose – power in from holding tanks and take center stage. For the next 20 minutes, their trainers will give signals to wave flippers, leap out of the water, jump over ropes, breach in unison, and throw their human buddies from their noses. Later, participants in the Trainer for a Day program come on stage to interact with the animals and the audience.

You can take all the time you wish with the dolphins next door at immensely-popular **Dolphin Cove ❸**, a saltwater lagoon containing a large pod of dolphins under the watchful eyes of the SeaWorld staff. The underwater viewing area offers a different perspective on these social creatures, but if getting close

enough to bond with a dolphin is your goal, go ahead and plop down $5 for a paper cone of four fish to feed the animals during one of the scheduled feedings. At other times, dolphins may get close enough for you to touch their neoprene-like skin. If your hands are empty, be prepared for dolphin derision – a disapproving shake of the head or a splash at close quarters.

Street performers are in abundance in this area. You can relax with fried conch and other island specialties at **Captain Pete's Island Eats** and listen to a calypso band while the children are entertained by jugglers, tightrope walkers, magicians, and other acts that require audience participation.

Troubled waters

Second in popularity only to the dolphins is **Stingray Lagoon ❹**, just to one side of Dolphin Cove. These strange but harmless fish float around the touch tank, tolerating endless petting of their wet-felt skin (the sting in their tail is a reflex to being stepped on – not a problem

here). At set times, you can purchase food and feed them. Tip: the toothless mouth is on the underside of these bottom-feeders. Don't try to feed them through the nose.

Less animated but no less fascinating are the residents of **Turtle Point ❺**, a modest exhibit that focuses on the lives of these highly endangered creatures. Sea turtles flock to Florida's white-sand beaches between May and August to nest. For centuries, hatchlings were guided back to the water by the light of the moon and stars, but now the bright lights of condos, hotels, and restaurants are leading them astray, often into busy highways. Only a handful survive each year.

An equally poignant story is told on the opposite side of the dolphin stadium at **Manatee Rescue ❻**. Some of SeaWorld's most important conservation work is with endangered manatees, which congregate around Florida's warm springs, rivers, and power plants every winter, where, unseen, they are frequently injured by boat propellers. Rescued manatees missing flippers and parts

Map on page 152

BELOW: visitors can feed and touch dozens of rays at the Stingray Lagoon.

of tails, and scarred badly on their backs, can be seen at this haunting exhibit, which re-creates a coastal wetland environment and chronicles the life cycle and incipient threats to manatees with excellent interpretive signs. A beautifully executed, three-minute multimedia film is shown in a walk-through theater. When it finishes, the doors open to reveal these gentle, torpedo-shaped giants from a rare underwater perspective.

Scream machines

The two rides in Key West are just around the bend. The first, **Journey to Atlantis ❼**, is a unique attraction that combines the thrills of a roller coaster with a water ride whose final 60-foot (18-meter) soaking plunge is one of the steepest in the world. There's a story line behind the ride having to do with the Lost Continent of Atlantis and a battle between the gods, but once your boat gets moving it's all secondary to the action. There's a barrage of lasers, holographs and other special effects and a rapid-fire succession of drops and dips, including two 60-foot (18-

meter) dives that will have your stomach doing somersaults. Expect to get drenched, especially in the front seats.

The only drawback is the long waiting time, which can be as much as an hour during the busy season. Your best strategy is to ride early in the morning or late in the afternoon. You exit the ride into **Jewels of the Sea Aquarium**, which sticks to the theme of the ride with a handful of displays of tropical fish in a sunken palace setting. As with other venues around SeaWorld, park photographers capture riders on film. You can buy these photos as well as other merchandise at booths near each attraction.

Kraken ❽, a 150-foot-high (46-meter), floorless roller coaster named after a legendary sea monster, will terrify the living daylights out of even seasoned riders. Raised seats allow your legs to dangle freely as this monster reaches speeds of 65 miles per hour (105 kph), creating a g-force that keeps you glued to your seat during a three-and-a-half-minute ride involving seven inversions (including a cobra roll, vertical loop, and flat spin),

BELOW:
Kraken rips through
seven inversions.

underground passages and a soaking in the eel-infested monster's lair.

Here, too, the lines can be daunting. Make a beeline to Kraken as soon as the park opens, or queue up in the hour before closing time.

Penguins, seals, and sharks

Near the entrance to Kraken is **Penguin Encounter** , where Magellanic penguins and puffins are kept safely behind glass. Viewing the exhibit feels a bit like window shopping, as you glide through a rather cramped, Antarctic dark chamber on a moving walkway, watching penguins fly through the water, mass on rocks, and waddle gracelessly on land. At the exit, interactive exhibits and staff educators will assure you that penguins are highly social, curious, and playful, and quite happy living in their odd storefront.

It's a whole lot noisier around the corner at **Pacific Point Preserve** ❿, a two-acre (1-hectare) re-creation of the wild, rocky Californian coast. The sea lions that inhabit Pacific Point know every trick in the book to attract fish at feeding time: flipper waves, rock-hopping, barks, and melting your heart with their large, bright eyes (a feature that allows them to see better underwater). Buy food for them, but watch out for aggressive egrets, gulls, and other seabirds that swoop down fast to steal fish right out of your hand.

In front of Pacific Point Preserve is the **Sea Lion and Otter Stadium** ⓫, home to the ridiculously goofy **Clyde and Seamore Take Pirate Island** show. Scripting a comedy routine around the unpredictable behavior of sea lions, otters, and a giant walrus is foolhardy at best and humiliating to the animals at worst, but the human players incorporate the goofs into the 30-minute show and you'll laugh in spite of yourself. The pirate ship set is one of the park's best, and it's remarkable to see the

animals sliding around the stage and into the tank in front as if Laurel or Hardy were their second names.

Even though this show may be an animal lover's least favorite, don't miss the preshow, which stars the SeaWorld Mime, a truly funny talent who mimics latecomers and others in classic street performance style.

Next to the stadium, you'll find **Shark Encounter** ⓬, a favorite with kids, who are transfixed by the hammerhead and other species of shark, as well as rays, puffer fish, moray eels, and other poisonous and predatory denizens of the deep. The wonder of this exhibit is how close you can get to these toothy terrors. View them from above or below, but don't miss actually moving among them via a mechanical walkway that passes through two 124-foot-long (38-meter) glass tunnels, an innovation that offers the illusion of proximity without the danger.

Chow time

Several restaurants are clustered around this area of the lagoon called the **Waterfront**. Shark Encounter

Map on page 152

The air inside Penguin Encounter is 30°F (–1°C), the water is 45°F (7°C), and 6,000 pounds (2,700kg) of man-made snow fall daily.

BELOW: sea lions inhabit Pacific Point Preserve, a re-creation of the California coast.

features the newly-opened **Sharks Underwater Grill** *(see page 161)*. **Smoky Creek Grill** has reasonably-priced Texas barbecue; the **Spice Mill** serves cajun grub; and **Mamma's Kitchen** offers a very limited menu which lacks either a proper kids' or vegetarian choice. **Seafire Inn** *(see page 161)* is the scene for daily **Music Maestro** lunch shows throughout the afternoon. The show is a quick musical tour around the Mediterranean and makes a pleasant setting for your meal. Reservations are required for the main evening event **Makahiki Luau**, a Polynesian themed dinner theater with elaborate costumes and Pacific Rim cuisine. The restaurants are busiest between noon and 4pm. A new attraction here is the **Oyster's Secret**. You can watch divers reclaim oysters from the enormous aquarium. The pearls are then turned into jewelry at the shop on land.

A few steps away is the **Dolphin Nursery** , another opportunity to meet dolphins, in this case mothers and newborns given time alone to bond. **Pets Ahoy!**, an endearing animal show held several times a day in the nearby **Seaport Theater** , features cats, dogs, pigs, and other animals rescued from shelters and trained to do remarkable tricks – and shtick. Kids love meeting the actors after the show.

To avoid long lines filled with cranky youngsters, you may want to head over to the attractive, modern **Anheuser Busch Hospitality Center**, a relaxing spot for a meal buffered from the rest of the park by lush vegetation and gurgling waterfalls. It's next to the **Clydesdale Hamlet** , home of some of the brewery's famous Scottish dray horses and one of the sweetest-smelling barns in the world. Admire the beautiful bell-bottomed creatures and the quick-with-a-pitchfork maintenance staff.

Inside the Hospitality Center, decorated with replicas of beer-making equipment, is **The Deli**, which serves hand-carved turkey and roast beef on crispy rolls, Caesar salads and a kid's Shamu Meal, consisting of a hot dog, chips, and a cookie in a collectible Shamu lunchbox. Adults can wash it all down with a nice cold beer, on the house. In case you've forgotten, SeaWorld is an Anheuser-Busch product, same as Budweiser, which is on tap along with several other brews. You can take your refreshments to an outdoor patio next to the fish ponds or watch the Clydesdale horses exercising outside the barn, perhaps getting hitched for a parade around the park.

For a lark, you can attend **Beer School**, a 30-minute class on beer brewing, which offers a brewmaster's certificate at the end.

On the way there, you pass **Odyssea** in the **Nautilus Theater** , the park's latest attraction. Though you no doubt came here

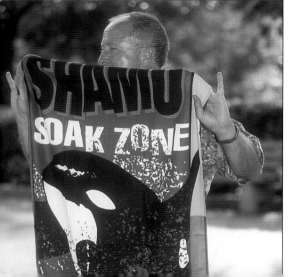

BELOW: sitting in the soak zone at Shamu Stadium? You may need a towel.

for the animal attraction, this circus show shouldn't be missed. Its elaborate costumes and set changes re-create an underwater fantasy world full of acrobats, mimes, and dancers.

Shamu's neighborhood

This side of the park has an open, spacious feel. **Shamu Stadium ⓱** seats thousands for SeaWorld's world-famous **Shamu Adventure Show**, a changing extravaganza that currently includes the patriotic entrance of a fish eagle and a large video screen, on which Jack Hanna, SeaWorld's resident naturalist, is your virtual guide to orca behavior, their habitats around the world, and threats to their survival. Most of Hanna's dialogue gets drowned out, though, as the crowd roars at the breathtaking feats of real orcas. You can end the afternoon with **Shamu Rocks America**, an upbeat 20-minute version of the daytime show.

While you're waiting for these big-ticket shows, there are plenty of distractions nearby. **The Atlantis**

Bayside Stadium ⓲ hosts special events. This is also a good spot to catch SeaWorld's big finale, the 15-minute **Mystify Fireworks Spectacular** over the central lagoon. For a small fee, you can ride to the top of the 400-foot-high (120-meter) **Sky Tower ⓳** for views over. Orlando or rent a **Flamingo Paddle Boat** for a leisurely tour around the lagoon. A **Games Area** and **Video Arcade** will satisfy bored teens, while the little ones have their own play area, **Shamu's Happy Harbor**, an outdoor climbing gym, complete with ropes, tunnels and a **Shamu Splash Attack** zone, where for $5 two buckets of water balloons offer yet another chance to cool off and have fun.

The park's third big ride, **Wild Arctic ⓴**, is also here. Unlike the other two, this attraction combines thrills with education. Fifty-nine passengers are strapped into a helicopter simulator for a choppy flight deep within the Arctic Circle. Along the way, you drop in on a polar bear family, dip below the waves to see a narwhal, are buf-

Map on page 152

SeaWorld's animals are served about 4,000 pounds (1,800 kg) of fish every day, a quarter of which is fed to the orcas.

BELOW: an underwater viewing area gives visitors a unique perspective on Sea-World's biggest star.

feted by gales, enter crevasses, and fly straight into an avalanche, before landing at an Arctic base station. The research station has been cleverly designed to look like it's built around the wrecked ships of real-life British explorer John Franklin, who disappeared in 1845 while searching for the fabled Northwest Passage.

During the course of the ride, you'll see beluga whales, walruses, and one of two pairs of polar bears, including the famous twins Klondike and Snow, born in the Denver Zoo, abandoned by their mother, and now residing in Orlando. If you're prone to motion sickness, skip the ride and choose the stationary version.

Two popular restaurants are located on this far side of the lagoon. **Mango Joe's Café**, near Wild Arctic, features fajitas, steak, fish, sandwiches, big salads and desserts. **Dine with Shamu** next to the underwater viewing area, the backstage area of Shamu Stadium, includes pasta, salads, chicken, and beef dishes, though the food here is beside the point: all eyes are on Shamu himself, swimming around his watery dressing room.

Discovery Cove

In 2001, SeaWorld opened what has been billed as the future in theme parks: Discovery Cove, a free-standing, all-inclusive resort-style park across the road from Sea-World. Up to a thousand lucky guests a day arrive at the attractive thatch-roofed tiki entrance to register for a day of sunbathing, swimming, interacting with tropical animals, and, the highlight, swimming with a dolphin.

All guests are checked in by efficient staff members upon arrival, given a useful identity/ swipe card to charge purchases, then whisked off to a small-group orientation and an individual photo that can be picked up after 2pm. Staff members hand out wetsuits and wet jackets (required for swimmers) and a string bag containing an eco-friendly sunscreen, complimentary snorkel, and mask that must be returned later.

TIP

Height requirements are 42 inches (107 cm) for Journey to Atlantis and Wild Arctic, and 54 inches (137 cm) for Kraken.

BELOW:
a trainer and guest interact with a dolphin at Discovery Cove.

Imported sandy beaches, deck chairs, cabanas, and refreshment stands surround the cool, saltwater **Coral Reef**, which has been stocked with stingrays and 6,000 tropical fish, as well as glassed-in sharks, a grouper and a moray eel. Nervous youngsters (and adults) can enjoy the stingray experience in a baby stingray pool adjoining the Coral Reef.

But if that's too much for some – as it may well be – plan on floating around the park in the warm, fresh-water **Lazy River**, passing water-falls and submerged ruins. The river will lead you to the **Aviary**, a hugely popular spot, where staff members answer questions and hand you cups of food for the toucans, ibises, sun conures, guineafowl, and even a tiny Muntjac deer. A substantial gourmet lunch, included in the fee, features above-average grilled salmon, faji-tas, stir fries, pasta, burgers, salads, and yummy desserts, served cafete-ria style.

While it's possible to enjoy all this and more by signing up for the less expensive **Non-Dolphin Swim** Package (about $140), you'll prob-ably kick yourself later if you don't take the opportunity to get into the water with one of the 30 dolphins. You can't change your mind when you arrive; the park is sold to capac-ity almost every day, and there are few last-minute cancellations. If you haven't made reservations, you're out of luck.

Included in the **Dolphin Swim** Package (about $240) is a 30-minute session interacting with a dolphin and two trainers in groups of no more than six people. Dolphin swims take place at specific time slots all day. You will be given your time when you arrive at the park and assigned a special cabana, where you will receive an orientation before getting into the water. The skill of the trainers makes this a very safe experience and great care is taken to give each guest ample one-on-one dolphin time. You'll get a chance to try out hand signals to get your dol-phin to roll, wave flippers, exchange kisses, and tow you along. And that, everyone seems to agree, is an expe-rience that is almost priceless.   ❏

Map on page 152

BELOW:
an Inca tern at the Discovery Cove aviary.

RESTAURANTS

Sharks Underwater Grill
An upscale eatery inside the Shark Encounter exhibit where you can enjoy a meal while sharks circle ominously all around. **$$$**

Seafire Inn
Serves Caribbean style food during the daily Music Maestro lunch shows. Reser-vations are required for Makahiki Luau, a Polynesian themed dinner theater. **$$**

Voyagers Wood Fired Pizza
Serves three types of pizza and half a dozen other entrees including grilled salmon, pastas, and salads. **$$**

● ● ● ● ● ● ● ● ● ● ● ● ● ● ● ● ● ● ● ●
Price includes dinner and a glass of wine (when available), excluding tip. **$$$** *over $30,* **$$** *between $20–30,* **$** *under $20.*

BEYOND THE THEME PARKS

Had enough of Disney and Universal? Explore the area's smaller attractions, ranging from water parks and dinner shows to old-time roadside wonders

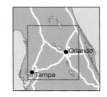

Walt Disney World may be the big cheese Orlando has been hosting since the 1970s, but there are plenty of other tasty hors d'oeuvres on the platter. Everything – from the weird to the wonderful – finds a home here: exotic zoos, gator wrestling, orchid farms, flight museums, and light entertainments such as stock car and go-cart racing, miniature golf, and water parks.

For a trip down memory lane to the Florida of old, nothing beats the quaint roadside attractions that have survived the onslaught of Disney-style tourism by doing one thing and doing it well. They provide a refreshing alternative to here-today, gone-tomorrow fakery and are worth a detour. International Drive has the atmosphere of a seaside carnival (minus the sea) that Disney and Universal sacrificed in exchange for technological wizardry and meticulous set design. An afternoon spent roaming its attractions is a more casual affair and waiting times are rarely long.

A religious experience

One of Orlando's most unique attractions is **Holy Land Experience ❶** (Mon– Thur 10am–7pm, Fri–Sat 9am–9pm, Sun noon–7pm, 4655 Vineland Road, exit 31 on I-4; tel: 866-USA-HOLYLAND or 407-367

2065; www.theholylandexperience. com) near Universal Orlando. No matter where you stand on the novelty of a Christian theme park, this $16 million, 15-acre (6-hectare) "Living Biblical Museum" is undeniably well-executed and uses effective multimedia presentations to interpret the roots of Christianity, albeit from a distinctly partial point of view.

The park reflects the combined efforts of Islands of Adventure design firm ITEC Entertainment and founder Marvin Rosenthal, a Jew-

Map on page 164

LEFT: alligator wrestling, Gatorland.
BELOW: Holyland Experience.

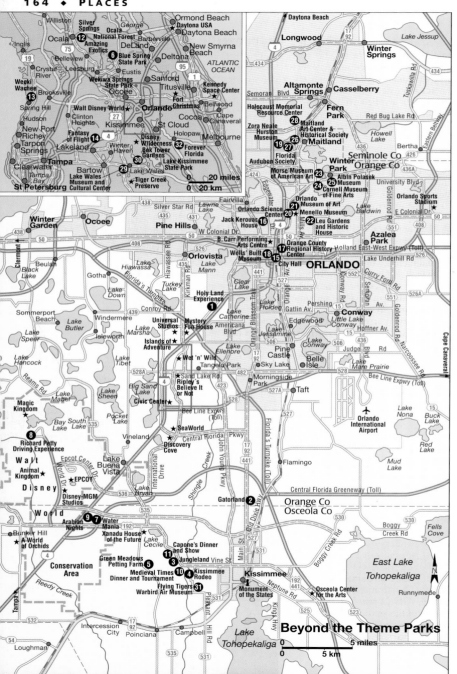

Beyond the Theme Parks

Map on page 164

ish-born Baptist minister. Rosenthal's motives for creating the park have been questioned since the project was announced in 1993. Some critics have accused him of using the park in a veiled effort to target Jews for conversion. Others object to the emphasis on links between Christianity and Judaism and the sale of such items as menorahs, prayer shawls, and other religious paraphernalia from Israel. None of this seems to bother Christian groups, though, who have made up the vast majority of visitors since the park opened in February 2001.

The core of the Holy Land Experience is a re-creation of the city of Jerusalem between 1450 BC and AD 66 and includes the world's largest scale model of the **Calvary Garden Tomb**, the **Wilderness Tabernacle**, and the **Qumran Dead Sea Caves**. A **Scriptorium** houses one of the world's largest private collections of original Biblical manuscripts and books. You can only see it via a 55-minute guided tour. Exhibits in the buildings, ongoing short presentations in indoor theaters, and a schedule of live performances focus on various aspects of the Christian message. A film entitled *Seed of Promise*, which tells the story of Christianity, from Adam and Eve to the sack of Jerusalem in AD 70, shows throughout the day. Live shows often take place in the **Plaza of the Nations** on the steps of the **Temple of the Great King**, a dramatic, six-story-high, one-half size representation of the temple where the boy Jesus reasoned with the scribes and Pharisees. Attention to detail is impressive. Landscaping focuses on plants native to the Holy Land. The **Oasis Palms Cafe** serves Middle Eastern dishes such as falafel, and cast members dressed as priests of the Herodic Temple blow a shofar, or ceremonial ram's horn, to announce shows.

Gator wrestling

Things are decidedly more funky at one of Orlando's oldest and least crowded attractions, the gloriously low-tech **Gatorland** ❷ (daily 9am–dusk, 14501 Orange Blossom Trail; tel: 800-393 5297 or 407-855 5496; www.gatorland.com).

Opened in 1949 by Kissimmee cattle rancher Owen Godwin, this 55-acre (22-hectare) combination gator farm, exotic zoo, and wetlands is still the best place to have your Florida alligator experience. This is a working gator farm, with about a thousand gators sent to market each week.

You can sample the taste of alligator meat in one of the restaurants, but don't miss classic entertainments like the **Gator Jumparoo Show**, where gators leap out of the water like trained dolphins to snag chickens from trainers' hands, and the **Gator Wrestling Cracker-style Show**, popular since Bunk Baxter first jumped astride a gator and opened its mouth for inspection in downtown Orlando in the late 1800s.

TIP

Fast food is sold at both Water Mania and Wet 'n' Wild, and visitors are permitted to bring coolers for a picnic.

BELOW: Before Disney there was Gatorland, entertaining tourists since 1949.

A word to the wise at Gatorland.

BELOW: even a litigious mouse seems timid next to Florida's native beasts.

These days, Gatorland uses more than half a century of experience with alligators to promote a strong conservation message. It also works with the University of Florida on alligator research.

Gators are also featured at another roadside attraction in Kissimmee. **Jungleland** ❸ (daily 9am–6pm, 4580 W. Irlo Bronson Highway; tel: 407-396 1012) is primarily an exotic zoo that houses some 300 animals in an intimate setting. African leopards, Bengal tigers, cougars, African caracols, and other members of the cat family are legion. Monkeys are also well-represented. Jungleland's 25-minute Bushmasters Gator Show takes place each afternoon. The show offers slightly different gator lore than Gatorland, including the fact that Seminole Indian hunters were the first to wrestle with gators, and lone hunters developed the trick of pulling the gator's head back and holding the jaws with their chin, so that they could tie the creature's jaws shut single-handedly and avoid sharing the bounty with a partner.

Bronc Busting

Wrangling of a different type takes place every Friday evening at the **Kissimmee Rodeo** ❹ (Fri 8pm, 958 S. Hoagland Boulevard; tel: 407-933 0020; www.ksarodeo.com). Not so long ago, Kissimmee was one of the country's largest cattle ranching areas, and folks around here like to celebrate the fact most weeks by taking part in a little friendly roping and riding. You'll see bareback riding, bull riding, bronco busting, and calf roping, as well as a calf scramble, in which kids from the audience chase a herd of young dogies. Concession stands sell cowboy hats and hot dogs, burgers, hot chocolate, and drinks.

If it's the real thing you're after, try to time your visit to Orlando for the Fourth of July, when the annual Silver Spurs Rodeo attracts professional rodeo riders from all over the United States.

Stomping around in the mud is part of the fun at the delightful **Green Meadows Petting Farm** ❺ (daily 9.30am–4pm, 1368 South Poinciana Boulevard; tel: 407-846 0770; www.

greenmeadowsfarm.com), a 40-acre (16-hectare) rural farm with 200 animals, south of U.S. 192. New arrivals are greeted by farm hands in jeans and rubber boots who conduct continuous two-hour tours and give the little ones plenty of time to chase the chickens, milk a cow, ride a pony, and enjoy an old-fashioned hay ride and a trip aboard a miniature train around the back forty. Spring is the best time to see baby animals. Stop by at Halloween to play in the pumpkin patch. A Cowboys and Indians festival takes place in November, featuring Seminole Indian dances and rope tricks. Bring food and drinks and enjoy a picnic. Only snacks are sold here.

If close-up animal encounters appeal to you, you're going to love **Amazing Exotics ⑥** (by appointment only; tours begin at noon, SR 452, Umatilla; tel: 352-821 1234; www.amazingexotics.com), a non-profit exotic animal rescue facility. This former macaque monkey-breeding farm on the remote northern fringes of Orlando now cares for tigers, lemurs, lynx, and other exotic beasts, many of them show-biz retirees, and also trains animal handlers for zoos and other animal preserves. Visitors get a firsthand look at wild-animal care on fascinating small-group insider tours, then have a chance to interact with small cats, big cats, and primates on one of the Safari, Encounter or Discovery Tours. Reservations are mandatory, and you will be required to sign a waiver. Your fee ($34–94, depending on tour) is treated as a tax-deductible contribution.

Water parks

On a hot, humid summer afternoon, you begin to understand why so many private homes in Florida have screened-in swimming pools. The Orlando area has several terrific water parks, where you can escape the heat on a variety of flumes, slides, and other aquatic thrill rides.

Kissimmee's 36-acre (15-hectare) **Water Mania ⑦** (6073 W. Irlo Bronson Highway; tel: 800-527 3092 or 407-396 2626; www.watermania-florida.com) has the usual rides and slides, as well as a few others, including a white-water tubing adventure; a float along an 850-foot-long (260-meter) river; and the Abyss, a 380-foot-long (115-meter) enclosed tube that spirals down to a plunge pool. Hurricane damage in 2004 forced the park to close temporarily.

Even more elaborate is **Wet 'n' Wild ⒶA** (daily 10am–6pm, extended summer hours, 6200 International Drive; tel: 800-992 9453 or 407-351 9453; www.wetnwild.com), near Universal Studios. A massive tower holds three rides: Mach 5, a spiraling flume; The Blast, their newest ride, which is your standard raft ride with added sound effects and water cannons that insure you get soaked; and the Flyer, a fast drop in a raft that offers the park's biggest thrills. The Surge, in a separate tower, offers another hairy ride, as your raft

Map on page 164&168

BELOW: bulls, broncs, and buckaroos strut their stuff at the Kissimmee Rodeo.

screams down a banked tube some five stories high. Small children have their own fun in the sun: a kiddie pool and a pint-size multilevel water play area that includes water cannons, slides, the mini Surf Lagoon wave pool, and a Lazy River that takes you through Florida's past. The water at Wet 'n' Wild is heated, and the park is open year-round, though you'll find the winter months quite chilly.

International Drive

Across from Wet 'n' Wild is **Skull Kingdom** Ⓑ (daily 6pm–midnight, kid-friendly tours 10am–5pm, 5933 American Way; tel: 407-354 1564; www.skullkingdom.com), a haunted-house attraction occupying a castle with an enormous skull-shaped entrance. Spine-chilling mechanical monsters, creepy, maze-like stage sets, and a ghoulish cast of live actors make it feel like Halloween here every day of the year.

The massive vertical wind tunnel at **SkyVenture** (Mon–Thur 2–10pm, Fri–Sun 12–10pm, 6805 Visitors Circle, tel: 407-903 1150) allows you the sensual experience of sky-diving without the fear of falling to the ground.

The Mediterranean-style **Mercado** Ⓒ restaurant and shopping complex, in the 8000 block of International Drive, offers several worthwhile attractions. Inside the courtyard is **Titanic – Ship of Dreams** (open 10am–8pm, 8445 International Drive; tel: 877-410 1912 or 407-248 1166; www.titanicshipofdreams. com), where fans of the movie take a virtual voyage aboard the *Titanic* and view artifacts, historic photos, and costumes from the film. Enthusiastic actors representing historical characters escort visitors through a re-created shipyard, a dock and staterooms, then leave you in the main exhibit room to read sample passenger

BELOW:
visitors cool off at Wet 'n' Wild water park.

Universal Studios
DOCTOR PHILLIPS
Downtown Orlando
Kirkham Road
Ⓗ Fun Spot Action Park
Ⓑ Skull Kingdom
International Drive
Ⓐ Wet 'n' Wild
Sandy Lake
TANGELO PARK
Carrier Drive
Republic Drive
Ⓘ Pirates Dinner Adventure
Sleuth's Ⓙ Mystery Show and Dinner
Lake Pat
Sand Lake Road
Ⓔ Ripley's Believe It or Not Odditorium
Hard Rock Vault
Mercado
Ⓒ Titanic-Ship of Dreams
Ⓓ Bergamo's Italian Restaurant
Pirates Cove Ⓖ Miniature Golf
Perimeter Road
Turkey Lake Road
Republic Drive
International Drive
Ⓕ WonderWorks
★ Pointe Orlando
N
International Drive
SeaWorld
0   1000 yds
0   1000 m
Disney World
Convention Center
528

biographies and view rescued artifacts. Most effective are the passenger dock (complete with foghorn), the life-sized grand staircase, and the chilly deck of the *Titanic*, with the fatal iceberg looming nearby. The exhibit's most poignant moment comes when you check the assigned passenger name on your boarding pass against the list of 2,000 *Titanic* passengers to see if you survived or perished. Eerily, you can book the museum for weddings, so long as starting your married life on a sinking ship doesn't bother you.

Just outside Mercado, in its own futuristic building, is the **Hard Rock Vault D** (daily 9am–midnight, 8437 International Drive; tel: 407-599 7625; www.hardrock.com), an interactive exhibition of rock 'n' roll memorabilia from the collections of the Hard Rock Café. Spread out inside the 17,000-square-foot (1,580-sq-meter) space is a timeline chronicling the evolution of rock music through various styles and periods such as the British Invasion, the Psychedelic Sixties, and the advent of Punk Rock, with special attention paid to major figures such as Elvis Presley, Bob Dylan, the Beatles, and the Rolling Stones. Among the items on display are Jim Morrison's leather pants, Elvis's rhinestone cape, B.B. King's guitar "Lucille," Buddy Holly's horn-rimmed glasses, and the motorcycle jacket worn by Bruce Springsteen on the cover of *Born to Run*.

If, on the other hand, you're in the mood for a walk on the weird side, head next door to **Ripley's Believe It or Not Odditorium E** (daily 9am–1am, 8201 International Drive; tel: 407-345 0501; www.ripleysorlando.com), housed in one of I-Drive's most memorable buildings: an ornate Italian villa sliding into a Florida sinkhole. Newspaper cartoonist Robert Ripley had a taste for natural and man-made oddities and made a fortune collecting bizarre artifacts from 198 countries. Prepare to be equally grossed out and intrigued by exhibits, such as a two-headed calf, a Mona Lisa re-created in small squares of toasted bread, and

Map on page 164&168

LEFT: Titanic – Ship of Dreams features a re-creation of the ill-fated ship's grand staircase.
BELOW: Skull Kingdom is housed in a spooky castle with a skull-shaped entrance.

a three-quarter-scale Rolls-Royce crafted from matchsticks. The topsy-turvy theme is carried through in skewed rooms, where things seem to roll uphill, and a disorienting catwalk, which appears to be stationary but is really moving.

If illusions and tilted buildings are your thing, don't miss **Wonder-Works**  (daily 9am–midnight, 9067 International Drive; tel: 407-351 8800; www.wonderworksonline.com), next to Pointe Orlando, another retail and entertainment complex. In typical Orlando one-upmanship, the three-story WonderWorks tops Ripley's by featuring a subsiding neoclassical building that is also upside down.

Inside, it's a gamer's heaven, with more than 100 games, science-museum-style hands-on experiments that teach physics, and the world's largest laser tag game. Other attractions let you design your own roller coaster, experience an earthquake or take part in virtual reality war. They've also joined the dinner show racket with the "Outta Control Magic Show" *(see page 176).*

Pirates and high-seas adventures are popular themes in spectacle-oriented Orlando. At **Pirates Cove Miniature Golf**  (daily 9am–11pm, 8501 International Drive; tel: 407-352 7378; also at I-4 at exit 27 in Lake Buena Vista, tel: 407-827 1242), you can play two enjoyable 18-hole courses – Captain Kidd's Adventure and Blackbeard's Challenge (the more difficult) – through caves, under waterfalls, over bridges, and around markers with real-life bios of famous pirates.

Pirates' newest competitor is **Tiki Island Adventure Golf** (open daily 10am–11.30pm; 7460 International Drive; tel: 407-248 8180) which recreates a Pacific Island theme. If you are able to score a hole in one on the final hole, a four-story volcano will erupt.

Well off the beaten I-Drive trail and located next to one of Orlando's newest super malls is **Millenia Gallery** (daily, 4190 Millenia Boulevard, tel: 407-425 5379, www.milleniagallery.com). This recent addition to the city's art scene is one of the largest galleries in the South-

Muvico Pointe 21, a cinema complex at Pointe Orlando on International Drive, has 21 state-of-the-art theaters, including a six-story theater for IMAX films.

BELOW: the FAO Schwarz toy store on International Drive.
RIGHT: Ripley's Believe it or Not Odditorium.

east with over 10,000 square feet (900 square meters) of exhibition space displaying sculpture and works from modern masters.

Start your engines

Young speed demons will enjoy **Fun Spot Action Park**  (Mon–Fri noon–11pm, Sat–Sun 10am–midnight, 5551 Del Verde Way; tel: 407-363 3867), at the intersection of International Drive and Kirkman Road. Four twisting, multilevel tracks make this one of the best go-cart speedways in Orlando (try the 1,375-foot/420-meter, three-level QuadHelix for real thrills), and there are also bumper car rides and other fairground attractions. For a change of pace, climb aboard the 101-foot-high (31-meter) Ferris wheel for panoramic views of I-Drive and Universal Orlando.

If Fun Spot is for the little ones, then the **Richard Petty Driving Experience** ❽ (daily 9am–5pm, 3450 N. World Drive, Walt Disney World Speedway, Lake Buena Vista; tel: 407-939 0130; www.

1800bepetty.com) is strictly for the big boy racers.

If you've always wanted to drive a souped-up 630-horsepower Pontiac Grand Prix at 125 miles per hour (200 kph), this NASCAR-affiliated racing school is the place. Choices range from a $100 three-lap shotgun ride with a professional driver to a $3,000 intensive two-day program that includes exercises in side-by-side driving and a final duel on the speedway between student and pro.

The most popular options are the $400 "Rookie" basic driving lessons, which consist of eight laps behind the wheel on the mile-long speedway.

Just in case you were wondering: no one gets to climb into one of these cars without signing a 19-point release form.

Race fans will also get a kick out of **Race Rock** (8986 International Drive; tel: 407-248 9876; www.racerock.com), a theme restaurant devoted to motor sports and packed floor to ceiling with racing memorabilia. Highlights include stock cars, funny cars, Formula 1 racers, dragsters, and motorcycles owned

Map on page 164&168

BELOW: Wonder Works, the only upside-down building on International Drive, features games, interactive exhibits and virtual-reality rides.

by racing superstars like Dale Earnhardt, Richard Petty, Don Prudhomme, and Michael Andretti, as well as Bigfoot, the world's largest monster truck. There's also an array of simulators and video games and, naturally, a well-stocked gift shop.

Dinner and a show

After an afternoon in the theme parks, it's time to think about dinner. Kissimmee has several popular – though pricey – dinner shows. "Show" is the operative word. No matter what the advertising says, the mass-dining experience has more in common with hotel convention food than gourmet dining. Don't get your hopes up. Yet what they lack in gourmet cooking they make up for with good-humoured entertainment. Themes vary but the experience is quite similar. So the choice is yours: a murderer or a buccaneer for dinner?

Most enchanting is **Arabian Nights ❾** (Wed–Sat 8.30pm, Sun–Tues 7.30pm; www.arabian-nights. com; *see page 176*), which stars 50 Arabian, Lippizaner, palomino and quarter horses that are put through their paces by skilled riders in an enormous arena. The story line involves the wedding of a prince and princess. The finale is worth the price of admission, featuring 15 riderless horses that prance around the arena as artificial snow falls.

Medieval Times Dinner and Tournament ❿ (call for show times; www.medievaltimes.com; *see page 176)* is another horsey extravaganza, set in the 11th century. It features a well-executed jousting tournament that pits six knights against each other while the audience cheers on their favorites. Avoid purchasing an upgrade to preferred seating; there are only five rows in the arena, and all offer good viewing.

The longest-running (and weakest) of the offerings is the amateurish **Capone's Dinner & Show ⓫** (call for show times; www.alcapones. com; *see page 176)*, set in a cheesy 1930s speakeasy behind a fake ice-cream parlor. Guys and Dolls this ain't, though the waiters are dressed as gun-brandishing gangsters, and you are ostensibly attend-

BELOW: Bigfoot on display at Race Rock.

Map on page 164&168

ing a celebration for the notorious hoodlum Al Capone.

The food is far better at **Bergamo's Italian Restaurant** (daily 5pm– 10pm; www.bergamos.com; *see page 176*). Not only are these some of the friendliest waiters around, but if you time your visit right the servers will assemble in the center of the room and perform glorious renditions of operatic classics, Neapolitan folk songs and show tunes. The quality of the food and service and the incomparable sound of trained voices effortlessly filling the room with Verdi or Puccini make this one dinner show you shouldn't miss.

The newest show on the circuit is **Dolly Parton's Dixieland Stampede** (shows daily, 8251 Vineland Avenue, tel: 866-443 4943; www.dixiestampede.com). Guests are divided between Union and Confederates (still a dangerous game to play in some Southern states) and the rivalry begins. Over thirty horses dance and prance while you are served a four course meal. Despite its name, Dolly Parton does not appear, but patriotic ferver is definitely in attendence.

A swashbuckling theme prevails at **Pirates Dinner Adventure** ❶ (daily show times vary, 6400 Carrier Drive; tel: 407-248 0590, 800-866 2369; www.piratesdinneradventure.com; *see page 176*), one block west of International Drive. This arena dinner show has one of Orlando's most impressive sets: a life-sized pirate ship, which serves as the centerpiece for an action-packed evening of pillaging, fighting on deck, and attempts to save Princess Anita. Expect to do plenty of oohing and aahing, cheering and singing of pirate songs. Pre-show attractions include gypsy fortune-tellers and face painting. A post-show Buccaneer Bash continues the silliness.

Also near International Drive is a dinner show that has grown in popularity in recent years. **Sleuth's Mystery Show and Dinner** ❷ (daily shows, times vary; www.sleuths.com; *see page 176*) involves the audience in solving a crime and is perfect for fans of murder mystery

LEFT: sunset at Cypress Gardens.

Birdies and Bogeys

With 150 courses to choose from, you could build an entire vacation around golf in Orlando. Disney World has five championship courses and 15 golf pros. Two courses near Disney, Villas at Grand Cypress Resort, with a 45-hole course designed by Jack Nicklaus, and Bay Hill Club and Lodge, with its Arnold Palmer Golf Academy, are top rated. Palmer also designed Orange Lake Resort and Country Club at the quiet end of International Drive, while Nick Faldo put his stamp on two courses at Marriott's Grand Vista Resort, also on I-Drive.

Just trying to squeeze in a round of golf? *Orlando* magazine voted Metrowest Golf Club, designed by Robert Trent Jones, the city's No. 1 course for its rolling fairways and stunning views of downtown. Jones also designed Celebration Golf Club, which has an unusual five tees at each hole and a three-hole junior course for kids.

Beyond Orlando, Saddlebrook Resort, 20 minutes north of Tampa, allows you to combine a visit to Busch Gardens with two 18-hole courses and the Arnold Palmer Golf Academy. Plus, you may glimpse tennis pros Pete Sampras and Martina Hingis practicing on the tennis courts.

weekends and whodunits. Guests seated at round tables to watch the first act, which gets the murdering over with and includes much ad-lib at the audience's expense. Each table then chooses a spokesperson who questions the actors as you try to solve the murder.

Cypress Gardens

One of Orlando's oldest attractions, **Cypress Gardens** (open daily from 10am, closing times vary; tel: 863-324 2111 www.cypressgardens.com) has been going through a tough patch recently. Closed down in 2001 due to a lack of revenue, the historic gardens reopened at the end of 2004. "Adventure Park" has been added to their title and dozens of amusement rides, animal attractions and shows have been built in the hope of rejuvenating this old timer on Orlando's vacation scene.

Silver Springs

Central Florida's crystalline springs have attracted people for thousands of years. In the mid-1800s, steamboats carried wealthy tourists down

the St John's and Oklawaha rivers to **Silver Springs** ⓬ (daily 10am–5pm, 5656 E. Silver Springs Boulevard; tel: 352-236 2121; www.silversprings. com), the world's purest and largest artesian springs.

Set in the rolling horse country of Ocala, northeast of Orlando, this 350-acre (140-hectare) nature theme park is to Orlando what Busch Gardens is to Tampa – albeit without the roller coasters (there is even a Jeep safari now). Now a state historic site, Silver Springs highlights Florida wildlife through natural zoo exhibits containing native spiders, snakes, alligators, birds of prey, and other animals, which are put through their paces by knowledgeable handlers at daily shows.

Look for 2,000-pound (900-kg) Sobek the crocodile, believed to be the world's largest croc in captivity; the largest bear exhibit of its kind in the United States, featuring spectacled bears and black bears; and rare Florida panthers.

Silver Springs' famous glass-bottom boats were invented here in 1878. No visit is complete without

BELOW: glass-bottom boats have been delighting tourists at Silver Springs for more than 120 years.

a slow-paced river ride aboard these historic boats to view the underwater life. Other boat rides include Jungle Cruises, for glimpses of free-ranging giraffes, zebras, gazelles, and other wildlife from six continents, and the Lost River Voyage, a look at the Florida of old amid cypress-lined waterways alive with alligators, osprey, and herons, including a stop at a wilderness outpost to learn more about the park's wildlife rehabilitation programs.

Weeki Wachee

If you enjoy Silver Springs, you may want to stop at **Weeki Wachee** ⓯ (call for hours, US Highway 19 and SR 50; tel: 352-596 2062; www.weekiwachee.com), a natural spring north of Tampa, where you can canoe, scuba dive, play on water slides, and try to spot manatees on the Wilderness Cruise on the Weeki Wachee River. In true Florida fashion, Weeki Wachee has a gimmick: mermaid shows featuring pretty girls in fishtails swim in a large aquarium. It's hokey but makes for family fun.

Flight of fancy

To find **Fantasy of Flight** ⓮ (daily 9am–5pm, 1400 Broadway Boulevard, Polk City; tel: 863-984 3500), exit 44 off I-4, just look for the crashed plane beside the road.

Vintage aircraft collector Kermit Weeks offers a first-class *Boy's Own* museum, split into three main areas. The first is a walk-through history of flight, featuring dioramas and film, that bring to life 19th-century balloon flight, airborne combat in World War I, and more. Weeks's collection of vintage aircraft is displayed in a hangar containing reproductions of the Wright Brothers' 1903 Flyer and Charles Lindbergh's Spirit of St Louis, a 1959 flying automobile Roadair, and the 1929 Ford Tri-Motor used in the film Indiana Jones and the Temple of Doom. Included in the price of admission is unlimited time aboard eight flight simulators in Fightertown. The authentic Art-Deco-style Compass Rose Restaurant serves tasty burgers, sandwiches, salads and desserts at rock-bottom prices and is a convenient stop for breakfast or lunch. ❑

Map on page 164&168

LEFT: wildlife from six continents is on show at Silver Springs.
BELOW: all tied up at Gatorland.

RESTAURANTS & BARS

Dinner Theaters

Arabian Nights
6225 W Irlo Bronson
Memorial Highway (US 192)
Kissimmee
Tel: 407-239 9223 or
800-553 6116
www.arabian-nights.com
Mainstream dinner fare includes your choice of chicken tenders, prime rib, and lasagna and, of course, wedding cake. Be warned: dinner is served at long benches around the arena in close proximity to the horses. **$$$**

Bergamo's Italian Restaurant
The Mercado
8445 International Drive
Orlando
Tel: 407-352 3805
www.bergamos.com

Bergamo's has earned kudos for an attractive ambience and beautifully-prepared pasta, steak and seafood (thankfully not overcooked, as is so often the case in Orlando). **$$$**

Capone's Dinner & Show
4740 W Irlo Bronson
Memorial Highway (US 192)
Kissimmee
Tel: 407-397 2378 or
(800) 220 8428
www.alcapones.com
Cafeteria-style Italian fare such as lasagna, ziti, spaghetti and baked chicken is the bill of fare at this amateurish dinner show, set in a cheesy 1930s speakeasy behind a fake ice-cream parlor. **$$$**

Medieval Times Dinner and Tournament
4510 W Irlo Bronson
Memorial Highway (US 192)
Kissimmee
Tel: 800-WE JOUST
www.medievaltimes.com
Dinner is served in a large arena at this horsey Medieval extravaganza complete with jousting knights and serving wenches. This is a satisfying experience for those who relish eating a whole roasted chicken or prime rib with their fingers in a rowdy atmosphere. **$$$**

The Outta Control Magic Show
Wonderworks
9067 International Drive
Orlando
Tel: 407-351 8800
www.wonderworksonline.com
One of the newest entries to the dinner theater scene. Food includes hand-tossed pizza and popcorn with unlimited beer, wine, and soda. Entertainment is a mixture of comedy, improv, and magic that precisely promises to "tickle your funny bone every eight seconds". **$$**

Pirates Dinner Adventure
6400 Carrier Drive
off I-Drive
Orlando
Tel: 407-248 0590 or

800-866 2469
www.piratesdinneradventure.com
Caribbean jerk chicken barbecued on pirate swords and rice with pineapple, followed by hot apple cobbler, add some spice to the gloomy and glutinous fare served at such shows. A post-show Buccaneer Bash continues the silliness. **$$$**

Sleuth's Mystery Show and Dinner
Republic Square
7508 Universal Boulevard
Orlando
Tel: 407-363 1985 or
800-393 1985
www.sleuths.com
Dinner here is lacking in mystery: you have your choice of lasagna and meatballs, Cornish hen, and prime rib, but it's done well and tastes fresh. **$$$**

Restaurants

Bahama Breeze
8849 International Drive
Orlando
Tel: 407-248 2499
8735 Vineland Avenue
Orlando
Tel: 407-938 9010
www.bahamabreeze.com
A taste of the Caribbean, from the coconut shrimp and paella to the piña colada bread pudding for dessert. Listen to the live band while you wait. **$$**

LEFT: trick riders perform at the Arabian Nights dinner show.

B-Line Diner
Peabody Hotel
9801 International Drive
Orlando
Tel: 407-345 4460
A cozy, 1950s-style
diner that's open 24
hours a day. Features
thick sandwiches, grid-
dle cakes, and a juke-
box with vintage tunes.
$

Cafe Tu-Tu Tango
8625 International Drive
Orlando
Tel: 407-248 2222
www.cafetututango.com
Serves wide variety of
tapas – small appetizer
dishes. Artists and per-
formers roam the restau-
rant. **$–$$**

Capriccio
Peabody Hotel
9801 International Drive
Orlando
Tel: 407-352 4000
Genuine Italian country
cooking with top-quality,
fresh ingredients. **$$$**

Dux
Peabody Hotel
9801 International Drive
Orlando
Tel: 407-345 4550
Elegant restaurant with
innovative American cui-
sine. No duck served,
respecting the hotel's
resident mascots. **$$$**

Macaroni Grill
5320 W Irlo Bronson
Memorial Highway (US 192)
Kissimmee
Tel: 407-396 6155

www.macaronigrill.com
Italian cuisine. Special-
ties include *scallopini di
pollo*, *saltimbocca* and
rack of lamb. **$–$$**

Ming Court
9188 International Drive
Orlando
Tel: 407-351 9988
www.ming-court.com
A fine variety of Chinese
food. Specializing in dim
sum. **$$$**

Pebbles
Crossroads
12551 SR 535
Lake Buena Vista
Tel: 407-827 1111
California cuisine meets
Florida ingredients. Try
the salmon sautéed
with artichoke hearts or
the Florida citrus
chicken with pecan
couscous. Four other
locations in the Orlando
area. **$$**

Plantation Room
Celebration Hotel
700 Bloom Street
Celebration
Tel: 407-566 6002
Affordable gourmet nou-
velle Florida cuisine,
including master din-
ners featuring every-
thing from gator to
kangaroo. Breakfast is
lovely and an excellent
value. **$$$**

Ran-Getsu
8400 International Drive
Orlando
Tel: 407-345 0044
www.rangetsu.com

Elegant setting for fine
Japanese food: sushi,
sukiyaki, tempura. **$$**

Wild Jacks
7634 International Drive
Orlando
Tel: 407-352 4407
A Western-style eatery
with mounted buffalo
heads on the walls and
an open-pit barbecue
(tangy grilled shrimp,
big steaks, Texas rice,
and sweet molasses
bread). **$**

Bars

Cricketers Arms
The Mercado
8445 International Drive
Orlando
Tel: 407-354 0686
www.cricketersarmspub.com
The epicenter of English
expats and visitors
caters to them with

warm ales and live
football (known as
soccer in these parts).
$

Lucky Leprechaun
7032 International Drive
Orlando
Tel: 407-352 7031
A traditionally American
version of a vintage Irish
pub. Along with a decent
Guinness, and live
English sport, you can
dig into bar snacks
including homemade
pies. **$**

RIGHT: Race Rock is packed to the rafters with racing
memorabilia, including several cars and motorcycles.

SOME LIKE IT HAUTE

Not to be left behind, culture presses onward and
upward in the region. Art stirs the spirit,
museums abound, and nature is heeded

Orlando's many theme parks offer funhouse rides through a variety of re-imagined worlds. It's a great escape, but the real Florida beyond the theme parks is at least as compelling as these recent experiments in virtual reality. Did you know, for example, that 74 million years ago, the Florida peninsula lay beneath a sea populated by gigantic gatorlike mosasaurs? Or that the state's highest point, 295-foot (90-meter) Lake Wales Ridge, south of Orlando, is an ancient sand dune ecosystem supporting endangered desert plants and animals similar to those found in Arizona?

Nor is Orlando the cultural wasteland that critics so often make it out to be. A great variety of museums and theaters have been quietly delighting residents for decades; others have only recently received infusions of public funds and now rank among the Southeast's most vital cultural institutions.

A home for the arts

A case in point is the multimillion-dollar revitalization of downtown Orlando, now the center of a vibrant arts scene. Galleries, nightclubs, coffeehouses featuring poetry slams, and fine restaurants are sprouting up along Orange Avenue around the beautifully-restored railroad depot, Church Street Station, an erstwhile entertainment complex. Also downtown is the new postmodern-style **Orlando City Hall** ⓑ (Mon–Fri 8am–9pm, Sat–Sun noon–5pm, 400 S. Orange Avenue; tel: 407-246 2121), which exhibits art in two galleries. Across from City Hall is the swank new **Westin Grand Bohemian Hotel** (325 S. Orange Avenue; tel: 407-313 9000), with rooms showcasing fine art by such luminaries as Gustave Klimt. There is also a retro bar and

Map
on page
164

LEFT: Tiffany glass at the Charles Hosmer Morse Museum.
BELOW: gilded goddess, downtown Orlando.

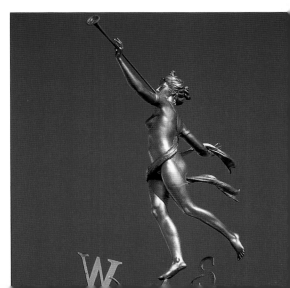

one of downtown's best gourmet restaurants, the critically-acclaimed The Boheme *(see page 191)*.

Nearby **Church Street Station** is a clear symbol of the difficulty communities outside the pale of Disney face to attract attention. In 2002, this famous nightspot – a collection of bars and restaurants – had nearly ceased to exist. Now it's on its way up, pulling in clientele from Orlando's young artists and classy business executives. Several store fronts remain unclaimed, as development plans have been held up with red tape. Nevertheless, it's again becoming a place for locals that tourists should get away from Disney to see.

The **Bob Carr Performing Arts Centre** (401 W. Livingston St; tel: 407-849 2020; www.orlandocentroplex.com) is home to some performances of the Orlando Philharmonic *(see page 183)* and seasonal theater productions. The **Dr Phillips Center for Performing Arts** (1111 N. Orange Avenue) is the home of the Southern Ballet Theatre (tel: 407-426 1733), one of the Southeast's major

dance companies, as well as Orlando Opera (tel: 407-426 1717). In Kissimmee, the **Osceola Center for the Arts** (2411 E. Irlo Bronson Hwy; tel: 407-846 6257; www.ocfta.com) is home to 10 visual and performing arts groups and has an art gallery, a 244-seat theater, and an art school with classes for children and adults.

Fans of Beat Generation literature may be surprised to learn that Jack Kerouac lived in the Orlando suburb of College Park in the 1960s, where in 11 frenetic days he wrote *Dharma Bums*, his sequel to *On the Road*. A grassroots effort to save the old **Jack Kerouac House** ⓰ at 1418 Clouser Avenue began in 1997 after an article in the *Orlando Sentinel* by reporter Bob Kealing led to the formation of the nonprofit Kerouac Project. An annual Jack Kerouac Festival, featuring poetry readings, jazz concerts, and house tours, is held in April. Serious writers completing books written in the Kerouac style may be interested in applying for the writer-in-residence program, which offers a three-month, rent-free stay in the house.

BELOW: endangered manatees are found in captivity throughout Florida but live in the state's warm coves and estuaries along the coast.

Manatees

One of Florida's star attractions is the gentle, slow-moving manatee. Manatees browse on vegetation growing along the coast and are attracted to the warmth of crystalline springs along coastal Florida. In winter, you can spot them in the warm-water outflows of power plants such as Indian River Lagoon in Fort Pierce at the Manatee Observation and Education Center (561-466 1600) which teaches visitors about the struggles manatees face. Lowry Park Zoo in Tampa rehabilitates injured manatees, as does SeaWorld, which features the animals in "Manatee Rescue." You can also see manatees at the Living Seas pavilion at Epcot.

Natural resources

Florida's spectacular natural environment hasn't been left out of the equation. State initiatives like Florida 2000 and the Florida Forever campaign have been enthusiastically supported by Floridians. They are designed to preserve the state's critical habitats and are slowly paying off. Public-private partnerships, such as those forged among the state, The Nature Conservancy, and corporations like Disney, have led to the preservation of more than a million acres (400,000 hectares) of sensitive Florida wildlands.

Outdoor enthusiasts can hike and camp overnight in **Ocala National Forest** (3199 NE Highway 315, Silver Springs; tel: 352-236 0288) to the north. The St John's River is a great place to canoe. If you're more interested in going underwater than above it, snorkeling and swimming in crystal clear springs at nearby **Blue Spring State Park** (2100 W. French Avenue, Orange City; tel: 386-775 3663) and **Lower Wekiva River Preserve State Park** (1800 Wekiva Circle, Apopka; tel: 407-884 2008) are also popular. At the start of the paved **West Orange Trail**, you can hire bikes and rollerblades and cruise for 19 miles (30 km) around Lake Apopka to Winter Garden.

A reconstructed Cracker Cow Camp at **Lake Kissimmee State Park** (14248 Camp Mack Road, Lake Wales; tel: 863-696 1112) is one of the draws in the Lake Wales area. In east Orange County, you can learn about life during the Seminole Wars and visit a traditional Cracker house and reconstructed 1837 fort at 25-acre (10-hectare) **Fort Christmas Historical Park** (daily 8am–6pm, 1300 Fort Christmas Road, Orlando; tel: 407-568 4149).

Several Nature Conservancy preserves offer glimpses of wild Florida. Look for the real Florida mouse and endangered skinks that "swim" under the sand at 6,000-acre (2,430-hectare) **Tiger Creek Preserve** (daily dawn–dusk, 155 Pfundstein Road, Babson Park; tel: 863-635 7506) just past Lake Wales. A state-of-the-art visitor center, restored wetland trails, and

Map
on page
164

For more information on Florida state parks go to www. floridastateparks.org

BELOW: hiking among cypress trees in the Disney Wilderness.

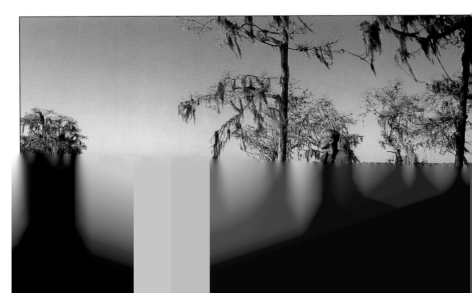

glimpses of white-tailed deer and extremely endangered Florida scrub jays are three excellent reasons to visit The Nature Conservancy's 12,000-acre (4,900-hectare) **Disney Wilderness** (2700 Scrub Jay Trail, Kissimmee; tel: 407-935 0002) – a nature refuge just minutes from Walt Disney World.

A complex history

Great museums abound. No visitor should miss the **Orange County Regional History Center** (Mon–Sat 10am–5pm, Sun noon–5pm, 65 E. Central Boulevard; tel: 407-836 8500; www.thehistory center.org), voted best museum by *Orlando* magazine in 2001. OCRHC now occupies the restored 1927 Orange County Courthouse in downtown's Heritage Square, the old Orlando town center. The museum features four floors of colorful exhibits covering central Florida's 12,000 years of history, from the state's first Indian residents to Spanish explorers and missionaries, British colonists, the Seminole Indian Wars, Cracker cowmen, citrus growers, tin can tourists, aerospace engineers, and Walt Disney. The area's little-known Indian cultures are particularly well interpreted, with dioramas showing an ancient shell midden, Timucuan chiefs in ceremonial attire, 3,000-year-old St John's pottery (probably the first to be made in North America), and contemporary Seminole culture, including a video of the Green Corn Ceremony held annually by the few hundred Seminoles still living in the Everglades.

A community museum in the best sense, OCRHC offers monthly socials and educational programs for people of all ages. Some of the best are for children. Camp-ins offer the opportunity to sleep overnight among the exhibits. Other school programs allow kids to perform mock trials of the Big Bad Wolf and other fairy tale characters in the original courtroom, where, less innocently, mass murderer Ted Bundy was tried and sentenced to death.

Life for African-Americans in the segregated Florida of the 1920s and

BELOW: a painting by Earl Cunningham at the Mennello Museum.

Map on page 164

1930s is explored at the 6,000-square-foot (560-sq-meter) **Wells' Built Museum of African American History and Culture**  (Mon–Fri 9am–5pm, 511 W. South Street, Suite 100; tel: 407-245 7535) in downtown Orlando.

The museum is housed in the historic Wells' Built Hotel, erected by a black doctor to provide lodging for black performers like Billie Holiday, who often performed in its casino and while touring the South on what was known as the Chitlin Circuit. Exhibits include a guest room with period furnishings from the 1930s, vintage photographs, slave records, and other artifacts including artworks by African-American artists.

Also devoted to African-American culture is the tiny **Zora Neale Hurston National Museum of Arts** ⑲ (daily 9am–4pm, 227 E. Kennedy Boulevard; tel: 407-647 3307) in nearby Eatonville, the first black township in the United States, established in 1887. Hurston, the noted Harlem Renaissance writer, anthropologist, and folklorist, was born in Eatonville in 1891. She celebrated rural Florida life in such books as *Their Eyes Were Watching God* and *Of Men and Mules*. Revolving exhibitions feature African-American art. Each January, Eatonville holds a festival in Hurston's honor, attracting such prominent artists as legendary Latino singer Celia Cruz.

Science and Shakespeare

Another must-see is the **Orlando Science Center** ⑳ (daily Tues– Thur 9am–5pm, Fri–Sat 9am– 9pm, Sun noon–5pm, 777 E. Princeton Street; tel: 407-514 2000; www.osc.org) in tree-shaded Loch Haven Park, a few miles north of downtown Orlando. Ten interactive exhibit halls cover everything from Florida's famous limestone sinkholes to its dinosaurs (courtesy of Disney World), an astronaut's life in zero gravity, and a journey through the human body. An eight-story CineDome shows giant-screen films, and daily sky shows are presented in the Planetarium, including one on Orlando's night sky, which can be viewed every Friday and Saturday evening through a giant telescope in the Crosby Observatory.

Soon after the Orange County Regional History Center *(see opposite)* vacated its building in nearby Loch Haven Park, it was refurbished and reopened as the **John and Rita Lowndes Shakespeare Center** (812 E. Rollins Street; tel: 407-447 1700), the fancy new home of Orlando's popular annual Orlando/UCF Shakespeare Festival. The Festival stages five major plays each season as well as PlayLab workshops and productions for children.

Also occupying the Lowndes Shakespeare Center is the **Orlando Philharmonic Orchestra** (407-896 6700), which performs regular concerts at the Bob Carr Arts Centre and other venues.

A robotic fly at the Orlando Science Center illustrates principles in computer science and electronics.

BELOW: visitors at the Orlando Science Center can explore prehistoric life.

A mural based loosely on Aztec art at the Maitland Art Center

Art and gardens

In the far opposite corner of Loch Haven Park is the **Orlando Museum of Art ㉑** (open Tues–Fri 10am–5pm, Sat–Sun noon–4pm, 2416 N. Mills Avenue; tel: 407-896 4231; www.omart.org), founded in 1924 and recently expanded. OMA's renovations now allow it to mount traveling exhibitions from major art museums like the Metropolitan in New York City. The Museum's own well-regarded collections include ancient artifacts from the American Southwest, Mexico, and Central and South America, works by 18th- to 20th-century American painters such as John Singer Sargent, Thomas Moran, Georgia O'Keeffe, and Robert Rauschenberg, and African art. Recent exhibitions have included Ancestors of the Inca, a collection of ancient jewelery, ceramics, and other artifacts from Peru, and the Holocaust Project's From Darkness Into Life, a gathering of works reflecting on the genocide and its aftermath. Call for a schedule of gallery talks and tours.

Across the street, in the former home of art patron Howard Phillips, is the **Mennello Museum of American Folk Art** (Tues–Sat 11am–5pm, Sun noon–5pm, 900 E. Princeton Street; tel: 407-246 4278; www.mennellomuseum.com), one of only a handful of American folk art museums. Much of the collection is devoted to the primitive paintings of Earl Cunningham, a self-taught artist and former sea captain whose long friendship with the Mennellos led to the founding of this museum.

Not far from Loch Haven is the **Harry P. Leu Gardens and Historic House ㉒** (daily 9am–5pm, 920 N. Forest Avenue; tel: 407-246 2620; www.leugardens.org), a former 19th-century cattle ranch where visitors can stroll 50 acres (20 hectares) of gardens displaying the most extensive collection of camellias and the largest formal rose garden in the South. A Tropical Stream Garden brims with exotic bromeliads, ferns, gingers, bananas, and flowering vines; a Palm Garden features not only palms from around the world but ancient cycads and 50 varieties of bamboo. Other highlights include an exquisite White Garden (a very popular spot for weddings) and herb and butterfly gardens. A boardwalk along the edge of Lake Rowena skirts an area of wetland and aquatic plants and is a convenient spot for spying waterbirds and the occasional alligator lazing on the shore. Special events here include evening concerts, flower shows and plant sales. Free 20-minute tours of the Leu house, built in 1888, are offered daily on the half hour. Now devoted to decorative arts, the house is beautifully appointed with Victorian, Chippendale, and other fine furnishings, and artworks collected by the property's last private owner,

wealthy Orlando-born business-man, Harry P. Leu.

In the small town of Clermont, east of Orlando, the **Lakeridge Winery and Vineyards** (Mon–Sat 10am–5pm, Sun 11am–5pm, 19239 US 27 North; tel: 352-394 8627) is the statesl largest winery and an award-winning one at that.

Free guided tours take you through their facilities and finish with wine tastings.

Small wonders

Central Florida culture benefited greatly from the wealthy Northern-ers who wintered and eventually retired here, following the arrival of the railroad in the 1880s. Exhibits about the railroad are on display in **Winter Park Historical Museum** (200 W. New England Avenue; tel: 407-647 8180) in downtown Winter Park.

Nearby, the **Charles Hosmer Morse Museum of American Art** ㉓ (Tues–Sat 9.30am–4pm, Sun 1pm–4pm, 445 Park Avenue North; tel: 407-645 5324; www. morsemuseum.org) features the world's most comprehensive col-lection of late-19th-century stained glass by Louis Comfort Tiffany. The centerpiece of the collection is the reconstructed Tiffany Chapel, designed for the 1893 World's Columbian Exposition in Chicago. The Museum was founded in 1942 by Jeannette Genius McKean and named for her industrialist grand-father, a Winter Park benefactor. The collections were assembled over 50 years by Mrs McKean and her husband Hugh McKean, Presi-dent of Rollins College in Winter Park, and include significant hold-ings of Arts and Crafts-style Rook-wood pottery.

The Museum recently moved from the college to an elegant new building near Central Park, where it presents a carol concert in December featuring Winter Park's renowned Bach Festival Choir. As a holiday treat, illuminated Tiffany windows are displayed in the park.

Though quite small, the **Cornell Museum of Fine Arts** ㉔ (closed for renovation until autumn 2005; tel: 407-646 2526 for more infor-

Map on page 164

The Charles Hosmer Morse Museum fea-tures an extensive collection of Tiffany stained glass.

BELOW: some 200 works are exhibited at the Albin Polasek Museum and Sculpture Garden.

mation; www.rollins.edu/cfam) on the gracious Mediterranean-style campus of Rollins College, is one of the finest and oldest art museums in the Southeast. Each year, the Cornell curates six to eight exhibitions drawn from its holdings of more than 6,000 European and American works of art. The collection encompasses paintings, drawings, and sculpture from the 1450s to the 1990s. At the start of the school year, one gallery is dedicated to exhibiting work by contemporary local artists.

Just down the road is the **Albin Polasek Museum and Sculpture Garden** ㉕ (Tues–Sat 10am–4pm, Sun 1pm–4pm Sept–June, 633 Osceola Avenue, Winter Park; tel: 407-647 6294; www.polasek.org). Listed in the National Register of Historic Places, the home of late Czech-American sculptor Albin Polasek is a peaceful 3-acre (1 hectare) retreat, with a studio, private chapel, gardens, and galleries. The collection of some 200 pieces are dominated by Polasek's works, many of them artfully displayed on the mani-

cured grounds. The museum also exhibits sculpture by American masters such as Augustus Saint-Gaudens.

Maitland museums

Tranquil grounds and art are also featured at the **Maitland Art Center** ㉖ (Mon–Fri 9am–4.30pm, Sat–Sun noon–4.30pm, 231 W. Packwood Avenue; tel: 407-539 2181; www.maitlandartcenter.org) in adjoining Maitland. This sprawling, 6-acre (2.5-hectare) art studio complex, on a quiet side street, was built in the 1930s by artist Jules Andre Smith. A formed concrete building decorated with an unusual Aztec-Maya frieze, it is considered one of the best surviving examples of fantasy architecture. Smith, a friend of Annie Russell, the New York actress who was professor of Theater Arts at Rollins College, moved to Maitland in the early 1930s, and designed sets for productions at the quaint Annie Russell Theater. In 1937, a donation from the wife of Edward Bok, the Dutch-born former editor of *Ladies' Home Jour-*

BELOW:
Below the Dam, 1916–19, by the American Impressionist Maurice Pendergast, at the Orlando Museum of Art.

nal, allowed Smith to build a "laboratory studio to be devoted to research in modern art." Now managed by the Maitland Historical Society, the little museum's galleries and grounds (reputed to be haunted by Smith's ghost) still retain an aging charm. Changing exhibitions are devoted to art representing many different ethnic traditions within the community.

The Maitland Historical Society also runs the charming **Telephone Museum** (Thur–Sun noon–4pm, 221 W. Packwood Avenue; tel: 407-644 1364) next door, which has a large collection of historic telephones and a working switch station, and staffs the late-19th-century **Historic Waterhouse Residence and Waterhouse Carpentry Shop** (Thur–Sun noon–4pm, 820 Lake Lily Drive, Maitland; tel: 407-644 2451), the home and woodworking shop of Maitland pioneer William H. Waterhouse.

Inadequate signposting can make some Maitland attractions hard to find. This is particularly true of the **Florida Audubon Society's Birds of Prey Center** ㉗ (Tues–Sun 10am–4pm, 1101 Audubon Way; tel: 407-644 0190; www.audubonofflorida.org), which is hidden in a residential area near Lake Sibelia. But don't let this dissuade you. The recently refurbished raptor rescue center offers an unforgettable experience. Audubon takes in about 600 injured birds a year and releases 40 percent of them. You won't see recuperating birds here – they are isolated to improve their odds of survival in the wild – but you will see members of some 32 raptor species whose injuries are so extensive they must remain in captivity. Ospreys, tiny screech owls, vultures, bald eagles, red-tailed hawks, kites, and other birds of prey live in aviaries and many have learned to do tricks. Daisy the barn owl does the polka, and Elvis the American kestrel wears blue suede shoes. A camera is set up in an eagle's nest so you can spy on an aerie. A program also allows you to adopt a particular bird (they all have names) to help the center with

Map on page 164

LEFT:
Bok Tower Gardens
BELOW:
a student examines
work by Tiffany at
the Charles Hosmer
Morse Museum.

its work. Guided tours for groups of 10 or more are available by reservation.

A more somber experience awaits visitors at the small **Holocaust Memorial Resource and Education Center of Central Florida** (Mon–Thur 9am–4pm, Fri 9am–1pm, Sun 1pm–4pm, 851 N. Maitland Avenue; tel: 407-628 0555). One room chronicles the History of the Holocaust with multimedia displays. Another room offers changing exhibits on aspects of the Nazi campaign to exterminate Jews, homosexuals, gypsies, and other minorities. A library holds 4,000 volumes dedicated exclusively to Holocaust history. Special events include a Kristallnacht Commemoration in November.

Around Lake Wales

Winter Park is the northern anchor of Orlando's cultural corridor; Lake Wales, 100 miles (160 km) to the south, forms the southern anchor, with both areas linked by railroad. **The Lake Wales Museum and Cultural Center** (Mon–Fri 9am–5pm, Sat 10am–4pm, 325 S. Scenic Highway; tel: 863-678 4209) in the railroad depot displays vintage railcars, photographs, antiques, and exhibits about the area's turpentine, lumbering, cattle ranching, railroading, and citrus industries.

The entire downtown region of Lake Wales is in the National Register of Historic Places. Another historic landmark is the delightfully quirky **Chalet Suzanne** (3800 Chalet Suzanne Drive, Lake Wales; tel: 800-433 6011; www.chaletsuzanne.com), a 30-room lakeside inn, renowned for its award-winning rich European dining and unique guest rooms. Although the orange groves that once surrounded it are giving way to housing developments, Chalet Suzanne retains its old-fashioned storybook charm, with dark woods, lace, antiques, and a warren of low-ceilinged rooms, each at a different level. The inn has catered to wealthy winter visitors since 1931, when founder Bertha Hinshaw began serving travelers in her home. One of her best customers was food maven Duncan Hines, whose raves drew many friends to this lovely area of hills, lakes, and unspoiled natural habitat.

Hines and Mr and Mrs Edward Bok, among others, created the exclusive Mountain Lake enclave designed by celebrated landscape architect Frederick Law Olmsted, Jr. In 1922, Edward Bok engaged Olmsted to design a retreat "of natural beauty, a refuge for the bird, a place for the student of southern plant and bird life" at adjoining 298-foot-high (91-meter) Iron Mountain.

Originally named Mountain Lake Sanctuary, the 200-acre (80-hectare) **Bok Tower Gardens** (daily 8am–5pm, 1151 Tower Boulevard, Lake Wales; tel: 863-676 1408; www.boktower.org) were opened by President Calvin Coolidge in 1929. These serene gardens have strong

European echoes, with the grounds laid out as a series of horticultural rooms linked by paths winding through azalea and camellia gardens, a magnificent grove of Spanish moss-draped live oaks, and other Southern plantings.

At the center is the famous Singing Tower, a 209-foot-high (64-meter) Arts and Crafts-style bell tower visible from miles away. Made of native Georgia sandstone and St Augustine coquina, the historic bell tower rises above a tranquil swan lake and houses one of only a few carillons in the United States. Recitals are given daily. Bok Tower Gardens is renowned nationally for its work to save endangered Florida plants. It propagates endemic plants like the Florida ziziphus and provides education through exhibits at the visitor center and Pine Ridge Nature Preserve, a typical Lake Wales sandhill community of longleaf pine, turkey oak, blazing star and other plants kept healthy through controlled burns. Hurricane damage in 2004 forced the sanctuary to close temporarily.

Kissimmee culture

If all of the offerings at Bok Tower have whetted your appetite for rare plants, don't miss **A World of Orchids** (Tues–Sun 9.30am–4.30pm, 2501 Old Lake Wilson Road, Kissimmee; free; tel: 407-396 1887). A thousand orchids, as well as ferns and tropical trees, including 64 varieties of palm and 21 varieties of bamboo, thrive in the steamy atmosphere of an expansive conservatory at this working nursery, which also features streams, waterfalls, koi ponds, and a small aviary.

Outside there is a 1,000-foot-long (300-meter) nature walk in a wooded area. For those with a particular interest in orchids, tours by knowledgeable guides are offered every Wednesday; call for reservations.

Warbirds and eco-cowboys

Florida was a popular training ground for US Army Air Corps pilots during World War II. One of those bases was located at Kissimmee Airport, which today houses **Flying Tigers Warbird Air Museum ㉛** (daily 9am– 6pm, 231 North Hoagland

Map on page 164

LEFT:
Harry P. Leu Gardens.

Orlando Cuisine

Viewed for years as a culinary wasteland, Orlando has come a long way toward pleasing discriminating palates. Disney led the way with its California Kitchen and $200-per-couple, six-course meals served by maids and butlers at Victoria and Albert's, the centerpiece of the Grand Floridian Hotel. But Disney is by no means the only game in town. Manuel's on 28th, Harry's Bistro, and the Boheme Restaurant feature superb dining in downtown Orlando, just to name a few.

Of particular note is the emergence of Floribbean cuisine, which draws inspiration from the state's Spanish, African, and Caribbean heritage. Fresh grouper, red snapper, conch, and other Florida seafood as well as local beef, chicken, and even alligator, are given a kick by Caribbean pepper marinades and tropical fruit salsas, and accompanied, often as not, by grits and greens, and other Southern staples. Cuban food also has a strong following. The Columbia Restaurant in Tampa's renovated Ybor City (and a satellite in Celebration) features fish with pepper-and-tomato sauces, paella, black beans, and a shredded-beef dish called *ropa vieja* (old clothes), all of it washed down with a mojito, Ernest Hemingway's favorite rum drink.

Map on page 164

Special events at Leu Gardens include a summer concert series featuring the Orlando Philharmonic Orchestra.

BELOW:
vintage aircraft are on display at the Flying Tiger Warbird Museum.

Boulevard; tel: 407-933 1942; www. warbirdmuseum. com), a combination air museum and restoration facility for old war planes (nicknamed Bombertown USA). Tom Reilly and his wife Sue have dedicated their lives to restoring historic fighters. Most are owned by private collectors, but you'll find a permanent display of 30 vintage planes, ranging from a 1909 wood-and-canvas pusher (so named because the engine sits behind the pilot and pushes the plane through the air) to an A4 Skyhawk (made famous in the movie *Top Gun*). Stroll around the hangar or, better yet, take a half-hour tour. Guides are full of fascinating facts and passion for old planes. Seriously intrigued? Consider a week-long vintage aircraft restoration course (about $1,000), culminating in a spin over Kissimmee in a B-25.

For a walk on the wild side, head to **Forever Florida and Crescent J Ranch ㉜** (daily 9am–5pm, 4755 N. Kenansville Road, St Cloud; tel: 407-957 9794). This 4,700-acre (1,900-hectare) nature preserve and working cattle ranch is about 24 miles (39 km)

east of Kissimmee and makes a great day out for the whole family. You can walk, ride a trail bike, or take a guided horseback tour (reservations required) along the extensive trail system to visit nine different Florida ecosystems. Most popular are mule-drawn covered wagon rides and the preserve's unique 10-foot-high (3-meter) open-air cracker coaches, which depart regularly from the visitor center. You'll avoid the afternoon heat and see more wildlife if you take a tour at dusk. White-tailed deer, wild turkeys, gopher tortoises and even elusive Florida panthers roam this preserve. Local guides really know their stuff and offer fascinating ecological information.

Forever Florida was begun by rancher and opthalmologist Dr Bill Broussard in honor of his late son Allen, a well-known Florida ecologist. A country restaurant serves cracker favorites like fried gator tail and catfish, biscuits, gravy, and grits. Special events and programs include sleepovers for kids, with a nighttime hike in search of nocturnal creatures. ❏

RESTAURANTS

Downtown Orlando

Boheme Restaurant
Grand Bohemian Hotel
325 S. Orange Avenue
Tel: 407-313 9000
www.grandbohemianhotel.com
A sumptuous art-filled dining room sets the stage for a selection of sophisticated Continental dishes complemented with an extensive choice of wines. The menu changes often, but past highlights include jumbo peeky toe crab cake, asparagus-crusted scallops, and pepper-seared Angus carpaccio. Soups and salads are equally delectable. The cognac lobster bisque is particularly satisfying. Breakfast, including a Sunday jazz brunch, is not to be missed. **$$$$**

Harvey's Bistro
390 N Orlando Avenue
Tel: 407-246 6560
www.harveysbistro.com
A little European style goes a long way at this welcoming bistro popular with business lunchers and nighttime revelers. Even pot roast and meatloaf are something special, not to mention more ambitious choices such as seared calf liver, crab cakes, roasted duck, and a variety of nicely-done pasta dishes. **$$$**

Maison et Jardin
430 Wymore Road South,
Altamonte Springs

Tel: 407-862 4410
www.maisonjardin.com
Three uniquely designed dining rooms. One recreates a Mediterranean chateau overlooking a tiered fountain. The restaurant also displays many museum quality pieces including Oriental rugs, Austrian crystal, and antique mirrors in frames taken from a 17th century Venetian palazzo. The menu features equally classic European cuisine plus an extensivve wine service. **$$$**

Manuel's on the 28th
390 N Orange Avenue
Orlando
Tel: 407-246 6580
www.manuelsonthe28th.com
Stunning views accompany your meal at this elegant restaurant on the 28th floor of the Bank of America building. Artfully presented entrées include asparagus-speared ahi tuna, phyllo-wrapped lamb loin with mint pesto, peppercorn filet mignon with smoked gouda potatoes, and more. **$$$**

Lake Wales

Chalet Suzanne Restaurant and Inn
3800 Chalet Suzanne Drive
Tel: 863-676 6011 or
800-433 6011
www.chaletsuzanne.com

Consistently voted one of Florida's best restaurants, the romantic dining room overlooking tiny Lake Suzanne offers full country breakfasts featuring the inn's famous Swedish pancakes and lingonberries. Six-course candelit dinners with classic entrees like king crab Thermidor, chicken Suzanne, filet mignon, lamb chop grille, and the inn's world-famous cream soups, canned on the premises – a favorite of astronauts, film stars and other celebrities. **$$$$**

Winter Park

Bubbalou's Bodacious Bar-B-Q
1471 Lee Road
Tel: 407-423 1212 or

(866) BUBBALOUS
www.bubbalous.com
Small, award-winning, Southern-style barbecue spot with very casual atmosphere and first-rate ribs. **$**

Park Plaza Gardens
319 S Park Avenue
Tel: 407-645 2475
www.parkplazagardens.com
Elegant garden courtyard restaurant. Sunday brunch is a highlight. Fine selection of dinner entrees. **$$$**

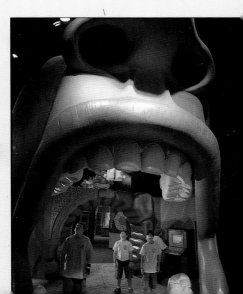

RIGHT: you are what you eat...

BUSCH GARDENS

Wildlife abounds at this zoological park in Tampa,
featuring wide-open savanna, a simulated safari,
and three of the wildest roller coasters in Florida

Africa is the overall theme here. The park's 335 acres (136 hectares) are laid out in 10 distinct areas – Morocco, Crown Colony, Edge of Africa, Serengeti Plain, Egypt, Nairobi, Timbuktu, Congo, Stanleyville, and Bird Gardens. Three of its five roller coasters – Montu, Kumba, and Gwazi – are musts for thrill-ride aficionados, with state-of-the-art features such as gravity-defying inversions, barrel rolls, and intertwining tracks. Busch Gardens' water rides (and those at its adjoining water park, Adventure Island) are guaranteed to soak you to the skin. And the innovative Rhino Rally leaves Disney's Animal Kingdom safari ride in the dust – literally – as it turns a rally car race across a corner of the Serengeti Plain into a swept-down-the-river adventure alongside real African animals.

Zoo-topia

All of this hoopla does nothing to obscure one basic fact: Busch Gardens is, quite simply, one of the nation's top zoos. Low-key but persistent messages about wildlife conservation can be found throughout the park. Educational programs, such as Summer Adventure Camps focusing on animal care and zoo careers, are available for participants age 10 and up. Schools working to restore

wildlife habitat in their backyards are recognized with annual awards. Busch Gardens (and its sister SeaWorld parks) has built the world's largest Internet Animal Information Database (www.buschgardens.org). Captive breeding takes place at the park under the Species Survival Program. And through its partnership with 14 conservation organizations, Busch Gardens funds and carries out research on gorillas, koalas, orangutans, pandas, and other animals on four continents.

Map on page 194

LEFT: Python tears through a barrel roll.
BELOW: Aviary Walk-Thru.

The park places its highest emphasis on quality visitor/wildlife interactions. More than 2,700 animals live in large, naturalized environments that consistently win industry awards for their authenticity. In the walk-through Edge of Africa exhibit, for example, lions climb over an abandoned Land Rover embedded in mud-colored concrete while you watch from the driver's seat behind a glass partition. Rare white tigers occupy the large Claw Island in Congo, protected by fine nets and a moat, but remain easily visible to visitors from an overhead walkway. Throughout the day, the park's conservation rangers (most with wildlife biology degrees and field research experience) offer animal shows, sporadic enrichment exercises timed to coincide with feeding, grooming, and caring for some of the 320 species that call the park home. And then, of course, there are the popular Serengeti Safaris, well worth the extra fee for an opportunity to interact with wild animals out in the open.

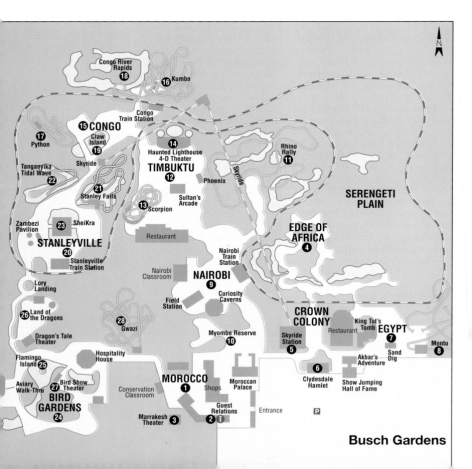

Busch Gardens

Plan of attack

The good news is that Busch Gardens is only 90 minutes west of Orlando and easily reached via I-4. The bad news is that it is a large park, crammed with too many must-see exhibits and rides. It is pretty much impossible to do everything in one day. A two-day visit is ideal, perhaps one for the animals, the other for rides. Two-day passes are a good deal, as are the discounted next-day passes sold at the exit.

Lines to enter the park at opening time are long, but with 5,000 parking places and an efficient tram system that deposits you right at the entrance, this is about the most time-consuming part of a visitor's day. Once inside, walking around the park is pleasant, with themed areas linked by pathways shaded by tropical plants and trees, and plenty of benches and food vendors in between. Wear comfortable shoes and take frequent breaks. Busch Gardens is a huge place with few shortcuts from one section of the park to another, so you'll be on your feet for the better part of the day.

Doing the rides at Busch Gardens will be a pleasant surprise for anyone used to the long lines at Disney World: typical loading times here are less than half those of Orlando theme parks, 45 minutes at most. Even with all the animal attractions, the rides are the main draw for many family members, so you may not get any peace until you've ridden the most popular ones. If that's the case, the best strategy is to knock off a few rides first thing in the morning and use the restful animal exhibits for downtime in between.

If you're in line and willing to return later, you may be able to receive a ride pass that will get you to the head of the line later on. Ask staff at the ride in question. If there are just two of you, another strategy to get on quicker is to hold up a couple of fingers and be willing to share a ride with another party.

If seeing wildlife is your priority, be sure to get to the park early. Animals from hot countries are more active in the cooler mornings. Later on, they tend to hide themselves behind bushes and snooze the afternoon away – a problem in a park where enclosures are large and so natural that it can be hard to see the animals. Serious wildlife watchers may want to bring binoculars.

Morocco

The park entrance is through **Morocco ❶**, which takes as its theme an Arabian bazaar. Before entering, consider whether you want to pay the hefty extra charge to have your own special guided tour of the park. Half-day and whole-day tours can be booked in the building on the right, which also has an ATM machine (there are others throughout the park). Once through the turnstiles, you'll find **Guest Relations ❷** on your left, and **Lost and Found** in the right-hand corner. Spend a few minutes getting oriented and checking that

Map on page 194

The park offers several guided tours, with a behind-the-scenes look at the wildlife exhibits, animal interactions, and priority access to some of the hottest rides. Call 813-984 4043 for information.

BELOW: an animal ambassador introduces park visitors to a koala.

you have everything for your visit: hat, sunscreen, layered clothing, bottled water, etc.

Strollers and wheelchairs can be rented next to **Sultan's Sweets**, a good place to tank up on coffee and pastries. Across the way is **Zagora's Café**, one of five restaurants in the park offering more substantial fare.

Pick up a free map and entertainment guide, which lists the times and locations of animal shows and stage events. Many visitors find that sitting down and taking in one of these offerings is a welcome respite from walking around in the hot sun and standing in line for popular rides.

You may be serenaded by a steel band called **Rhythms and Steel**, playing at various times in Stanleyville, Congo, and Crown Colony; **Men of Note**, an a cappella singing group that strolls around Morocco and Crown Colony; or **Mystic Sheiks of Morocco**, a world-renowned marching band that puts you immediately in mind of the last days of 19th-century imperialism, performing choreographed standards in Morocco, Stanleyville, and Timbuktu.

Most stage shows get going around noon. If you pick only one, try **KATONGA**, a musical celebration of animal folklore. More hokey is **Moroccan Roll**, a Moroccan-themed song-and-dance show featuring hits like *Rock the Casbah* (quite unrecognizable as a punk Clash hit here), presented in the **Marrakesh Theater ❸**, to the left of the entrance past Guest Relations and a clutch of shops.

Edge of Africa

Visitors wishing to do one of the five daily Serengeti Safaris should head immediately to **Crown Colony** on arrival and sign up for a tour in the Edge of Africa Store, one of several shops in the park selling attractive, reasonably-priced safari-style clothing and African souvenirs. The limit per safari is 20 people, and the first-come, first-served places fill quickly.

If Serengeti Safari is sold out or you would rather not pay the extra fee, the next-best thing is a walk through **Edge of Africa ❹** just across the railroad tracks. It features nose-to-nose encounters with baboons, Nile crocodiles, hippos, a lion and lioness, hyenas, vultures, and meerkats in enclosures designed to get you right next to the animals. Hidden behind hedgerows, it's easy to miss.

As you enter the exhibit, stop at the wildlife education table on the left. Staff members here will answer animal questions and give you free copies of *Ranger Rick* magazine and Jack Hanna's *Wildlife Guide*, an informative foldout brochure that mimics a safari journal. Based on the television show *Jack Hanna's Animal Adventures*, which is taped on a random schedule in the Bird Gardens, this pamphlet enhances a visit to Edge of Africa by sharing fun facts and turning wildlife-watching into a game of skill and observation.

Clearly-posted signs guide visitors around the park.

BELOW: the Mystic Sheiks of Morocco march through Zagora's Café.

Everything in Edge of Africa rewards observation. Tents contain hands-on exhibits such as bones and skins. Animal tracks in the concrete pathways teach wildlife identification. Underwater aquarium-style views of tropical fish in the hippo pond (some of the most entrancing in the park) communicate how much more graceful hippos are in water than on land.

Abandoned Land Rovers are all open for exploration and have special brass plaques with wildlife conservation messages that can be rubbed into the wildlife guide. Animal Ambassadors with snakes and birds and other wildlife wander around and talk about their charges. All in all, time spent here is relaxing and educational.

Crown Colony

Return to Crown Colony the way you came, stopping perhaps at the **Skyride Station ❺**, a four-person aerial tram that affords sweeping views of the Serengeti Plain and the big coasters. The trip takes about 4 minutes and leaves you at Congo.

Unfortunately, there are no round-trips without exiting and reboarding.

Across the path is the **Crown Colony House Restaurant**, the only eatery with table service and, with grandstand views of the Serengeti Plain, the most pleasant place for a meal. Expect a wait during the busy season. Disappointingly, there are no African restaurants at Busch Gardens (nor any real effort to extend the African theme to highlight the human cultures of the continent).

Horse lovers will appreciate the **Clydesdale Hamlet ❻**, just across the plaza, where the magnificent dray horses of the kind that pulled beer carts for Anheuser-Busch in the 1800s are stabled. **The Show Jumping Hall of Fame**, next door, is mostly of interest to equestrians.

Egypt

Just a short walk away, in an area of the park called **Egypt ❼**, is the most popular of Busch Gardens' big-deal roller coasters. Named for an Egyptian god, **Montu ❽** is one of the tallest and longest inverted coasters in the world. It is clearly visible as

Map on page 194

There are free lockers in Egypt, Morocco, Timbuktu, Congo, or Stanleyville if you'd like to store any items.

BELOW: feeding giraffes on the Serengeti Safari.

TIP

Height requirements
are 54 inches (137 cm)
for Kumba and Montu,
48 inches (122 cm) for
Gwazi, Python, Phoenix,
and Tanganyika Tidal
Wave, 46 inches (117
cm) for Stanley Falls; 42
inches (107 cm) for
Congo River Rapids,
Akbar, and Scorpion,
and 39 inches (99cm)
for Rhino Rally.

BELOW:
hieroglyphics adorn
the highly-stylized
entrance to Montu.

you enter the park and beckons right
away to ride fans, who are strapped
into open-air, pedestal-like seats
secured only by shoulder restraints.
Feet dangling in the air, passengers
are thrown around 360-degree, stom-
ach-churning loops at a top speed of
more than 60 miles per hour (96
kph), creating a g-force of 3.85. This
monster is not for the uninitiated. Old
hands will scream for more.

There are two other attractions in
Egypt, neither very compelling.
Open seasonally, **Akbar's Adventure**, the park's only simulator ride,
takes you on a madcap Egyptian
adventure with comedian Martin
Short. **King Tut's Tomb**, reproduced
exactly as explorer Howard Carter
found it, is probably the park's least
interesting attraction. Better to spend
some time with the kids unearthing
fake antiquities in the **Sand Dig** in
the shadow of the Sphinx.

Nairobi

From Egypt, backtrack through
Crown Colony to a fountain near the
entrance to **Nairobi** ❾, pausing for
a few minutes to view the nearby

Florida alligators, for once not
required to wrestle with humans or
perform circus tricks for tourists.

To one side of the alligators is the
entrance to the **Myombe Reserve**
❿, the park's award-winning 3-acre
(1.2-hectare) great apes exhibit.
Even if you're not here for the zoo,
on no account should you miss
Myombe. The warm, steamy environment of the African jungle is lovingly re-created with lush plantings,
waterfalls and strategically-placed
misters. A tranquil, meandering
pathway draws you deeper into the
exhibit past chimpanzees and sil-
verback gorillas that are, quite simply, thrilling to see close up. Visitors
can observe the great apes eating
fruit and leaves, grooming one
another, hanging from branches, and
mugging for cameras on the other
side of a glass partition. Closed-cir-
cuit cameras show gorillas wandering through deep undergrowth in the
back of the enclosure – very *Gorillas in the Mist*. A video and beauti-
fully-rendered interpretive signs
explain ape behavior and character-
istics. An explorer's area displays
casts of gorilla footprints and other
exhibits, as well as data from Busch
Gardens' ongoing research on lowland gorillas in the Congo.

Nairobi also contains reptile,
tortoise, and elephant displays.
Curiosity Caverns is your typical
reptile room, but also includes a por-
cupine and lemurs. **Field Station**
gives you a chance to get a closer
look at animals such as llamas,
macaws, and pot-bellied pig. Try to
time your visit to watch the elephants being bathed by their keep-
ers – the high point of the day for
creatures that seem sadly at loose
ends compared with their free-ranging buddies on the Serengeti Plain.

For still more wildlife watching,
hop aboard the **Serengeti Express**,
a miniature train done up like a colo-
nial-era locomotive. The train puffs

Map on page 194

slowly around the edge of the Serengeti Plain, making this your best bet for viewing impala, eland, zebra, and other animals outside of a Serengeti Safari tour. Cape buffalo and camels come into sight as you approach Congo, and you'll see orangutans climbing over a giant play set near Stanleyville. The entire journey takes about 30 minutes, with stops at the Nairobi, Stanleyville, and Congo train stations. Seats on the left-hand side of the train offer the best views.

Rhino Rally

The ride is a heck of a lot bumpier on **Rhino Rally** ⓫, a short walk from the Nairobi train station. This 10-minute, off-road safari experience combines the controlled adventure of a thrill ride with the bonus of real wild animals. It's the closest to an actual four-wheel-drive safari some people will ever experience.

Each of the 17-passenger Land-Rovers (all following a ride track) is participating in a race across Africa and encounters washed-out roads, mud slides, collapsing bridges, and dangerous wild animals. One passenger is commandeered as map reader (and will receive mock derision when the car gets lost and things go awry). Volunteer for this position, if you can. It's the best seat in the vehicle.

The ride starts out as a slip-and-slide, off-road drive past rare white rhinos and other African animals, pointed out by the driver. The adventure gets crazy when a shaky pontoon bridge collapses, plunging the Land-Rover into a raging, crocodile-infested river. The vehicle is buffeted from bank to bank and passes under a waterfall (window seats will get wet). Eventually, the panicked driver is able to pull the truck up a steep bank and finish the race. Some drivers work hard to get passengers into the spirit of the ride;

others project a rather ho-hum, "it's just a job" attitude. In either case, don't miss it.

Timbuktu

Exit Rhino Rally, stay to the right of the elephants, and pass through the dramatic arched gateway to **Timbuktu** ⓬, modeled after the ancient African trading center, although this version is devoted mostly to rides. **Scorpion** ⓭, one of the park's smaller coasters, is perfect for those who don't meet the height restrictions or have the stomach for the big guns. But don't mistake it for a kiddie coaster. With a 60-foot (18-meter) drop, a 360-degree loop, three 360-degree corkscrews and a top speed of 50 miles per hour (80 kph), it's plenty frightening in its own right.

Other attractions in Timbuktu are jazzed-up versions of traditional amusement-park rides, though the **Phoenix**, a pirate ship that swings around in a complete circle, is more than a little unnerving. A carousel, several kiddie rides, and midway games will keep

BELOW: children love to climb on the bronze gorilla and other statues at Myombe reserve.

BELOW: a tender
moment between the
tigers of
Claw Island.

young children occupied while
older siblings take on something a
bit more challenging.

**R. L. Stine's Haunted Light-
house** is shown in the Haunted
Lighthouse 4–D Theater. Considering it's the most recently-opened 3-
D plus special effects show in
Florida, it's disappointingly hokey
and will only hold the attention of
the youngest. At the opposite end of
Timbuktu is the cavernous, 1,000-
seat **Desert Grill Restaurant**,
designed (somewhat incongruously)
after a German beer hall. The menu
features corned beef and turkey
sandwiches, baby back ribs, and a
few Italian dishes, all served with
tall glasses of – what else? –
Anheuser-Busch beer. More puz-
zlingly is the live show featured here
– **Irish Thunder**, a shortened take
on the *Riverdance* theme. Exactly
how all this ties into the African
theme is as much your guess as ours.

Congo

The next area, **Congo** ⓯, is dominated by a trio of popular rides.
Kumba ⓰, a steel roller coaster in

the same league as Montu, is the
biggest of the three. After an initial
135-foot (40-meter) drop, riders
plunge 110 feet (34 meters) into a
diving loop, experience a full 3
seconds of weightlessness while
spiraling 360 degrees, and tear
through one of the world's largest
vertical inversions.

Python ⓱, a much smaller
coaster, seems like a cakewalk in
comparison, though it may feel quite
different when you're ripping through
two vertical loops at speeds in excess
of 40 miles per hour (64 kph).

Situated between the coasters is
Congo River Rapids ⓲. For many
visitors this is the water ride of
choice, offering a free-floating,
bumper-car experience, with passengers seated in a large round raft
and buffeted from side to side as
they bounce over waves and under
waterfalls. A rain poncho may help
keep you dry, but don't count on it.
Short of wearing a wetsuit, there's
not much you can do to avoid a
good soaking.

The animal stars of Congo are
rare white tigers on **Claw Island** ⓳.
These are denizens of India, not
Africa, but why nitpick? Three big
cats – one orange-striped, one all
white, and one black-and-white-
striped – lie on their backs, paws in
the air, in their huge enclosure,
sleeping the afternoon away as cameras click. Get here in the morning
and you may catch them at feeding
time – a bloodcurdling sight.

Congo also has bumper cars and
a few kiddie rides, perfect for
entertaining young children while
the big kids are occupied elsewhere. **Vivi Restaurant** has sandwiches, chicken fajitas, salads, and
a variety of dessert treats.

Stanleyville

The pathway to **Stanleyville** ⓴, the
next area in the circuit, is flanked by
two more water rides. To the left is

Stanley Falls ㉑, a fairly standard water flume. This is one of those slow-build affairs, where passengers sit in a four-passenger hollowed-out log that inches along, makes a few bumpy drops and turns, then does a final bobsled-like freefall into the pond below.

The real soaker, however, is **Tanganyika Tidal Wave** ㉒, a devilish piece of engineering that starts out as a tranquil jungle cruise and ends with a sudden plunge down a 55-foot (17-meter) chute, creating a tidal wave that gets everyone sopping wet. Gluttons for punishment can stand on the walkway at the end of the ride for a second drenching.

Stanleyville is also home to Florida's newest and perhaps scariest rollercoaster – **SheiKra** ㉓. It is North America's only diving rollercoaster. This means that after your initial ascent you are dropped down at 90 degrees and over 70mph (110kph) before encountering a climbing carousel, an underground tunnel and a splash down into an artificial lake.

Bird Gardens

Bird Gardens ㉔ is the most restful area of Busch Gardens, with many photo opportunities amid tropical plants and exotic birds. A rather incongruous koala exhibit is situated in a corner of the gardens, featuring koalas, kangaroos, and other Australian animals that sometimes come out for curtain calls with TV host Jack Hanna. Set in the middle of a large lake, **Flamingo Island** ㉕ hosts flocks of eye-popping flamingos, as well as herons, egrets, and other visiting Florida waterfowl (how nice it would be if Florida wildlife was interpreted as well as the African wildlife at this park). Elegant roseate spoonbills can be seen in the **Aviary Walk-Thru** as well as **Lory Landing**, an aviary tricked out as a shipwreck site and home to lorikeets, halfway between a parakeet, and a parrot. The birds flutter around, landing on hands, heads and shoulders, and investigating bags.

Sheltered from most of the traffic is **Land of the Dragons** ㉖, a children's play area with a pint-size Ferris wheel and water flume. Near the

Taking the plunge at Stanley Falls.

Map on page 194

BELOW: a tower rises above the entrance to Timbuktu.

Map on page 194

Try out the climbing wall near Gwazi.

entrance are real-life dragons, actually large lizards. On display in these cages are rhinoceros, iguanas, and Komodo dragons, the latter known for an unnerving habit of killing and summarily disposing of humans in their native Indonesia.

Bird shows highlighting raptors and parrots frequently take place in the **Bird Show Theater ㉗**, adjacent to Flamingo Island. Some of the scripting is a bit silly, but no amount of hokum can ruin the magnificence of a bald eagle in flight, the paintbox plumage of a parrot, or the genuine rapport between the birds and their well-trained handlers.

Just across the plaza is the **Hospitality House** and **Budweiser Beer School**, where you can sample free beer (restricted to guests over 21), order up a pizza or sandwich, and enjoy a grownup mix of jazz and ragtime at an open-air stage.

There's only one major ride in this area, but it's a doozy. **Gwazi ㉘** is an old-fashioned wooden roller coaster that, in the opinion of some enthusiasts, is even more thrilling than the modern variety, due partly

to the fact that wood shakes much more than steel; the noise alone is deafening. This is one of the largest and fastest wooden coasters in the Southeast, boasting more than 1.25 million board feet of lumber and 2 million bolted connections (that makes you feel safer, doesn't it?).

Named after a fabled lion with a tiger's head, Gwazi actually has two separate but intertwining tracks. Riders have their choice: **Gwazi Tiger** that gives riders a slalom sensation, more like a bobsled; **Gwazi Lion** features a stomach-turning series of spirals. The coasters rocket passengers over nearly 7,000 feet (2,130 meters) of track and six flyby maneuvers in which trains pass within feet of each other at crossing speeds of 100 miles per hour (160 kph).

Lines for Gwazi tend to be quite long. Your best bet is to ride first thing in the morning or in late evening – or both. The experience takes on a new dimension after dark.

Next to Gwazi is the **Family Water Game** featuring water balloons, a trampoline, a climbing wall and several midway-style games. ❑

RESTAURANTS

St Pete Beach

Crabby Bill's Seafood Restaurant
5100 Gulf Boulevard
Tel: 727-360 8858
www.crabbybills.com
Very popular, casual restaurant known for its crab dishes, of course, and seafood. No reservations possible so there are often long lines. **$$**

Hurricane
807 Gulf Way
Tel: 727-360 9558
One of the most durably popular restaurants on

the Gulf Coast, with multiple bars, great seafood and sunset views. **$–$$**

Leverock's on the Beach
10 Corey Avenue,
Tel: 727-367 4588
www.leverocks.com
Inexpensive but very good seafood specialties. **$$**

Tampa

Columbia Restaurant
2117 E 7th Avenue
Tel: 813-248 4961
www.columbiarestaurant.com
Founded in 1905 as a corner café by Cuban

immigrant Casimiro Hernandez, Sr., the block-long Columbia Restaurant is the oldest restaurant in Florida and the largest Spanish restaurant in the world. A perennial award winner for its Iberian meat and seafood cuisine as well as its extensive wine list. **$$$**

Crawdaddy's
2500 Rocky Point Drive
Tel: 813-281 0407
A funky hangout much favored by locals that serves up fried alligator and all sorts of other regional delicacies. **$$$**

Donatello
232 N Dale Mabry Highway
Tel: 813-875 6660
The quiet atmosphere, attentive staff, and northern Italian food make for a fine meal. You can choose from linguine to lobster or veal. **$$–$$$**

Shula's Steak House
4860 W Kennedy Boulevard
Tel: 813-286 4366
www.donshula.com
Named for a well-known former football coach, and themed with football memorabilia, Shula's serves a predictable but tasty diet of steaks and more steaks. **$$–$$$**

Tampa

Tampa Bay is named for the 398-square-mile (1,030-sq-km) body of water that constitutes Florida's largest open-water estuary. Here, several rivers empty into the turquoise waters of the Gulf of Mexico. Thirty-five miles (56 km) of white-sand beaches lie along some 20 barrier islands, linked by majestic bridges. It is a stunning natural area – home to endangered nesting sea turtles, dolphins, manatees, and dozens of bird and fish species.

Overlooking Tampa Bay is the Florida Aquarium (tel: 813-273 4000), home to about 5,000 aquatic creatures, including sandbar sharks, stingrays, and leafy sea dragons. Daily eco-cruises take passengers into the bay for glimpses of dolphins and wintering manatees.

Manatee sightings are guaranteed at Lowry Park Zoo (tel: 813-935 8552), one of only three manatee rescue facilities in Florida. You can even dine in front of the manatee tank.

Tampa Bay's recorded history began nearly 500 years ago, when Spanish conquistador Hernando de Soto landed on these shores to a decidedly unenthusiastic welcome from the area's Indian residents, whose fishing village, Tanpa, or "sticks of fire," gave the city its name. The often-overlooked De Soto National Memorial in Bradenton commemorates De Soto's landing with artifacts, living-history presentations, and a film. Downtown, the Tampa Bay History Center (tel: 813-228 0097) offers an introduction to the area's history, while at the Henry B. Plant Museum (tel: 813-254 1891), housed in a 19th-century hotel, Tampa's Victorian era is the focus.

The contributions of a larger-than-life visionary are explored at Sarasota's John and Mable Ringling Museum of Art (tel: 941-359 5700), built by circus magnate John Ringling in 1930 to showcase his love of Italian art and architecture. It fea-

tures a series of large-scale Rubens and other Baroque masterpieces, and a reproduction of Michelangelo's David in graceful, European-style gardens. Arrive early to tour the delightful Ringling mansion, Ca d'Zan. Its setting, overlooking Sarasota Bay, is straight out of Venice, Italy.

When the sun sets over the Gulf, Tampa's historic Ybor City comes to life. Once the Cigar Capital of the World, Ybor City was founded by Don Vicente Martinez Ybor, a Cuban exile, in 1885 and quickly attracted Cuban, Spanish, and other immigrants. Renovated cigar factories and tiny "shotgun" houses are the setting of Tampa's hottest nightclubs, bars, and restaurants.

To learn more, hop aboard a newly-restored 1892 electric streetcar in downtown Tampa and visit the Ybor City State Museum (tel: 813-247 6323), housed in a former bakery.

No visit is complete without a meal at the landmark Columbia Restaurant (tel: 813-248 4961) on bustling Seventh Avenue. Opened in 1905 by a Cuban immigrant, Casimiro Hernandez, Sr., it features an old-fashioned cigar bar, two floors of dining rooms and flamenco shows. ❏

RIGHT: skyscrapers in Tampa's downtown district reflect in the Hillsborough river.

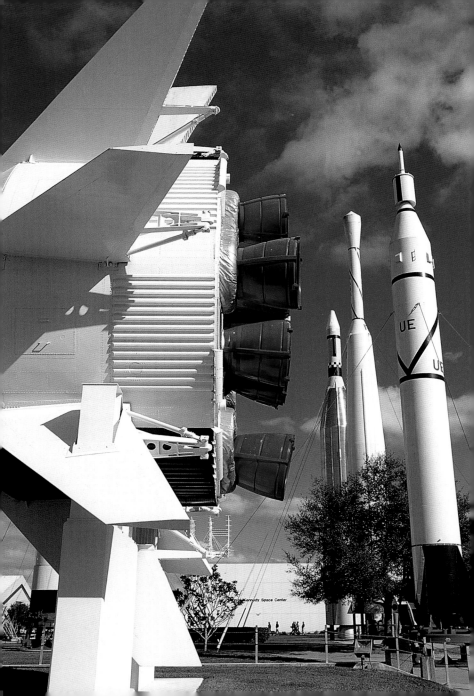

THE SPACE COAST

Kennedy Space Center, at the heart of the NASA's launching pad into the heavens, tells the story of America's adventure into space

"The gun must be fired perpendicularly to the plane of the horizon, that is to say, toward the zenith. Now the moon does not traverse the zenith except in places between 0° and 28° of latitude." With those parameters in mind, members of the Observatory of Cambridge in Jules Verne's 1873 book *De La Terre à la Lune* advised that their manned projectile Columbiad should begin its journey to the moon from either southern Texas or southern Florida.

In the book, Texans were aghast, arguing that Florida, "a mere peninsula confined between two seas," could never sustain the shock of the discharge, that it would "bust up" at the very first shot.

"Very well, let it bust up!" replied the Floridians. And on December 1, 1873, before a vast assemblage of 5 million people, "the discharge of the Columbiad was accompanied by a perfect earthquake. Florida was shaken to its very depths." But it didn't bust up in the book – or in real life.

The National Aeronautics and Space Administration (NASA) continues to shake up Florida's east coast each time it launches rockets from Kennedy Space Center, just about 100 miles (160 km) from the spot the prescient Mr Verne chose to launch the Columbiad. The Center is at the heart of the Space Coast, a

40-mile (65-km) swath of land that stretches from its northern terminus in Titusville through Cocoa Beach and south to the Melbourne-Palm Bay area.

Kennedy Space Center

Cape Canaveral has been associated with the space program ever since NASA's manned flights began in the early 1960s. Space Coast nomenclature can get a bit confusing, however, and some clarification is in order. Cape Canaveral has long been the

Map on page 209

LEFT: Saturn 1B booster in the Space Center's rocket garden. **BELOW:** moon gravity simulator.

BELOW: a sign lures visitors to Mad Mission to Mars, a live show that takes guests on a voyage through the cosmos.

name of the peninsula that extends south from Merritt Island and east of the Banana River. (Its name was changed to Cape Kennedy after the president's 1963 assassination, but was changed back to Canaveral in 1973.) It's the site of Cape Canaveral Air Force Station, where the earliest experimental American military rockets were launched. **Kennedy Space Center** ❶ (daily 9am–dusk, NASA Parkway; tel: 321-449 4444), including launch pads for the Space Shuttles, is on Merritt Island. It lies, in fact, within Merritt Island National Wildlife Refuge.

Although the space center is a government facility, the **Visitor Complex** is operated by a private company without the benefit of taxpayer funds. The complex sprawls across a landscaped campus, incorporating nearly a dozen buildings and several outdoor exhibits. Begin by getting oriented at **Information Central**, where a multimedia presentation introduces the themes and attractions within the complex. Use the schedules for films, live events, and tours poster here to plan your day.

The Red Planet and beyond

Robot Scouts, located in the opposite wing of the main building, is a walk-through exhibit that takes a whimsical look at the role of robot probes in interplanetary exploration. Adjacent is the **Universe Theater**, where the film *Quest for Life* chronicles the effort to answer the most compelling of questions: are we alone?

Mad Mission to Mars 2025 is the title of a live-action stage show using theme-park techniques and 3-D computer animation to teach an audience of "astronaut trainees" essential facts about physics, rocketry, and living in space. The show is aimed at kids, but adults come away with a better understanding of what will be involved in the first interplanetary journey.

At the **Nature and Technology** exhibit, visitors are brought back to Earth – in fact, to the diverse environment in which the Space Center is located. Some 5,000 alligators make their home in Merritt Island National Wildlife Refuge – they've been known to loll alongside the 15,000-foot (4,600-meter) runway where Space Shuttles land – and this exhibit explains how an almost primeval environment coexists alongside a realm of advanced technology.

Exploration in the New Millennium takes a slightly more serious approach to the next phase of space exploration. The presentation starts with terrestrial voyages of discovery such as the Vikings' adventures in Greenland and Iceland a thousand years ago, then speculates on the logistics of travel to Mars and beyond. A small chunk of Mars, incidentally, is on the premises: this is the only place in the world where it's possible to touch an actual piece of the Red Planet, which fell to Earth as a meteorite. Afterwards, you can send a bit of your own identity Mars-ward, by creating an electronic signature to be stored on a microchip that will one day make the interplanetary journey.

Meet and greet

At the **Astronaut Encounter**, offered several times a day, NASA astronauts discuss space travel with visitors. Representing the fewer than 500 men and women who have flown in space, the astronauts answer questions, narrate videos, and invite a young audience member onto the stage to become part of the presentation.

To get up close and personal with one of the space-traveling elite, make a reservation to **Dine with an Astronaut**. Offered at 1pm Monday through Friday, this extra-cost option (about $30 for adults, $20 for children) is exactly what it says it is: an opportunity to join a crew member for a multicourse lunch, complete with a briefing, conversation, and photo-and-autograph session. (As occasionally astronauts are not available; it's advisable to make reservations well in advance.)

The Space Center is home to the only back-to-back **IMAX theaters** in the world. Two films are shown throughout the day on 5½-story screens: *The Dream Is Alive*, a paean to space flight filmed by shuttle astronauts and narrated by Walter Cronkite; and *Space Station*, a remarkable 3-D look at the shape, character, and challenges of life in the international space station.

Anyone who remembers listening to a live report of Alan Shepard's 1961 suborbital flight on a tinny transistor radio or black-and-white television knows that space exploration, though only a recent development, has a remarkably rich and vivid history. At the **Early Space Exploration** exhibit, visitors can watch a re-creation of a Project Mercury launch, see the mission control-room consoles used by ground crews during Mercury and Gemini missions, and even examine the interiors of the tiny capsules from those pioneering days.

Heavy lifting

Just outside is the **Rocket Garden**, resembling nothing so much as a display of stark modern sculpture. Eight rockets, all but one mounted vertically as if ready to soar skyward, trace the evolution of the technology that made manned space flight possible. Here are the Redstone, Atlas

Map on page 209

A re-entry capsule in a Space Center exhibit.

BELOW: rockets on display that carried Mercury, Gemini, and Apollo astronauts.

and Titan models, including an example of the Mecury-Atlas engine that blasted John Glenn into orbit in 1962. The one horizontal specimen is a Saturn 1B, an enormous vehicle designed by NASA (the others were adapted from military rockets) and originally built as a rescue vehicle rocket for Skylab astronauts in the 1970s; it later served as a backup for the Apollo-Soyuz project.

By the way, if you're still around the Visitor Complex at dusk, head over to the Rocket Garden for a look at the dramatic lighting display.

Another impressive outdoor display dominates the opposite corner of the campus. This is **Explorer**, a full-size replica of a space shuttle. Climbing aboard is as close as most space enthusiasts will come to riding in a real shuttle. There's an accurate mockup of the flight deck and of mid-deck working and living areas (and you'll learn how toilets work in weightless conditions), and a cargo bay equipped with the famed, versatile robot arm and gold-foil-covered cradle used to position satellites. Near the shuttle are the familiar orange fuel tanks and twin solid rocket boosters used in the early stages of launch. The boosters, incidentally, are recovered after being jettisoned; boats dedicated to this function are moored in the Banana River nearby.

If clambering through Explorer whets your appetite for information on the real-life shuttle, head next door to the **Launch Status Center**, which offers live briefings on recent launches and missions in progress. If a shuttle is in orbit at the time of your visit, you'll be able to watch live images broadcast from space.

From the Launch Status Center, it's a short walk to the **Astronaut Memorial**, dedicated in 1991 to honor Americans who lost their lives in service to the space program. Elegant in conception, the memorial consists of a highly polished, 50-

foot-high (15-meter) granite space mirror in which the astronauts' names are incised. The granite surface reflects passing clouds, so names appear to float in the heavens.

Restricted area tour

After touring the Visitor Complex, board a bus for a narrated tour of outlying Space Center facilities that play a vital part in NASA operations. (Itineraries may be altered or tours suspended, depending on mission schedules. As of this writing, the last stop on the tour – the International Space Station Center – has been removed indefinitely. Call 321-449 4444 for more information.)

The first stop is **Launch Complex 39**, the most exciting part of the tour and the area most directly involved with shuttle launches. The route then passes at the three-bay **Orbiter Processing Facility**, where shuttles spend several months for maintenance and repair. This is one of the few places, outside of space itself, where shuttle cargo doors can be opened and closed. The spacecraft are then transported to the 525-foot-tall (160-meter), 8-acre (3-hectare) **Vehicle Assembly Building**, the largest building by volume in the world. This is where shuttles are outfitted with twin solid rocket boosters and an external fuel tank. Nearby is the **Launch Control Center**, familiar from television coverage of final countdowns.

Equally impressive, if only for their sheer size, are the **Crawler Transporters**, two 6-million-pound (2.7-million-kg) tracked vehicles built to carry assembled shuttles along the 3½-mile (5.5-km) route to the launch pads. In service for more than 30 years, the Crawlers travel at 1 mile per hour (1.6 kph) when carrying a shuttle, boosters, and a fuel tank.

The **LC 39 Observation Gantry**, a 60-foot (18-meter) platform that affords a sweeping view of the

Map on page 209

FAR LEFT: the space shuttle Atlantis rises on a plume of fire.
BELOW: costumed astronauts greet visitors.

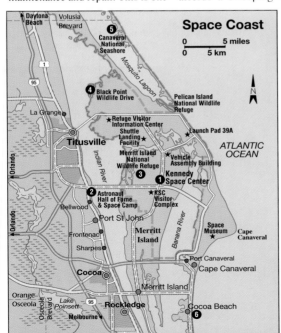

launch pads, Vehicle Assembly Buildings, and the surrounding area. On exhibit is a 7,000-pound (3,200-kg) shuttle main engine, and a model re-creation of a launch countdown. A 6-minute film presents a briefing by astronaut Marsha Ivins on how a shuttle is prepared for launching.

Launch Pads 39A and **39B** are historic structures – they were used for the Apollo moon launches – now adapted to the needs of the shuttle program. With their service structures towering alongside, the massive concrete pads are rivaled only by the spacecraft themselves as emblems of modern space exploration.

After a look at the **Shuttle Landing Facility**, one of the longest airstrips in the world, the tour continues to the **Apollo/Saturn V Center**, dedicated to the men and machines whose work culminated in the moon landings of 1969 and 1971. A video presentation reviews the early phases of the Apollo program, prior to a re-creation of an Apollo launch in the firing room. Still the main attraction here is a re-creation of the July, 1969, Apollo 11 landing

presented in the **Lunar Theater**. The Center houses the original **Lunar Module** and **Command Service Module** and one of only three Saturn V rockets still in existence. When the first of the rockets was fired in 1967, it created the loudest noise ever made by human beings.

Viewing a launch

For many travelers, the high point of visiting the Space Coast is viewing an actual launch. There is truly nothing like it. You stand amid an expectant throng, listening to a radio or loudspeaker, or just waiting, as the countdown clock ticks off the remaining minutes. Miles away stands a gleaming white space shuttle, with a large rust-colored external tank. It releases clouds of vapor like a dragon about to wake from a deep slumber. Then, as the anticipation becomes almost unbearable, the countdown reaches its final seconds.

There is a burst of fire from the shuttle's main engines, and for a few long seconds the beast stays where it is, its engines building up thrust, billowing clouds of steam and smoke.

The space shuttle travels at 17,500 miles per hour (28,200 kph) about 10 times faster than a bullet.

BELOW: Apollo 14 command module, Astronaut Hall of Fame.

Finally, the two solid rocket boosters ignite with a flame so bright that it seems to rival the sun, and the shuttle quickly leaves the Earth. The cheers of the crowd are soon drowned out as the roar of the shuttle's engines reaches you while the magnificent flying machine heads for space.

How can you experience this cosmic departure? Like thousands of others, you could simply find a good spot along US Hwy 1 in Titusville or Hwy A1A in Cape Canaveral or Cocoa Beach. Or, if you're going to be at the Kennedy Space Center on launch day, purchase a Launch Viewing ticket (first-come, first-served), which allows you to ride a bus to a viewing site about 6 miles (10 km) from the launch pad. Don't forget to bring a pair of binoculars.

If you're coming to the Space Center specifically to view a launch, it's a good idea to plan on staying a few extra days, in case there's a delay. There are no guarantees, however; launches are sometimes postponed for weeks. Call 321-449 4444 for information or buy launch tickets online at www.ksctickets.com.

Astronaut Hall of Fame

"[T]he surface was beautiful, beautiful… Magnificent desolation." So wrote Buzz Aldrin in a 1972 letter describing how it felt to walk on the moon. The document, on exhibit at the **Astronaut Hall of Fame ❷** (daily 9am–5pm, 6225 Vectorspace Boulevard, Titusville; tel: 321-269 6100) about 6 miles (10 km) west of the Kennedy Space Center, is just one artifact among thousands that are gathered here to tell the story of the American experience in space.

But there's a lot more here, including a Mercury trainee capsule, the command module from Apollo 14, and wheels from the moon rover. One of the highlights here is the state-of-the-art Simulator Station interactive area, where visitors can experience firsthand a variety of astronaut-training devices. Among them is a g-force centrifuge that creates the sensation of gravity four times that on Earth, a moon walk simulator, and a shuttle simulator that allows visitors to test their piloting skills. Special activities are arranged for viewing shuttle launches, and

Space suits and other artifacts are exhibited at the US Astronaut Hall of Fame.

LEFT: future astronaut makes repairs at Space Camp.

Space Camp

Your kids wonder if they have the right stuff to be astronauts? If they're between the ages of 9 and 14, they can find out at Space Camp Florida. Held at the Astronaut Hall of Fame, the intensive, five-day program shows kids what it takes – mentally, emotionally, and physically – to become a member of the American space program.

Youngsters bunk in dorm-style "space habitats" and prepare for space missions on state-of-the-art simulators, including the Five Degrees of Freedom simulator, which prepares them for working in zero gravity, and the One-Sixth Gravity Trainer, which teaches them how to walk on the moon. They also build and launch model rockets, attend lectures on the principles of space science, conduct experiments, and direct a mock shuttle mission. Tuition, ranging from $700 to $800, includes meals, lodging and all program materials. There are also Parent/Child weekend programs for children aged 7–11, an Advanced Space Academy for ages 15–18, and a program solely for adults. Other locations include Huntsville, Alabama, and Mountain View, California. Call 800-63-SPACE or go to www.spacecamp.com for more information.

Waterbirds like this white heron abound at Merritt Island National Wildlife Refuge.

RIGHT: a leatherback hatchling takes its first swim.

astronauts occasionally drop by for a visit. The Hall of Fame is also headquarters of **Space Camp Florida** *(see panel, page 211),* which offers educational programs and "astronaut training" for children and adults.

Back to nature

In contrast to all this high-tech adventure are two nearby nature preserves. At the 140,000-acre (57,000-hectare) **Merritt Island National Wildlife Refuge ❸** (daily dawn–dusk, closed several days before launches, PO Box 6504, Titusville; tel: 321-861 0667), adjacent to Kennedy Space Center, endangered West Indian manatees loll peacefully in brackish lagoons, sea turtles waddle ashore to lay eggs on pristine beaches, and alligators bask in the sun on creek banks. The refuge lies along a prime migratory flyway, and the sky is filled in early spring with warblers and shorebirds while, on the ground, egrets, and herons are in breeding plumage, wood storks and ospreys build nests, and bald eaglets test their wings.

The mild climate and varied environment of marshes, hardwood hammocks, pine forest, scrub and coastal dunes sustain more than 500 species of wildlife, including more than 20 on the Endangered or Threatened Species List. This is one of the most important nesting areas in the country for loggerhead, green and leatherback turtles. Much of the wildlife can be spotted along 7-mile (11-km), one-way **Black Point Wildlife Drive ❹**, a self-guided auto tour through salt- and freshwater marshes. The entrance is on SR 406, a mile east of the intersection with SR 402. Manatees, most prevalent in the spring and fall, can be best viewed from the observation area near Haulover Canal Bridge on SR 3.

The best time to visit the refuge is during the off-season, when wildlife populations are at their highest and mosquitos, high temperatures and thunderstorms are least likely to present a problem. The Visitor Information Center, east of Titusville on SR 402, has wildlife displays, educational resources, fishing information, and trail maps. Nearby **Pelican Island National Wildlife Refuge** is accessible via a boardwalk over the

Turtle walks

I t is one of the most riveting beachside spectacles served up by nature: a 600-pound (270-kg) loggerhead sea turtle trudges ashore in the moonlight and, in a grueling act of devotion that can last as long as two hours, digs a sandy nest in which she deposits as many as 100 Ping-Pong-ball-sized eggs. Rear flippers working counterpoint to cover up her handiwork, then carving out a shallow, false nest to trick yolk-hungry predators, the turtle finally crawls back to the ocean and lets destiny take its course.

To see this or maybe even the hatchlings emerge two months later, there's no better place than Canaveral National Seashore on Florida's Atlantic coast. While it is a violation of federal law to harm a sea turtle or disturb its nest – the beach is zealously patrolled during nesting season to make sure the curious keep their distance – the park sponsors occasional evening turtle walks. After locating a female that has already begun laying eggs and is not likely to be spooked, rangers escort small groups to witness the ritual.

Tours start around 8pm and last until midnight. Reservations can be made in May or June by calling 386-428 3384 ext 18.

ocean which offers stunning views of the island (tel: 772-562 3909). This bird rookery – the nation's first National Wildlife Refuge – was established in 1903. **Space Coast Nature Tours** (tel: 321-267 4551) offers 90-minute wildlife cruises of the Indian River Lagoon aboard a 49-passenger vessel.

Beauty and the beach

Adjacent to the wildlife refuge is 57,000-acre (23,000-hectare) **Canaveral National Seashore ❺** (daily 6am–8pm, 308 Julia Street, Titusville; tel: 386-428 3384), whose miles of barrier dunes and sea-swept beaches are a haven for beachcombers and nature lovers. Two of the beaches, **Apollo** and **Playalinda**, at the northern and southern tips of the Seashore, have restrooms, boardwalks and, from May 30 to September 1, lifeguards. In between, the landscape has been left untouched. Portions of the seashore may be closed for days before shuttle launches or when parking lots are full.

Another word of caution – or recommendation, as the case may be:

Canaveral is the destination of choice for Florida's nude sunbathers, who are constantly at odds with local authorities. The legal wrangle over whether Florida's laws against public nudity can be enforced on federal land has been going on for years. If you want to chuck your clothes, you'll have plenty of company. But there's no guarantee that a deputy sheriff won't slink out of a palmetto thicket and slap you with a citation.

Those who prefer beaches in a more developed setting will find **Cocoa Beach ❻** to their liking – an old-time seaside town with an abundance of chain motels, restaurants, and souvenir shops, as well as first-rate beaches. The biggest attraction is the **Ron Jon Surf Shop** (daily 24 hours, 4151 N. Atlantic Avenue, Cocoa Beach; tel: 321-799 8888), a neon-lit palace devoted to bikinis, boogie boards, surfboards, scuba equipment, and other beach and surf gear. Famous surfers occasionally drop in for autograph sessions; scuba diving and surfing lessons are also available. ❑

Map on page 209

LEFT: Ron Jon Surf Shop, open daily around the clock, carries everything for the well-equipped beach goer.

RESTAURANTS

Barnhill's Buffet
800 S Babcock Street
Melbourne
Tel: 321-728 8813
A bottomless buffet of sirloin steaks for big eaters. **$$**

Gregory's Steak and Seafood Grille
900 N Atlantic Avenue
Cocoa Beach
Tel: 321-799 2557
Open for dinner only and serving prime grade beef and fresh, local seafood. **$$$**

Mango Tree Restaurant
118 N Atlantic Avenue
Cocoa Beach
Tel: 407-799 0513

A romantic, tropical setting of fresh flowers, wicker furniture and white linen. Serves fine American cuisine and fresh seafood specialties. **$$$**

Punjab
520 Causeway
Cocoa Beach
Tel: 321-799 4696
Fine Indian cuisine open for lunch and dinner with many special discounts available. **$$**

Thai Thai Restaurant and Sushi Bar
2447 N Wickham Road
Melbourne
Tel: 321-253 2353
Fresh and authentic Japanese and Thai cuisine. **$$**

TRANSPORT

GETTING THERE AND GETTING AROUND

GETTING THERE

By Air

Most major US and international carriers serve Orlando. Fare prices are competitive, so shop around before buying a ticket. A variety of discount fares and "package deals," which can significantly cut round-trip rates, are also available. Many scheduled services are supplemented by charter flights.

Orlando (McCoy) International Airport (code MCO) is 9 miles (15 km) south of downtown Orlando and about 25 miles (40 km) from Walt Disney World Resort. Spacious, glittering, and constantly expanding, it has three terminals, with satellite gates reached by "people-mover" shuttle trains. Disney characters often make appearances during the day.

A lot of package flights land at Sanford Airport, about 30 miles (48 km) north of Orlando. During the busy summer months this small airport is utilized to cope with the large numbers of tourists, and lines at immigration can be long. Furthermore, the extra distance can be a costly inconvenience if you plan to use taxi or shuttle bus to reach Orlando. One advantage of Sanford, however, is that the car rental outlets are right outside the terminal building.

The telephone numbers of the main airports are:
● Orlando International Airport, tel: 407-825 2001.
● Sanford Airport, tel: 407-585 4000.

Post 9/11

Security at airports since September 11, 2001, has become a serious matter indeed. As long as you give yourself plenty of time, remain patient and take absolutely no chances, you should be fine.

Ensure that you are not taking any sharp objects onto the plane with you. Along with obvious weapons such as knives or scissors, nail clippers, jewelery with spikes on it and even tweezers may be confiscated.

Arrive early enough to deal with all the random searches. Three hours should be the norm now. Also be prepared for searches that may be embarrassing and or offensive. Unfortunately, not all staff protecting the airports are as courteous as they might be. Remain calm and don't take it personally, they are only doing their jobs. Doing so will also get you through quicker and with fewer hassles.

AIRLINES

Telephone numbers of major airlines serving Florida, numbers are US unless stated:
American West
Tel: 800-235 9292
www.americawest.com
American
Tel: 800-433 7300
www.aa.com
British Airways
Tel: 800-247 9297
UK Tel: 0870-850 9850
www.britishairways.com
Continental
Tel: 800-523 3273
www.continental.com
Delta
Tel: 800-241 4141
www.delta.com
Lufthansa
Tel: 800-645 3880
UK Tel:0870-837 7747
www.lufthansa.com
Southwest
Tel: 800-435 9792
www.southwest.com
United Airlines
Tel: 800-864 8331
www.ual.com
USAir
Tel: 800-428 4322
www.usairways.com
Virgin Atlantic
Tel: 800-862 8621
UK Tel: 0870-380 2007
www.virgin-atlantic.com

Domestic flights

Air travel is by far the quickest and most convenient way of getting around the US. Travelers from abroad can buy a Visit USA ticket, which gives substantial discounts and sets no fixed program. To benefit, you must buy these before you enter the country, or within 15 days of arrival. Fares change constantly, so it's wise to consult travel agents for the latest on special deals.

By Rail

Amtrak offers slow but leisurely service from America's Midwest, Northeast and South – and connecting service from points west – to certain Florida cities. There is daily service from New York City to Miami or Tampa on the Silver Service. The Sunset Limited travels from Los Angeles via New Orleans. For those who want to take their car along too, Amtrak offers an Auto Train service from Lorton, Virginia (near Washington, DC), to Sanford, Florida, near Orlando.

Amtrak services within Florida are not extensive, being most useful for destinations along the east coast and in parts of central Florida. There are plans for a high-speed rail link between Miami and Orlando, but at this stage they are just that.

For information on all rail services, call Amtrak at 800-872 7245 or www.amtrak.com.

By Road

Greyhound provides bus services to Florida and all over the state. While some inter-city bus services include many stops en route which make long distances seem interminable, there are also express buses which take in fewer stops.

Many bus terminals, including the one in downtown Orlando, are in a dodgy area of town, so take care when traveling to or from stations.

Bus & rail information

For bus information, call the national Greyhound number 800-229 9424 or www.greyhound.com.

GETTING AROUND

To/From the Airport(s)

Taxis and less expensive shuttle minibuses run between the airports and Walt Disney World locations, International Drive, downtown Orlando, Kissimmee, and Cocoa Beach. Some hotels operate free shuttle services to and from the airports; if you are on a package tour, airport transfers may be included. There's a public bus Lynx no. 42 to International Drive that departs every 30 minutes from 5.15–12.15am.

Check-in time

Arrive at least two hours before domestic and international flights (airlines now suggest three hours, see page 214). For flight information, telephone your airline.

Miami, Tampa, Fort Lauderdale, West Palm Beach, and Key West also have international airports.

Orientation

Like most American cities, Orlando suffers from urban sprawl. I-4 connects the Disney resort in the south, to Downtown Orlando in the north with International Drive, SeaWorld, and the Universal resort gathered together in a band about halfway between them. To the east of this is Orlando International Airport.

Public Transport

Disney transportation

The Walt Disney World Resort transportation system is complex, as are the rules about who can use it. They include those staying at Disney accommodations, at the Plaza hotels, or those carrying four- or five-day passes. Additionally, those with Magic Kingdom tickets can use the monorail or ferry to get to its entrance.

Disney buses connect all areas within the Walt Disney World Resort. They all look the same, but have electronic destination displays in the windo to identify them. Bus stops outside parks and resorts are clearly labelled. If in any doubt, ask the driver. He or she will ever-so-happily tell you where they're going, in between wishing everyone a magical day as they board.

The Disney World Monorail links Disney's Magic Kingdom resorts with the Magic Kingdom and Epcot.

Ferries run between the Ticket & Transportation Center (TTC) and the Magic Kingdom; between the Contemporary Resort, Magic Kingdom and River Country; and between the Swan, Dolphin and Yacht and Beach Club, BoardWalk Inn and Disney-MGM Studios.

Lynx buses

Like most cities in the United States, public transportation exists in Orlando but offers only infrequent service and only to major destinations. Luckily, this is usually along the tourist route. If you are staying along I-Drive, in Kissimmee or in downtown Orlando, service is adequate to other major areas only. Ask your hotel which bus takes you where, though be prepared for odd responses – most concierges are never asked for bus information. Your best bet is to call the Lynx information line at 407-841 5969 or www.golynx.com. Lynx runs a downtown service dubbed Lymmo that circles the city until late in the evening (10pm most nights, midnight on Friday and Saturday).

I-Ride Trolley

Additionally, the I-Ride Trolley goes up and down I-Drive and Universal Boulevard from

8am–10.30pm. A single fare is .75$ but exact change is required. They will (graciously) accept $1 to get you on your way, but you won't receive any change.

TIPS FOR MOTORISTS

● When you first arrive, ask for advice from the car rental agent about the best route from the airport to your hotel. Better still, arrange to pick up your rented car from an agency near your hotel on the morning after you arrive, rather than tackle unfamiliar routes when very tired. Many rental agencies will deliver your car to your hotel at no (or only a small) extra charge.
● Use a map to plot out your route before you begin any journey, to prevent going astray.
● Ignore any pedestrian or motorist who tries to stop you, for example by indicating some supposed fault on your vehicle or even by bumping your car from behind.
● Always keep your car doors locked, windows closed and valuables out of sight while driving.
● Avoid unfamiliar shortcuts in urban areas. If you get lost, drive to a well-lit and preferably busy area before stopping to look at your map.

Taxis
Taxis are available in all the main tourist centers. They tend to be expensive, and you usually have to telephone in advance for pick-up. Your hotel should call for you; otherwise, numbers are listed in the Yellow Pages. Don't stand by the side of the road and expect to hail a passing cab.

Driving

Driving is the most popular way to travel to and around Orlando. More than 20 million visitors enter the Sunshine State by car every year – about twice as many as those entering by plane. Unless you plan to remain within Disney World or Universal Orlando during your entire stay, a car is the most convenient way to get around. Bus, train, and taxi service is quite irregular and slow to cover the vast distances encompassed by Disney World and Orlando.

Car rental
Renting a car is by far the easiest way to explore the Orlando area beyond Disney World and Universal, allowing you to zip quickly between the major parks, unless of course you encounter one of the many traffic jams that snarl the area's major roads. If possible, avoid driving the I-4 corridor during rush hour.

Conditions: Most rental agencies require that you are at least 21 years old (sometimes 25), have a valid driver's license and a major credit card. Some will take a cash deposit in lieu of a credit card, but this might be as high as $500. Travelers from some foreign countries may need to produce an international driver's license from their own country.
Arrangements: Visitors wishing to rent a car after arriving in Orlando will find rental offices at the airports, at downtown locations, and even at some hotels. Rates are cheap by US and international standards, but you should shop around for the best rates and features. Local rental firms outside the airports are often less expensive than the national companies and can be more convenient if you want a car only for a day or two. The cost of insurance is usually tacked on to the rental fee, so be sure to check insurance provisions before signing anything.

If you are traveling from overseas, it is normally cheaper to arrange car hire in advance. You should also check with your airline or travel agent for special package deals that include a car, since rental rates can be reduced by about 50 percent if you buy a so-called "fly-drive" deal. However, be wary of offers of "free" car hire, which do not include extras like tax and insurance.

Available rental vehicles range from modest economy cars to luxury convertibles and vans.
Car insurance: Be sure to check that your car rental agreement includes Loss Damage Waiver

DRINK DRIVING

Florida has some of the toughest laws in the US against driving under the influence of alcohol. The maximum level permitted is so small that you are advised to drink no alcohol at all if driving.

CAR RENTAL AGENCIES

These rental agencies may be contacted within the US and from abroad:

Alamo
Tel: 800-462 5266
www.alamo.com

Avis
Tel: 800-230 4898
www.avis.com
UK: 08700-100 287
www.avis.co.uk

Budget
Tel: 800-527 0700
UK: 01344-484 100
www.drivebudget.com

Dollar
Tel: 800-800 3665
www.dollar.com

Hertz
Tel: 800-654 3131
www.hertz.com
UK: 08708-44 88 44
www.hertz.co.uk

National
Tel: 800-227 7368
www.nationalcar.com

Thrifty
Tel: 800-847 4389
www.thrifty.com

If you're travelling from the United Kingdom, try to book your car hire before departing as many rates available to overseas customers are much less expensive than the best US deals.

Limits change suddenly and for only short distances, so pay attention to signs. The Highway Patrol is good at enforcing limits, including minimum speeds: signs along interstates sometimes oblige motorists to drive at over 40 miles per hour (64 kph).

Maps: Most service stations and convenience stores sell maps. Florida tourist offices (including overseas) often distribute the Official Transportation Map of Florida, which has city plans, free of charge.

Parking: All theme parks provide extensive facilities for car parking. There is usually a charge, although at Disney parks it is free if you are staying at Disney-owned accommodations and display the card that you are given when you register. If you do have to pay a parking fee, keep the ticket, since it is valid at all parks for that day. Remember to make a careful note of the exact location where you leave your car. After a few days of parking in vast lots that all look the same, it's easy to become confused.

(LDW), also known as Collision Damage Waiver (CDW). Without it, you will be liable for any damage done to your vehicle in the event of an accident, regardless of whether or not you were to blame. You are advised to pay for supplementary Liability Insurance on top of the standard third-party insurance. Insurance and tax charges com-

bined can add $35 to each day's rental.

Speed limits: American states set their own speed limits. In Florida they are:

● 55–70 miles per hour (90–112 kph) on highways.

● 20–30 miles per hour (32–48 kph) in residential areas.

● 15 miles per hour (24 kph) near schools.

TRANSPORT

ACCOMMODATIONS

ACTIVITIES

A – Z

ACCOMMODATIONS

SOME THINGS TO CONSIDER BEFORE YOU BOOK THE ROOM

Choosing a Hotel

Accommodations in Orlando range from luxury resorts that cater to your every whim to modest mom-and-pop motels, cozy, antique-filled bed & breakfast inns, youth hostels, and campgrounds.

Although standards for service and facilities are generally quite high, there is the occasional bad apple. Indeed, some of the cheapest accommodations offered by tour operators are positively miserable, so be sure you know what you're getting into before signing on the dotted line.

Reservations and Prices

Reservations are generally required, and if you are traveling during the high season you should book several months ahead if you have your heart set on a particular hotel or if you want to stay inside Walt Disney World.

Room rates vary enormously between the high season and the off season. Peak periods in Orlando are: mid-December to early January; February–April (including Easter); and early June–late August. At other times, prices are slightly lower at some Disney accommodations and may be much lower at non-Disney properties.

The cost can rise by 30 percent or more during the peak tourist months. There is plenty of scope to ask for a discount if you are staying for a week or more, or if you are visiting during the off-season, which for many hotels is a lean time.

Florida also imposes a resort tax, in addition to the usual sales tax, which is added to the price of all hotel rooms. It varies from county to county and ranges from between 2 and 5 percent.

Chain Hotels and Motels

These are both common and popular. Some people dislike chains because they offer no variety and lack a personal touch; the plus point is that once you have been to a hotel run by a particular chain, you can predict what kind of service and facilities to expect wherever else you are in the state.

Bed & Breakfasts

Bed & breakfasts vary greatly in terms of price and quality, but the thing they have in common is that they are almost always in a private and/or historic home. Few have restaurants and the facilities will not be as good as in a regular hotel, but some travelers prefer the more personal ambience (and the often wonderful homecooked breakfasts).

The Florida edition of the Charming Small Hotel Guides series published by Duncan Petersen is a good source for travelers wanting a personal touch. The Southeast edition of the Bed and Breakfast USA guide also lists B&Bs. Agencies specializing in finding B&B-style accommodations include:

Bed & Breakfast Co. – Tropical Florida, tel: 305-661 3270, which covers the whole state.

Camping

Fort Wilderness Resort within Walt Disney World has more than 800 campsites for tents and RVs. Another option is to rent a trailer (decked out like a log cabin) that sleeps up to six people and has air-conditioning, color TV, radio, cookware, and linen, i.e. all the equipment you'll need. The resort is located amid 650 acres (263 hectares) of woods and streams on Bay Lake, east of the Magic Kingdom.

For information and reservations, write to Walt Disney World Central Reservations, PO Box 10,000, Lake Buena Vista, FL 32830, or call 407-824 2900.

WALT DISNEY WORLD

HOTELS

Disney's Animal Kingdom Lodge
Tel: 407-938 3000
Animal Kingdom
Built to resemble a southern African game lodge, the hotel has an elaborately furnished lobby with a four-story observation window looking out onto a 33-acre (13-hectare) savanna, which teems with wildlife. All standard and deluxe rooms have handcrafted furniture and traditional tapestries, and balconies; most have two queen beds. Many of the balconies overlook the savanna. Amenities include three restaurants, several bars, a children's play area that opens at 4:30pm, a health club, playground, shopping area, video arcade, and outdoor pool. Buses transport guests to the parks. 1,293 rooms. **$$$–$$$$**

Disney's BoardWalk and Villas
Tel: 407-939 5100
Epcot
Elaborately detailed buildings with turreted, brightly-colored facades and twinkling lights recreate an East Coast boardwalk circa 1920. Spacious rooms with ocean-blue and sea-green furnishings have two queen-size brass beds, daybeds and ceiling fans; two-story garden suites have private gardens.

The villas – Disney Vacation Club time-share units – sleep 4 to 12 and have kitchens, laundries, whirlpool tubs, and VCRs. Nightclubs, restaurants, midway games, and shops line the boardwalk. There's a supervised evening children's program, a health club, and a large swimming pool with a 200-foot water slide. Ferry boats and buses serve the parks. 372 rooms, 520 villas. **$$$–$$$$**

Disney's Caribbean Beach
Tel: 407-934 3400
Epcot
Each of the five areas at this brightly-colored resort that circles 45-acre (18-hectare) Barefoot Bay re-creates a Caribbean island and has its own pool, beach, and laundry room. Accommodations in each of the two-story buildings are the same: two double beds, a table and chairs, a coffeemaker, and bath. Rates vary only according to view. A food court and several casual restaurants cater to the resort's family-oriented clientele, and there are water sports, bike rentals, playgrounds, a shopping complex, and a video arcade. Buses serve the parks. 2,112 rooms. **$$–$$$**.

Disney's Contemporary Resort
Tel: 407-824 1000
Magic Kingdom
The monorail passes

through the middle of this 15-story A-frame built a quarter-century ago. Most rooms have two queen-sized beds and a daybed. Tower rooms have private balconies overlooking the Magic Kingdom or Bay Lake; those in the Garden Wings have nice views but are somewhat distant from the central property. There are several bars and restaurants, including the elegant California Grill – a popular spot for watching Magic Kingdom fireworks. Amenities include a supervised evening children's program, salon, water activities, a health club and tennis center, several swimming pools and a video arcade. The monorail serves the parks. Wheelchair access. 1,030 rooms. **$$$–$$$$**

Disney's Grand Floridian Resort & Spa
Tel: 407-824 3000
Magic Kingdom
The Victorian era in all its splendor is re-created at Disney's flagship property, an elegant confection of glistening white, wooden buildings with red shingled roofs, gracious verandas, and turrets. Open-cage elevators in the plant-filled, five-story, chandeliered lobby serve second-floor shops and restaurants. Most rooms in the four- and five-story lodge buildings have two queen-size beds and a daybed; many overlook

Map, page 58

the Seven Seas Lagoon. Amenities include six restaurants (one requiring jackets), several bars, a supervised evening children's program, a health club and spa, several swimming pools, and water activities. The monorail, buses, and water launches serve the parks. Wheelchair access. 901 rooms and suites. **$$$–$$$$**

Disney's Old Key West Resort
Tel: 407-827 1198
Downtown Disney
Although it's miles from the ocean, this hotel's color scheme and architecture bear an uncanny resemblance to buildings in the seaside resort town far to the south. Studios have two queen-size beds, tables and chairs, small refrigerators,

PRICE CATEGORIES
Price categories are for a double room without breakfast:
$ = under $100
$$ = $100–$150
$$$ = $150–$200
$$$$ = more than $200

microwaves, and coffeemakers. One-bedroom villas have king-size beds in the main bedroom and queen-size sleeper sofas in the living room. Two- and three-bedroom villas have full kitchens and porches or balconies. All units except studios have private whirlpool tubs. There are grills and picnic tables, several restaurants, a health club, swimming pools, shopping, tennis courts, a video arcade, and playgrounds. Buses serve the parks, and water launches go to Downtown Disney. Wheelchair access. 709 villas. **$$$–$$$$**

Disney's Polynesian Resort
Tel: 407-824 2000
Magic Kingdom
One of Disney's most authentic theme hotels re-creates a Pacific Islands retreat. The centerpiece is the Great Ceremonial House, a tropical extravaganza of plants and waterfalls. Rooms, in 11 two- and three-story "longhouses," vary in size, but most have two queen-size beds, a daybed and balconies. Those overlooking the Seven Seas Lagoon afford front row seats for Magic Kingdom fireworks. There are several restaurants and bars, two pools, a playground, supervised evening children's programs, and water activities. The monorail, buses, and motor launches serve the parks. **$$$–$$$$**

Disney's Wilderness Lodge and Villas
Tel: 407-824 3200
Magic Kingdom
A skillful blending of wood and stone replicates the look of an early 20th-century National Park lodge. Although the eight-story lakefront dwelling appears rustic, accommodations are anything but. Most rooms have two queen-size beds, tables and chairs, and balconies. Villas, in a five-story adjoining tower, range from studios with kitchenettes to two-bedroom units with dining areas, kitchens, whirlpool tubs, and VCRs. There are several restaurants and bars, a supervised evening children's program, a health club, video arcade, swimming pool, sand beach, and boat rental. Boats sail to the Magic Kingdom; buses serve the other parks. 728 rooms; 181 villas. **$$$–$$$$**

Disney's Yacht & Beach Club and Beach Club Villas
Yacht Club
Tel: 407-934 7000
Beach Club
Tel: 407-934 8000
Both at Epcot
Each of the three properties overlooking a 25-acre (10-hectare) lake has a distinct theme but share many facilities. Yacht Club rooms are finished in a nautical motif; those in the Beach Club are reminiscent of a private seaside retreat. Most, however, have either one king-sized or two queen-size beds (some with daybeds), ceiling fans, and a table with chairs. The studios and one- to three-bed-

room villas sleep up to eight. The resort's highlight is Stormalong Bay, an elaborate swimming area with whirlpools, water slides, and a private beach. In addition, there are several pools, a miniature golf course, a health club, restaurants and bars, boating, a supervised evening children's program, a salon, tennis courts, a video arcade, and shops. Buses and ferry boats serve the park. Wheelchair access. 1,213 rooms, 208 villas. **$$$–$$$$**

Hilton
1751 Hotel Plaza Boulevard, Lake Buena Vista, FL 32830
Tel: 407-827 4000
www.hilton.com
Newly renovated resort across from Downtown Disney with convention center, recreation, pools, nine restaurants, and child care. Wheelchair access. 814 rooms. **$$$$**

Walt Disney World Dolphin
Tel: 407-934 4000
Epcot
Two 56-foot-high (17-meter) dolphins and hundreds of seven-story banana leaves festoon the facade of this 27-story, triangular, turquoise hotel with four nine-story wings. The lobby has a circus theme, and the spacious rooms, with turquoise and peach furnishings, have two queen-size beds, desks and chairs. Some have balconies. There is a supervised evening children's program. In addition to the seashell-shaped pool there are several restaurants and

lounges on the property, which is within walking distance of Epcot and the BoardWalk; buses and ferries provide transportation to the other parks. Wheelchair access. 1,509 rooms and suites. **$$$–$$$$**

Walt Disney World Swan
Tel: 407-934 3000
Epcot
Just across the road from the Dolphin is this Westin property, topped by two 47-foot-tall (14-meter) swans. Rooms in the 12-story main building and two seven-story towers are a bit smaller in size than those in the Dolphin, but similar in color and amenities. There's a pool as well as several restaurants and bars, and a supervised evening children's program. Buses and boats provide transportation. 758 rooms. **$$$–$$$$**

Wyndham Palace Resort & Spa
1900 Lake Buena Vista Drive, Lake Buena Vista, FL 32830
Tel: 407-827 2727 or 800-996 3426
www.wyndham.com
A sprawling property within Walt Disney World (but not run by Disney), with more than 1,000 spacious suites, pools, tennis courts, a health club and a game room. Ideal for large families. **$$$$**

Moderate

Best Western Lake Buena Vista Resort
2000 Hotel Plaza Boulevard, Lake Buena Vista, FL 32830
Tel: 800-348 3765
www.orladoresorthotel.com

Caribbean-style resort with 18th-floor nightclub overlooking Disney World, plus swimming pool, playground, and shopping. Wheelchair access. 325 rooms. **$$$**

Disney's All-Star Movies, Music & Sports

All-Star Movies
Tel: 407-939 7000
All-Star Music
Tel: 407-939 6000
All-Star Sports
Tel: 407-939 5000
Animal Kingdom

Disney's only budget complex (until the Pop Century opens) has 30 three-story buildings divided by themes. Each has a distinctive facade, but aside from a few decorative touches, the size and decor of most rooms are identical: they're 260 square feet (24 sq meters), have two double beds, small bureaus, a table with chairs, and bathrooms with separate vanity areas. Popular with families, the resort has a game room, playground, outdoor pool, shopping, and food court. Buses transport guests to the parks. 6,000 rooms. **$–$$**

Disney's Coronado Springs Resort

Tel: 407-939 1000
Animal Kingdom

The American Southwest and Mexico are elaborately re-created at this lakefront complex with outdoor fountains, a Mayan pyramid, and the country's largest ballroom (the property is a popular spot for conventions). Each of three buildings is evocative of a differ-

ent setting – the oceanfront, the city, and the countryside – with rooms decorated accordingly. Standard rooms have two double beds: some queens and kings are also available. There are several pools, a large whirlpool, a health club and spa, a playground, video arcades, shops, a restaurant and food court, several bars, and water sports. Buses serve the parks. Wheelchair access. 1,921 rooms. **$$–$$$**

Disney's Port Orleans – Riverside

Tel: 407-934 6000
Downtown Disney

The former Dixie Landings has been renamed but retains the feel of the Old South. Accommodations are in two- and three-story buildings divided into "parishes." All rooms are the same size and most have two double beds. Mansion rooms are in antebellum-style "estates," while Bayou rooms are in rustic-appearing buildings surrounding Man Island, a sprawling water complex. Only mansions have elevators. Amenities include six swimming pools, a restaurant and food court, bars, bike and boat rentals, fishing excursions, and shops. Buses serve the parks; a riverboat goes to Downtown Disney. Wheelchair access. 2,048 rooms. **$$–$$$**

Disney's Fort Wilderness

Tel: 407-824 2900
Magic Kingdom

Large lots with grills and picnic tables, air-condi-

tioned comfort stations with private showers, and landscaping combine to make this a first-rate option for trailer and tent campers. Some sites have electric and cable TV hookups, water and sanitary disposal; pets are welcome for $3/day. Well-appointed trailers with kitchens sleep up to four adults; and six-person log-cabin-like buildings have TVs, VCRs, picnic tables and charcoal grills. There's a restaurant, several swimming pools, tennis courts, arcades, and bike and horse rentals, as well as scheduled evening activities. Buses and watercraft serve the parks. Wheelchair access. 784 campsites. **$–$$$$**

Grosvenor Resort

1850 Hotel Plaza Boulevard, Lake Buena Vista, FL 32830
Tel: 407-828 4444
Downtown Disney
www.grosvenorresort.com

One of several hotels on Disney property but not actually operated by the Disney Company, the Grosvenor is a middle-of-the-road lakeside resort with convention facilities and comfortable, if not lavish, rooms. A variety of recreational facilities and restaurants is available. There is also a murder mystery dinner show on Saturday night. Wheelchair access. 620 rooms. **$$$**

Hotel Royal Plaza

1905 Hotel Plaza Boulevard, Lake Buena Vista, FL 32830
Tel: 800-248 7890

Close to Downtown Disney, this 17-story hotel features dining, enter-

tainment, recreation, and meeting facilities. Wheelchair access. 394 rooms. **$$$**

Perri House

10417 Vista Oaks Court, Lake Buena Vista, FL 32836
Tel: 800-780 4830
www.perrihouse.com

A chance to get away from it all without leaving the Disney area. This small country inn is secluded on a quiet 16-acre (7-hectare) nature reserve adjacent to Walt Disney World. **$$$**

Pop Century

901 Century Drive, Lake Buena Vista 32830.

Encompassing 20 four-story buildings, this resort will be divided into two sections: the Legendary Years, depicting the first 50 years of the 20th century, and the Classic Years, depicting the second 50 years. "Time capsules" representing various aspects of pop culture will be used to carry the themes. Rooms, smaller than at other Disney properties at 260 square feet (24 sq meters), will have two double beds, bathrooms with a separate vanity area, and small dressers, tables, and chairs. Each section will have a food court, several pools, a playground, a shopping area, and a video arcade. Buses will serve the parks. 5,760 rooms. **$–$$**

PRICE CATEGORIES

Price categories are for a double room without breakfast:
$ = under $100
$$ = $100–$150
$$$ = $150–$200
$$$$ = more than $200

CLOSE TO WALT DISNEY WORLD/KISSIMMEE

HOTELS

Expensive

Hyatt Regency Grand Cypress Resort
One Grand Cypress Boulevard, Orlando, FL 32836
Tel: 407-239 1234 or 800-554 9288
www.grandcypress.com
This luxurious resort has a lush garden setting near Downtown Disney. Amenities include golf, a racquet club, windsurfing on the lake, a "Kid's Club," and an equestrian center as well as convention facilities. Wheelchair access. 750 rooms and suites. **$$$$**

Marriott Orlando World Center
8701 World Center Drive, Orlando, FL 32821
Tel: 407-239 4200 or 800-621 0638
www.marriottworldcenter.com
A towering resort hotel near Disney complete with a convention center, golf and tennis facilities, pools, and gardens. Wheelchair access. 1,500 rooms. **$$$$**

Moderate

Celebration Hotel
700 Bloom Street, Celebration
Tel: 407-566 6000 or 888-499 3800
www.celebrationhotel.com
Located in the Town of Celebration, this quietly elegant, out-of-the-way boutique hotel feels like a million miles away from Disney World, which is just next door. Guests feel like they are stepping back into Old Florida. Registration is concierge style in the low-key lobby, which features comfy sofas, fans, a bar, and hand-painted murals and handtinted photos of orange groves, wildlife, and other historic scenes. The peaceful terrace has rocking chairs and overlooks the pool, lake, and adjoining workout room. The 115 rooms have a classic Southern feel, with pin-striped wallpaper, reproduction antique furnishings, CD players, interactive televisions, and high-speed Internet and e-mail access; some have balconies. Guests may play Celebration's renowned 18-hole golf course and work out at the state-of-the-art Fitness Center at the hospital. **$$$**

Days Inn Maingate East
5840 W Irlo Bronson Memorial Hwy (US 192), Kissimmee, FL 34746
Tel: 407-396 7969 or 800-327 9126
www.daysinn.com
Budget hotel with pools. Close to the Magic Kingdom. Wheelchair access. 604 rooms. **$$**

Doubletree
1249 Apopka-Vineland Road Lake Buena Vista, FL 32836
Tel: 407-239 4646
www.doubletreeclublbv.com
One of the more upscale chains in the Orlando area. Most of the hotels in this chain cater to Orlando's hectic conference schedule. This one, however, makes a special effort to cater to children and guests who've come to Orlando for amusements, not meetings. All rooms have cable TV with in-room movie and video games, and newspaper delivery. The pool downstairs can help you relax or keep fit and the internet café will keep you in touch with those back home. Shuttle service available. **$$$**

Seralago Suites Maingate East
5678 W Irlo Bronson Memorial Hwy (US 192), Kissimmee, FL 34746
Tel: 407-396 4488 or 800-366 5437
www.orlando-family-fun-hotel.com
Large family-oriented hotel near the Magic Kingdom, with pools, children's entertainment, and special "kid suites" for children. Wheelchair access. 614 rooms and suites. **$$**

Orange Lake Resort & Country Club
8505 W Irlo Bronson Memorial Hwy (US 192), Kissimmee, FL 34747
Tel: 407-239 0000 or 800-877 6522
www.orangelake.com
A lakeside resort complex of villas near the Magic Kingdom, with water sports, tennis courts, pools, and a golf course. Wheelchair access. 1,344 studio villas and 1-, 2- and 3-bedroom villas. **$$**

Ramada Resort Maingate
2950 Reedy Creek Boulevard,

Orlando

Kissimmee

Map, page 164

Kissimmee, FL 34747
Tel: 407-396 4466 or 800-365 6935
www.ramada.com
Comfortable, family-oriented lodging near the Magic Kingdom, with swimming pools and tennis courts. Wheelchair access. 278 rooms. **$$**

Inexpensive

Howard Johnson Inn Maingate East
6051 W Irlo Bronson Memorial Hwy (US 192), Kissimmee, FL 34747
Tel: 407-396 1748 or 800-288 4678
www.hojomge.com
Motel with pool near the Magic Kingdom. Children under 12 eat meals at no charge. Wheelchair access. 567 good-sized rooms. **$**

Park Inn Suites
6075 W Irlo Bronson Memorial Hwy (US 192), Kissimmee, FL 34747
Tel: 407-396 6100
www.parkinn.com
Budget hotel. Pool and hot tub. Handy for Magic Kingdom. Wheelchair access. 120 rooms and suites. **$**

UNIVERSAL AND I-DRIVE

HOTELS

Expensive

Portofino Bay Hotel
5601 Universal Boulevard,
Orlando FL 32819
Tel: 888-273 1311
This is such a beautifully designed and constructed re-creation of the real Portofino, you'd be forgiven for calling out *buon giorno* from your window first thing in the morning, especially after that first cup of stiff Italian coffee. Set on a harbor filled with fishing boats, the hotel offers some of the most luxurious accommodations in Orlando, with large, sumptuous rooms, three elaborate pools, a spa, an indoor children's play area, and several restaurants, including the elegant Delfino Riviera. Very expensive but worth it. Free water taxis transport guests between the theme parks and the three Universal hotels. Best of all, guests at all on-site hotels are given express access to nearly all rides and attractions. **$$$$**

Hard Rock Hotel
5800 Universal Boulevard,
Orlando FL 32819
Tel: 888-273 1311
Not quite as lavish or expensive as the Portofino, the accommodations at this Mission-style hotel range from very comfortable standard rooms to large and opulent

suites. An eclectic array of rock and roll memorabilia is displayed tastefully around the building, which nearly surrounds a huge pool with a sandy beach, water slide, and underwater sound system. Several restaurants and bars, a fitness room, an indoor play area, and a Hard Rock store round out the picture. **$$$$**

Royal Pacific Resort
6300 Hollywood Way,
Orlando, FL 32819
Tel: 888-273 1311
Attempting to re-create the South Pacific in central Florida, this resort – opened in 2002 – is centered around a lagoon-like pool fringed with palm trees, waterfalls, a sandy beach and cabanas. Accommodations are priced slightly lower than the Hard Rock Hotel but sacrifice little in the way of comfort or amenities, which include six restaurants and bars, a children's activity room, a fitness room, and convention facilities. **$$$$**

The Peabody Orlando
9801 International Drive,
Orlando, FL 32819
Tel: 407-352 4000 or
800-732 2639
www.peabodyorlando.com
A 27-story landmark hotel in the tourist corridor, with an Olympic-size pool and convention center. Known for its twice-daily "March of the Peabody Ducks" and high tea Mon–Fri. Wheelchair access. 891 rooms and suites. **$$$$**

Moderate

I-Drive Inn
6323 International Drive,
Orlando, FL 32819
Tel: 407-351 4430
www.enjoyfloridahotels.com
Newly refurbished hotel located across from Wet 'n' Wild water park. Some rooms feature a microwave oven and refrigerator. Wheelchair access. 218 rooms. **$$**

Renaissance Orlando Resort
6677 Sea Harbor Drive,
Orlando, FL 32821
Tel: 407-351 5555 or
800-468 3571
www.renaissancehotels.com
This elegant 10-story tower and convention complex is perfect for business travelers as well as families. Rooms are huge and well-appointed, and the service is first rate. A grand, sunlit atrium with sleek glass elevators and what appears to be acres of marble flooring encompass meeting facilities, waterfalls, goldfish ponds and several shops, and restaurants, including the Atlantis, which offers fine Continental dining in a warm and welcoming atmosphere. A coffee shop and deli are good for a quick breakfast or lunch. The location is ideal for guests who want to explore several parks. The hotel is across the street from SeaWorld and Discovery Cove and 15 minutes away or less from Universal Orlando and Disney

Maps, pages 164 & 168

World. Amenities include a pool, an exercise room, a nearby spa, tennis courts, and more than 40 meeting rooms. All in all, it's a great value in a prime location. Wheelchair access. 780 rooms. **$$$**

Sheraton World Resort
10100 International Drive,
Orlando, FL 32821
Tel: 407-352 1100
www.sheratonworld.com
Low-rise buildings surrounded by gardens and located near SeaWorld. Amenities include three pools and miniature golf. A refrigerator and coffeemaker are in each room. Wheelchair access. 789 rooms. **$$**

Sheraton Studio City Resort
5905 International Drive,
Orlando, FL; 32819
Tel: 407-351 2100
www.sheratonstudiocity.com

ACCOMMODATIONS

ACTIVITIES

A – Z

An economical, 21-story round hotel evoking Hollywood of the 1940s and 50s, across from Universal Orlando. Pools. Wheelchair access. 302 rooms. **$$**

Wyndham Resort
8001 International Drive
Tel: 407-351 2420

www.wyndham.com
One of the best of the many choices along International Drive, this is a vast place but surprisingly quiet, with more than 1,000 spacious rooms and pleasant swimming pools. **$$$**

Inn of America
8342 Jamaican Court,
Orlando, FL 32819
Tel: 407-363 1944
www.innofamerica.com
Cozy hotel with free continental breakfast. Close to SeaWorld. Wheelchair access. 134 rooms. **$**

Howard Johnson Plaza Resort
7050 Kirkman Road, Orlando, FL 32819
Tel: 407-351 2000
www.hojo.com
Family-oriented economy hotel with two pools near Universal Orlando. Wheelchair access. 354 rooms. **$**

FURTHER AFIELD

HOTELS

Cocoa Beach

Cocoa Beach Oceanside Inn
1 Hendry Avenue
FL 32931
Tel: 800-874 7958
www.cocoabeach oceansideinn.com
Forty rooms on the beach with fishing, a pool, a restaurant, and shuttle bus service. **$$**

Comfort Inn and Suite Resort
3901 N Atlantic Avenue FL 32931
Tel: 321-783 2221
Ninety-four rooms on the beach with restaurant, lounge, pool. **$–$$**

Doubletree
2080 North Atlantic Avenue FL 3291
Tel: 321-783 9222
www.cocoabeachdoubletree.com
Located directly on the beach of the Atlantic Ocean with balconies overlooking the pool. It's just an upscale chain hotel, but it's got a fantastic location. **$$**

Kissimmee

Clarion Hotel
7675 W Irlo Bronson Memorial Highway
FL 34747
Tel: 407-396 4000
www.clarionhotelmaingate.com
Popular with families, this five-story hotel is close to major theme parks. **$$**

Doubletree Resort Orlando – Villas at Maingate
4787 W. Irlo Bronson Highway, US 192
FL 34746
Tel: 407-397 0555
Just minutes from the Walt Disney World resort. **$$$**

Super 8 Maingate
7571 W Irlo Bronson Memorial Highway
FL 32747
Tel: 407-396 7500
www.super8.com
A comfortable, modest hotel near Walt Disney World with 281 rooms, pool, restaurant, game room and shuttle service. **$**

Lake Wales

Chalet Suzanne Restaurant and Country Inn
3800 Chalet Suzanne Drive
FL 33853
Tel: 863-676 6011 or 800-433 6011
www.chaletsuzanne.com
Voted one of Florida's Top Ten Most Romantic Places by *Woman's Day* magazine, the legendary Chalet Suzanne, owned and operated by the Hinshaw family since 1931, is like a vacation with your favorite fussy Swiss aunt. Thirty homey yet elegant guest rooms, decorated in sunny yellows and creams, and furnished with antiques, lace, quilts, and rockers, cluster around the original inn. The chateau-style building has grown organically over the years to include seven unique rooms overlooking tiny Lake Suzanne and its fast-disappearing orange groves. The award-winning restaurant is renowned for its extravagant Continental cuisine and superb service. Amenities include a swimming pool, ceramics studio, gift shop, and special romantic getaway packages. **$$$$**

Ocala

Seven Sisters Inn
820 SE Fort King St,
FL 34471
Tel: 352-867 1170 or 800-250 3496

Maps, pages 56–57

www.sevensistersinn.com
A Victorian mansion transformed into a charming inn with seven rooms, period antiques, and gourmet breakfasts. **$$**

Downtown Orlando

Orlando International Youth Hostel
4840 W Irlo Bronson Memorial Parkway
FL 32801
Tel: 800-909 4776
Sitting across from downtown's Lake Eola, this hostel is housed in a beautiful old house with 40 private and shared rooms, kitchen facilities and park. Inexpensive, and children are welcome. **$**

Orlando Marriott Downtown
400 W Livingston Street
Orlando, FL 32801
Tel: 407-843 6664

www.marriott.com
A 15-story downtown hotel across from the Orlando Arena and the Carr Performing Arts Center. Casual dining, signature sports bar. Wheelchair access. 290 rooms. **$$$**

Veranda Bed & Breakfast
115 N Summerlin Avenue
FL 32801
Tel: 407-849 0321 or 800-420 6822
www.theverandabandb.com
Five 1920s homes in downtown Orlando have been turned into a delightful B&B, with hardwood floors and period furnishings. **$$**

Westin Grand Bohemian Hotel
325 S Orange Ave.
Orlando, FL 32801
Tel: 407-313 9000
www.starwood.com
This high-style, Bohemian-themed hotel, across from City Hall, calls itself "An Experience in Art and Music." More than 100 pieces of rare artwork, including drawings by Gustav Klimt and Egon Schiele, are displayed. The Klimt Rotunda offers nightly entertainment on one of only two Imperial Grand Bosendorfer pianos in the world. The 250 guest rooms and suites are dramatically furnished in dark Java wood tones, soft red and purple velvet fabrics, silver paint, Tiffany-style lamps, and the luxurious all-white Heavenly Bed, featuring a custom mattress, three high-thread-count sheets, a down blanket, down comforter, and five pillows. All rooms have CD players, high-

speed Internet and e-mail access, three telephones (two with data ports), and interactive TV. The intimate Bosendorfer's Lounge and elegant four-star Boheme Restaurant attract downtown's business and arts community. Starbucks coffee shop, heated outdoor pool, spa, massage room, workout room and guest privileges at nearby Citrus Athletic Club. **$$$**

St Petersburg

Bayboro House Bed and Breakfast
1719 Beach Drive SE,
FL 33701
Tel: 877-823 4955
www.bayborohousebandb.com
A charming Victorian inn overlooking Tampa Bay with three cozy rooms, generous breakfasts and an airy veranda. **$$**

Renaissance Vinoy Resort
501 Fifth Avenue NE
FL 33701
Tel: 727-894 1000 or 800-468 3571
www.renaissancehotels.com
When it opened in 1925, this was the first hotel in the US with steam heat in every room. Now it's a lush restored resort – with guided tours daily of the old haunted nooks and crannies. **$$$**

St Pete Beach

Don CeSar Beach Resort
3400 Gulf Boulevard FL 33706
Tel: 866-728 2206
www.doncesar.com
A shocking pink 1920s resort on the beach,

with 277 luxurious rooms, a pool, a beach, tennis courts, a fitness center and a restaurant, plus sailing, windsurfing, and scuba lessons. **$$$**

Tampa

Double Tree Guest Suites
3050 N Rocky Point Dr West
FL 33607-5800
Tel: 813-888 8800
www.doubletreehotels.com
The only full-service, all-suite, waterfront property in Tampa. **$$$**

Hilton Garden Inn
1700 E 9th Avenue
FL 33605
Tel: 813-769 9267 or 800-221 2424
www.hiltongardeninn.com
The first hotel built in historic Ybor City in a hundred years. Now visitors can spend the night and enjoy a "cooked-to-order" breakfast. **$$**

Hyatt Regency Tampa
2 Tampa City Center
FL 33602
Tel: 813-225 1234 or 800-233 1234
www.tampa.regency.hyatt.com
A modern high-rise hotel in the heart of downtown Tampa; 517 rooms, pool, and exercise room. **$$–$$$**

Saddlebrook Resort Tampa
5700 Saddlebrook Way
Wesley Chapel, FL 33543
Tel: 813-973 1111 or 800-729 8383
www.saddlebrook.com
Golf and tennis are the main draws at this relaxing 480-acre (194-hectare) resort and spa, 12 miles (19 km) north of Tampa. World headquarters for the Arnold Palmer Golf Academy, Saddlebrook

offers year-round golf clinics on two 18-hole championship golf courses surrounded by lagoons, tall cypresses and palm trees, and 45 Grand Slam tennis courts popular with touring pros as well as those participating in The Hopman Tennis Program, founded by legendary Australian Davis Cup coach Harry Hopman. Daily tennis instruction is also available at Saddlebrook Preparatory School. The resort's 800 deluxe guest rooms and one-, two- and three-bedroom suites all have kitchens. Suites have balconies overlooking the golf courses, 270-foot-long (80-meter) SuperPool or nature areas. The Spa at Saddlebrook features 12 treatment rooms, whirlpools and a variety of unisex treatments. Amenities include a wellness center, fitness center, five restaurants and extensive conference facilities and meeting rooms. **$$$$**

Tahitian Inn
601 S Dale Mabry Highway FL 33609
Tel: 800-876 1397
www.tahitianinn.com
A comfortable, budget 79-room motel that caters to families; swimming pool. **$–$$**

PRICE CATEGORIES

Price categories are for a double room without breakfast:
$ = under $100
$$ = $100–$150
$$$ = $150–$200
$$$$ = more than $200

ACTIVITIES

THE ARTS, NIGHTLIFE, FESTIVALS, SHOPPING, AND SPECTATOR SPORTS

THE ARTS

Despite initial impressions, entertainment in Orlando is not an unadulterated diet of kitsch and theme park razzmatazz. The city has a vibrant cultural scene, with everything from Broadway shows to opera and orchestral music.

As far as the performing arts are concerned, the majority of the top-quality shows are staged between October and April, although there is plenty to choose from year-round. The main venues are listed below, alphabetically by region.

Museums & Art Galleries

Charles Hosmer Morse Museum of American Art
445 North Park Avenue
Winter Park, FL 32789
Tel: 407-645 5324
www.morsemuseum.org
The world's most comprehensive collection of works by Louis Comfort Tiffany, including jewelery, pottery, paintings, and glassworks.
City Hall of Orlando – Terrace Gallery
400 S Orange Avenue
Orlando, FL 32801
Tel: 407-246 2121
Showcases Florida artists and traveling exhibits.

Orange County Regional History Center and Heritage Square
65 East Central Boulevard
Tel: 407-836 8500
www.thehistorycenter.org
Set in the 1927 Orange County Courthouse, this award-winning museum explains Florida's diverse history from Native Americans to cartoon heroes.
Orlando Museum of Art
2416 North Mills Avenue
Tel: 407-896 4231
www.omart.org
Collections of American, African, and ancient American art plus touring international art exhibits.
Orlando Science Center
777 East Princeton Street
www.osc.org
Tel: 407-514 2000 or
888-672 4386
Dozens of interactive exhibits that keep all ages entertained plus an eight-story CineDome screen, the world's largest domed theater and planetarium.

Theaters

Cirque Du Soleil
Downtown Disney West Side
Tel: 407-939 7600
www.cirquedusoleil.com
Don't be misled by the name. This is much more than a mere circus. Outrageous costumes (and prices) and outlandish acts make this a very memorable

evening indeed.
Surfside Playhouse
Brevard Avenue and
South 5th Avenue
Cocoa Beach
Tel: 321-783 3127
www.surfsideplayers.com
A community theater featuring first-rate performances.
Broadway In Orlando
201 South Orange Avenue,
Suite 101
Tel: 407-423 9999 or
800-950 4647
Presents a series of national touring Broadway productions at the Bob Carr Performing Arts Center.

Ballet

Central Florida Ballet
4525 Vineland Road,
Suite 204, Orlando, FL 32811
Tel: 407-849 9948

Opera

Orlando Opera
Dr Phillips Center
Tel: 407-426 1717 or
800-336 7372
Celebrating over 40 years of performing in central Florida.

Concerts

Bob Carr Performing Arts Center:
401 Livingston Street, Orlando

Tel: 407-849 2070
A year-round community auditorium that hosts regional and national musical, theater, and dance performances.
TD Waterhouse Center
600 W Amelia Street
Orlando
Tel: 407-849 2020
One of the main concert venues in the area.

NIGHTLIFE

Introduction

Orlando's theme parks do an excellent job of keeping their clientele after hours, which is a shame, as downtown (Orlando's not Disney's) is worth the excursion. Downtown Disney and City-Walk, on the other hand, have restaurants, bars, and clubs all centrally located with transportation back to resort hotels until late evening, so you need not worry about drink driving. Downtown Disney can still be too pristine for an evening and both seem to be taken over by local teens during the weekend. Downtown Orlando is exactly what you'd expect from a bustling city: a mixture of stylish clubs and bars, some characterful watering holes, and a large variety of independent restaurants. The choice – something never in short supply in Orlando – is yours.

Nightclubs

Adventurers Club
Downtown Disney
Modeled after a gentlemen's sport club of the 1930s, this bar and nightclub offers eccentric live stage shows in four different rooms.
8TRAX
Downtown Disney
Relive the disco days of the 70s.
Mannequins Dance Palace
Downtown Disney
Once voted the Southeast's best dance club. Spinning dance floor and state-of-the-art light and sound systems keep crowds going.
the groove
CityWalk
A hip dance club with a throbbing sound system frequented mostly by young singles on the make.

Pubs & bars

Jimmy Buffett's Margaritaville
CityWalk
A spin-off of Jimmy's original Key West booze house. The original is the biggest tourist trap in Key West. This one has the best margaritas in CityWalk.
Cricketer's Arms
8445 International Drive
The Mercado
Tel: 407-354 0686
A taste of England serving 15 imported beers and four hand-drawn ales.
Lucky Leprechaun Irish Pub
7032 International Drive
Tel: 407-352 7031
Irish beer, song, and cheer.

8 Seconds
100 W Livingston Street
Tel: 407-839 4800
A rodeo bar with a mechanical bull and dance lessons.

Music Venues

Pleasure Island Jazz Company
Downtown Disney
Features current jazz stars and local artists in a relaxed environment.
Pat O'Brien's
CityWalk
A copy of New Orleans' famous watering hole, featuring dueling pianos and its trademark Hurricane, a potent rum concoction.
CityJazz
CityWalk
Hosts live performances of fine jazz musicians.
Latin Quarter
CityWalk
Sexy salsa served with stiff drinks. The live performances draw a big crowd.
The Social
54 N Orange Avenue
www.theorlandosocial.com
Tel: 407-246 1419
Nightly live music from local and national acts.

Comedy Venues

Comedy Warehouse
Downtown Disney
The Who, What, and Warehouse Players offer hilarious improv every night.
SAK Comedy Lab
380 W Amelia Street
Tel: 407-648 0001
www.sak.com
Improvisational comedy show.

CINEMA

Universal Cineplex
CityWalk
Tel: 407-354 5998
AMC
Downtown Disney
Tel: 407-298 4488

Enzian Cinema
1300 South Orlando
Avenue, Maitland
Tel: 407-629 1088
www.enzian.org
Florida's only not-for-profit cinema
and the best place to see films off
the beaten blockbuster path.

CHILDREN'S ACTIVITIES

Little

Theme parks...
The Magic Kingdom in general,
and its dark rides, such as **Peter
Pan's Flight** and **it's a small
world...**, are a big hit with the
smallest of fans but can be a bit
too tedious for those who've
out-grown the characters they
feature. Said characters are
especially entertaining at character dining experiences held at
Cinderella's Castle and **Crystal
Palace**, amongst other locations.
Check times when entering parks.
Islands of Adventures' **Seuss
Landing** and Universal Studios'
Woody Woodpecker's Kidzone
are both brilliant jungle gyms by
any other name.
Unexpectedly, many tots find
most of the 3-D attractions in
Orlando a bit too terrifying as
some sort of bug scampering up

your legs is a standard gag. Plus,
the graphics are so realistic they
may forget that it's just a film.
The exception to this is **Mickey's
PhilHarmagic** in the Magic Kingdom, which is just as entertaining as other films, but enjoyable
for all ages.

...and beyond
If seeing only animatronic animals or those in captivity leaves
your child wanting more, the
Green Meadows Petting Farm
(see page 166) gives kids the
chance to milk a cow, ride a pony,
go on a hay ride, and get up close
to over 200 animals.

Medium

Theme parks...
Disney-MGM and Animal Kingdom
are the most appealing Disney
Parks for those young children
who want to relive the adventures
of movies and see wildlife, but
are still too timid for thrill rides.
Don't forget to take along an
autograph book and pen to
gather lasting memories of character greetings. The compulsion
to collect can also be quenched
by trading pins at stalls located
throughout the Disney resort.
Stunt shows such as the **Wild
Wild Wild West Stunt Show** at Universal and **Indiana Jones Epic**

Stunt Spectacular at Disney-MGM
are great for those too big to be
scared by loud noises but not big
enough to see through the stunts
(and they are performed in shaded
pavilions and last long enough for
you to get a bit of a rest).
It may be impossible to pull
kids away from **Nickelodeon Studios** at Universal. When taping,
they can see all their favourite
shows (and stars) live. **Discovery
Cove**, where you get a hand-
shake and a kiss from a dolphin
before it swims you back to
shore, is something most children could only dream of. It's
expensive, but travel agents
often offer specials and the
memory is irreplaceable.

...and beyond
If you've got a young one who's
taste for the disgusting and
bizarre seems insatiable, **Ripley's Believe or Not Odditorium**
(see page 169) may be just the
place for them. Exhibits include a
two-headed calf, among other
oddities.
Really for all ages, the **Orlando
Science Center** (see page 183)
is a must-see, with interactive
exhibits covering everything from
life in zero gravity to a journey
through the human body.

Teens

Theme parks...
Assuming your teen wants to push
the limits of motion sickness, Universal's Islands of Adventure with
the **Incredible Hulk** and **Dueling
Dragons** roller coasters, plus the
**Amazing Adventures of Spider-
Man** and other disorienting
rides should be top of their list.
Disney-MGM (**Twilight Zone Tower
of Terror** and the **Rock 'n' Roller
Coaster**) is the next best stop.
Epcot has two fantastic thrill rides
in **Test Track** and **Mission: SPACE**,
but the other exhibits are likely to
bore even the most inquisitive
adolescent.
As far as nightlife goes,
CityWalk and **Downtown Disney**

both provide a safe environment for teens to mingle (and get away from their parents).

Though entrance is expensive, the amusements at **DisneyQuest** could entertain a teen for the entire day (or evening) and there are plenty of places nearby (House of Blues just across the street) that could allow adults the comfort of mind and the relaxing beverages needed after a day at the parks.

...and beyond

For those desperate to get behind the wheel of a car, **Fun Spot Action Park** *(see page 171)* provides bumper cars and four multi-level tracks for go-cart racing.

SHOPPING

What to Buy

If you are into kitsch – plastic flamingo ashtrays, canned sunshine, orange perfume, and the like – you will find Florida a veritable treasure house. From roadside shacks to massive, futuristic malls, stores carry plenty of traditional souvenirs. (Don't be surprised if your souvenir plate has a sticker on the bottom that says "Made in Taiwan".) And then, of course, there are the homegrown souvenirs like oranges, tangerines, limes, kumquats, and grapefruits that can be shipped home for a small fee.

But if you look a little harder, Florida also has an array of quality goods to take home from a trip. There are shops worth seeking out that sell designer clothing at factory prices, fascinating examples of Haitian art, Art Deco, and old Florida antiques, Native American crafts, and shells that forever smell of the sea.

For more humdrum shopping and for everyday necessities, there is the usual array of convenience stores, drugstores, department stores, and supermarkets.

Many Floridians do their shopping in malls, which contain the usual mix of department stores, boutiques, chain stores and one-of-a-kind shops. Just ask the staff in your hotel for details of the best malls in your area. Hours vary, but most shopping centers are open seven days a week.

Where to Buy

Belz Factory Outlet Mall
5211 International Drive
Tel: 407-352 9611
www.belz.com
Open 10am–9pm Mon–Sat,
11am–6pm Sun.
Supposedly the second most-visited attraction in Orlando after Walt Disney World, Belz is a bargain bonanza. This large, indoor mall is one of the best places in Florida to shop for designer clothes – Anne Klein, London Fog, Christian Dior, and many more – and for just about every brand of jeans, sneakers, and casual wear at discounts of up to 75 percent.

The Florida Mall
8001 South Orange
Blossom Trail
Orlando FL 32809
Tel: 407-851 6255
www.simon.com
Open Mon–Sat
10am–9pm, Sun 12–6pm
The area's most popular shopping destination, with over 200 shops and six major department stores (Saks Fifth Avenue, Dillard's, Sears, JC Penney, Parisia, and Burdines).

Historic Downtown Kissimmee
Main to Broadway to
Emmett Street
Features men's and ladies' clothiers, western wear and collectibles in an old-fashioned atmosphere.

Lake Buena Vista Factory Stores
15591 Apopka Vineland Road,
Orlando, FL 32821
Tel: 407-238 9301
www.lbvfs.com
Open Mon–Sat 10am–9pm, Sun 10am–6pm
Manufacturer-direct prices on designer brands.

Mercado Mediterranean Village
8445 International Drive.
Tel: 407-345 9337.
www.themercardo.com
Open 10am–10pm daily.
More than 60 specialty shops along a series of brick streets with an atmosphere of a Mediterranean village. Arts, crafts, jewelry, clothing, and leather goods.

Orange World
5395 W Irlo Bronson Memorial Highway, Kissimmee.
Tel: 407-396 1306.
Open 8am–11pm daily.
www.orangeworld192.com
You can't miss the building – shaped like a gigantic orange – and inside is an assortment of fresh-picked fruits, citrus candies, and orange blossom honey. All available to be shipped to friends and family back home.

Pointe Orlando
9101 International Drive,
Orlando.
Tel: 407-248 2838.
www.pointeorlando.com
Open 10am–10pm Sun–Thur and 10am–11pm Sat and Sun.
An outdoor shopping plaza with upscale retailers such as Armani, Abercrombie & Fitch and chi-chi toy store F.A.O. Schwarz, as well as a huge cineplex, Muvico Pointe 21, featuring an IMAX theater.

Downtown Disney

Though shopping opportunities abound in Disney World, this area has more specialty items and a wider selection than most. Highlights include a Virgin Megastore, the Lego Imagination Center, and the largest Disney store in the world.

Disney & Universal

You can't walk two steps at Disney World or Universal Orlando without bumping into a shop of some kind. The trick is finding the interesting ones. Here are a few suggestions.

Magic Kingdom
Disney Clothiers
Main Street USA
Everyone's first stop for textiles with trademark ears.

Ye Olde Christmas Shoppe
Liberty Square
Decorations for the most magical of days sold year-round.
Pooh's Thotful Shop
Fantasyland
Pick up the best in Pooh goods.

Disney-MGM Studios
Tatooine Traders
Star Tours
Vintage Star Wars dolls on sale.
Stage 1 Company Store
Muppet Vision 3-D
Muppet madness, souvenirs for all of Henson's creations.
Sid Cahuenga's One-of-a-Kind
Entry Plaza
Celebrity memorabilia, including clothing worn by the stars.
Beverly Sunset
Sunset Boulevard
Souvenir shop dedicated to Disney villains.

Downtown Disney
Sosa Family Cigars
West Side
The only tobacco shop in Disney World, featuring high-quality, hand-rolled cigars. The trick is finding a place to smoke one.
Suspended Animation
Pleasure Island
A gallery of Disney animation celebs.

Universal Studios
Silver Screen Collectibles
Hollywood
Gifts based on vintage stars such as Lucille Ball and Betty Boop.
Brown Derby Hat Shop
Hollywood
An assortment of hats from all eras.

Islands of Adventure
Mulberry Street Store
Seuss Landing
Cat in the Hat clothing and souvenirs.
Historic Families
The Lost Continent
Explore the history of your family name.
Gasoline Alley
Toon Lagoon
Featuring PEZ Candy collectibles.

Comic Book Shop
Marvel Super Hero Island
Get the latest editions and collectibles of your favorite characters.

SPORTS

Participant Sports

Orlando and the Disney resorts provide plenty of opportunity for every type of active recreation, with state-of-the-art facilities for jogging, swimming, fishing, cycling, boating, and so on.

Fishing
For information about fishing licenses, locations and limits on fish or closed seasons on certain species, you must contact the Florida Fish and Wildlife Commission (tel: 888-347 4356; www.floridafisheries.com) A 7-day freshwater license costs around $17.

Golf
Florida is one of the top golfing states in the country – it is said that one out of every ten golf games in the US takes place in Florida, and few states have more courses. There are more than 150 courses within a 45-minute drive of downtown Orlando.

Many of the courses are private, but there are enough public courses for out-of-towners who don't have a friend at a local country club. And don't think that because Florida is flat its courses lack challenge and rolling beauty. Many courses were designed by experts who have created beautiful man-made undulations, hills, and bluffs amid the greens. There are more than 30 golf resorts registered with the Orlando Visitors Bureau.

Green fees vary from over $75 per person at the more exclusive, private courses to less than $20 per person at the public courses. Fees are often higher in winter, when northerners flock to the state. For information on location of courses, fees, and regulations call the Florida Sports Foundation, tel: 850-488 8347, for a free copy of the Official Florida Golf Guide.

Tennis
Walt Disney World resorts contain 25 high-quality tennis courts. Disney's Raquet Club at the Contemporary Resort is the highlight. It contains six clay courts and a professional shop. Call for reservations at 407-WDW-PLAY (939 7529). You can also make reservations for the courts at the Yacht and Beach Club by calling the number above. Courts at the Grand Floridian, Fort Wilderness, BoardWalk, Old Key West, and the Swan and Dolphin are on a first-come, first-served basis.

Courts open 7am–7pm with the exception of the Swan and Dolphin, which opens 24 hours. Play is often limited to two hours and there are fees at the Contemporary, Grand Floridian, and Swan and Dolphin. Disney also offers a rotating program of training sessions. Call the number above for details.

Orlando Tennis Service provides reservations, lessons, and equipment rental for visitors to the Orlando area. For information, contact the Orlando Tennis Service, 9801 International Drive, Orlando; Tel: 888-958 0487; www.orlandotennis.com

Jogging/running
Several scenic jogging paths wend through Disney World. Summer heat and humidity can be extreme, so drink more water than usual and adjust your pace and distance accordingly. Try one of the interesting paths listed below:
● The 1.4 mile (2.3 km) promenade around the Caribbean Beach Resort Lake.
● 75 mile (1.2 km) route around Crescent Lake, accessible to the Swan and Dolphin, Yacht and

TRANSPORT

Beach Club, and BoardWalk Resorts.

● 75 mile (1.2 km) path around Lago Dorado at Coronado Springs.

● 75 mile (1.2 km) path at Wilderness Lodge, with fitness stations.

● 1–3 mile (1.6–5 km) scenic routes around Old Key West and Port Orleans Resorts.

● 1.5 mile (2.4 km) path from Universal City Walk to Portofino Bay Hotel via the Hard Rock Hotel.

Boating

Many WDW resorts rent watercraft and there is no shortage of artificial lakes to explore. You can explore Bay Lake from the Contemporary Hotel, Wilderness Lodge or Fort Wilderness. Seven Seas Lagoon is accessible from the Polynesian and Grand Floridian Resorts. The Caribbean Beach Resorts have a marina, Barefoot Bay, worth exploring, while the Yacht and Beach Club, BoardWalk, and the Swan and Dolphin all have access to Crescent Lake. From Port Orleans, Old Key West, and Downtown Disney you can access waterways connected to Lake Buena Vista and from Coronado Springs explore tiny Lago Dorado. You will need a resort ID and a driver's license to hire any watercraft.

Canoeing

Canoes are available from the Caribbean Beach and Port Orleans resorts. A better option is renting one from Fort Wilderness and exploring its wooded canals.

Ocean kayaks

Available at Coronado Springs and Port Orleans.

Canopy boats

These accommodate up to eight people and are suited for cruising. Available at Downtown Disney, Polynesian, Contemporary, Grand Floridian, Wilderness

Lodge, Yacht and Beach Club, Old Key West, Port Orleans, and Caribbean Beach marinas.

Other watercraft

Pedal Boats, Hydro Bikes and Pontoon Boats are available throughout the resort. Parasailing is available at the Contemporary resort only.

Spectator Sports

Football

Orlando's closest team in the National Football League is the Tampa Bay Buccaneers, but Florida's favourite team is the Miami Dolphins. The season runs Sep–Dec.

College games draw almost as many (highly partisan) fans as the NFL matches. The Citrus Bowl held in Orlando at the New Year is one of the top matches in the football season.

Baseball

As the official spring training grounds for 18 major league teams, Florida from February through March is the place to watch your favorite players warm up for the summer season. Visiting teams also meet in friendly games in the so-called Grapefruit League, which draws big crowds.

Basketball

The Orlando Magic is the city's professional basketball team. They play at the TD Waterhouse Center. The season begins in September and runs through May. Call the box office 407-896 2442 for information and tickets.

Horse Racing

Thoroughbred Horse Racing
● Tampa Bay Downs, 12505 Racetrack Road, Tampa, tel: 813-855 4401. Dec–Apr.

Greyhound racing

● St Petersburg Kennel Club: 10490 Gandy Boulevard, St Petersburg, tel: 727-576 1361.

● Sarasota Kennel Club: 5400 Bradenton Road, Sarasota, tel: 941-355 7744.

● Tampa Greyhound Track: 8300 Nebraska Avenue N, Tampa, tel: 813-932 4313.

Sporting Events

January

Florida Citrus Bowl (Orlando). Nationally televised college football bowl game featuring teams from the Southeastern and Big Ten Conferences. Some years it decides the National Champion.

February

Silver Spurs Rodeo (Kissimmee). Late February.

March

Winter Equestrian Festival (Tampa). Late March.

April

Easter Surfing Festival (Cocoa Beach). Early April.

July

Central Florida Soap Box Derby (Sanford). Mid-July.

September

Labor Day Rodeo and Parade (Okeechobee). Early September. Power Boat Racing (Sanford). Late September.
Triathlon (Sarasota). Late September.

October

Airboat Races and Festival (Okeechobee). Mid-October. Kissimmee Boating Jamboree. Late October.

November

St Petersburg Boat Show. Late November.

December

Central Florida Sailfest (Sanford). Early December. Sandy Claws Beach Run (Sarasota). Early December. Kissimmee Warbird Weekend. Late December.

ACCOMMODATIONS

ACTIVITIES

A – Z

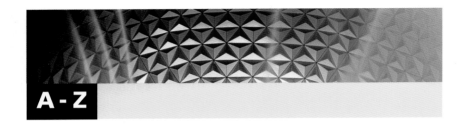

DIRECTORY OF PRACTICAL INFORMATION

B Budgeting for Your Trip 232
Business Hours 232
C Climate 233
Crime and Safety 233
Customs Regulations 233
D Disabled Travelers 234
E Electricity 234
Embassies/Consulates 234
Emergencies 234
Entry Requirements 234

Etiquette 235
G Gay & Lesbian Travelers 235
H Health & Medical Care 235
I Internet 236
L Left Luggage 236
M Maps 236
Media 236
Money 236
P Photography 237
Postal Services 237

Public Holidays 237
Public Toilets 237
R Religious Services 238
S Student Travelers 238
T Telephones 238
Tickets 238
Travel Agents 238
Tourist Offices 238
U Useful Numbers 239
W What to Bring 239

B udgeting for Your Trip

If you're looking for a hotel with an acceptable minimum level of comfort, cleanliness, and facilities, a reasonable starting point for the price of a double room is $50 in budget-class hotels: going up from there to around $80 should make a significant difference in quality. For between $100 and $150 a whole range of hotels opens up, ranging from bland business-traveler places to characterful establishments.

Food costs range from a couple of dollars for a bagle and coffee, through $25–40 for a 2–3-course meal at a standard (often chain) restaurant. Finer fare begins at $40 and can be as pricey as you can handle, at a fine restaurant.

Getting around by Disney transport and hotel shuttles to the park is free. Lynx buses cost a couple of dollars depending on distance and taxis, due to the distance inherent in most journeys through Orlando, are expensive. Expect to spend at least $30.

Business Hours

Most businesses are open 9am–5pm, with many of the shopping malls open as late as 10pm. Many large supermarkets and numerous restaurants stay open 24 hours.

Banks usually remain open until at least 4pm from Monday through Thursday, and until 6pm on Friday. Some banks are open for a short time on Saturday.

During some public holidays, some or all state, local, and federal agencies may be closed. Local banks, businesses, shops, and attractions may also stop operating during some public holidays.

Park opening hours
Opening hours at all Orlando parks are calculated on a complex matrix that attempts to maximize the use of park staff and other resources. This makes for such a complicated and unpredictable schedule that

you are strongly advised to consult the parks shortly before visiting. The easiest way is via the Web; www.disneyworld.com and www.universalorlando.com provide up-to-date information on hours and entertainment schedules. For those without Web access, telephone Disney at 407-939 4636 or Universal at 407-363 8000.

C limate

Winter is usually delightful in central Florida, but there are rainy and cold spells – temperatures can dip to freezing. On the other hand, winter temperatures can reach 80°F (30°C). It's best to pack clothing for layering if temperatures drop.

Summer ranges from hot to very hot, with high humidity. From June to October, it rains heavily but briefly most days. For a weather report, dial 407-824 4104.

Rainfall
Orlando's hottest months are also the rainiest. Thunderstorms occur with such regularity each day that you can set your watch by them. There is little rain in November and December: only 2 inches (5 cm) of rain falls on average across the whole state.

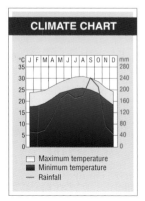

CLIMATE CHART

□ Maximum temperature
■ Minimum temperature
— Rainfall

Tornadoes
Florida ranks eighth in the list of US states with the most tornadoes per year, but they're not nearly as bad as the awesome twisters that assail the Midwest. Trailer parks are vulnerable.

Lightning
Florida is unofficially dubbed the "lightning capital of the country." The state records an average of 10 deaths and 30 injuries from lightning each year. This is attributed to the hot, wet air that lies close to the ground and unstable atmospheric conditions that exist mainly from May until September.

Lasting just 1/1000th of a second, a bolt of lightning delivers a shock of 6,000–10,000 AMPS that can paralyze vital functions. Even so, two-thirds of those hit by lightning in Florida survive, but are later removed from the electoral rolls.

If you see dark clouds and lightning bolts approach, take cover. If in a car, stay inside until the storm passes. If in a building, don't "make a run for it." Many lightning victims are killed when getting into or out of their cars. Boaters should head for the nearest place they can tie up and evacuate the boat. During any nearby lightning storm, parks will close their outdoor attractions.

When to visit
Plan your visit to Orlando very carefully. Visiting during the least crowded seasons usually makes for a far more pleasant experience at the theme parks. Crowds and waiting times are daunting during the busy seasons. The obvious times to avoid are those coinciding with school vacations. During the summer break (mid-June to late August), spring break and Easter periods (March/April) and Thanksgiving or Christmas you will encounter the heaviest crowds and priciest hotel rooms.

From September until Thanksgiving, crowds are light, as they are in January, and between the holiday weekends of Thanksgiving and Christmas.

Crime and Safety

The big theme parks have their own security personnel. They are so discreet that you are hardly aware of their presence, but they'll be on hand if you need them. Walt Disney World is among the safest environments on Earth, but – as always – you should look after your property and keep a close eye on young children.

Having said that, it should also be acknowledged that Florida does not have a squeaky clean reputation when it comes to crime. Attacks committed against tourists periodically ruin the state's idyllic vacation-in-the-sun image. The authorities have come up with various safeguards designed to protect visitors. Many of these are aimed at motorists, particularly in Miami, where some violent assaults occurred because jet-lagged tourists disembarked from long flights, missed the highway signs for Miami Beach, and found themselves in a dangerous part of town.

Car rental agencies have removed the special license plates which formerly earmarked rental cars and replaced them with standard-issue plates used by residents. Pedestrians should use common sense:
● don't carry around large sums of money or expensive video/camera equipment or jewelry;
● know where you're going and how to get there;
● don't travel alone at night;
● ask your hotel staff for advice about areas that should be avoided.

Customs Regulations

All articles brought into the US must be declared to customs. You will be given a special form to fill in before you enter the country. Articles brought into the US are subject to duty or internal revenue tax, but visitors are given an allowance of exempted goods.

Prohibited goods

Articles which visitors are forbidden to take into the United States include:
● Liquor-filled chocolates or candy.
● Dangerous drugs.
● Obscene publications.
● Hazardous articles (e.g. fireworks).
● Most fresh food products, unless you have an import permit.
● Narcotics. Travelers using medicines containing narcotics (such as tranquilizers or cough medicine) should carry a prescription and/or a note from their doctor, and should take only the quantity required for a short stay.

Full details of customs requirements are available from your nearest US Embassy or Consulate.

Customs allowances

Articles brought into the United States are subject to duty or internal revenue tax. Visitors, however, are given an allowance of exempted goods. These include:
● Money. There is no limit on the amount of money − US or foreign traveler's checks or money orders − that you may bring into or take out of the US. But you must declare amounts exceeding $10,000 or the foreign currency equivalent.
● Alcohol. Visitors over the age of 21 are permitted to bring in 1 liter (34 fl oz) of alcohol for their personal use. Excess quantities are subject to duty and tax.
● Cigars and cigarettes. Visitors may bring in not more than 200

EMERGENCIES

In case of emergency, dial 911 to be connected to fire, police, or ambulance.

cigarettes (one carton), 50 cigars (as long as they are not Cuban), or 4.4 lbs (2 kg) of smoking tobacco, or proportionate amounts of each. An additional 100 cigars may be brought in under your gift exemption.
● Gifts As a visitor to the US, you can claim on entry up to $100 worth of merchandise, free of duty and tax, as gifts for other people. Such articles may have to be inspected, so do not gift-wrap them until after you have entered the country.

D isabled Travellers

Accessibility and facilities are excellent at the theme parks and other attractions in Orlando. Special parking is available near the entrances to each park, the hotels, and other facilities.

Disney publishes *The Guidebook for Guests with Disabilities*. Ask at City Hall in the Magic Kingdom and at Information/Guest Services desks in other areas.

Wheelchairs are available for rent in limited numbers in several locations, usually outside or just inside the entrance. For some attractions and rides, guests may remain in wheelchairs. For others, they must be able to leave the wheelchair. Regulations are clearly indicated in leaflets and at the appropriate entrance. Some motorized wheelchairs are available for rent, and nearly all buses and launches can accommodate conventional wheelchairs. Wheelchair access is available at toilets in all the theme parks.

For hearing-impaired guests, there is a *TDD* at City Hall in Magic Kingdom, at Guest Services in Disney-MGM Studios, Epcot and Animal Kingdom, and at both Universal parks. Many rides and attractions have closed captioning. A sign-language interpreter is available for theater shows.

Sight-impaired guests can borrow complimentary cassettes

and tape recorders at the same locations. A deposit is required.

E lectricity

110−115 volts; flat two or three-pronged plugs.

Embassies and Consulates

Few English-speaking countries have a consulate in Florida. These are the nearest ones to contact:
● Australia: 2103 Coral Way, Suite 108; Tel: 305-858 7633.
● Canada: 200 South Biscayne Boulevard, Suite 1600, Miami, Florida 33131. Tel: 305-579 1600.
● New Zealand: Embassy, 37 Observatory Circle, NW, Washington DC 20008. Tel: 202-328 4800.
● Republic of Ireland: 345 Park Avenue, 17th Floor, New York, NY 10022. Tel: 212-319 2555.
● South Africa: 333 East 38th Street, 9th Floor, New York, NY 10016. Tel: 212-213 4880.
● United Kingdom: 245 Peachtree Street Center Ave., Atlanta, GA 20303. Tel: 404-524 5856 Fax: 404-524 3153.

Entry Requirements

Most foreign visitors need a machine readable passport (which should be valid for at least six months longer than their intended stay) and a visa to enter the United States. You should also be able to provide evidence that you intend to leave the United States after your visit is over (usually in the form of a return or onward ticket), and visitors from some countries need an international vaccination certificate.

Certain foreign nationals are exempt from the normal visa requirements. Canadian citizens with a valid Canadian passport need no visa. Nor do Mexican citizens provided they have a Mexican passport and a US Border Crossing Card (Form I-186 or I-586), and as long as they are residents of Mexico.

A special "visa-waiver" program means that citizens of some countries do not require a visa if they are staying for less than 90 days and have a round-trip or onward ticket. These include New Zealand, Japan, the UK, and about 18 other European nations.

Mistakes are not accepted on immigration forms you fill in during the flight. So don't cross anything out – ask for a new form. Note that immigration officials are entitled to ask for proof of solvency on your arrival in the United States. You will also be fingerprinted and have an iris scan upon arrival.

Those requiring a visa or visa information can apply by mail or by personal application to their local US Embassy or Consulate.

Vaccination certificate requirements vary, but proof of immunization against smallpox or cholera may be necessary.

Etiquette

Liquor laws
The legal drinking age in Florida is 21. Liquor can be purchased on any day of the week, but note that some municipalities do not permit retail stores to sell liquor until after 1pm on Sundays.

Smoking
Smoking is not permitted on any attraction, ride, or in any waiting area in theme parks. All Disney restaurants are smoke-free. Other restaurants in town have taken that lead, though many eateries have designated smoking and non-smoking areas; be sure to mention your preference before being seated. Non-smoking rooms are available at most hotels; ask when you make your reservation or when you check in.

G ay & Lesbian Travelers

Gay Day
Each June, Orlando and its amusement parks are host to Gay Day. This event attracts over 100,000 gay and lesbian people along with their friends and families. Special events are held at Walt Disney World, Universal Studios, and throughout Orlando and its many theme parks.

H ealth and Medical Care

Most visitors to Florida will have no health problems during their stay: sunburn and mosquito bites in summer are the main nuisance for the majority. Even so, you should never leave home without travel insurance to cover both yourself and your belongings. Your own insurance company or travel agent can advise you on policies, but shop around since rates vary. Make sure you are covered for accidental death, emergency medical care, trip cancelation, and baggage or document loss.

Medical assistance
In the event you need medical assistance, ask the reception staff at your hotel or consult the local Yellow Pages for the physician or pharmacist nearest you (in large cities, there is usually a physician referral service number listed). The larger resort hotels may well have a resident doctor.

If you need immediate attention, go directly to a hospital emergency room (ER). Most emergency rooms are open 24 hours a day.

There is nothing cheap about being sick in the US – whether it involves a simple visit to the doctor or a spell in a hospital. The initial ER fee charged by a good hospital might be $250, and that's before the additional cost of X-rays, medicines and so on have been added. It is essential

to be armed with adequate medical insurance, and to carry an identification card or policy number at all times.

Health hazards and insects
The two most common health hazards in Orlando are sunburn and heat exhaustion; both are easily avoided. Biting and stinging insects are a nuisance more than a hazard but are still well worth avoiding.

Sunburn
An early overdose of sun can ruin in a few short hours a vacation that involved months of planning and saving. One of the most common sights in Florida is an over-baked tourist painfully trying to sit or walk without rubbing against anything.

If you are set on getting a suntan, do so gradually. Begin with a high-factor sunscreen and work up to less protective lotions. Don't neglect to apply lotion on overcast days; the sun's ultraviolet rays still penetrate the clouds, and the shade can lull you into staying outside for too long.

The heat alone can be a danger, especially for the elderly or those with a pre-existing medical condition. Dehydration and salt deficiency can lead to heat exhaustion. The main symptoms are headache, weakness, light-headedness, muscle aches, cramps, and agitation. Make a point of drinking plenty of non-alcoholic fluids (before you get thirsty) and take periodic breaks in the shade or an air-conditioned environment.

If untreated, heat exhaustion can escalate to a far more serious case of heat stroke, which means that the body's temperature rises to dangerous levels. In addition to the symptoms listed above, people suffering from heat stroke may exhibit confusion, strange behavior, and even seizures. If you suspect a companion is suffering from heat stroke, get them to a cool place, apply cold damp cloths, and call for a doctor immediately.

Insects

People aren't the only creatures attracted to Florida's sun and sand. Dozens of insect species, from mosquitoes and fleas to bees and fire ants, can bite or sting and cause a great deal of annoyance and discomfort.

Florida is infamous for the great swarms of mosquitoes that can take the joy out of watching summer sunsets. Most big cities have mosquito-control programs that have effectively curtailed the pest's activities. Walt Disney World sends out teams to spray the whole park on a daily basis in summer, but pack a bottle of insect repellent just in case. Sunrise and sunset are the worst times, so splash on repellent, and cover up at these times.

Entomologists call them bibinoid flies, but to most Floridians they are simply known as love bugs – because you will usually find them "flying united" right into your hair, face or windshield. Love bugs don't bite. They are too busy mating. But they can cause trouble between May and September. In moist, wooded hammock areas, black clouds of love bugs may hang over highways, slowing down traffic as they clog car radiators and splatter against windshields.

If you are exploring off the beaten track, you might want to tread carefully, particularly when barefoot. Grassy fields are prime locations for mounds of fire ants. These tiny red ants inflict a burning sting and leave a reddish welt that turns into a chickenpox-like blister. This can become infected if scratched. Some people are allergic to the sting of a fire ant and can suffer nausea or dizziness that needs prompt medical attention.

Visitors new to tropical or subtropical regions may be startled by the local cockroaches. Often called palmetto bugs, they grow to sizes unheard of in colder cli-

mates, usually resembling miniature armored patrol cars as they dart under the carpet or disappear into cracks in the wall. They will eat virtually anything, but steer clear of people.

Ticks attach themselves to the skin of humans and animals and feed on blood. There are basically two kinds in Florida. A dog tick is fairly large and easily removed with fingers or tweezers. A deer tick is much tinier (about the size of a poppy seed) and can transmit bacteria that causes Lyme disease. The primary symptom of Lyme disease is a distinct bull's-eye rash. Later symptoms resemble the flu. Contact a physician if you suspect you may have contracted Lyme disease or you've found a tick and need help identifying which type it is.

nternet

Walt Disney World
disneyworld.disney.go.com/
waltdisneyworld/index
Universal Studios
themeparks.universalstudios.
com/orlando/website/index.htm
SeaWorld
www.buschgardens.com/
seaworld/fla/
Busch Gardens
www.buschgardens.com
Orlando Visitors Bureau
www.orlandoinfo.com
Florida Tourist Board
www.flausa.com
Golf in Orlando
www.orlandgolf.com/tourism
Hotel Discounts
www.orlandohoteldiscounts.com
Restaurants in Orlando
orlando.diningguide.net/
Orlando Nightlife
www.orlando.nightguide.com
Kennedy Space Center
www.ksc.nasa.gov/

L eft Luggage

Most theme parks have locker rental at the entrance. Charges vary but they are invariably helpful.

M aps

If renting a car, you should be supplied with a basic map of the Orlando area. It's important to familiarise yourself with the major interstates near your hotel. Once you've done this, driving in Orlando – though time consuming – is much easier than navigating the parks.

In addition to the maps provided in this book, highly detailed maps are available at the entrance of each park and often include showtime information. Take one of these to plan your trip and learn more about shopping and food outlets.

Media

Television
Hotel rooms usually have cable TV, but you often have to pay to watch movies. Newspapers list TV and radio programs.

Newspapers
Local newspapers and the national daily *USA Today* are sold in drugstores, grocery stores, and from vending machines. Special newsstands carry *The New York Times*, *The Wall Street Journal*, and *The Miami Herald*, as well as a variety of other newspapers. The *Orlando Sentinel* provides information about central Florida and gives TV programs, opening hours of attractions, pages of grocery store bargains, and coupons for price reductions at various restaurants. Newspapers and magazines from Britain, Germany, France, Italy, etc., are usually available the day following publication in some big supermarkets, shops, and hotels.

Money

Foreign visitors are advised to take US dollar travelers' checks to Orlando, since exchanging foreign currency –

TRANSPORT

whether as cash or checks – can prove problematic. An increasing number of banks, including the First Union National Bank, Nations Bank and Sun Bank chains, offer foreign exchange facilities, but this practice is not universal. Some department stores offer foreign currency exchange.

Most shops and restaurants accept travelers' checks in US dollars and will give change in cash. Alternatively, checks can be converted into cash at the bank.

Credit cards are very much part of daily life in Orlando and can be used to pay for pretty much anything, and it is also common for car rental firms and hotels to take an imprint of your card as a deposit. Rental companies may oblige you to pay a large deposit in cash if you do not have a card.

You can also use your credit card to withdraw cash from ATMs. Before you leave home, make sure you know your pin number and find out which ATM system will accept your card. The most widely accepted cards are Visa, American Express, MasterCard, Diners Club, Japanese Credit Bureau, and Discovery.

Tipping
Service personnel expect tips in Orlando. The accepted rate for baggage handlers in airports is about $1 per bag. For others, including taxi drivers and waiters, 15–20 percent is the going rate, depending on the level and quality of service. Sometimes tips are included in restaurant bills when dining in groups.

Moderate hotel tipping is around 50 cents per bag or suitcase handled by porters or bellboys. You should tip a doorman if he holds your car or performs other services. It is not necessary to tip chamber staff unless you stay several days.

P hotography

Realizing the importance of good background in your memories, Disney and Universal have dotted their parks with signs alerting you to good photographic locations. The advice is free, but the film and batteries, if you should run out, are distributed with much less generosity. In other words, stock up before you arrive. Additionally, there are Kodak quick processing outlets throughout Disney parks.

Postal Services

Post offices
The opening hours of post offices vary between central, big-city branches and those in smaller towns or suburbs; but all open

ACCOMMODATIONS

PUBLIC HOLIDAYS

- January: New Year's Day (Jan 1); Martin Luther King's Birthday (Jan 15).
- February: Presidents' Day (third Monday).
- May: Memorial Day (last Monday).
- July: Independence Day (July 4).
- September: Labor Day (first Monday).
- October: Columbus Day (second Monday).
- November: Veterans Day (Nov 11), Thanksgiving (fourth Thursday).
- December 25: Christmas Day.

Monday to Friday and some open on Saturday mornings. Hotel or motel personnel will know the opening hours of the post office nearest you.

Drugstores and hotels usually have a small selection of stamps, and there are stamp-vending machines in some transport terminals.

Delivery services
For the best service, you should pay for Express Mail via the US postal service, which guarantees next-day delivery within the US and delivery within two to three days to foreign destinations. Privately owned courier services, which offer next-day delivery to most places, are also very popular.

Telephone numbers for the main courier services are:
FedEx: 800-238 5355.
DHL: 800-345 2727.
UPS: 800-272 4877.

Public Toilets

These are never in short supply at the theme parks, but are often tucked behind creative landscaping. This should be a relief to everyone. All parks are especially considerate to the needs of wheelchair users and anyone needing to change babies.

ACTIVITIES

A – Z

Photo Spot ◄

R eligious Services

**First Baptist Church
at Lake Buena Vista**
11511 North CR 535
Tel: 407-239 6030
Service Sunday 11am
**Southwest Orlando Jewish
Congregation – Ohalel River**
11200 South Apopka-Vineland
Tel: 407-239 5444
**Church of the
Ascension (Episcopal)**
4950 South Apopka – Vineland
Tel: 407-876 3480
Services Sunday 8.30am;
traditional service 10.30am
**St Luke's United
Methodist Church**
4851 South Apopka – Vineland
Tel: 407-876 4991
Services Sunday 8.15am,
9.30am and 11am

S tudent Travelers

If you're looking to do Orlando on the cheap, you can succeed so long as you keep your expectations realistic. During the low season many budget hotels can have very affordable rates (especially if sharing) and transport to Disney or Universal is available via Lynx, so long as you plan well. Food purchased outside the park can be inexpensive. And though there is no way to avoid paying a lot for your entry tickets, once inside there is no need to spend a penny.

T elephones

You'll find public telephones in hotel lobbies, restaurants, drugstores, garages, roadside kiosks,

TIME ZONE

Eastern Standard Time (EST), is 3 hours ahead of San Francisco and 5 hours behind Greenwich Mean Time (GMT). Set your clocks and watches an hour ahead for Daylight Saving Time, which begins in early May and finishes at the end of October.

convenience stores and other locations throughout the state.

The cost of making a local, three-minute call from a pay phone is 35 cents. To make an international call from a pay phone you'll need a heap of quarters, so for long-distance calls you would do best to use a card: either a pre-paid telephone debit card (available in airports, post offices, and a few other outlets), usable at a growing number of public phones, or your credit card, which you can use at any phone: dial 1-800-callatt, key in your credit card number, and wait to be connected.

Avoid making calls from your hotel room since you will have to pay vastly inflated rates. Long-distance calling rates decrease in the evening and on weekends and holidays, but the specific time varies depending on the destination of your call.

Businesses, including hotels and tourist attractions, often have toll-free numbers – prefixed by 800 or 888. Note that if you are phoning from abroad, the call will not be free of charge.

Ticketing

There is an enormous variety of tickets offered at both Universal Studios and Walt Disney World Parks. Disney guests travelling from the US or purchasing tickets on the day of arrival can buy a one day, one park pass for about $60 or a Park Hopper pass that allows you access to more than one park and ranges in price from $95 for one day to $250 for ten days.

Disney has recently introduced the *Disney's Ultimate* ticket for UK guests only. It is tailored to suit long holidays and lasts 14 or 21 days and costs £181–199. A shorter ticket, *Disney's Premium* is valid for 7 or 5 days and costs £165–167. Any of these passes give unlimited access to the four main parks. The *Ultimate* ticket also offers unlimited access to other attractions including the Water Parks

and *Downtown Disney*, while the *Premium* ticket offers three or five entries respectively to these other attractions.

Universal Studios has a more straightforward approach with a one day, one park ticket costing $60, but teams up with SeaWorld, Busch Gardens and Wet n Wild to offer 14 day passes ranging from $184–224. They also regularly offer special deals on the website www.universalstudios.com.

Travel Agents

Virgin Holidays
www.virginholidays.com
Perhaps the best trans-Atlantic service. Professional, reasonably priced, and stylish too.
**American Express
Travel Services**
7618 West Sand Lake Road,
Orlando
Tel: 407-264 0104
www.americanexpress.com

Tourist Information Offices

Below is a list of tourist information offices in and around Orlando.

Orlando
● Orlando/Orange County Convention and Visitors Bureau
8723 International Drive, Suite 101, FL 32819
Tel: 407-363 5800
www.orlandoinfo.com
● Walt Disney World Co
PO Box 10000,
Lake Buena Vista,
FL 32830-1000
Tel: 407-934 7639.
● Universal Studios
1000 Universal Studios Plaza,
Orlando, FL 32819
Tel: 407-363 8000.

St Petersburg
● St Petersburg/Clearwater Area Convention and Visitors Bureau
14450 46th Street, Ste. 108,
Clearwater, FL 33762
Tel: 727-464 7200 or
800-354 6710
www.stpeteclearwater.com

Tampa

- Tampa/Hillsborough Convention and Visitors Bureau 400 N. Tampa Street, Ste. 1010, Tampa, FL 33602 Tel: 813-223 1111 or 800-826 8358 www.gotampa.com

Space Coast

- Titusville Area Chamber of Commerce 2000 S. Washington Avenue Tel: 321-267 3036.
- Cocoa Beach Area Chamber of Commerce, 400 Fortenberry Road, Merritt Island Tel: 321-459 2200.
- Melbourne Chamber of Commerce 1005 E. Strawbridge Avenue Tel: 321-724 5400.
- Palm Bay Area Chamber of Commerce 1153 Malabar Road NE Tel: 321-951 9998.

U seful Numbers

- Local directory inquiries: 411
- International directory inquiries: 00
- Local operator: 0
- International operator: 00
- International direct-dial calls: dial 011 + the code of the country, followed by the area or city code minus the first 0. Some country codes:
Australia: 61
Germany: 49
Ireland: 353
New Zealand: 64
United Kingdom: 44
- Police, ambulance or fire service: 911.

W hat to Bring

Light-colored, lightweight clothing is the norm in Florida. Most attractions permit shorts and sportswear, and at beach resorts people walk around the streets in just a swimsuit. Note that topless bathing is illegal.

There is little need for formal clothes, except at restaurants in the most sophisticated resorts. The Grand Floridian Resort's Victoria & Albert requires jackets for men. Otherwise, a sports coat with an open-neck sports shirt is fine for men, and women can wear just about anything as long as the effect is moderately respectable.

Take a light raincoat or umbrella, particularly in the wet summer months, and a sweater or jacket in case of cold spells during the winter. A light sweater comes in handy during the summer, when air-conditioning can be very chilly.

A few essentials are sunscreen, bug spray, and sunglasses. Of course, the most important item of all is a pair of comfortable walking shoes. There's a lot of walking in Orlando.

ART & PHOTO CREDITS

Map Production: Dave Priestley and Stephen Ramsay

©2005 Apa Publications GmbH & Co. Verlag KG, Singapore Branch

Desktop Production:
Linton Donaldson, Sylvia George

ORLANDO STREET ATLAS

The key map shows the area of Orlando covered by the atlas
section. An index of street names and places of interest
shown on the maps can be found on the following pages.
For each entry there is a page number and grid reference

Map Legend

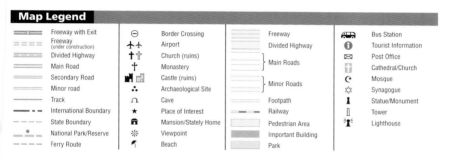

Freeway with Exit	⊖ Border Crossing	Freeway	🚌 Bus Station	
Freeway (under construction)	✈✈ Airport	Divided Highway	❶ Tourist Information	
Divided Highway	✝⛪ Church (ruins)	} Main Roads	✉ Post Office	
Main Road	✝ Monastery		🏛 Cathedral/Church	
Secondary Road	🏰 Castle (ruins)		☾ Mosque	
Minor road	∴ Archaeological Site	} Minor Roads	✡ Synagogue	
Track	∩ Cave	Footpath	🛉 Statue/Monument	
International Boundary	★ Place of Interest	Railway	🗼 Tower	
State Boundary	🏠 Mansion/Stately Home	Pedestrian Area	🕯 Lighthouse	
National Park/Reserve	☀ Viewpoint	Important Building		
Ferry Route	⚑ Beach	Park		

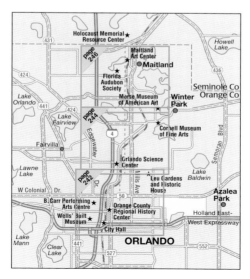

A   B

Yates St

Jack Kerouac House
Shady Lane Dr.
Guernsey St
Golfview St
Maxwell St
Oak St

ADAIR PARK

Reading Dr.
Clouser Ave
Edgewater Dr

Mercedes Pl.

Edgewater Ct

Orange Blossom Trail
441

Lake Adair

IVANHOE PLAZA PARK
Greely St
Sheridan Blvd
Desoto Cir.
Lakeview St

Lake Ivanhoe

LAKE IVANHOE PARK

Depauw Ave

Shore Dr.

4

527

Alden Rd

LAKE IVANHOE PARK

Ivanhoe Antique Row

Lake Ivanhoe

Orange Avenue

Alden

Ivanhoe Blvd

Dr Phillips Center for Performing Ar

Seville Pl.
Alameda St
Alba Dr.
Boardman St

Elwood Ave
Westmoreland Dr.
Cordova Dr.
Edgewater Dr.

Lake Concord

Peachtree Rd

Weber St
Pasadena Pl.
Marks St

LAKE HIGHLAN PARK

Magnolia Ave

Orange Avenue

Park Lake St

Irma Ave
Highland Ave

Park Lake

Colonial Drive
50

Colonial Drive
50

Cheney Pl.
Garland

527

Arlington St
Concord St

Hillcrest St

Lake Dot

Concord St

Concord St

Magnolia Ave

Broadway Ave

526

Givens St
Amelia St
Federal St

Orange Blossom Trail

TD Waterhouse Centre

Orlando Centroplex

Paramore Dr.

Studio Theater

Bob Carr Performing Arts Centre

Hughey Ave

4

Hibiscus Ct
Amelia St

Orange County Court House

Livingston St
Ridgewood Ave

Livingston St
Bentley St

Robinson St

526

Chatham Ave

Garland Ave

Dupont Center

Orange Ave

Palmetto Ave

LAKE EOLA PARK

Lake Eola

Polk St
Washington St
526

Macbro Ct

Federal Building

Orange County Regional History Center
527

Magnolia Ave

Court Ave

Rosalind Ave

Lake Eola Amphitheater
Founta

Central Blvd

Central Blvd
Pine St

Orange Blossom Trail
441

Pine St
Church St
Jackson St

Westmoreland Dr.
Paramore Dr.

Lime Ave

Terry Ave
Pine St
Division Ave
Bryan Ave

Hughey Ave

Terror on Church Street
SunBank Center
Church Street Station

Garland Ave

Pine St
Church St

Mariposa S
Jackson St

South St

South St
Colyer St
Randall St
Anderson St
Long St

Glenn Alley

Wells Built Museum of African-American History & Culture

City Hall

4

UNION PARK

East West Expressway
408

Lake Lucerne

A   B

LEU BOTANICAL GARDENS

Nebraska St

Ferris Ave
Asher Ln.
Dauphin Ln.
Haven Dr.
Flamingo Dr.
Gay Dr.

idway

Virginia Dr.
Brookhaven Dr.

Virginia Dr.

Weltin St

Montana St
Montana St

Mills Ave

Fern Creek Ave

Hampton Ave

Georgia Blvd

Asbury Ave
Cole Rd

Lake Dee

Asbury Ave

Gale St

Plaza Terrace Dr.
El Paso St

Lake Highland Dr.

Terrace Blvd

ake Highland
Lake Highland

Oregon St

Canton St

Vivada St

Druid Lake

Oregon St

Coy Dr.

Weber St

BIG TREE PARK

Garvin St

Weber St

Forest St

Eola Dr.

Hyer Ave.

Thornton Ave.

Mills Ave

Marks St
Illinois St

Shine Ave.

Fern Creek Ave

Hampton Ave

Illinois St

Illinois St

Garden Plaza

Jamie Cir.

Bumby Ave

Coy Ave

Marks St

Primrose Ave

Woodward St

Park Lake St

Woodward St

Colonial Drive

Hillside Ave

Colonial Drive

50

Colonial Plaza

Irving St
Lakewood Dr.

Hillcrest St

Hillcrest St

Concord St

Cathcart Ave

Summerlin Ave

arwood St

Hyer Ave.

Mills Ave

Mt Vernon St

Amelia St

Fern Creek Ave

Altaloma Ave

Hampton Ave

Amelia St

Bumby Ave

Livingston St

Livingston St

Graham St

Primrose Ave

Ridgewood Ave

Robinson St

LAKE EOLA PARK

Hill Ave.

Mills Ave

Robinson St

Jefferson St

526

DICKSON PARK

Robinson St

Forest Ave

Glenwood Ave

Washington St

Kilgore St

Eola Dr.

Summerlin Ave

Central Blvd

LAKE LAWSONA PARK

Lake Lawsona

Langford Park

Church St

Reeves Ct.

Hampton Ave

Central Blvd

Pine St

Bumby Ave

Graham St

Primrose Ave

Lake Olive

LAWSON PARK

South St

South St

Anderson St

408 East West Expressway

GREENWOOD URBAN WETLANDS

Greenwood Urban Wetlands Ponds

GREENWOOD CEMETERY

0   600 yards

0   600 m

D   E

A   B

Carew Ave
Canovia Ave
Alton Ave
Santee St
Euston Rd
Salisbury Blvd
Roxbury Rd
Eli St

Euston Rd
Salisbury Blvd
Roxbury Rd

Lake Killarney

Fairbanks Ave
Riddle Dr.

Killarney Dr.
Staunton Ave
Formosa Ave
Ohio St
Karolina Ave

Blue Heron Dr.
Kilshore Ln.

1

Little Lake Fairview

Driver Ave
Overspin Dr.

Fairbanks Ave

Kentucky Ave
Oglesby Ave
Crandon Ave

Clay St

Jackson Ave

Minnesota Ave

Crandon Ave
Post Ln.
Minnesota Ave

Michigan Ave
Miller Ave
Indiana Ave
Pelham Rd
Harmon Ave

Dubsdread Country Club Pond

2

DUBSDREAD COUNTRY CLUB

Midiron Dr.

Clay St

Edgewater Dr.

Westchester Ave

Par St
Par St
Preston St
Preston St
Hazel St
King St
Clayton St
Winter Park St
Bryn Mawr St
Vassar St
Smith St

Harrison Ave
Helen Ave
Oberlin Ave
Amherst Ave
Depauw Ave

Hazel St
Evans St
King St
Spruce St
Winter Park St
Oglethorpe Pl.
Orlando St

Cornell Ave

Hazel St
Guava St
King St
Spruce St

Berkshire Ave
Westminster St

Orange Ave

Lake Winyal

Florida Hospital Medical Center

3

Bryn Mawr St
Edgewater Dr.
Rugby St
Vassar St

Elizabeth Ave

Formosa Ave

Rollins St

McRae Ave
Alden Rd
Camden Rd

4

Harvard St
Yale St
Stetson St
COLLEGE PARK PLAYGROUND
Dartmouth St

Princeton St

Harrison Ave
Ivanhoe Rd

Harvard St
Yale St
Vanderbilt St
New Hampshire

Orange Ave

Menello Museum of America Folk A
Theater Downtown

Alden Rd

Lake Formos

A   B

Lake Osceola

Lake Mensden

Morse Blvd

Charles Hosmer Museum of American Art

Albin Polasek Museum & Sculpture Garden

Osceola Ave

Winter Park Historical Museum

New England Ave

Lyman Ave

Comstock Ave

Fairbanks Ave

Cornell Fine Arts Museum

Holt Ave

Kentucky Ave

Arogan Ave

Rollins College

Minnesota Ave

Lake Virginia

Oxford Rd

Harmon Ave

Stirling Ave

Orchid Ave

Virginia Dr

Garden Dr.

MEAD BOTANICAL GARDEN

Virginia Dr.

Grover Ave

Lake Sue Ave

Nottingham St

Kings Way

Chichester St

Reading Way

Wilkinson St

Ayrshire St

Run

Munster St

Lake Sue

Lake Estelle

Lake Forest

John & Rita Lowndes Shakespeare Center

Wright Ave

Orlando Museum of Art

Norris Ave

Edyth Bush Theater

Parkland Dr.

Lake Rowena

Leu Rd

LEU BOTANICAL GARDENS

Corrine Dr.

0   600 yards

0   600 m

Denning Dr.

Halper St

Bruce Ave

Capen Ave

Pennsylvania Ave

Virginia Ave

New York Ave

Knowles Ave

Center St

Interlachen Ave

Park Ave

Orange Ave

Orlando Ave

Vivian Ave

Denning Dr.

Pennsylvania Ave

Fawsett Rd

Glencoe Ave

Winter Park Rd

Laurel Rd

Forrest Rd

Turky

Howard Dr.

Middlesex Rd

Norfolk Rd

Shrewbury Rd

Shoreham Rd

Lakeshore Dr.

Lakeside Dr.

Randall Rd

Winter Park Rd

Mills Ave

Gay Dr.

Woodlawn Dr.

Oak Ln.

Palm Ln.

Lake Sue Rd

Maitland Blvd

Maitland Blvd (414)

Lake Destiny Rd

LAKE LUCIEN
CEMETERY

Sandspur Rd

White Oak Cir.

Lake
Sybelia

Lake Sybelia Dr.

Maitla
Art Cer

Lake Lucien

Wymore Rd

Banbury Trail

Covewood Trail

Willowbrook Trail

Lake Sybelia Dr.

Boynton Rd

Lake Destiny Rd

Lake Jackson

Brook Dr.

Cranes Ct

Cranes Ct

Lake
Catherine

Lucien Way

Carver Ave

Rogers Ave

Ford Ave

Florida Audubon
Society Center
for Birds of Prey

Deacon Jones Blvd

Washington Ave

Lincoln Blvd

Lake
Hungerford

Eaton St

Lake Sybelia Dr.

Lake
Lalia

Toni St

Campusview Dr.

Kennedy Blvd

EATONVILLE

Kennedy Blvd

Lord Ave

Lake Ave

Zora Neale
Hurston National
Museum of
Fine Arts

West Ave

East Ave

Grove St

Park Lake

Wymore Rd

Lake
King

Ruffel St

Fitzgerald
Dr.

Monroe Ave

Alfred Dr.

Baltimore Dr.

Malone Dr.

Alloway St

Diplomat
Cir.

Lake Bell

Margaret
Sq.

Turner Pl.

G
L.

Bennett Ave

Lee Road

Early Ave

Albert Lee Parkway

Adanson Ave

Hanover
Ave

Gloriosa
Ave

Lee Road

Lee Road

Blossom Ln.

Rippling Ln.

Audrey
Ave

Courtland St

Neuse Ave

Carlson Dr.

FAIRVIEW SHORES

Timor Ave

Eli St

Roxbury St

Santee St

Naples Dr.

Carew
Ave

Lake Fair

Lot A Fun Ave

Euston Rd

Lake Killarney

Euston Rd

Lake Minnehaha

MAITLAND

rge Ave
Maitland Ave
atio Ave
kson St
**Maitland
Historical Museum**
Packwood Ave

Horatio Ave

Algonquin Trail

Seneca Trail

Thistle Ln.

Horatio Ave

Old
Club
Pt.

Howell Branch Rd

King Arthurs Cir.

Adams Dr.

Trotters Dr.

Shell Pt.

Lake
Ninja

Ventris Ave

Live Oak St.

Lake
Lily

Eastwind
Ln.

Venetian Way

Orlando Ave

Leslie Trail

Circular Dr.

Azalea Ln.

Magnolia Rd

Legion Dr.

Summerland Ave

Lake Maitland

PineTree Rd

Via Lugano

Ridge Wood

Lyndale Blvd

Sunnyside Dr.

Dixie Pkwy

Alpine
Dr.

Williams Dr.

Park Ave

Pennsylvania Ave

Raintree
Ct

KRAFT AZALEA
PARK

Valencia Ave

Alabama Dr.

Orlando Ave

Benjamin Ave

del Pkwy

n Ave

Solana Ave

Pansy Ave

Beloit Ave

Beloit Ave

Palmer Ave

Keyes Ave

Park Ave

Georgia Ave

Seminole
Dr.

Railroad Ave

Tatum Ave

**WINTER PARK
GOLF COURSE**

Webster Ave

Lake
Francis

Webster Ave

Orlando Ave

Denning Dr.

Capen Ave

Pennsylvania Ave

New York Ave

Swoope Ave

Lake Osceola

rovillion
Ave

Rd

Swoope Ave

Depugh St

Cole
Ave

**Morse
Museum**

Interlachen Ave

Canton Ave

Virginia Ave

Center St.

Knowles Ave

0   600 yards

English Ct

Symonds Ave

Symonds Ave

0   600 m

STREET INDEX

A

Adams Drive 247 E1
Adanson Avenue 246 A4
Adanson Street 246 A4
Alabama Drive 247 E3
Alameda Street 242 A2
Alba Drive 242 A2
Albert Lee Parkway 246 B3
Albin Polasek Museum &
  Sculpture Garden 245 E1
Alden Road 242 C1
Alfred Drive 246 A3
Algonquin Trail 247 E1
Alloway Street 246 A3
Alpine Drive 247 C3
Altaloma Avenue 243 D3
Alton Avenue 244 A1
Amelia Street 242 A3–C3, 243
  D3–E3
Amherst Avenue 244 B3
Anderson Street 242 A4, 243
  C4
Arlington Street 242 A2
Arogan Avenue 245 C2
Asbury Avenue 243 E1
Asher Lane 243 C1
Audrey Avenue 246 A4
Ayrshire Street 245 C3
Azalea Lane 247 C2

B

Baltimore Drive 246 A3
Banbury Trail 246 B1
Beloit Avenue 247 D3
Benjamin Avenue 247 C3
Bennett Avenue 246 C3
Bentley Street 242 A3
Berkshire Avenue 244 C3
Blossom Lane 246 B4
Blue Heron Drive 244 C1
Boardman Street 242 A2
Bob Carr Performing Arts Centre
  242 B3
Boynton Road 246 C1
Broadview Avenue 245 C1
Broadway Avenue 242 C3
Brook Drive 246 B1
Brookhaven Drive 243 C1
Bruce Place 245 D1
Bryan Avenue 242 B4
Bryn Mawr Street 244 A4
Bumby Avenue 243 E1–E4

C

Camden Road 244 C4
Campusview Drive 246 A2
Canovia Avenue 244 A1
Canton Avenue 247 D4
Canton Street 243 D1
Capen Avenue 245 D1
Carew Avenue 244 A1
Carlson Drive 246 A4
Carver Avenue 246 A2
Cathcart Avenue 243 C3
Center Street 245 E1
Central Avenue 247 C1
Central Boulevard 242 A4–C4,
  243 D4–E4
Charles Hosmer Museum of
  American Art 245 E1
Chatham Avenue 242 B3
Cheney Place 242 B2
Chichester Street 245 C3

Church Street 242 A4–C4, 243
  D4
Church Street Station 242 B4
Circular Drive 247 C2
City Hall 242 B4
Clay Street 244 C1–B2
Clayton Street 244 A3
Clouser Avenue 242 A1
Cole Avenue 247 D4
Cole Road 243 E1
Colonial Drive 242 A2–B2, 243
  D2–E2
Colonial Plaza 243 E3
Colyer Street 242 A4
Comstock Avenue 245 D1
Concord Street 242 A2–B3–C2,
  243 D2
Cordova Drive 242 A2
Cornell Avenue 244 B3
Cornell Fine Arts Museum 245
  E1
Corrine Drive 245 E4
Court Avenue 242 B4
Courtland Street 246 A4
Covewood Trail 246 B1
Coy Avenue 243 E2
Coy Drive 243 E1
Crandon Avenue 244 B2
Cranes Court 246 B1, B2

D

Dartmouth Street 244 A4
Dauphin Lane 243 C1
Deacon Jones Boulevard 246 A2
Denning Drive 245 D2, 247 D4
Depauw Avenue 242 B1, 244 B3
Depugh Street 247 D4
Desoto Circle 242 B1
Diplomat Circle 246 A3
Division Avenue 242 B4
Dixie Parkway 247 D3
Dr Phillips Center for
  Performing Arts 242 C1
Driver Avenue 244 A1
Dupont Center 242 B3

E

Early Avenue 246 B3
East Avenue 246 B2
East West Expressway 242 A4,
  243 E4
Eastwind Lane 247 E2
Eaton Street 246 A2
Edgewater Court 242 A1
Edgewater Drive 242 A1, 244
  A2–A4
Edyth Bush Theater 245 C4
El Paso Street 243 E1
Eli Street 244 A1
Elizabeth Avenue 244 A3
Ellwood Avenue 242 A2
Elvin Avenue 247 C3
English Court 247 D4
Eola Drive 243 C2–C4
Euston Road 244 A1–B1
Evans Street 244 B3
Executive Drive 246 C4
Expo Centre 242 B3

F

Fairbanks Avenue 244 A1–B1,
  245 D1
Fawsett Road 245 D3

Federal Building 242 B3
Federal Street 242 A3
Fern Creek Avenue 243
  D1–D3
Ferris Avenue 243 C1
Fitzgerald Drive 246 B3
Flamingo Drive 243 D1
Florida Audubon Society Center
  for Birds of Prey 246 B2
Florida Hospital Medical Center
  244 C3
Ford Avenue 246 B2
Forest Avenue 243 E3
Forest Street 243 E2
Formosa Avenue 244 B1–B4
Forrest Road 245 E3

G

Gale Street 243 D1
Garden Drive 245 C2
Garden Plaza 243 E2
Garland Avenue 242
  B2–B3–B4
Garvin Street 243 D2
Gay Drive 243 D1
Gay Road 247 C4
Gene Street 245 C1
George Avenue 247 C1
Georgia Avenue 247 C4
Georgia Boulevard 243 E1
Givens Street 242 A3
Glencoe Ave 245 E3
Glencoe Road 245 E3
Glenn Alley 242 A4
Glenwood Avenue 243 E3
Gloriosa Avenue 246 B3
Golfview Street 242 A1
Graham Street 243 E3–E4
Greely Street 242 A1
Grove Street 246 B2
Grover Avenue 245 C3
Guava Street 244 B3
Guernsey Street 242 A1

H

Hampton Avenue 243 D1–D4
Hanover Avenue 246 B3
Harmon Avenue 244 C2, 245
  C2
Harper Street 245 C1
Harrison Avenue 244 A3–A4
Harvard Street 244 A4–B4
Harwood Street 243 C3
Haven Drive 243 C1
Hazel Street 244 A3–B3
Helen Avenue 244 B3
Hibiscus Court 242 C3
Highland Avenue 242 C2
Hill Avenue 243 C3
Hillcrest Street 242 C2, 243
  C2–D2
Hillside Avenue 243 E2
Holt Avenue 245 D1
Horatio Avenue 247 C1–D1–E1
Howard Drive 245 E3
Howell Branch Road 247 E1
Hughey Avenue 242 B3–B4
Hyer Avenue 243 C2–C3

I

Illinois Street 243 D2–E2
Indiana Avenue 244 C2
Interlachen Avenue 245 E1
Irma Avenue 242 C2
Irving Street 243 E2
Ivanhoe Antique Row 242 C1
Ivanhoe Boulevard 242 B1
Ivanhoe Road 244 B4

J

Jack Kerouac House 242 A1
Jackson Avenue 244 C1
Jackson Street 242 A4–C4, 247
  C1
Jamie Circle 243 E2
Jefferson Street 243 D3
John & Rita Lowndes
  Shakespeare Center 245 C4

K

Karolina Avenue 244 B1
Kennedy Boulevard 246 A2–B2
Kentucky Avenue 244 B1, 245
  C1
Keyes Avenue 247 E4
Kilgore Street 243 E3
Killarney Drive 244 B1
Kilshore Lane 244 C1
Kindel Parkway 247 C3
King Arthurs Circle 247 E1
King Street 244 A3–B3
Kings Way 245 E3
Knowles Avenue 245 E1

L

Lake Avenue 246 B2–C2
Lake Destiny Road 246
  A1–A2–B1–C1
Lake Eola Amphitheater 242 C3
Lake Highland Drive 243 C1
Lake Sue Avenue 245 E3
Lake Sue Drive 245 E4
Lakeshore Drive 245 D4
Lakeside Drive 245 D4
Lakeview Street 242 B1
Lakewood Drive 243 E2
Laurel Road 245 E4
Lee Road 246 A3–B4–C4
Legion Drive 247 D2
Leslie Trail 247 C2
Leu Road 245 D4
Lewis Drive 247 C3
Lime Avenue 242 A4
Lincoln Boulevard 246 A2
Live Oak Street 247 C2
Livingston Street 242 A3–C3,
  243 D3–E3
Long Street 242 A4
Lord Avenue 246 B2
Loren Avenue 246 C3
Lot A Fun Avenue 246 A4
Lucien Way 246 A2
Lyman Avenue 245 D1
Lyndale Boulevard 247 D3

M

Macbro Court 242 A3
Magnolia Avenue 242 B2–B4
Magnolia Road 247 C2
Maitland Art Center 246 C1
Maitland Avenue 247 C1
Maitland Boulevard 246 A1–B1
Maitland Historical Museum 247
  C1
Malone Drive 246 A3
Margaret Square 246 B3
Mariposa Street 242 C4
Marks Street 242 C2, 243
  D2–E2
Maxwell Street 242 A1
McRae Avenue 242 B1
Menello Museum of American
  Folk Art 244 C4
Mercedes Place 242 A1
Michigan Avenue 243 E2
Middlesex Rd 245 D3
Midiron Drive 244 B2

Midway Drive **243** C1
Miller Avenue **244** C2
Mills Avenue **243** D1–D3, **245** C4
Minnesota Avenue **244** B2–C2, **245** D2
Monroe Avenue **246** C3
Montana Street **243** D1–C1
Morse Boulevard **245** D1
Morse Museum **247** E4
Mount Vernon Street **243** D3
Munster Street **245** C3

N
Naples Drive **246** A4
Nebraska Street **243** D1
Neuse Avenue **246** A4
New England Avenue **245** E1
New Hampshire Street **244** B4
New York Avenue **245** D1
Norfolk Road **245** D3
Norris Avenue **245** E4
Nottingham Street **245** C3

O
Oak Lane **245** E4
Oak Street **242** A1
Oberlin Avenue **244** B3
Oglesby Avenue **244** B2
Oglethorpe Place **244** B4
Ohio Street **244** B1
Old Club Point **247** E1
Orange Avenue **242** C1–B2–B3, **244** C3–C4, **245** D2
Orange Blossom Trail **242** A2–A4
Orange County Court House **242** B3
Orange County Regional History Center **242** B3
Orchid Avenue **245** C2
Oregon Street **243** D1–E1
Orlando Avenue **245** C2, **247** C2–C4
Orlando Centroplex **242** A3
Orlando Museum of Art **245** C4
Orlando Science Center **245** C4
Orlando Street **244** B4
Osceola Avenue **245** E1

Overspin Drive **244** B1
Oxford Road **245** D2

P
Packwood Avenue **247** C1
Palm Lane **245** D4
Palmer Avenue **247** E3
Palmetto Avenue **242** B3
Pansy Avenue **247** D3
Par Street **244** A3–B3
Park Avenue **245** E1, **247** D3–E4
Park Lake Street **242** B2, **243** D2
Parkland Drive **245** E4
Parramore Street **242** A3–A4
Pasadena Place **242** C2
Peachtree Road **242** B2
Pelham Road **244** C2
Pennsylvania Avenue **245** D1–D2, **247** D3–D4
Pine Street **242** A4–B4–C4, **243** E4
Pinetree Road **247** E2
Plaza Terrace Drive **243** E1
Polk Street **242** A3
Post Lane **244** A2
Preston Street **244** A3–B3
Primrose Avenue **243** E2–E4
Princeton Street **244** B4

R
Railroad Avenue **247** D4
Raintree Court **247** D3
Randall Road **245** E4
Randall Street **242** A4
Reading Drive **242** A1
Reading Way **245** E3
Reeves Court **243** D4
Riddle Drive **244** A1
Ridge Wood **247** C3
Ridgewood Avenue **242** C3, **243** D3
Rippling Lane **246** B4
Robinson Street **242** A3, **243** C3–D3–E3
Rogers Avenue **246** B2
Rollins College **245** E2
Rollins Street **244** C4

Rosalind Avenue **242** C4
Roxbury Road **244** A1–B1
Ruffel Street **246** B2
Rugby Street **244** A4

S
Salisbury Boulevard **244** A1–B1
Sandspur Road **246** B1
Santee Street **244** A1
Seminole Drive **247** E4
Seneca Trail **247** E1
Seville Place **242** A2
Shady Lane Drive **242** A1
Shell Point **247** D1
Sheridan Boulevard **242** A1
Shine Avenue **243** D2
Shore Drive **242** C1
Shoreham Road **245** D4
Shrewbury Road **245** D4
Smith Street **244** A4
Solana Avenue **247** C3
South Street **242** A4–C4, **243** D4–E4
Spruce Street **244** B3
Staunton Avenue **244** B1
Stetson Street **244** A4
Stirling Avenue **245** E2
Studio Theater **242** B3
Suffolk Road **244** C2
Summerland Avenue **247** D2
Summerlin Avenue **243** C3–C4
SunBank Center **242** B4
Sunnyside Drive **247** D3
Swoope Avenue **247** D4
Symonds Avenue **247** C4–D4

T
Tatum Avenue **247** D4
Terrace Boulevard **243** C1
Terror on Church Street **242** B4
Terry Avenue **242** B4
Theater Downtown **244** C4
Thistle Lane **247** E1
Thornton Avenue **243** D2
Timor Avenue **246** A4
Toni Street **246** A2
Trotters Drive **247** D1
Trovillion Avenue **247** C4

Turkey Run **245** E3
Turner Road **246** B3

V
Valencia Ave **247** E3
Vanderbilt Street **244** B4
Vassar Street **244** A4
Venetian Way **247** E2
Ventris Avenue **247** C1
Ventris Court **246** C2
Via Lugano **247** E3
Virginia Avenue **245** D1
Virginia Drive **243** C1–D1, **245** E2
Vivada Street **243** E1
Vivian Avenue **245** C2

W
Washington Avenue **246** A2
Washington Street **242** A3
Waterhouse Centre, TD **242** A3
Weber Street **242** C2, **243** D2–E2
Webster Avenue **247** D4–E4
Wells' Built Museum of African-American History & Culture **242** B4
Weltin Street **243** D1
West Avenue **246** B2
Westchester Avenue **244** C2–C3, **245** C3
Westmoreland Drive **242** A2–A4
White Oak Circle **246** B1
Wilkinson Street **245** C3
Williams Drive **247** D3
Willowbrook Trail **246** B1
Winter Park Historical Museum **245** D1
Winter Park Road **245** E3 E4
Winter Park Street **244** A3–B4
Woodlawn Drive **245** E4
Woodward Street **243** C2–D2
Wright Avenue **245** E4
Wymore Road **246** A1–A2

Y–Z
Yale Street **244** A4–B4
Yates Street **242** A1
Zora Neale Hurston National Museum of Fine Arts **246** B2

GENERAL INDEX

A

accommodation 9, 218–25
Adventure Island 193
Adventureland (Magic Kingdom) 64–6
Adventurers Club 109
Africa (Animal Kingdom) 89–91
air travel 214–15
Akbar's Adventure (Busch Gardens) 198
Albin Polasek Museum and Sculpture Garden 185–6
alcohol 38, 216, 235
Amazing Adventures of Spider-Man 8, 44, 117, **142**, 143, 228
Amazing Exotics (Umatilla) 167
American Adventure 81
American Film Institute Showcase 102
Amity (Universal Studios) 125–6
Anandapur (Animal Kingdom) 91
Andersen, Martin 25, 28
Anheuser-Busch 29
Animal Kingdom 59, **85–93**, 228
Africa 89–91
Anandapur 91
Asia 91–2
Backstage Safari **90**, 108
The Boneyard 92
Camp Minnie-Mickey 88–9
Character Greeting Trails 89
Chester & Hester's Dino-Rama 93
Conservation Station 91
Cretaceous Trail 93
DinoLand U.S.A. 92–3
Dinosaur ride 87, 91, **92–3**
Discovery Island 88–9
Expedition Everest 92
Fastpass 87
Festival of Lion King 89

Flights of Wonder 91
Habitat Habit 91
height requirements 91
It's Tough to be a Bug! 88
Kali River Rapids 87, **91–2**
Kilimanjaro Safaris 87, **90**
Maharajah Jungle Trek 92
The Oasis 87–8
Pangani Forest Exploration Trail 90
parades 90
Pocahontas and Her Forest Friends 89
Primeval Whirl 91, **93**
Rafiki's Planet Watch 90–91
restaurants 93
Tarzan Rocks 93
Tree of Life 88
TriceraTop Spin 93
Wild by Design 108
Wildlife Express 91
Animal Planet Live **124**, 126
Arabian Nights (Kissimmee) 171–2
art galleries see museums and art galleries
arts, the 180, 183, **226–7**
Asia (Animal Kingdom) 91–2
Astro Orbiter **71**
Astronaut Encounter (Kennedy Space Center) 207
Astronaut Hall of Fame 211, **212**
Astronaut Memorial (Kennedy Space Center) 209

B

Back to the Future...The Ride 8, 117, 121, **124–5**, 126
Backlot Tour (Disney-MGM Studios) 102
Backstage Safari (Animal Kingdom) 90

Bartram, William 23
Bavar, Emily 25
Beastly Kingdom 37, 87
Beauty and the Beast: Live on Stage 98
bed & breakfast 218
Beetlejuice's Graveyard Revue 126, **128**
behind-the-scenes tours 49, 75, 90, 102, **108**, 151, 195
Bergamo's Italian Restaurant 172
Big Thunder Mountain 64, **66–7**
Bird Gardens (Busch Gardens) 201–2
Black Point Wildlife Drive 9, **213**
Blizzard Beach 45, **113–14**
Blue Spring State Park 6, 181
Bob Carr Performing Arts Center **180**, 183, 226–7
Bob Marley – A Tribute to Freedom 146
Body Wars (Epcot) 77
Bok Tower Gardens 6, **188–9**
The Boneyard 92
Bongos Cuban Cafe 106–7
Bowlegs, Billy 19
Brock, James 24
budgeting 232
Burns, Haydon 25
Busch, Augustus 25
Busch Gardens 18, 29, 149, **193–202**
Akbar's Adventure 198
behind-the-scenes tours 195
Bird Gardens 201–2
Claw Island 200
Clydesdale Hamlet 197
Congo River Rapids 198, **200**
Edge of Africa 196–7
Egypt 197–8
Family Water Game 202
Flamingo Island 201
Guest Relations 195–6

Gwazi ride 42, 193, 198, **202**
height requirements 198
Kumba ride 193, 198, **200**
Land of the Dragons 201–2
Montu ride 8, 42, 193, 197–8
Morocco 195–6
Myombe Reserve 198
Nairobi 198–9
Phoenix ride 198, **199**
Python ride 198, **200**
Rhino Rally 198, **199**
Scorpion ride 198, **199**
Serengeti Safaris 196
SheiKra **201**
Skyride Station 197
Stanley Falls 198, **201**
Stanleyville 200–01
Tanganyika Tidal Wave 198, **201**
tickets and passes 200
Timbuktu 199–200
Buzz Lightyear's Astro-Blaster (Downtown Disney) 107
Buzz Lightyear's Space Ranger Spin (Magic Kingdom) 64, **71**

C

Camp Jurassic 140
Camp Minnie-Mickey 88–9
camping 218
Canada! (Epcot) 80
Canaveral National Seashore 212, **213**
Cape Canaveral 205–6
Capone's Dinner & Show 172
car rental 216–17
Caribbean cruises 112
Caro-Seuss-el **135**, 136
Castaway Cay 112
The Cat in the Hat 135–6
Celebration residential community 25
Chalet Suzanne 188, 191
character dining 8, **64**
Character Greeting Trails 89

Charles Hosmer Morse
Museum of American
Art 9, 149, **185**,
226
Chester & Hester's
Dino-Rama 93
children
see also **height
requirements**
activities for 6, 117,
228–9
character dining 8, **64**
overnight adventure,
Kennedy Space Center
206
survival strategies 47, 49
China (Epcot) 82
Church Street Station
181
Cinderella's Castle 8,
64, 228
Cinderella's Golden
Carousel 69
cinemas 227–8
Cirque du Soleil **105–6**,
226
City Hall (Magic
Kingdom) 63
CityWalk 117, **145–7**,
229
Claw Island (Busch
Gardens) 200
climate 233
Clydesdale Hamlet
(Busch Gardens) 197
Cocoa Beach 224
Comedy Warehouse 109
Congo River Rapids
(Busch Gardens) 198,
200
conservation 88
Conservation Station
(Animal Kingdom) 91
Cornell Museum of Fine
Arts 9, **185**
Cranium Command 77
credit cards 237
Crescent J Ranch 190
Cretaceous Trail 93
crime 233
crowd control 39
cruises **112**
Crystal Palace **64**, 228
Curious George Goes to
Town 123
CyberSpace Mountain
44, **107**
Cypress Gardens 18,
173, 174

D

A Day in the Park with
Barney **124**, 126
De Soto National
Memorial (Tampa) 203
dinner shows 171–3
DinoLand U.S.A. 92–3
Dinosaur ride (Animal
Kingdom) 87, 91,
92–3
disabled travellers 234
Discovery Cove
(SeaWorld) 6, 149,
152, **160–61**, 228
Discovery Island (Animal
Kingdom) 88–9
Disney Cruise Line 112
Disney, Roy 26, 34, 55
Disney, Walt 24–7, 29,
34–5, 38, 61, 127
Epcot concept 73
invents theme parks
15
Disney Wilderness 181
Disney Wildlife
Conservation Fund 88
Disney World *see* **Walt
Disney World**
Disney-MGM Studios 59,
95–103, 228
American Film Institute
Showcase 102
Backlot Tour 102
Beauty and the Beast:
Live on Stage 98
behind-the-scenes tours
108
compared with
Universal Studios 101
Echo Lake 99–100
Fantasmic 98
Fastpass 99
Great Movie Ride 97–8
height requirements 101
Hollywood Boulevard 97
Honey, I Shrunk the
Kids Movie Set
Adventure 101
Indiana Jones Epic
Stunt Spectacular 99,
100, 228
Lights, Motors, Action!
Extreme Stunt Show
100
Magic of Disney
Animation 103
Muppet Vision 3-D 99,
101

Playhouse Disney – Live
on Stage 103
Rock 'n' Roller
Coaster Starring
Aerosmith 8, 43, **99**,
101, 228
Sorcerer's Hat 97
Sounds Dangerous 100
Star Tours 44, 99, **100**,
101
Sunset Boulevard 98
Twilight Zone Tower of
Terror 8, 43, **98–9**,
101, 228
Voyage of the Little
Mermaid 99, **103**
Walt Disney: One Man's
Dream 102
Who Wants To Be a
Millionaire – Play It!
99, **102**
DisneyQuest 107
Disney's Boardwalk
110–11
DiveQuest (Epcot) 78
Doctor Doom's Fearfall
43
Dolphin Cove (SeaWorld)
154–5
Dolphin Swim Package
(SeaWorld) 161
Downhill Double Dipper
113
Downtown Disney
105–11, 229
Adventurers Club 109
Buzz Lightyear's
Astro-Blaster 107
Cirque du Soleil 105–6
Comedy Warehouse 109
CyberSpace Mountain
107
DisneyQuest **107**, 229
Disney's Boardwalk
110–11
Guitar Gallery 108
House of Blues 106
Lego Imagination
Center 110
Mannequins Dance
Palace 109
Planet Hollywood 108
Pleasure Island 108–9
Rock 'n' Roll Beach
Club 109
Sosa Family Cigar
Company 108
Starabilia 108
Wolfgang Puck 106

World of Disney 110
Dr Doom's Fearfall **142**,
143
Dr Phillips Center for
Performing Arts 180
drink driving 217
driving 216–17
Dudley Do-Right's
Ripsaw Falls **141**, 143
Dueling Dragons 8, 42,
136, **138**, 228
Dumbo the Flying
Elephant 69

E

Earthquake – The Big
One 126, **127**
Echo Lake 99–100
Edge of Africa (Busch
Gardens) 196–7
Egypt (Busch Gardens)
197–8
Eighth Voyage of Sinbad
136, **137**
Eisner, Michael 28, 36, 95
electricity 234
Ellen's Energy Adventure
76–7
embassies and
consulates 234
emergencies 234
Enchanted Tiki Room
65–6
Epcot 59, **73–83**, 228
American Adventure 81
behind-the-scenes tours
75, 108
Body Wars 77
DiveQuest 78
Ellen's Energy
Adventure 76–7
Fastpass 75, 78
Future World 75–80
Global Neighborhood 76
height requirements 77
Honey, I Shrunk the
Audience 75, **80**
IllumiNations 73
Imagination! 80
Innoventions 78–9
The Land 79
Living with the Land 75,
79
Living Seas 79
Mission: SPACE 8, 73,
75, **77–8**, 228
restaurants and bars
83

Soarin' ride 76
Spaceship Earth 75–6
Test Track 75, 77, **78**, 228
Universe of Energy 76–7
Wonders of Life 77
World Showcase 73, **80–82**, 83
E.T. Adventure 123–4
events 7
sporting events 231
Everglades 19
Expedition EVEREST 92

F

Fairytale Garden 70
Family Water Game (Busch Gardens) 202
Fantasmic 98
Fantasy of Flight 174–5
Fantasyland (Magic Kingdom) 68–70
Festival of the Lion King 89
festivals 7
Fievel's Playland 123
fireworks 70, 73, 97, 123, 128
Flamingo Island (Busch Gardens) 201
FlexTicket 9, 36
Flights of Wonder (Animal Kingdom) 91
Florida Aquarium (Tampa) 203
Florida Audobon Society's Birds of Prey Center 9, 88, **186–7**
Flying Tigers Warbird Air Museum (Kissimmee) 189–90
Flying Unicorn 136, **138**
Food Rocks (Epcot) 79
Forever Florida 190
Fort Christmas Historical Park 181
Fort Gatlin 19
France (Epcot) 81
Frontierland (Magic Kingdom) 66–8
Fun Spot Action Park **170**, 229
Future World (Epcot) 75–80

G

Gatorland 7, 18, 29, 149, **165–6**
gay and lesbian travellers 7, **235**
Germany (Epcot) 82
Global Neighborhood (Epcot) 76
golf 114, 170, **173**, 230
Goofy's Country Dancin Jamboree 67
Grant, President Ulysses S. 23
Great Movie Ride 97–8
Green Meadows Petting Farm **166**, 228
Guiness World Records Experience 149
Guitar Gallery 108
Gwazi ride (Busch Gardens) 42, 193, 198, **202**

H

Habitat Habit (Animal Kingdom) 91
Hall of Presidents 68
Hamilton, Finley 26
Hard Rock Cafe (CityWalk) 147
Hard Rock Vault (I-Drive) 169
Harry P. Leu Gardens and Historic House **184–5**, 186
Haunted Mansion 64, **67–8**
height requirements 67, 77, 91, 101, 121, 138, 143, 160, 198
Henry B. Plant Museum (Tampa) 203
Historic Waterhouse Residence and Waterhouse Carpentry Shop (Maitland) 186
Hollywood Boulevard (Disney-MGM Studios) 97
Hollywood (Universal Studios) 121–3
Holocaust Memorial Resource and Education Center 187
Holy Land Experience 163–4
Honey, I Shrunk the Audience (Epcot) 75, **80**

Honey, I Shrunk the Kids Movie Set Adventure (Disney-MGM Studios) 101
hotels 8, **218–25**
privileges for guests 39, 48–9, 117
House of Blues 106
Hurston, Zora Neale 24

I

If I Ran the Zoo 136
IllumiNations 73
Imagination! (Epcot) 80
Incredible Hulk Coaster 8, 41–3, **143**, 228
Independence Day 7, 128
Indiana Jones Epic Stunt Spectacular 99, **100**, 228
Indians 19–22
Indy Speedway 67, **71**
Innoventions (Epcot) 78–9
insects 236
International Drive 26, 55, **168–70**
accommodation 223–4
restaurants and bars 176–7
Internet 236
Islands of Adventure 55, 117, **133–43**, 228
Amazing Adventures of Spider-Man 8, 44 117, **142**, 143, 228
Camp Jurassic 140
Caro-Seuss-el **135**, 136
The Cat in the Hat 135–6
Dr Doom's Fearfall **142**, 143
Dudley Do-Right's Ripsaw Falls **141**, 143
Dueling Dragons 8, 42, 136, **138**, 228
Eighth Voyage of Sinbad 136, **137**
Flying Unicorn 136, **138**
height requirements 138, 143
If I Ran the Zoo 136
Incredible Hulk Coaster 8, 41–3, **143**, 228
Jurassic Park River Adventure 45, 138, **139–40**
landscaping 141

The Lost Continent **136–7**, 138
Marvel Super Hero Island 141–3
One Fish, Two Fish, Red Fish, Blue Fish **135**, 136
Popeye & Bluto's Bilge-Rat Barges **140–41**, 143
Port of Entry 133–5
Poseidon's Fury 136, **137**
Pteranodon Flyers **140**
Seuss Landing 6, 117, 133, **135–6**, 228
Storm Force Accelatron 143
Toon Lagoon **140–41**, 143
Triceratops Discovery Trail 139
Universal Express 136, 142
Italy (Epcot) 81–2
it's a small world 6, 40, 45, **68**, 228
It's Tough to be a Bug! 88

J

Jackson, Andrew 18, 22
Japan (Epcot) 81
Jaws (Universal Studios) 126
Jernigan, Aaron and Isaac 19
Jimmy Neutron's Nicktoon Blast 130–31
Journey to Atlantis 45, **156**, 160
Jungle Cruise (Magic Kingdom) 64–5
Jungleland (Kissimmee) 166
Jurassic Park (Islands of Adventure) 138–40
Jurassic Park River Adventure 45, 138, **139–40**

K

Kali River Rapids 87, **91–2**
Kennedy, President John F. 25
Kennedy Space Center 149, **205–11**

Astronaut Encounter
207
Astronaut Memorial
209
children's overnight
adventure 206
Explorer (Space Shuttle
replica) 208
IMAX theaters 207
Mad Mission to Mars:
2025 206
restricted area tour
209–11
Rocket Garden 208
viewing a launch
211
Kerouac House 9, 180
**Key West Dolphin
Stadium (SeaWorld)**
154
Kilimanjaro Safaris 87,
90
**King Tut's Tomb (Busch
Gardens)** 198
Kissimmee 189–90
accommodation **222**,
224
dinner shows 171–2,
176
Rodeo 7, **166**
Kraken ride 8, 42, 153,
156–7, 160
**Kumba ride (Busch
Gardens)** 193, 198, **200**

L

Laemmle, Carl 119, **127**
**Lake Kissimmee State
Park** 181
Lake Wales 187–9, 224
**Land of the Dragons
(Busch Gardens)** 201–2
The Land (Epcot) 79
Le Moyne, Jacques 20
left luggage 236
Lego Imagination Center
110
Liberty Belle **Riverboat** 67
Liberty Square 67–8
**Lights, Motors, Action!
Extreme Stunt Show**
100
**Living with the Land
(Epcot)** 75, **79**
Living Seas (Epcot) 79
lockers 49, 236
**Lost Continent, The
136–7**, 138

**Lower Wekiva River
Preserve State Park**
181
**Lowndes Shakespeare
Center** 183
Lowry Park Zoo (Tampa)
203
Lucas, George 95, 100
Lucy: A Tribute 121

M

**Mable Ringling Museum
of Art** 203
**Mad Mission to Mars
2025 (Kennedy Space
Center)** 206
Mad Tea Party 69
**Magic Carpets of
Aladdin** 65
**Magic of Disney
Animation** 103
Magic Kingdom 35–6,
38, 59, **61–71**, 228
Adventureland 64–6
Astro Orbiter 71
Backstage Magic 108
Big Thunder Mountain
64, **66–7**
Buzz Lightyear's Space
Ranger Spin 64, **71**
character dining 8, **64**
Cinderella's Castle 8,
64, 228
Cinderella's Golden
Carousel 69
Country Bear Jamboree
67
Disney's Family Magic
108
Dumbo the Flying
Elephant 69
E-rides night 48
Enchanted Tiki Room
65–6
Fairytale Garden 70
Fantasyland 68–70
Fastpass 64
Frontierland 66–8
Goofy's Country Dancin
Jamboree 67
Haunted Mansion 64,
67–8
height requirements 67
Indy Speedway 67, **71**
it's a small world 6, **69**,
228
Jungle Cruise 64–5
Liberty Square 67–8

Mad Tea Party 69
Magic Carpets of
Aladdin 65
Main Street U.S.A. 61–4
Many Adventures of
Winnie the Pooh 64, **69**
Mickey's PhilHarmagic
6, **68**
Mickey's Toontown Fair
70
parades 63, **64**
Peter Pan's Flight 6,
64, **68**, 228
Pirates of the Caribbean
65
Snow White's Scary
Adventure 69–70
Space Mountain 8, 64,
67, **71**
Splash Mountain 45,
64, **66**, 67
Swiss Family Treehouse
64
Sword in the Stone
Ceremony 68
Tom Sawyer Island 67
Tomorrowland 71
Walt Disney's Carousel
of Progress 71
**Maharajah Jungle Trek
(Animal Kingdom)** 92
**Main Street, U.S.A.
(Magic Kingdom)**
61–4
Maitland Art Center 186
manatees 155–6, **180**,
203, 212
Manatee Rescue 155–6
**Mannequins Dance
Palace** 109
**Many Adventures of
Winnie the Pooh** 64, **69**
maps 236
Mardi Gras 7, 128
**Marketplace (Downtown
Disney)** 110
**Marvel Super Hero
Island** 141–3
**Medieval Times Dinner
and Tournament** 8,
172
**Men in Black: Alien
Attack** 121, 124, **125**,
126
**Menendez de Aviles,
Pedro** 17, 20
**Mennello Museum of
American Folk Art**
184

Mercado 9, **168–9**,
176–7, 229
**Merritt Island National
Wildlife Refuge** 6,
212–13
Mexico (Epcot) 82
MGM Studios *see*
Disney-MGM Studios
Mickey Mouse 27, 64
Hidden Mickeys 68
Mickey's PhilHarmagic
6, **68**, 228
Mickey's Toontown Fair
70
Mission: SPACE (Epcot)
8, 73, 75, **77–8**, 228
Montu ride 8, 42, 193,
197–8
**Morocco (Busch
Gardens)** 195–6
Morocco (Epcot) 81
Mount Gushmore 113
Muppet Vision 3-D 99,
101
**Murvico Pointe 21
(cinema complex)** 170
**museums and art
galleries** 9, 179–80,
182–90, 226
**Myombe Reserve (Busch
Gardens)** 198

N

Nairobi (Busch Gardens)
198–9
NASA 78, 205, 208
**New York (Universal
Studios)** 128–30
newspapers 236
Nickelodeon Studios
119, **131**, 228
nightlife 227

O

**The Oasis (Animal
Kingdom)** 87–8
Ocala 224
Ocala National Forest 6,
181
Odyssea (SeaWorld)
159
**One Fish, Two Fish, Red
Fish, Blue Fish 135**,
136
opening hours 232–3
Orange County 18, 22,
26, 28, 29

Orange County Regional History Center 7, 55, **182**, 226
orange-growing 15–19
Orlando 55, 149
accommodation (Downtown) 224–5
arts and museums 179–80, 182–90
best of 6–9
cuisine 189
history 18–19, 22–9
restaurants and bars 176–7, 191
Orlando City Hall 9, **179–80**, 226
Orlando Convention and Visitors Bureau 36
Orlando Museum of Art 9, 55, 149, 182, **183–4**, 226
Orlando Science Center 6, 149, **183**, 226, 228
Osceola Center for the Arts 9, **180**
Outpost (Epcot) 82

P

Pacific Point Preserve 157
Pangani Forest Trail 90
Panton, Leslie Company 21
parades 63, 64, 90
parking 217
Pelican Island Wildlife Refuge 213
Penguin Encounter 157
Peter Pan's Flight 6, 64, **68**, 228
Phoenix ride (Busch Gardens) 198, **199**
photography 237
Pine Castle Army Air Field 26
Pirates of the Caribbean **65**
Pirates Cove Miniature Golf 170
Pirates Dinner Adventure 8, **172–3**
Planet Hollywood 108
planning your visit 46–9
Playhouse Disney – Live on Stage 103
Pleasure Island 108–9
Pocahontas and Her Forest Friends 89

Ponce de Leon, Juan 20
Popeye & Bluto's Bilge-Rat Barges **140–41**, 143
Port of Entry (Islands of Adventure) 133–5
Poseidon's Fury 136, **137**
postal services 237
Primeval Whirl 91, **93**
Production Central (Universal Studios) 130–31
Pteranodon Flyers 138, **140**
public holidays 237
public transport 9, 215–16
pubs and bars 227
Python ride (Busch Gardens) 198, **200**

Q

queues 39, 48–9, 61, 79, 97, 117, 195

R

Race Rock 171
Rafiki's Planet Watch 90–91
rail travel 215
Reedy Creek Improvement District 26, 35, 55
religious services 238
Remington, Frederic 23
restaurants 47–8, 189
see also under individual parks by name
CityWalk 147
Downtown Disney 115
Downtown Orlando 191
Space Coast 213
Tampa and St Pete Beach 202
Rhino Rally (Busch Gardens) 198, **199**
Richard Petty Driving Experience 170–71
rides 8, 40–45
see also individual rides by name
Ripley's Believe It or Not Odditorium 55, 149, **169–70**, 228
R.L. Stine's Haunted Mansion (Busch Gardens) 199–200

road travel 215
Rock 'n' Roll Beach Club 109
Rock 'n' Roller Coaster Starring Aerosmith 8, 43, **99**, 101, 228
Rocket Garden (Kennedy Space Center) 208
roller coasters 8, 40–44
Royal Pacific Resort 39, **223**

S

St Pete Beach 202, 225
St Petersburg 225
San Francisco (Universal Studios) 127–8
Sanford, General Henry 18, 22
Scorpion ride (Busch Gardens) 198, **199**
SeaWorld 38–9, 55, 149, **151–61**
Backstage Tours 151
Discovery Cove 6, 149, 152, **160–61**, 228
Dolphin Cove 154–5
Journey to Atlantis 45, **156**, 160
Key West 154–7
Kraken ride 8, 42, 153, **156–7**, 160
Manatee Rescue 155–6
Odyssea 159
Pacific Point Preserve 157
Penguin Encounter 157
restaurants 158, 161
Shamu Stadium 159
Shark Encounter 157–8
Stingray Lagoon 155
Trainer for a Day 6, **151**
Tropical Reef 154
Turtle Point 155
Waterfront **157**
Wild Arctic 154, **159–60**
security, airport 214
Serengeti Express (Busch Gardens) 198–9
Serengeti Safaris (Busch Gardens) 196
Seuss Landing 6, 117, 133, **135–6**, 228
Shamu Stadium 159
Shark Encounter (SeaWorld) 157–8

Shark Reef (Typhoon Lagoon) 114
SheiKra **201**
shopping 229–30
Shrek 4-D 130
Silver Springs 7, 29, **173–4**
Ski Patrol Training Camp 114
Skull Kingdom 168
Skyride Station (Busch Gardens) 197
Sleuth's Mystery Show and Dinner 8, **173**
Slush Gusher 113
smoking 235
Snow Stormer 113–14
Snow White's Scary Adventure 69–70
Soarin' ride 76
Sorcerer's Hat 97
Sosa Family Cigar Company 108
Sounds Dangerous 100
Space Camp Florida **211**, 212
Space Coast 205–13
Space Coast Nature Tours 213
Space Mountain (Magic Kingdom) 8, 64, 67, **71**
Space Shuttle 208–11
Spaceship Earth (Epcot) 75–6
spas 111
speed limits 217
Splash Mountain 45, 64, **66**, 67
sports 230–31
Stanley Falls (Busch Gardens) 198, **201**
Stanleyville (Busch Gardens) 200–01
Star Tours 44, 99, **100**, 101
Starabilia (Downtown Disney) 108
Stingray Lagoon (SeaWorld) 155
Storm Force Accelatron 143
strollers 49, 119
student travellers 238
Summerlin, Jacob 22
Summit Plummet 45, 113
sunburn 235–6
Sunset Boulevard (Disney-MGM Studios) 98

Swiss Family Treehouse 64

Sword in the Stone Ceremony 68

T

Tampa 149, **203**
accommodation 225
restaurants 202
Tampa Bay History Center 203
Tanganyika Tidal Wave (Busch Gardens) 198, **201**
Tarzan Rocks 93
taxis 216
Teamboat Springs 113
Telephone Museum (Maitland) 186
Terminator 2: 3-D Battle Across Time 122, 126
Test Track 75, 77, **78**, 228
tickets and passes 9, 36, 48–9, 200
Disney Transportation and Ticket Center 61
Fastpass 48, 61, 64, 75, 78, 93, 99
Flexticket 9, 36
meal reservations 47–8
Universal Express 48, 126, 136, 142
Tiger Creek Preserve 6, 181
Tikes Peak 114
tipping 237
Titanic – Ship of Dreams 168–9
Mr Toad 67
Toboggan Racers 113
toilets 237
Tom Sawyer Island 67
Tomorrowland (Magic Kingdom) 71
Toon Lagoon 140–41, 143
tourism 23–9, 34–9
tourist information offices 238–9
Town Square Exposition Hall (Magic Kingdom) 63
transport 214–17
travel agents 238
Travelocity.com 36
travelers' checks 236–7

Tree of Life (Animal Kingdom) 88
TriceraTop Spin (Animal Kingdom) 93
Triceratops Discovery Trail (Islands of Adventure) 139
Tropical Reef (SeaWorld) 154
Turtle Point (SeaWorld) 155
turtle walks 212
Twilight Zone Tower of Terror 8, 43, **98–9**, 101, 228
Twister…Ride It Out 126, **129**
Typhoon Lagoon 45, 113, **114**

U

Universal Cineplex (CityWalk) 145
Universal Horror Make-Up Show 122–3, 126
Universal Orlando 28–9, 38–9, 55, **117**
see also **CityWalk; Islands of Adventure; Universal Studios**
accommodation 223
opening hours 232–3
shopping 229–30
Universal Express 48, 126, 136, 142
Universal Studios 95, 117, **119–31**
Amity 125–6
Animal Planet Live **124**, 126
Back to the Future… The Ride 8, 117, 121, **124–5**, 126
Beetlejuice's Graveyard Revue 126, **128**
compared with Disney-MGM Studios 101
Curious George Goes to Town 123
A Day in the Park with Barney **124**, 126
Earthquake – The Big One 126, **127**
E.T. Adventure 123–4
Fievel's Playland 123
Universal Horror Make-Up Show **122–3**, 126

Hollywood 121–3
Jaws 126
Jimmy Neutron's Nicktoon Blast 130–31
Lucy: A Tribute 121
Men in Black 121, 124, **125**, 126
New York 128–30
Nickelodeon Studios 119, **131**, 228
Production Central 130–31
San Francisco 127–8
Shrek 4-D 130
Terminator 2: 3-D Battle Across Time **122**, 126
Twister…Ride It Out 126, **129**
Universal Express 126
Wild Wild Wild West Stunt Show **126**, 228
Woody Woodpecker's Kidzone 6, 101, 117, **123–4**, 228
Woody Woodpecker's Nuthouse Coaster 121, **124**
World Expo 124–5
Universe of Energy (Epcot) 76–7

V

VIP Tour Experience 49
Virgin Megastore 108
Voyage of the Little Mermaid 99, **103**

W

Walt Disney: One Man's Dream 102
Walt Disney World 34–8, 55, **59–115**
see also **Animal Kingdom; Blizzard Beach; Disney-MGM Studios; Downtown Disney; Epcot; Magic Kingdom; Typhoon Lagoon**
accommodation 219–21
Disney transportation 63, **215**
Fastpass 48, 61, 64, 75, 78, 93, 99
opening hours 232–3
shopping 229–30

Walt Disney's Carousel of Progress 71
Washington, President George 68
Water Mania (Kissimmee) 45, **167**
water parks 45, **111–14**, 167–8
water-rides 45
see also individual rides by name
Weeki Wachee 7, 149, **174**
Wells' Built Museum of African American History and Culture 182–3
West Orange Trail 181
Wet 'n' Wild 45, 117, **167–8**
Who Wants To Be a Millionaire – Play It! 99, **102**
Wild Arctic (SeaWorld) 154, **159–60**
Wild Wild Wild West Stunt Show 126, 228
Wildlife Express (Animal Kingdom) 91
Winter Park Historical Museum 185
Winter Summerland Miniature Golf 114
Wolfgang Puck 106
Wonderland Tea Party 8
Wonders of Life (Epcot) 77
WonderWorks 170
Woody Woodpecker's Kidzone 6, 101, 117, **123–4**, 228
Woody Woodpecker's Nuthouse Coaster 121, **124**
World of Disney 110
World Expo (Universal Studios) 124–5
World of Orchids (Kissimmee) 189
World Showcase (Epcot) 73, **80–82**, 83, 108

Y–Z

Ybor City (Tampa) 203
Zora Neale Hurston National Museum of Arts 7, **183**